Heroes of the Nations

A Series of Biographical Studies presenting the lives and work of certain representative historical characters, about whom have gathered the traditions of the nations to which they belong, and who have, in the majority of instances, been accepted as types of the several national ideals.

FOR FULL LIST SEE END OF THIS VOLUME

Heroes of the Nations

EDITED BY

H. W. C. Davis

FACTA DUCIS VIVENT, OPEROSAQUE
GLORIA RERUM———OVID, IN LIVIAM, 255.
THE HERO'S DEEDS AND HARD-WON
FAME SHALL LIVE

WILLIAM THE SILENT

WILLIAM OF NASSAU, PRINCE OF ORANGE, AET. C. 24

WILLIAM THE SILENT
PRINCE OF ORANGE
[1533–1584]
AND THE REVOLT OF THE NETHERLANDS

BY

RUTH PUTNAM

AUTHOR OF "A MEDIÆVAL PRINCESS," "CHARLES THE BOLD," "WILLIAM THE SILENT," ETC.

ILLUSTRATED

G. P. PUTNAM'S SONS
NEW YORK AND LONDON
The Knickerbocker Press
1911

COPYRIGHT, 1911
BY
RUTH PUTNAM

The Knickerbocker Press, New York

PUBLISHERS' NOTE

THE following biography has, in accordance with an engagement of some years' standing, been prepared specifically for the "Heroes of the Nations Series." In preparing the text for the present volume the author has made use of the material collected for her *Memoir of William of Orange* published in two volumes in 1895, but the present narrative is entirely rewritten, and in its preparation the author had the advantage of certain later information and fresh material which were not available in 1895. It was essential for the completeness of the "Heroes of the Nations Series," and under the general plan of the undertaking, that it should include a biography of the great leader of the sixteenth century who has been so definitely accepted as the national hero of Holland.

NEW YORK, February, 1911.

PREFACE

AN empty niche in the gallery of the *Heroes of the Nations*, long since dedicated to the figure of William of Orange, is the excuse for the appearance of a fresh biography within the narrow compass of a single volume. At Halle, Felix Rachfahl passed the milestone of his sixteen hundredth page when volume ii. (1906) of his *Wilhelm von Oranien und der Niederländische Aufstand* left his narrative at 1567, with seventeen years of complicated events still to be treated before the death of Orange in 1584. His completed book promises, therefore, to reach a size that would be formidable were it not adequate to the scale.

Between John Lothrop Motley, who introduced the English reading world to the Netherland struggle, and the German specialist, now exploiting the same field with intensive labour, Dutch, Belgian, German, French, and English writers, editors, and commentators have contributed to the literature and to the attainable sources of the subject. Frederic Harrison's monograph is charming and illuminating in the midst of the mountain of publications that has been piled up since my own *William the Silent* and all alike demanded some consideration before the story could be retold.

During the necessary review in the libraries here, in Oxford, in Paris and in London, it has been my good fortune to have much kindly assistance for which it would be difficult to give specific recognition, but certainly I owe especial thanks to Professor Blok of Leiden, whose lectures I followed for one semester, and to his former students, Drs. Japikse and Colenbrander. Then, too, I count myself peculiarly fortunate that the visit to the Dutch university happened during Robert Fruin's lifetime. Several interviews with the generous old professor emeritus were experiences never to be forgotten.

The most agreeable part of the direct preparation for this revised memoir, was reading and handling manuscript matter in the archives of several cities. The originals contain a personality difficult to reproduce. Handwriting, spelling, erasures, and the very folding of the papers add a quality that eludes print. This was especially the case in The Hague, where the more personal Orange-Nassau correspondence is now easily accessible to the student through the kindness of her Majesty, Queen Wilhelmina. To Dr. Krämer of the *Koninklijke Huisarchief* I would express my especial gratitude and no less to Dr. Bijvanck of the Royal Library. The treasures under their respective charges made the limitations of the

Preface

work in hand very trying, even as a summary. So much had to be ignored.

I should have preferred changing the title, having searched in vain for any contemporaneous justification of the adjective "Silent" as applied to the man. It was the Prince's political critics of a later period who instituted its use as a derogatory term. His own friends would never have recognised it. But as English readers have adopted it quite without the association of a hostile slur, no alteration is made. It seemed wiser not to incur the risk of confusing this William of Orange with a later king by using the formal title alone.

R. P.

WASHINGTON, *January, 1911.*

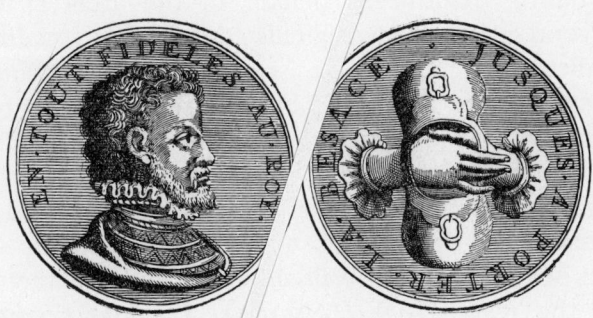

BEGGARS' MEDAL

CONTENTS

	PAGE
INTRODUCTION: THE HERITAGE OF PHILIP II OF SPAIN	1

CHAPTER I
THE NASSAU FAMILY—1200–1533 . . . 8

CHAPTER II
THE PRINCE'S YOUTH—1533–1551 . . . 30

CHAPTER III
MILITARY TRAINING—1551–1558 . . . 44

CHAPTER IV
DIPLOMATIC EFFORTS—1558–1559 . . . 67

CHAPTER V
THE PRINCE IN 1559 81

CHAPTER VI
THE SECOND MARRIAGE—1560–1561 . . 91

CHAPTER VII
THE NOBLES AND THE CARDINAL—1561–1564 . 112

Contents

	PAGE
CHAPTER VIII	
THE GROWTH OF POPULAR DISCONTENT—1564–1566	146
CHAPTER IX	
THE PARTING OF THE WAYS—1566–1567	168
CHAPTER X	
THE EXILE—1568–1570	185
CHAPTER XI	
THE CAPTURE OF THE BRILL AND AFTER—1572–1573	223
CHAPTER XII	
THE BATTLE OF MOOK HEATH—1574	253
CHAPTER XIII	
THE SIEGE OF LEIDEN—1574	271
CHAPTER XIV	
NEW ALLIANCES—1574–1575	288
CHAPTER XV	
THE PACIFICATION OF GHENT—1577	333
CHAPTER XVI	
SOME FAMILY LETTERS—1576–1578	358
CHAPTER XVII	
THE UNION, THE BAN, AND THE ABJURATION—1578–1581	379

CHAPTER XVIII
THE FRENCH PROTECTOR—1581–1582 . . 411

CHAPTER XIX
ANJOU'S FAILURE—1582–1583 . . . 432

CHAPTER XX
THE ASSASSINATION—1584 455

WILHELMUSLIED 495
BIBLIOGRAPHY 497
INDEX 507

ILLUSTRATIONS

PAGE

WILLIAM, PRINCE OF ORANGE, COUNT OF NASSAU, CATZENELLENBOGEN, ETC. . *Frontispiece*
    From a photograph of the painting in the museum at Cassel. This was a copy made in 1582 for William of Hesse from an original loaned by Count John of Nassau. Original was burned in 17th century.

GENEALOGICAL TABLES 8

CHARLES V., EMPEROR OF GERMANY, IN 1548 . 12
    From a photograph of the painting by Titian in the Pinakothek at Munich.

COUNT WILLIAM OF NASSAU, CALLED THE ELDER 18
    From a photograph of the original in great hall of Groningen.

THE RUINS OF DILLENBURG CASTLE IN 1825 . 26

NASSAU PALACE IN BRUSSELS . . . 38
    From *Bruxelles à travers les âges*, by Louis Hymans.

ANNA OF EGMONT (COUNTESS OF BUREN), PRINCESS OF ORANGE 46
    From a photograph of drawing at Arras.

Illustrations

	PAGE

FACSIMILE OF LETTER, PRINCE OF ORANGE TO HIS WIFE 58
    From photograph from original in Orange-Nassau family archives.

PHILIP II. AS PRINCE OF SPAIN, 1548 . . 74
    From a photograph of the painting by Titian in Madrid.

VIEW OF BREDA 88
    Redrawn from an old print.

WILLIAM OF NASSAU, PRINCE OF ORANGE, ÆT. c. 28 100
    From a photograph of the original in the *Mauritshuis* at The Hague. It was bought from the *Secrétan* collection in Paris, 1889. The inscription is *Antoninus Moro pingebat A? 1561*. It is not quite certain that it represents Orange.

ANNE OF SAXONY, PRINCESS OF ORANGE . . 124
    From an old print.

FACSIMILES OF LETTERS 158

ALLEGORY. NETHERLAND LION SYSTEMATICALLY CRUSHED BY SPANISH OFFICIALS . . 174
    From an old print.

COUNT JOHN OF NASSAU 180
    From an old print.

ADOLPH OF NASSAU 198
    From a photograph of the monument erected on battlefield of Heiligerlee, 1868.

Illustrations

	PAGE
FACSIMILE OF LETTER OF ANNE OF SAXONY	210
ALLEGORY. THE NETHERLANDS ARE PERSONIFIED AS ANDROMACHE BOUND TO A TREE. ORANGE COMES AS PERSEUS TO RESCUE HER FROM THE SPANISH MONSTER. THE INDIVIDUAL PROVINCES ARE IN A GROUP ON THE RIGHT	230

From an engraving of 1572.

PHILIP MARNIX, SEIGNEUR DE STE. ALDEGONDE . . . 244
From Boland's copy of an engraving by John Weirix.

COUNT LOUIS OF NASSAU 260
From an old print.

FACSIMILES OF LETTERS AND AUTOGRAPHS . 290
From photos of originals at The Hague.

ALLEGORY. THE PACIFICATION OF GHENT . 334
From a print of 1576.

ENTRY OF THE PRINCE OF ORANGE INTO BRUSSELS, 1577 348
From a contemporaneous print.

JULIANA OF STOLBERG, COUNTESS OF NASSAU . 364
From photo of original kindly procured by A. V. L. of Holland.

FACSIMILE OF LETTER OF CHARLOTTE DE BOURBON TO PRINCE OF ORANGE . . . 368
From a photograph of original in the *Huisarchief*, The Hague.

Illustrations

	PAGE
MAP SHOWING THE SITUATION IN 1576 AFTER THE PACIFICATION OF GHENT . . .	382

MAP SHOWING THE UNIONS, MAY, 1579 . . 382

WILLIAM OF NASSAU, PRINCE OF ORANGE, ÆT. 48   400
> From a photograph of engraving by H. Goltzius, 1581. In print cabinet, Rijksmuseum, at Amsterdam.

CHARLOTTE DE BOURBON, PRINCESS OF ORANGE, ÆT. 31 408
> From a photograph of original engraving by H. Goltzius, 1581. In print cabinet, Rijksmuseum, Amsterdam.

LOUISE DE COLIGNY, PRINCESS OF ORANGE . 446
> From an old print.

WILLIAM OF NASSAU, PRINCE OF ORANGE, ÆT. *c.* 50 466
> By M. J. Miereveld. Free composition after a lost portrait by Cornelis Visscher. From photo of original in the Rijksmuseum at Amsterdam. Greek inscription is from the *Medea:* "Jove, let it not escape thy eye who is the cause of these misfortunes." There are copies of this portrait at The Hague, at Leeuwarden, at Delft and Amersfoort, without the Greek.

STAIRCASE AT THE PRINZENHOF . . . 488
> From an etching.

MAP OF THE NETHERLANDS AND REGIONS ADJACENT . . . . *At End*

MEDALS

PAGE

The story of the revolt of the Netherlands is illustrated by a series of medals struck successively by Beggars and royalists, by regents and States-General, by individual provinces and towns. The designs were not always new for each occasion. Frequently one reverse was made to do repeated service. The following are chosen as typical:

BEGGARS' MEDAL, 1566 v

> Immediately after the name of *Gueux* or Beggars was assumed by the petitioners the first medals were struck, which were imitated in various forms. This has the bust of Philip II. with the legend, *En tout fidel au roy.* On the reverse: *Jusques à porter la besace,* "In all faithful to the king even to carrying the beggar's wallet." Two hands clasped hold a double wallet. The medal is evidently imitated from one struck in 1559 showing Philip's head with the legend, *Philippus Hispaniorum et novi occidui rex.* The reverse shows two hands clasped, signifying there the eastern and western hemispheres.

REGENT'S MEDAL, 1566 29

> Struck by the Duchess after she had averted rebellion by the Accord. Legend: "Margaret of Austria, etc.—Governess of the Netherlands"; encircles the regent's bust. Reverse.— Amazon crowned with laurel, a sword in her

right hand, an olive and a palm branch in the other. Legend: *Favente Deo*.

LEIDEN MEDAL, 1574 29
Face, bust of Adrian van der Werf with octrain describing his virtues. Reverse.—Siege of Leiden.

SIEGE OF HAARLEM, 1573 43

ORANGE MEDAL, 1572 66
The Prince's bust with his titles of Orange and Nassau. Reverse.—An old oak tree with the roots bare. Legend (Virg., *Æn.*, x., 284): *Audaces Fortuna juvat*. Copied from a Spanish medal.

HAARLEM SIEGE MONEY, 1573 66

ORANGE MEDAL, 1568 80
One of the first medals struck by the Prince. Around his bust is the legend in abbreviated Latin: "William, by the grace of God Prince of Orange, Count of Nassau." Reverse.—A kingfisher's nest floats on the sea. Four winds are turned aside by an arm out of the sky and lose their force against a high cliff. Legend: *Sævis tranquillus in undis*, "Calm in the cruel waters."

SIEGE MONEY, 1573 90
Money coined during siege of Haarlem.

BEGGARS' MEDAL, 1566 111
Later form. The inscription in abbreviated Latin signifies, "Philip by the grace of God King of Spain, Count of Holland." *En tout fidel. au roy* is the protestation of fidelity

Medals   xix

PAGE

to him in spite of opposition to his measures. Reverse.—Legend continues as on first specimen, but two figures replace the clasped hands. Both carry beggar's wallets; one has his hand significantly on his sword. A tiny cup is appended to the medal.

SIEGE MONEY, 1574   111

Money coined during siege of Leiden. Lion of Holland holds city arms in one hand, a pole with the liberty cap in the other. Legend: *Hæc libertatis ergo*, 1574. There were several other coins with inscriptions indicating resistance.

BEGGARS' MEDAL ON CHAINS WITH CUPS PENDANT   130

BEGGARS' MEDAL, 1567   200

A very rare heart-shaped Beggars' medal preserved in the Royal Cabinet at The Hague Library. On the face, Iconoclasm and *Neerlandia* trying to obtain mercy. Legends: *Vive Dieu, la santé du roi et la prosperité des Gueux* and *Niet voor deught*. Reverse.—4 scenes, very small but clear. One of the legends is, *Libertas patriæ*.

HALF MOON MEDAL, 1574   200

One of the Beggar medals that became very popular. They were called *Halve Maene*, "Half Moons," though the Turks' crescent was indicated by their shape. Legend: *Liever Turcx dan Paus*, "Better Turks than Pope," shows the increased sentiment of hatred towards the Pope and there is no protestation of fidelity to the king as in the earlier medals. Sometimes the legend is in French: *Plutôt le Turcque que le Pape*.

xx   *Medals*

                                                                PAGE
ROYAL MEDAL, 1568 230
    The emblematic aspersions of the rebels were
answered by a crop of medals applauding
Alva's actions and supporting Philip's course.
The one given here shows Philip with an un-
sheathed sword in one hand and a laurel
crown in the other. Legend: *Pœna et Prœmio*,
"By punishment and reward." Reverse.—
An unbridled horse. Legend is from Lucan's
Pharsalia: Libertas libertate perit, "Liberty
perishes through license."
    NOTE.—Bizot gives this as an Orange medal
struck after the defeat of Tholouse.

BEGGARS' MEDAL, 1572 230
    Struck after the capture of The Brill. It shows
a sword between two human ears; on the
sword's point is a penny, nine more lie at one
side. On the other, spectacles and a flute.
Legend: *En tout fidelles au roy* 1572. Reverse.—Two nobles with medals on their
necks and a beggar's wallet in their hands.
Legend continues: *Jusques à porter la besace.*
The ears and flute indicate the oft-repeated
phrase, "Sweetly sounds the flute when the
fowler snares the bird."

ORANGE MEDAL, 1574 270
    Face.—A pyramid, symbol of David. Legend:
Lapis rejectus caput anguli, "The stone which
was rejected becomes the corner-stone."
Reverse.—Jehovah in Hebrew. Legend in
abbreviated Latin: "God did this and
became admirable in the eyes of men. 1574."

RELIEF OF LEIDEN, 1574 287
    The face shows Jerusalem besieged by Sennach-
erib, King of Assyria, while an angel destroys

his soldiers. The inscription is *Ut Sanherib a Jerusalem. 2 Reg. 19.* The inscription on the reverse continues, *sic Hispa a Leyde noctu. fug.* "As Sanherib from Jerusalem so the Spaniards fled from Leiden in the night." Oct. 3, 1574.

HOLLAND MEDAL, 1575 287

Medal struck by the Estates of Holland and West Friesland. Face.—A book aflame. It is the book sealed with seven seals mentioned in the Apocalypse. It is open at the words, *Lex crucis testimonium Domini.* Legend: *Sermo Dei, ignis inextinguibilis.* Reverse.—Several hearts aflame. Legend: *Tua manus fecit hoc. Domine,* "Thy hand hath wrought this, Lord."

ORANGE MEDAL 332

Face.—Orange as David prepared to rescue Belgian lion chained near the feet of Goliath. Legend: *Confidens Domino non movetur in æternum,* "Who trusts in God will never be confounded." Reverse.—Story of Mucius Scævola. Legend: *Pro libertate Patriæ agere aut pati fortiora,* "To work for national liberty or to suffer worse things."

UNION OF HOLLAND AND ZEALAND, 1576 . . 357

Face.—Lion rampant within the hedge, naked sword in one paw, a bundle of arrows in the other. Legend: *Securius bellum pace dubia.* Reverse.—A hat above clasped hand. Legend: *Libertas concordia vindicata.* This commemorates the rupture of the Breda peace conference and the union of Holland and Zealand.

ROYAL PEACE MEDAL, 1577 378

Commemorates Peace of Marché-en-Famine from royalist point of view. Justice enthroned.

Peace is burning arms on her right. Abundance is on her left. Legend: *Justitia pacem, copiam Pax attulit.* Reverse.—Liberty holding in one hand a palm and a sword near which are chains and broken irons. Her other hand holds a hat above two olive branches springing from a crown above a heart which rests on hands clasped over a lion couchant.

MEDAL OF STATES-GENERAL, 1579 . . . 410

Struck by States-General after rupture of peace negotiations at Cologne. Face.—The Pope and Philip II. The King caresses the Belgian lion, offering it an olive branch with one hand while the other hides a collar. Legend: *Liber leo pernegat revinciri,* "The free lion refuses to be bound again." Reverse.—The Inquisition on a pillar to which a lion is attached. A mouse gnaws his chain. Legend: *Rosis leonem loris mus liberat.*

UNION OF UTRECHT, 1579 410

Face.—Two vessels approaching each other. Utrecht in the distance. Legend: *Frangimur si collidimur,* "We shall be shattered if we collide." Reverse.—A yoke of oxen dragging a cart. Legend: *Trahite æquo jugo,* "Draw with an equal yoke." The emblems are a warning of the dangers of division.

ANJOU MEDAL, 1582 416

Belgian lion couchant appeals to Anjou flying down to the rescue. The name of Jehovah is above him. Legend: *Belgia renascere.* Reverse.—Three small circles. 1st shows a horse without a driver and an overturned waggon. Legend: *Vis consilii expers mole ruit sua,* "Strength

Medals

without judgment is destroyed by its own weight." 2d. Horse and waggon with a driver. Legend: *Deus vim tempera [tam] provehit,* "God transports tempered strength." 3d. Arms of the Duke of Brabant. Legend: *Res parvæ crescunt concordia,* "Little things wax great through harmony."

ORANGE MEDAL, 1582 416

Jaureguy's attack. Assassin in act of shooting. Legend: *Proditione non armis agitur,* "It is done by treachery not arms." Reverse.—Three figures with Jehovah above. Legend: *Proditor tandem luct,* "The traitor finally makes atonement."

ANJOU MEDAL, 1582 436

There were numerous Anjou medals. This shows him bareheaded surrounded by his titles, including the new ones of Flanders and Brabant. Reverse.—A sun. Legend: *Fovet et discutit,* "He cherishes and dissipates." The fervour did not last long.

ANJOU'S TREACHERY, 1583 436

The Netherlands appear as a woman held fast by Anjou aided by King of Spain. But a lion leaps on the scene [the courage of the people] and rescues her [another form of this shows the astonished Prince of Orange as a spectator]. Legend: *Ubi rex in populum tiranus* 1583. Reverse.—Neerlandia tramples shackles under foot, snatches her right hand from Anjou's and shows him a broken ring. Legend continues: *Populo jure divino et humano divortiam,* "Wherever a king is a tyrant to the people a divorce [is permissible] to the people by law divine and human."

                                                        PAGE
ORANGE MEDAL, 1584 493

    The death of the Prince of Orange was commemorated by several medals. One shows Gérard saluting Orange. Behind the former stands Philip who is authorising the crime with his sceptre. Legend: *O dirum scelus, non manebit inultum*, "O dreadful deed, it will not remain unavenged." Reverse.—A shepherd in the midst of his flock attacked by a wolf. Legend: *Ne vos credite lupo—pastorem occidit*, "Do not trust the wolf. He has slain the shepherd."

MEDAL OF STATES-GENERAL, 1584 . . . 493

    Official medal struck by the States-General. Head of Orange with an encircling inscription in abbreviated Latin signifying "William, by the grace of God Prince of Orange, Count of Nassau, born at Dillenburg, 1533, has governed these provinces during 15 years with the greatest prudence and has died in an unfortunate manner at Delft in the year 1584." Inscription under the bust signifies, "Although the bones fall to ashes, his valour will survive." Reverse.—The halcyon on the ocean, Jehovah indicated above, The Prince's device as inscription: *Sævis tranquillus in undis*. Design almost identical with that used in 1568.

ZEALAND'S MEDAL 496

    Reverse of above is repeated in main details. Face shows arms and device of the province: *Luctor et emergo*. Another shows the same reverse, while the face depicts the actual scene of the assassination with the figure of Philip in the background.

ERRATA

Page 37, footnote—*For* Landgrave *read* Landgraf.
" 77, line 14, page 104, lines 15 and 16—*For* Martigny *read* Montigny.
" 166, line 26—*For* June 8th *read* April 8th.
" 194, line 5—*For* curamos *read* curamus.
" 207, line 5—*For* making saltpetre *read* working saltpetre.
" 277, footnote—*For* Prinz Willen *read* Prinz Willem.
" 302, footnote, line 2—*For* Qeen *read* Queen.
" 308, line 21—*For* Frederick will not wrong me *read* you will not wrong me.
" 354, line 24—*For* aivisan *read* avisan.
" 372, line 25—*For* will, *read* will
" 445, footnote—*For* Bewij's *read* Bewijs.

Proper names occur in various forms in quoted matter.

WILLIAM THE SILENT

INTRODUCTION

THE HERITAGE OF PHILIP II. OF SPAIN

ON Easter Sunday, in the year 1521, mass was celebrated on the Pacific island of Cebu, in the presence of awestruck natives beholding for the first time the mystic rites of the Roman Church. Then the Portuguese Ferdinand Magellan watched with reverent eyes the elevation of a mighty cross on a mountain side, rejoicing that it cast the shadow of the Faith upon the pagan strand.

The temporal jurisdiction of the island group he claimed for the King of Spain, Charles I., better known as the Emperor Charles V., whose gracious patronage had enabled the venturous navigator to reach the far East by dint of sailing persistently westward through the sea beyond the straits which preserve the memory of his name. To the explorer, the East proved the final goal of his course. His attempts to exalt a chief, an imperial god-child newly baptised as Don Carlos, to a supremacy over his fellow chiefs brought on a wretched little native war, wherein Magellan lost his life. But the enterprise he had set in motion was carried out by at least one ship of his outward bound fleet. The *Victoria* returned to Seville (September, 1522) to prove that the globe could be successfully circumnavigated, and that the Spanish flag and the message of the Church had been carried to the uttermost parts of the earth.

While the realm of Charles V. and the spiritual jurisdiction of the Pope were thus being extended, the ultimate authority of both potentates was exposed to danger in Germany. During the very Easter tide of 1521 when Magellan raised his cross, the famous diet was sitting at Worms. In the fortnight following the festival, Luther's protests were heard and the cleft in the political Church universal began to be visible.

It chanced that these two widely separated events are both mentioned when still fresh, in some pleasant letters between the Italian Bishop Chiericati and Isabella d'Este. The prelate, a pious and sincere son of the Church, had been entrusted with a special mission to Germany to smooth over the theological disputes spreading from Würtemberg to other quarters of the empire. "A noble mission" is the comment of the Dutch Erasmus.

On his northward journey the good man cherished hope of success. Then came disappointment. He was in the habit of corresponding with the cultivated Duchess on many matters of general interest, and it is in one of these leisurely friendly epistles that he writes (1522):

I assure your Excellency that Luther's doctrine has already so many roots in the earth that a thousand persons could not pull them up. Certainly I alone could not. But I will do what little I can, although threats and persecutions are not wanting. Every day I am subjected to villainous insults, but I try to take all these things patiently for the love of God, knowing that *they will be counted to me as martyrdom.* . . . Now they have begun to preach that the sacrament of the altar is not a true sacrament, and is not to be worshipped, but only celebrated in memory of Christ. And they say that the Blessed Virgin has no merit as the Mother of Christ, and that she bore other sons to Joseph. Every day things go from bad to worse. I pray God to put forth His hand.

Then the faithful and devoted prelate tells Isabella how much he is distressed at the secular spirit of the northern clergy. But the writer checks himself in this out-pouring, conscious that theological topics will only excite a languid though polite interest in the lady of the Renaissance. He turns to other subjects to fill out his letter and touches on the wonderful tales brought home by his Vicentine servant, Antonio Pigafetta, who had been with Magellan on the Easter Sunday of 1521.

I send your Excellency an account of the Spanish

expedition ... and I hope that in a few days your Excellency may have the great pleasure of speaking with my servant, who has just returned from this voyage around the world. For certainly this journey is a greater one than any man has ever taken before, since he and his comrades circumnavigated the whole of the globe, ... sailing ... until they reached the Canary Islands, returning to their own land by the opposite way, having gained not only great riches but what is worth more—immortality.

For surely this has thrown all the deeds of the Argonauts into the shade. Here we have a long account of the expedition which his Cæsarian Majesty has sent to the Archduke Ferdinand, who has kindly shown it to me, and has also given me some of the spices which were brought from those parts, with boughs and leaves of the trees from which they are made. Cæsar has also sent his Serene Highness a painted map of the course pursued and a very beautiful bird which the kings of those countries bear with them when they go to battle and say they cannot die as long as it is by their side. It seems to be a very rare bird and here they call it a phœnix; *et de his ratio.*

A few weeks later, Isabella receives Pigafetta's itinerary from Chiericati, and on February 3, 1523, she writes:

If your servant who has returned so full of knowledge from those parts and whom, indeed, we envy greatly, should happen to come this way, we shall be delighted to see him for, as you will understand, it is a far greater pleasure to hear of these new marvellous lands from a living person than merely to read about them. So if you can send him to Mantua, we shall be deeply indebted to you.

At the same time the lady courteously congratulated the bishop on his success in persuading the German princes to take arms against the Turk, and condoled with him over the difficulties which he had encountered at Nuremberg.

May our Lord God give you the power necessary to extinguish that shameful and diabolical Lutheran sect. You must not allow yourself to be disheartened by the insults and opposition that you receive, remembering that it is the same in all important undertakings and that the greater your difficulties are, the greater will be your glory.

The wonderful voyage bore fruits. Twenty-one years later, the great group of islands within which Magellan's cross had stood, the advance-guard of Rome in the Orient, was classed as belonging to the Western Hemisphere and received a new name as the adopted daughter of Spain. It was at the command of Ruy Lopez de Villabos, following the trail blazed by Magellan, that a portion of the archipelago was christened *Las Felipinas*, in honour of "our fortunate prince," later Philip II. of Spain, whose name thus remains commemorated by that of the latest comer into the circle of the dependencies of the United States of America.

In 1543, what prince could have seemed more fortunate than this same godfather to an archipelago? Was not his wonderful heritage well supported? Had not Alexander VI. issued a valid deed in his papal bulls of May, 1493, definitely dividing "the world like an orange,"[1]—all the countries not held by Christian princes,—between Spain and Portugal? And half a century later the actual extent of this land grant was realised. Such is the popular estimate of the famous Line of Demarcation. The beneficiaries, to be sure, seemed to base their practical rights rather on their own treaty of Tordesillas than on Alexander's donation, but of such rights they certainly had no doubt. The result of bulls and treaties was that the pale between the powers was considered to be a line 370° west of the Cape Verde Islands, Spanish property lying west, Portuguese east of the boundary. Out of all South America, Brazil fell to Portugal's share. In the Orient the Philippine Islands were juggled within Spanish claims, and for more than three centuries the island clocks ticked sixteen hours later than Madrid time instead of eight hours earlier. From 1543 to 1555, while a Spanish king still wore the imperial crown, the nominal jurisdiction of that monarch was the widest. With the abdication of Charles V. the area began to shrink. Since then other territories outside of the peninsula have fallen off, one by one. The Philippine archipelago was the last to be detached from their

[1] *Sabese la concession del Papa Alexandro; division del mundo como una naranjo.* Letter of Alonzo De Zuazo to Charles V., Jan. 22, 1518.

Spanish allegiance in 1898. The process has been slow.

At the moment (1555) when the "fortunate prince" Philip took over the sovereignty of the Netherlands from his father, the Emperor was supported in his physical feebleness by a pleasant faced youth, devoted to his service, a youth equally fortunate in his own sphere of worldly prosperity, William of Nassau, Prince of Orange. Between the two princes, the greater and the lesser, arose a contest over the extent to which he of Spain might exert that inherited sovereignty after the ruler had left the northern lands and the Burgundian tradition and was devoting himself to being the most Catholic King of Spain and of the Indies and to enforcing the observation of one universal religion in every corner of his dominions.

Behind monarch and noble is the background of the facts of the world discoveries and of the insistance of the Protestant Revolt, facts just beginning to be felt when these two men were born, —facts that differentiated their sixteenth century from its predecessors. That background and the political setting of Europe are taken for granted in this volume. This is the personal story of William of Nassau, titular sovereign of the tiny principality chiefly renowned on account of this man—always an absentee, yet the best known to fame of the long line of Princes of Orange.

CHAPTER I

THE NASSAU FAMILY

1200–1533

THE acknowledged founder of the Dutch Republic, William of Nassau, may be said to have had two lines of forbears, each affecting his life, one directly, one politically, and from both were handed down traits and tendencies potent in their influence on his own independent career as in their contribution to the fortunes and to the titles that determined his rank and position. These two strands of the family past were woven closely into his personality. The man could hardly have been the individual that he was, had a single thread of that double gift of ancestors and predecessors been omitted from his heritage.[1]

The Nassaus were an old, well established clan of German nobles. There had been one emperor among them, but they were not of the very

---

[1] This chapter is based on Arnoldi, *Geschichte der Oranien-Nassauischen Länder und ihrer Regenten*, vol. iii.; also Rachfahl, *Wilhelm v. Oranien*, vol. i., books i. and ii. and Jacobs's *Juliana v. Stolberg*, p. 45, etc.; and the Orange-Nassau family archives at The Hague. Notes in Nyhoff's Dutch translation of Putnam's *William the Silent* have also given valuable suggestions.

HOUSE OF NASSAU-DILLENBURG
(1247–1401)

Otto I.
1247–1289
d. before March 3, 1290,
m. Agnes, daughter of Count Emich of Leiningen

├── Henry I.
│   1285, d. 1343,
│   m. Adelheid, dau. of Diedrich, Lord of Heinsberg
└── five other children

Otto II.
1318, d. Jan. 25, 1351,
m. Adelheid, sister of Count Henry of Vianden

├── John I.
│   1351, d. bet. March 8 and Nov. 30, 1416,
│   m. Margaret, dau. of Count Adolf of the Mark
├── Henry
│   1351, d. 1402
├── Otto
│   1351, d. 1384
└── ten other children

├── Adolf
│   1384, d. June 12, 1420,
│   without male issue
├── John II.
│   surnamed "With the Helmet"
│   d. 1443
└── Engelbert I.
    1401, d. May 3, 1442,
    m. Johanna, dau. and heiress of
    John III., Lord of Polanen
    and Leck

├── Henry
│   1401
└── John III.
    d. 1430

(over)

HOUSE OF NASSAU-DILLENBURG
(1401-1606)

Engelbert I.
b. about 1388, d. May 3, 1442,
m. Johanna, dau. and heiress of John III., Lord of Polanen and Leck

Children: John IV., Henry II., Margaret, William, Maria, Philip

---

John IV.
b. Aug. 1, 1410, d. Feb. 3, 1475,
m. Maria, dau. of John, Lord of Loon and Heinsberg,
b. 1424, m. 1440, d. 1501 or 1502

Children: Anna, Johanna, Adriana, Engelbert

Henry II.
b. Nov. 9, 1455, d. July 30, 1516,
m. Elizabeth, dau. of Landgrave Henry of Hesse,
m. 1482, d. Jan. 17, 1523

Children:

John V.

Ernest
b. April 9, 1486,
d. Oct. 21, 1486

William
b. April 10, 1487,
d. Oct. 5, 1559,
m. 1. Walpurge, dau. of Count John of Egmont, 1506,
d. March 7, 1529,
m. 2. Juliana, dau. of Count Botha of Stolberg,
and widow of Count Philip of Hanau, 1531.
d. June 18, 1580

Elizabeth
b. 1488, d. June 3, 1559,
m. John, Count of Wied, 1506,
d. 1533

Maria
b. Feb., 1491
d. after 1542,
m. Jodocus, Count of Holstein-Schaumburg, 1506,
d. June 5, 1532

Children of William:

Henry
b. Jan. 12, 1483,
d. Sept. 13, 1538,
m. 1. Frances, dau. of Duke James of Savoy, 1504,
d. Sept. 17, 1511,
m. 2. Claudia, dau. of Prince John of Chalons and Orange, 1515,
d. May 31, 1521,
m. 3. Menzia of Mendoza, 1524

Elizabeth (1)
b. Oct., 1515,
d. Jan., 1523

Magdalena (1)
b. Oct. 6, 1522,
d. Aug. 18, 1567,
m. Herman, Count of Moers and Nuenar, 1538,
d. 1578

William (2)
b. April 25, 1533,
d. July 10, 1584,
Prince of Orange,
(for family see table Vol. II.)

Hermanna (2)
b. Aug. 9, 1534,
d. soon after

John VI. (2)
b. Nov. 22, 1536,
d. Oct. 8, 1606
(reigning family of Holland)

Louis (2)
b. Jan. 10, 1538,
d. April 14, 1574

Maria (2)
b. March 18, 1539,
d. 1599,
m. William, Count de Berghes, 1556,
d. May 24, 1586

Anna (2)
b. Sept. 21, 1541,
d. Feb. 12, 1616,
m. Albert, Count of Nassau-Saarbrück, 1559,
d. Nov. 11, 1593

Elizabeth (2)
b. Sept. 25, 1542,
d. Nov. 18, 1603,
m. Conrad, Count of Solms-Braunfels, 1554,
d. Dec. 27, 1592

Catherine (2)
b. Dec. 29, 1543,
d. Dec. 25, 1624,
m. Gunther, Count of Schwarzburg, 1560,
d. May 15, 1583

Juliana (2)
b. Aug. 10, 1546,
d. Aug. 31, 1588

Magdalena (2)
b. Dec. 15, 1547,
d. 1630,
m. Wolfgang, Count of Hohenlohe, 1567,
d. March 28, 1610

Henry (2)
b. Oct. 15, 1550,
d. April 14, 1574

René
b. 1518
Prince of Orange, 1530,
d. July 15, 1544,
m. Anna, dau. of Duke Anthony of Lotharingia, 1540,
she m. 2. Philip of Aerschot,
d. 1568

Maria
b. 154-, d. three weeks after birth

Adolf (2)
b. July 11, 1540, d. May 24, 1568

Ottilie (child of John V.)

GENEALOGICAL TABLE.

HOUSE OF ORANGE-NASSAU.

WILLIAM, COUNT OF NASSAU, CALLED TACITURNE, OR THE SILENT.

b. April 24, 1533, at Dillenburg; after 1544 Pr. of Orange; assassinated at Delft, July 10, 1584.
m. 1. Anne of Egmont, dau. of Maximilian, Count of Buren, m. July 7, 1554, d. March 24, 1558,
  2. Anne, dau. of Maurice, Elector of Saxony, m. Aug. 24, 1561, divorced, 1571, d. Dec. 18, 1577.
  3. Charlotte of Bourbon, dau. of Louis, Duke of Montpensier, m. June 12, 1575, d. May 5, 1582.
  4. Louise, dau. of Gaspar Coligny, Admiral of France, widow of Charles Teligny, m. April 12, 1583, d. Oct. 9, 1620.

(children of 1st marriage)

1. Philip William
b. 1554, d. 1618.
m. Eleanor, dau. of Prince of Condé

2. Marie
b. 1556
m. Philip, Count of Hohenlohe, d. 1616

(children of 2d marriage)

1. Anna
b. 1562
m. Count William Louis of Nassau-Dillenburg, d. 1588

2. Maurice
b. 1564, at Breda,
d. after a brief existence

3. Maurice
b. 1567, at Dillenburg,
d. 1625, at The Hague

4. Emilie
b. 1569,
m. Emanuel, Prince of Portugal, d. 1629

(children of 3d marriage)

1. Louise Juliana,
b. 1576,
m. Frederic IV., Elector Palatine, d. 1644

2. Elizabeth
b. 1577,
m. Henry, Duke of Bouillon, Marshal of France, d. 1642
[one son was Marshal Turenne]

3. Catherine Belgia
b. 1578,
m. Ludwig, Count of Hanau-Münzenberg, d. 1648

4. Charlotte Flandrina
b. 1579,
Abbess of Poitiers, d. 1640

5. Charlotte Brabantina
b. 1580,
m. Claudius, Duke of Trémoille, d. 1631

6. Emilie Antwerpiana
b. 1581,
m. Frederic Casimir, Count Palatine of Zweibrücken, d. 1657

(child of 4th marriage)

1. Frederic Henry
b. 1584,
m. Amalie of Solms-Braunfels, d. 1675

  1. William II.
  b. 1626,
  m. Mary Stuart, dau. of Charles I., King of England, d. 1650

    William III.
    b. 1650,
    after 1688, King of England,
    m. Mary Stuart, dau. of James, Duke of York, later James II. of England, d. 1702.

  2. Louise Henrietta
  b. 1627,
  m. Frederic William, Elector of Brandenburg, d. 1667
  [From her descends the present royal family of Prussia]

  3. Henrietta Emilie
  b. 1628, d. 1642

  4. Isabella Charlotte
  b. 1634, d. 1642

  5. Albertina Agnes
  b. 1634,
  m. William Frederic, Prince of Nassau-Dietz, d. 1696
  [From her descends the present royal family of Holland]

  6. Henrietta Catherine
  b. 1637,
  m. John George II., Prince of Anhalt-Dessau, d. 1708

  7. Marie
  b. 1642,
  m. Louis Henry, Count Palatine of Zimmern, d. 1688

highest rank in the empire. From the eleventh century on, their lineage is written in clear characters. The family tree was a flourishing growth in the lovely land of Nassau, a pretty hill country not far from Coblence and Frankfort, watered by the Lahn, a Rhine tributary,—a land rich in wonderful, beneficent springs. Tradition, indeed, carries the roots of this genealogical tree back to Roman times, but the most veracious chroniclers, while eager to render all honour to the illustrious race, declare that the renown of the descendants is sufficient to allow that claim to be rated as unproven, though highly probable.

Strict primogeniture did not prevail in the House of Nassau. The eldest sons were not exclusive heirs. All brothers received a portion and all wore the title. As the family ramified within the little stretch of territory, the title was existent in more than one of various castles perched on the rounded hill-tops congenial to the mediæval builder.

There were two main limbs of the ancient, ancestral tree, the Walramian and the Ottonian. The Nassau-Dillenburg branch of the Ottonian stem, from which sprang William the Silent, had a peculiar history of its own.

Just at the dawn of the fifteenth century there were four brothers with no prospect of heirs to any. One of these, Engelbert, was on the eve of taking Holy Orders, a profession to which he had been dedicated from birth, when he changed his mind, abandoned his celibate calling, and married (1404) Johanna, sole heiress of the Lord of Polanen, Leck, and Breda, rich estates in and near Brabant, far down the Rhine, remote from the hills and valleys of Nassau, and under wholly different political influences.

Engelbert's two sons, John and Henry, became heirs to their childless uncles and to their father. Henry had no issue and John's two sons, Engelbert II. and John V., divided the estates, the former taking the lands west, the latter those east, of the Rhine. Moreover, in 1475, a definite pact was made providing that this rule of partition should be adopted in perpetuity—failure of heirs in one branch throwing the property into the other, but for division, not consolidation, and the agreement was duly carried out. The successive Nassaus who inherited the lower German estates entered upon larger fortunes, however, than mere fruitful acres and revenues continually augmented by the dowries of rich brides.

The first Engelbert began his political career in the service of Jacqueline,[1] the luckless Countess of Holland, Duchess of Brabant, etc., and ended it in the more lucrative employ of her ambitious cousin, Philip of Burgundy. The second Engelbert of Nassau-Breda played an important part in the suite of Charles the Bold, was captured at Nancy (1477), and forced to leave a heavy

---

[1] See *A Mediæval Princess*, Ruth Putnam.

ransom with the Swiss before he could return to the Netherlands, where he did faithful service to Mary of Burgundy, and to Maximilian after her, until the day of his own death (1504).

In provision for that event, Engelbert, having no son, had taken under his charge his eldest nephew, Henry, whom he educated as his own heir, while Henry's brother, Count William, was content to succeed their father, John V., in the enjoyment and administration of the Nassau-Dillenburg estates, in accordance with the division of family property that had become traditional.

William was the father, but Henry was the political predecessor, of the subject of this biography, and a slight outline of his career is an essential part of the story. Born in Nassau in the same year as Luther, 1483, Count Henry spent nearly his whole life in the court atmosphere into which he was introduced by his uncle Engelbert at a very early age. He was one of the foremost nobles among the Knights of the Golden Fleece during the period of Maximilian's regency. He was stadtholder, envoy, state councillor, military commander, in turn, besides being temporarily one of the young king's guardians, but his greatest personal success was the service he was able to render at the time of the imperial election in 1519.

After Maximilian's death, the accession of his grandson to the empire was by no means a foregone conclusion. Henry VIII. of England and

Francis I. of France were also candidates for the imperial crown, and the latter was, for a time, rather a formidable rival. Henry of Nassau was appointed head of an embassy sent by Charles to Germany to look after his interests. Practically, the Count was chairman of a National Committee selected by the candidate with special reference to the local political conditions in the empire. Henry's duty was to interview each individual elector, ascertain how he intended to cast his vote, and use his influence to turn his choice to Charles.

Charles had considered that Henry's wide acquaintance in Germany might be a very important factor in affecting the campaign. In an autograph letter he promises the Count two thousand guilders for his journey, besides his expenses, while he wrote to his aunt, the Regent Margaret: "This matter of the imperial crown is the most important question that has arisen in our regard, and we must employ the best servants that stand at our service."

Englishmen there were who sneered at Henry's diplomatic powers, ranking him as inferior to the French and papal envoys, but he accomplished his object. The Elector of Mayence was the first one to be "convinced," and then more electioneering followed before the votes were cast at Frankfort. The electors of Trier and of Brandenburg were inclined toward Francis I. The Elector of Saxony was asked to be a candidate

CHARLES V., 1548
BY TITIAN

himself, but he declined definitely in favour of Charles, and that decided the matter. The election was finally unanimous. In the debates, a national sentiment was invoked. Much stress was laid on the German descent of Charles, his Spanish blood was made little of, while Francis was characterised as a foreigner to all things German. For Henry's efficiency in the campaign he was not only ready to receive credit but counted it one of the proudest achievements of his life.

As a military commander, the Count displayed a certain amount of ability, but his last offensive expedition against France did not add greatly to his reputation. He certainly ranked higher in diplomacy than in military science. That is, he was of a distinctly different type from Maximilian van Buren, for example, whose soul was in the field. He was always statesman rather than general.

Henry was present at Worms in 1521, and saw the beginnings and first seventeen years of the Protestant revolt; but he had not the slightest leaning toward the new ideas as they gradually took shape. Nor were his sympathies in the least inclined towards the reforming party from political reasons. He was a Burgundian in so far as that term may be used to denote a member of the never stationary Austro-Burgundian court. His interests were bound up with those of his imperial master rather than with any land, and he respected legitimacy in Church and State. To him the Protestant movement was simply a manifestation of unruly anarchy.

His advice to the priests who complained of the encroachments of Lutheranism upon their domain was simple: "Go and preach the message of Christ like Luther, only louder, and yield to no one." He agreed with Margaret of Austria, aunt of Charles V., that learned churchmen could eventually command more attention than a single unscholarly monk (*ungelehrter Mönch*) if they only exerted themselves to good purpose.

Henry's first marriage with Francesca of Savoy brought him neither children nor permanent riches, as the dowry had to be returned to her family on the death of the young wife. After a brief widowerhood, the hand of his second wife, Claudia of Orange-Chalons, was given to him by King Francis in acknowledgment of Count Henry's services in smoothing over difficulties between him and the Emperor. Claudia was an excellent *partie*, and the one son, René, whom she bore to Count Henry, became sole heir to her brother Philibert, Prince of Orange, an event of permanent moment in the Nassau family history.

The Burgundian court had known several successive Princes of Orange, just as it had the divers counts of Nassau, so that René united two lines of courtiers in his person. When René succeeded his father, in 1538, as Count of Nassau, he had already been Prince of Orange for eight years, his uncle Philibert having died in 1530.

The young Prince was then twenty years old and free from guardianship, but he turned to his Nassau uncle for advice, and Count William hastened down to Brabant to give his nephew counsel, and to remind him that there were Nassau claims which he must consider in entering on his new heritage.

René had troubles of his own. The French King was disposed to make serious difficulties about his accession to the Orange-Chalons estates. Countess Menzia, Henry's third wife, claimed more than her step-son thought just, and there were various other obstructions bristling in his path to ease. On his part, his uncle, Count William, pointed out to him that he had carried a large share of burdens, of which Henry should have taken a portion—allowances to the women of the family, the legal expenses of a certain lawsuit that had afflicted the family for many long years, etc.

Count William of Nassau was called the Rich, but he was often closely pressed for cash and found it very hard to meet his obligations. He was interested in furthering an alliance for his nephew that would bring fresh money to the family coffers and he made a journey to France which led to a marriage between René and Anne of Lorraine.

René entered into public life at a school-boy age. His two famous lines of predecessors left empty offices behind them. He was only twelve

years old when appointed Stadtholder of the
Franche-Comté. This Burgundian post, formerly
filled by the French Prince of Orange, bestowed
emoluments upon the minor long before he could
assume the duties. At twenty-two, René received the Order of the Golden Fleece and the
appointment as Stadtholder of Holland, Zealand,
Friesland, and Utrecht. In discharge of the
latter office he was plunged into immediate conflict with the troops of Guelderland under Martin
van Rossem, a formidable antagonist for the
youth described by Brantôme as "a very young
prince, inexperienced though courageous and
brave like all the members of his House."

The hostilities recurring periodically between
Francis I. and Charles V. were active in 1544.
The latter began aggressive operations in France,
and among the generals of the invading army was
René of Nassau, Prince of Orange. This was not
long after the death of his one little legitimate
daughter, at three weeks of age. René was thus
without direct heirs, but sound health and the
flush of youth seemed to promise long life with
all its possibilities.

What then led to the testamentary disposition
of his heritage? Count William of Nassau was
the legal heir-at-law to a portion of this, in accordance with the ancient family pact of 1475.
But by this date his theological proclivities were
well known. He was ranged among the Protestants, the party of the opposition, and it is very

probable that when Charles V. gave permission to Prince René, in May, 1544, to bequeath his estates to the eldest son of his father's brother, to William of Nassau-Dillenburg,—then eleven years of age,—he was actuated by a definite purpose, a desire expressly to exclude the convinced father in favour of the malleable son. On the testator's part it may have been a mere conventionality to make a will before exposing himself to danger. Assuredly there could have been little expectation that the almost impromptu document, signed by René on June 20th, would ever have to be proved.

On July 8th the invading imperial forces reached St. Dizier which it was determined to reduce by siege. After a week of waiting, Prince René was ordered by Gonzaga, in command of the expedition, to take up a position by the Marne, to repulse a possible sally of the besieged. A skirmish ensued in which René was hit by a cannonball. He was carried into his tent, and received the most tender care, the Emperor himself visiting him. It was evident that the wound was mortal and the imperial kiss of sympathy was a last farewell. After lingering until July 21st the Prince died, and his residuary legatee, the boy cousin referred to, came into the title, which he was to make more widely known than it had ever been in the possession of his predecessors.[1]

[1] There was an article in René's will providing for one illegitimate son, known as Palamede of Chalons.

During the years that Henry of Nassau played out his part in pompous Burgundian pageants on a European stage, his brother William had pursued a less eventful existence, first under the guidance of, and then as successor to, their father, Count John, whose death, in 1516, left him the headship of the German Nassaus, formally renounced by Count Henry for himself and his heirs.

There were several castles used by the family, Siegen among them, but in the sixteenth century the chief residence of Count William's branch was Dillenburg, charmingly situated on a hill, overlooking a fertile rolling country. The little river Dill flowed at the base on one side and a cluster of houses nestled on the other. Certain sovereign rights over village and district were enjoyed by the counts of Nassau and many responsibilities besides those of county magistrate fell upon their shoulders as they were accountable to the Emperor alone in temporal matters.

Affairs did not always run smoothly during the forty-three years of Count William's administration, and he often had to struggle with serious pecuniary difficulties. One particular lawsuit already mentioned dominated his career and furnished him engrossing occupation. His mother's brother, the Landgrave of Hesse, had died without children; and the Nassaus urged that the Hesse-Cassel cousin succeeding to the landgraviate had no claim to certain Catzenellenbogen

COUNT WILLIAM OF NASSAU
CALLED THE ELDER

estates derived from the mother of the childless landgrave and of Elizabeth of Hesse, Countess of Nassau. The suit brought against the Hesses to support this claim began with the sixteenth century and had been pending fifteen years when Count John died. Count William took up the suit and carried it on for forty-two years. During the whole period when it was in litigation, over half a century, no diet was held without a presentation of the merits of the case. The Protestant revolt came, passed through various phases, and was rooted firmly in Germany while the lawsuit languished on, hampering both litigants in other matters, and costing, all told, several tons of gold!

At the beginning, the case was in the supreme court of the empire, later (1520), Charles V. assumed personal jurisdiction over it, as was within his prerogative to do. He was not, however, in residence anywhere long enough for any hearing to be completed, therefore he appointed a special commission to settle the issue. More complications ensued as the commission had no power of enforcing the opinion it pronounced, and its term was limited. Successive commissions, indeed, expired without any result to their labours.

The final agreement reached was contained in a voluminous document, overweighted with details, of which the gist was that to the Hesses was adjudged the major part of the landed estates of Catzenellenbogen-Dietz, charged, however, with an indemnity to the Nassaus. The latter were entitled to the arms and title of Catzenellenbogen, while the Hesses were to wear those of Dietz. In case of the extinction of the Nassau-Dillenburg family, the Hesses were to have the option of redeeming the ceded land. Thus the suit ended, and its conclusion satisfied no one except possibly the arbitrators!

Landgrave Philip, the opposing party in the suit, was a hard fighter. He was called the Magnanimous, and became a leader of the Protestant party, but many of his methods were far from magnanimous, and he lost no opportunity of showing his ill-will toward Nassau.

In 1521, Count William was present at the Diet of Worms in the interest of this lawsuit, and chanced to hear Martin Luther's sturdy defence of his own position and his protest against ecclesiastical abuses, made in a fashion so strenuous that attention was enforced to ideas which had, indeed, been repeatedly formulated in various shapes by divers reformers during the sixteen centuries of the Christian Church, but hitherto swept aside as the murmurs of insignificant heretical dreamers,—to be ignored or punished by lay authorities on the recommendation of ecclesiastics.

Count William was inclined to agree with Luther on certain points. He had, indeed, been fighting the sale of indulgences within his own jurisdiction since 1518. But he did not at once

throw in his fortunes with the protesting princes.
His reform measures were slow to come and were
such as any fair-minded non-militant country
gentleman might have adopted. He stood so
long indeed at the parting of the theological ways
that he was a target for both parties. Count
Henry, solicitous for his brother's worldly interests,
and desirous of keeping him from alienating the
Emperor, wrote several earnest letters eloquent
in arguments against the dangerous "novelties."
On the other hand, the Protestant princes in
Germany were equally solicitous to win a convert.
In the spring of 1526, Duke Hans Frederick of
Saxony visited Dillenburg to bring his influence
to bear upon the hesitating noble. After his
departure he sent various polemical pamphlets
to the Count to reinforce his verbal arguments.
With the first packet the Duke sent the following
note: "As I promised to give you some of Luther's
writings, I despatch herewith as many as I can
lay my hands upon at this moment. Out of
these and with God's help, I hope to make a good
Christian of you."

Another seven years passed, however, during
which mass continued to be celebrated in the
Dillenburg chapel. Meanwhile, other visitors
brought other arguments whose purpose was to
turn Count William in the opposite direction to
that desired by the Duke of Saxony.

In 1533, Hartmuth of Cronenburg arrived
at Dillenburg as a special messenger from the

Emperor's nephew, Ferdinand, to induce Count William to accept the imperial nomination to the Order of the Golden Fleece. But the statutes of the Order, which the envoy had to show the nominee, made it plain that an acceptance of the flattering invitation would imply adherence to the tenets of the ancient Catholic faith with all its doctrines, just as subscription to the Augsburg Confession was an essential step to belonging to the League of Schmalkald. The knight's collar was intended to yoke Count William to the imperial service; it was a direct bid to keep him out of the Protestant League. William made his choice in declining the proffered honour.

When at last the first definite steps in regard to the adoption of a new ritual in Nassau took place in 1533, the year of this refusal to enter the Order, there were no violent reform measures. Portions of the Roman ceremonial were retained and each pastor followed his own methods without precise definition of creeds or usages. Some confusion resulted, and as time passed Count William felt called upon to bring order from chaos. In 1536, a handbook for the pastors was prepared, containing the "Nassau Church Regulations," to which William himself wrote the introduction. After mentioning the abuses that had crept into the Church services, he states that the Nuremberg Confession contained all that was needful for religious instruction, and added that he was displeased to note that the pastors had not adhered to it faithfully but had permitted to their people the "familiar leaven and yeast of their inherited fables," though perhaps rather from simplicity than from lack of understanding. "And as we are unwilling to permit the handful of subjects committed to our charge by God to suffer deprivation of His eternally blessed word, we have considered it necessary to come to the aid of your ignorance with a little commentary for your illumination and instruction."

The Regulation prescribed the use of German in the rite of baptism, the communion in both kinds, and the instruction of the youth in the true meaning of the sacraments. After the communion, the mass was to be celebrated in "ordinary clothing and with innocent ceremonies." The elevation of the Host was expressly forbidden, as well as private or week-day masses. In the early morning there might be a brief sermon or the reading of the Scripture, or an epistle with an exposition of the same and a prayer.

In places where week-day mass was not usually celebrated, there should be a Wednesday sermon. Auricular confession was forbidden. Both confession and absolution were to be general. The religious education of the children was strictly prescribed as well as the number of festivals (26) to be observed annually, and Lenten fasts were prohibited. The education and life of the pastors were prescribed and marriage recommended. In every church there were to be two Bibles, one

Latin, one German. A synod of pastors was to assemble twice a year, alternately in Dillenburg and Siegen, to discuss improvements, etc., and a superintendent was to visit the parishes at stated times.

As early as 1526, the petty princes of Germany had begun to exercise the right, claimed at the Diet of Speier, of regulating ecclesiastical matters, each within his own territory. A State Church had been organised in Hesse, Nassau's nearest neighbour, in 1526–28. Other independent organisations had followed in various quarters of Germany, so that Count William was justified by precedent in thus becoming the paternal director of theological matters in his domain. "As the prince, so shall the land be," was an attractive doctrine long before the phrase was formulated at the Peace of Passau.

The story of how a nunnery at Keppel slipped easily into a Protestant sisterhood is typical of the Reformation as it passed in Nassau. There was no question of scattering the inmates, none of confiscation and desolation of the community property. The cloister, which had existed from the thirteenth century on, offering dignified refuge to the noble Nassau daughters who sought a vocation in the Church, never fell into ruin,—a change in creed and regulations permitted the latter-day maidens to come to its shelter and to devote themselves to good works, yet unhindered by perpetual vows from returning to the world again if cloister life palled upon them or a suitable marriage presented itself.

Count William's assumption of jurisdiction over the consciences of Nassau was not unquestioned by the Church of Rome. The attempts of the Archbishop of Mayence to reassert his sway within his allotted diocese, were aided and abetted by the Landgrave Philip, that most protesting Protestant of them all, but so good a hater withal that he was satisfied to forget his scruples if, by so doing, he could annoy his dearest foe, with whom he was outwardly at peace. But Hesse and Nassau were constitutionally at odds, and a new cause of irritation also arose between them from the fact that the reform was not prosecuted in the same spirit, the old Landgrave being, at the outset, inclined to extreme measures, while Count William was very moderate. The differences between the two wings of the reformers were beginning to be as bitter as between Protestants and Catholics. When the Protestant League of Schmalkald was formed among the German princes, the Count refused to join for some time. In 1535 he was at last ready to change his mind and offered to endorse all action hitherto taken. But although accepted as a member he never became fully identified with its proceedings. Owing to the unfriendly insinuations of the Landgrave he was not invariably notified of the meetings and felt that he was treated with indignity. When the disaffection in the empire swelled to organised rebellion on the part of the leaguers against Charles V., Count William succeeded in retaining his foothold on neutral ground and in warding off engagements on Nassau territory.

Within Count William's household there was a pleasant and wholesome atmosphere, fair balance to the worldliness and bickerings, theological and political, without. In his nineteenth year Count William was married to Walpurga of Egmont (1506), who died in 1529, leaving one daughter. Various brides were immediately proposed to the widower, according to the mode of the day, when the funeral baked meats often might have served for the marriage feasts. Count Henry was interested and entreated his brother not to ally himself with the Protestant Houses of Saxony and Würtemburg as that might alienate the Emperor. In regard to a princess of Lorraine, suggested as a suitable *partie*, Count Henry warns William that the maiden is deformed, and that a rich dowry would ill compensate for weakly offspring.

Then, as it chanced, business matters brought William into the society of the young widow of a former ward of his own, Philip of Hanau, to whose children he was called upon to act as guardian on Philip's death in 1529. Juliana of Stolberg, Countess of Hanau, was then only twenty-five, though mother of five children. It was not unnatural that an alliance should result between widow and guardian. Negotiations would have

DILLENBURG CASTLE IN 1825.

needed no intermediary, and were, probably, short. A betrothal took place at Königstein, the residence of Juliana's kinsmen, on September 21, 1531; the wedding followed speedily and Count William took his wards and their mother home to the pleasant Dillenburg castle, renovated and improved to fit it for the life of the large family it was to shelter.

Neighbours of similar rank were far away, so that the inmates of the castle were thrown upon their own resources for entertainment. The habitation was fairly luxurious for the times, for there were marble statues in the court and foreign shrubs in the garden. The decorations within the house included tapestry whereon was depicted the battle of Pavia, then a very recent event.

Shortly after Juliana's installation, a library was fitted up "for the teaching and improvement of the Christian life as well as for the general good and for the amateurs of all good art," as Count William states. Latin and German books stood side by side on the shelves. The Count had endeavoured to exercise the greatest discretion in their selection and to banish those volumes, "learned though they might be, in which evil was mingled with the good."

Juliana was a woman of exceptional character, taking the responsibilities of wife, mother, and chatelaine as a serious profession to which she devoted herself. In her two marriages she bore seventeen children, nearly all of whom grew to

maturity, in itself a remarkable event in those
days of infant mortality,—a fact showing that
the offspring had sound inheritance and good care.
As a rule, the baptisms recorded in any family
annals are out of proportion to the children surviving their parents.

It was well that Dillenburg was a capacious
domicile as it often was called upon to give hospitality to large parties of guests. Once a certain
Duke of Brunswick was entertained there with
one hundred and fifty retainers in his suite, and
there were many other visitors with large trains,
from time to time, pausing on their way to various
diets or to Italy.

Those were transient guests, but the castle was
not left to solitude between the chance visits of
passing strangers. The school established by
Juliana for the benefit of her own charges won
so much reputation that pupils flocked in from
neighbouring castles. The training to be had
at Dillenburg, social and intellectual, was highly
prized, and the influence of Juliana of Stolberg
was felt in a wide circle.

Every bit of testimony, direct and indirect,
about this mother of William the Silent indicates
a charming personality and a sturdiness of character that impressed itself upon her children and
grandchildren. These numbered one hundred and
sixty before her death, and they have carried good
blood into every reigning family in Europe.
Juliana's husband and eldest son were often

biassed in their religious views by political reasons. Not so Juliana; she based her actions upon the religious principles that were part of her life, and she saw her sons go out to war with the firm conviction that they were fighting God's battles.

REGENT'S MEDAL

LEIDEN MEDAL

CHAPTER II

THE PRINCE'S YOUTH

1533–1551

THE first child of Juliana and William of Nassau came into the world at the castle of Dillenburg on Thursday, April 24, 1533. It was a boy baby, "whose name shall be called William," are the words written in the handwriting of Count William himself.[1]

This was the year in which the father refused the tempting collar of the Order of the Golden Fleece, the year when his sympathies took a definite turn toward the Protestant party. Nevertheless the christening of this eldest son on Sunday, May 4th, was celebrated not with the new rites for infant baptism instituted by Martin Luther, but in general conformity with orthodox usages, except for certain slight differences and variations symbolic of the doubts affecting the parental mind. Philip von Königstein, Philip von Rheineck, and Amelia, the widowed Countess of Isenburg, were god-parents. Juliana's mother and brother were at Dillenburg to meet various members

---

[1] MS. Orange-Nassau family archives, The Hague.

of the Nassau clan and apparently they all heard mass sung at eight o'clock. When that was over the *Kindlein* was brought into the chapel, and a sermon was preached with special reference to the occasion.

By the time the younger William was old enough to learn, methods of religious instruction, closely interwoven with general education, were formulated in the Nassau Church handbook already described. As Count William was sufficiently versed in letters to select his own library and to instruct his spiritual shepherds exactly how the ignorant flock should be pastured, he probably had his own theories of education when he found time to exploit them. But leisure was not an abundant commodity with him. There were many demands upon his time and his exchequer, and he was not wealthy enough to meet them easily in spite of the adjective attached to his name. In offspring he was rich indeed. John, Louis, Maria, Adolph, Anna, Elizabeth, Catherine, Juliana, Madeleine 2nd, and Henry followed their brother into the world. With such a small army of claimants for the good things of this life, the news of René's bequest, which turned young William of Nassau into the Prince of Orange, independent of the paternal purse, gave cause for rejoicing. But there were certain details about the succession that probably mitigated the father's satisfaction in the boy's fortune. He was himself ignored when he had every reason

to expect to be heir, at least to the Nassau-Breda
estates in accordance with the ancient family
pact. Furthermore his own son and heir, only
eleven years old in the year of his Orange inheritance, was to be removed from parental care
and brought up as though he were an orphan, as
ward of the empire. And this meant that the
minor was to be held strictly to the creed of the
ancient Church which Count William had abandoned for himself and for his own people. It was
a difficult problem to be faced by a father who
desired preferment and wealth for his children
and who yet had standards of conduct and reason
to fear the Greeks bearing gifts.

Count William's first step was to hasten to
Brussels to put in a plea in behalf of his own
rights. The tempting revenue would naturally
be far more available within his own hand. But
he soon became convinced that there was not the
slightest chance of breaking René's will and he
changed his tactics with that readiness to accept
the next best thing which was in later years a
marked characteristic of his famous son. It was
no easy matter but there were certain favourable
circumstances in the situation. At the epoch
in question, Marie, widowed Queen of Hungary,
sister to Charles V., was Regent of the Netherlands.
She was one of the most intelligent members of
the Habsburg family and an able executive in
her brother's behalf, so far as she was allowed to
work her own will in the administration. It is

she whom Erasmus addressed as the "Christian Widow." The Emperor was a flitting presence, an inconstant element in the court where the minor Prince of Orange was to be a ward. Possibly it was confidence in Queen Marie, whose sane and intelligent attitude towards reform was fairly congenial to Count William, that reconciled the latter to fulfilling the terms of René's will and to paying the stipulated price for his son's principality. Certainly, whatever his reasons, he consented to entrust the child's up-bringing to alien hands.

When the Prince published (1580) his famous *Apology*[1] for his own revolt against Philip II., he declared (or approved the statement) that the fact that he was permitted to enter on his inheritance unchallenged called for no special gratitude on his part toward Charles V. He says that there was no one with the shadow of a right to contest Prince René's will except his own father, "who took the pains to come to ask that I should be placed in possession, and there were none impudent enough to oppose except President Schoore, who said in council that a heretic's son ought not to succeed (*filius hæretici non debet succedere*)." In further explanation of his legal rights the Prince continues:

Moreover what can be answered when I point out that my cousin's will was a military testament, . . .

[1] Dumont, *Corps universel diplomatique*, v., p. 386.

and although I am no great doctor in law I can remember perfectly well hearing various learned personages, discussing this subject in my father's presence, affirm that not only military testaments but simple memoranda made on the eve of battle are of perfect validity. According to imperial laws if any warrior before his death had made the slightest manifestation of his intentions, the very faintest sign that could be imagined, such as tracing with his blood on his shield the name of the person he wished to appoint, or as merely scratching on the ground with a halberd or sword point,—then this indication of his last will is inviolable and is preferred to every other direction, according to the ancient privileges of those of high military rank. Assuredly the courtesy usual to others would have been unhesitatingly accorded to a valiant prince and gentle cavalier.

The validity was, however, not assumed without some considerable pressure, in which the Regent Queen Marie joined her entreaties to those of Count William. The Emperor was persuaded to fulfil the solemn promises he had made to Prince René, but he remained inexorable in regard to the exclusion of the father from the slightest jurisdiction over his son's person or his property. The former's pitiful protests against having his child separated from his oversight obtained no further concession than permission to submit a list of names whence the Emperor should select the guardians, and the right of drawing up an *Instruction* for the guidance of these gentlemen when appointed—a document which the deposed father could hardly expect to be very potent. The commission of guardianship thus formed consisted of the imperial chamberlain, Johann van Merode, Claude Bouton, Seignior of Cabazan, and Count Adolph of Holstein-Schaumburg, the coadjutor of Cologne, a kinsman of the Nassaus—all three being faithful to the Catholic Church. The first two named bore the burden of the task as it was fulfilled.

In the spring of 1545, the ward of the empire was established in his own house at Breda, sharing his lessons with the young counts of Westerburg and Isenburg—the latter his godmother's son. The tutor of the three boys received the munificent salary of 100 guilders. The education given was certainly far better than that furnished to many princes of royal blood,—especially in languages. Orange spoke German, French, Flemish, Spanish, and some Latin and could write all five, though with varying ease. His spelling is not standardised, *h's* crop up unexpectedly in his French (*habbandon* for *abandon*, etc.), and his style is never graceful, though often forceful.

When he was fifteen he met his father at the Diet of Augsburg, where family affairs were considered in the midst of the settlement of the political confusion arising after the battle of Mühlberg. The Prince was judged old enough to bear a part in the discussions and the Count was eager in urging that his son's voice should be heard,—for he was weary of being held at a distance from the

boy's affairs. The minority had been much
more trying to the father than to the ward, who
passed his time pleasantly enough between
Breda and the court, well looked after by the
Regent, petted by the Emperor himself, and
learning, incidentally to his formal education,
many of the ways of "practical" statecraft; for it
seems that he was often permitted to remain
in the council chamber during meetings of the
imperial cabinet. And he was quite intelligent
enough to recall in later years what he had then
heard without comprehending. Certainly the
family discussions at Augsburg were not in the
least too abstruse for the fifteen-year-old boy to
follow. The burden of them was the need of
money and the annoyances attendant on the
interminable litigation.

Count William cherished high expectations of
the advantages to accrue to the Nassau interests
from his son's close relations with the Emperor,
but disappointment after disappointment had
continued to curb his hopes of a settlement of
the Catzenellenbogen suit. When Charles V.
requested him to make out an itemised list of the
expenses forced upon him by the long process, he
thought the end was surely at hand, as he did
again when his friends attempted to push through
a private adjustment. Martin Bucer was convinced of the justice of the Nassau claim and took
it on himself to urge the Landgrave to accept an
accommodation:

Because Count William is a right pious gentleman, of kin to your princely Grace, a neighbour, and a brother in religion and in truth well affected toward your Grace, because the nobles who have adopted the evangelical confession look to your Grace as the one prince who can bring consolation to the whole German nation and to whom all wish well, pray consider the matter, etc.[1]

The Landgrave would not yield and at the Augsburg Diet of 1548 the threadbare topic was still demanding consideration.

When the Prince was seventeen an imperial general made a proposal greatly to his advantage. Maximilian, Count of Buren, designated Orange as the husband whom he desired for his daughter Anna of Egmont, sole heiress to the rich paternal estate. There was no objection from any one to an alliance eminently suitable from all worldly motives and from age also, as the two young people were born in the same year. When the matter was practically settled, it was urged that the time was ripe for giving the Prince an independent establishment. The Regent demurred, saying that this step could be postponed for a time, considering his youth, but finally gave her sanction. A governor of rank too was deemed desirable and Jerome Perrenot, Seignior of Champagny, was selected for the post, in spite of the guardians' protests, who declared that a more venerable and dignified personage was needed

[1] Lenz, *Briefwechsel, Landgrave Philipps mit Bucer*, ii., p. 172.

to give dignity and weight to the immature
household. The appointment was significant of
the influence exerted in the Prince's affairs by the
elder brother of this Champagny, Anthony Perrenot, Bishop of Arras, better known by his later
title of Cardinal Granvelle. High in credit with
the Regent Marie, the Bishop succeeded in carrying
his point and in controlling this responsible and
lucrative position in a way to keep him in touch
with the Prince's affairs. This appointment was
only one of the items upon which there was
clashing over the minor's interests.

While the final settlement was pending, Orange
had the privilege of entertaining that other fortunate prince, the Infante Philip, at his own
Breda, where for two evenings there were brilliant
illuminations. This was the time when the
Emperor's heir was making his first progress
through the provinces under escort of his aunt,
and the festivities were part of a long series given
in honour of the future ruler in Brabant and
elsewhere.

During these years of tutelage it is evident
that, as regards his religious status, the attitude
of the Prince of Orange was one of simple, unquestioning conformity. His baptism was accepted as valid and undoubtedly he took his first
communion at the usual age like a good Catholic.
No child finds it extraordinary that people think
and do one thing in one place, another in another.
Then as the boy grew into young manhood an

NASSAU PALACE IN BRUSSELS.

indifference toward all religion was the outcome of his familiarity with the formal observances in which he participated, combined with his knowledge that his own people held opinions completely at variance with those of the imperial household. And certainly the variations between the more moderate wings of the schools of faith were not made of tremendous weight just at that crisis. The atmosphere of the court was still non-militant. The Erasmian period had, it is true, passed, and the adherents of the Dutch scholar had been practically forced into taking sides with the new congregations that were forming or with the venerable institution which they criticised without utterly condemning. The major part of the Erasmians adopted the second alternative and it was they who coloured the court atmosphere with moderation that tended towards indifference. It is also true that, in other circles, evangelical and anti-papal opinions were steadily gaining ground between 1544 and 1555, and that, while strict laws for the repression of free thought stood on the imperial and municipal statute books, as a rule, these laws were not enforced. The penalties imposed were so terribly severe that the civil authorities refrained from taking cognisance of the infractions of which they were aware. This was the more possible because, in spite of his general formulas, the Emperor was long looked upon as a potential leader of an anti-papal party. It often happened that he was sufficiently in opposition to the Pope to be lenient towards reformers and liberal towards the Germans. John Calvin could write to him: "Up to now, Cæsar, you have not been against us. Even if the sword has, so to speak, been put in your hand you have still retained your moderation."

Many years later (1580) the Prince stated in reference to this period of wardship in the Emperor's court: "At that time my head was filled with thoughts of arms, of hunting and of other amusements natural to young men of rank, rather than of anxiety about my salvation." Though this assertion occurs in the *Apology*—a document teeming with unintentional inaccuracies —it may be accepted as fairly true. When acting as page and as gentleman-in-waiting, Orange followed the Emperor to church as to table and fulfilled the etiquette in both cases in simple obedience to the authorities whom his own father had bidden him accept.

Towards the close of the year 1550, Charles V. gave his sanction to the proposed alliance between his ward and Anna of Egmont. The marriage settlements were drawn up with due regard to the groom's interests and on July 6, 1551, the nuptials were celebrated most splendidly and the Prince was emancipated from the last vestiges of his minority and from the uncomfortable trammels of his wardship. No one was more pleased with the match than Granvelle, who was proud of the valuable aid he had given toward its consummation. He wrote to the Elector of Cologne:

As I worked zealously for this event it is a satisfaction to me that we have gained what we wished and to so much advantage for the House of Nassau. The labour that we have expended in the complicated state of affairs is well repaid, as I believe, in so far as we have been successful in our efforts.[1]

Thus the Prince of Orange was placed in a singularly advantageous position at the threshold of his career—surrounded by powerful friends, young, accomplished, independent, yet with a living father, a man whom the son liked and respected and with whom he was thrown into a peculiar kind of comradeship because both felt equally harassed by the interference of the younger man's guardians. There was something unique in that relationship. The friendship between father and son was really augmented by the barrier erected between them. Instead of the junior feeling hampered by the jurisdiction of the senior, the two actually made common cause against a common foe, who had endeavoured to keep them apart.

Maximilian of Egmont, Count of Buren, who selected the Prince of Orange for a son-in-law, was a very different type of man from the opportunist and diplomatic Nassaus. He was a rough and ready soldier, seriously criticised by his fellow knights of the Golden Fleece for his tendency

[1] Quoted Rachfahl, i., p. 165.

to good round oaths. When the Prince was negotiating his second marriage he refers to his first father-in-law as having been inclined to the reformed faith and *nevertheless* high in the Emperor's favour. This must be set down as one of the statements facilely used by Orange to point an argument, when it was very far from being the whole truth. Maximilian's utter indifference to Catholicism was noted. His fellows of the Order reproved him for neglecting mass and fasts. But he was equally indifferent to the new teaching and in the political split he commanded the imperial troops against the Protestant leaguers of Schmalkald in the war when Count William of Nassau managed to maintain a convenient neutrality. Maximilian might have had a dukedom as a reward for his services in this war, but the omission of revenues as part of the gift made him prefer to remain a rich count rather than to become a poor duke.

The story is told that Maximilian was afflicted with a throat disease which Vesalius himself pronounced fatal. Knowing his serious condition, he arranged a great feast to which Charles V. was invited and came. The host seized the opportunity to ask the Emperor's consent to the marriage of his heiress with the young Prince of Orange. When that was accorded, Maximilian felt at peace with the world and shortly afterwards, dressed in full armour, he breathed his last. He was far more like the Emperor from whom he received his name than he was like Charles V., his own sovereign. There was no glint of the modern in the Count of Buren. He would have had little in common with the clever, facile son-in-law whom he had selected for the sweet-faced maiden Anna. She seems to have shown excellent executive ability as head of the house at Breda, and as manager of her husband's finances, even though she had no voice in choosing her career.

1573
SIEGE OF HAARLEM

CHAPTER III

MILITARY TRAINING

1551–1558

A CERTAIN Frenchman has woven a vivid little picture of the Prince of Orange at eighteen into his memoirs, written down a long time after the events described. Memory must have played the writer false as to circumstances, but the inserted portrait is so lifelike that it is difficult to pass it by without a glance. This François de Scépeaux, Marquis de Vieilleville,[1] claims to have been present when an embassy from the anti-imperial German coalition of 1551 was received at the French court, and when Henry II. lent complaisant ears to the representations that his friend Charles V. had reduced the worthy nobles of the empire to an humiliating condition of ignoble servitude. The Marquis states that among the visitors was William of Nassau, accompanied, moreover, by the Emperor's ward, the younger William, Prince of Orange, whom Vieilleville recognises as a cousin from the connection between his house and that of Orange-

[1] *Mémoires*, p. 353, etc. (Petitot's Col., vol. xxvi.).

Chalons. He takes a great fancy to the youth who is handsome, intelligent, and charming, and he urges him to become a "good Frenchman" because his titular estates lie within the realm.

That is true [said the Prince], but it is not the larger portion nor the sixth part of my property in the Netherlands. Nevertheless there is one point that seems to urge me to consent to a French allegiance—which is that the Prince of Spain, without any apparent cause, cannot endure me and it is impossible for me to please him. I am unable to discover the reason for his animosity, being unconscious of having offended him.

Orange further acknowledges that he has heard dire prophesies of misfortunes in store for him at Philip's hand but he remains steadfast in his resolve to stay by the Emperor.

The Marquis ceases to urge a transference of allegiance, and proceeds to entertain the youth and his father to the best of his ability. The conferences between the disaffected German nobles and the French King ended with a banquet and a

ball at which the Queen and court ladies appeared so gorgeously apparelled that the Germans were filled with astonishment. The King led the first dance and then German dances followed, because better understood by the guests, with an occasional galliard to display to better advantage the disposition and grace of our French youth.

In the figures that followed none of the strangers

participated except the Prince of Orange, who acquitted himself very dexterously and would have won the prize for the galliard, if with his postures, capers, turns and evolutions, his countless flourishes, gambols, agile bounds and springs, *he had only kept time to the music!*

An embassy certainly made its way from Germany to France at this time; and Maurice of Saxony, the Prince's future father-in-law, rather the father of the future Princess of Orange, was among the German nobles to despatch it and later to cause Charles V. bitter mortification and chagrin. But quite as certainly the prudent William of Nassau held aloof from the cabal and still more certainly his son had no opportunity to dance for a prize at Fontainebleau in that month of October, 1551.

On July 7th of that year, his marriage with Anna was celebrated with much splendour, and in September the Prince received his first commission as captain of two hundred horse. The Queen of Hungary was his immediate chief, and under her direction he had his first military experience of frontier warfare in the campaigns forced upon Charles V. by the league between the recalcitrant German nobles and the French King. In the spring of 1552, the Regent gathered all the forces she could muster and prepared to repulse an expected French invasion. From her camps the Prince writes frequently to his young wife at Breda. A few letters may serve to give

ANNA OF EGMONT
PRINCESS OF ORANGE

glimpses of these years. The following, written in a large immature writing, is delightfully boyish[1]:

My wife: This is both to ask your counsel as to whether you think it would help matters if I were to write to Mme. our mother; considering that I promised Mme. our grandmother to send her occasional news of myself. I would not wish the said mother to be dissatisfied, and to tell you that Mons. de —— was very pig-headed [in a dispute] with Mons. Vandermer and myself and lost his knife on a wager. [Some garrison gossip follows.]

Mons. de Champagny told me to write you the whole story but as I am very sleepy I will not make it longer. So begging your advice about whether your mother would be pleased by a letter from me—for until I have heard from you again I shall be worried for the reason that you told me, I am, etc. [conventional phrases].

From Thore, June 7th. Pray give my compliments to all the company.

Your very good husband,
GUILE. DE NASSAU.[2]

The next is a more coherent document.

My wife: This is to inform you that yesterday I received letters from the Queen, the kindest, I think, she has ever written to any one of any rank whatsoever, for she expressed her approval of my capacity, desires me always to display the same zeal, and assures me of her entire confidence in me. I pray the Creator to give me grace to deserve this good repu-

[1] MS. Orange-Nassau family archives, The Hague.
[2] His usual signature. It is translated elsewhere for uniformity.

tation. I leave to-morrow for camp and shall sleep at a place near Tongres, where I must wait for five of my companies, hoping that our Lord will permit me to return in good health, so that we shall have better opportunity of enjoying each other's society. My wife, I beg you to make my excuses to Mmes. our grandmother and our mother for not having written to them. I will wait until later, for knowing no news now, I am afraid of boring them with my letters, but I will write as soon as I have anything to tell. In the meantime I beg you to present my humblest respects to all our friends at Breda and pray you to give them such good cheer that they will bear you company longer and keep you from the loneliness you would otherwise feel. Praying the Creator to give you all your desires, etc.

Your very good husband,
WILLIAM OF NASSAU.

To MME. THE PRINCESS OF ORANGE.
From Thore, June 10th.[1]

The young officer found camping no summer pastime, and grumbled freely and boyishly over the various discomforts. The following note was written on July 6th, when there seemed immediate danger of the French penetrating into Brabant:

My wife: This is to inform you that I am in camp with seven companies, where we are very comfortable except that it is rather cold to sleep in tents. . . . I think we will make an advance to-morrow, to

---

[1] MS. Orange-Nassau family archives, The Hague. Printed in Groen, *Archives*, i., p. 1.

prevent the enemy from entering Brabant. I can well believe that you are afraid, like the rest of the world, and that the fugitives from Brussels and elsewhere have infected you with their terror, but I hope there is no danger. My wife, I wish I could be with you on the 7th for our wedding anniversary.[1]

Affairs went from bad to worse. The question of supplies was a constant anxiety, disease was rampant in the ill-organised camps among the ill-fed soldiers, while the poor natives of the soil suffered equally on the advance of either party, as neither Marie nor Henry had the slightest scruple in taking all they could get, or in burning any unoffending town that might offer a foothold to their opponent. The notes from Orange to the Princess continue:

My wife: I received to-day two of your letters, and assure you that nothing more agreeable could happen to me than to have tidings from you and to be advised of your health, but I must tell you what news the Queen has received to-day, which is that the galleys have arrived with a goodly number of Spanish soldiers, about nine thousand, and a supply of money, about two millions of gold. I hope now that the courage of the Germans and French will be dashed . . . and that the agreement which is said to have been made between the Emperor and Duke Maurice will be broken, which will be much more profitable for our cause of Catzenellenbogen, for I hope that the Emperor will remember the rest of us in case that he

[1] MS. Orange-Nassau family archives, The Hague. Printed in Groen, *Archives*, i., p. 6.

prospers, as I trust he will by God's favour, also according to the good omens that I see, for he has already assembled sixty-five companies of German foot-soldiers, who have followed the others to Ulm, and forty more are expected, besides the Spaniards who arrived in the galleys. Therefore, I pray, have good courage and hope that we will succeed in our enterprise, and that we will make them stop their cackle.

Your very good husband,
WILLIAM OF NASSAU.

From Mons, July 11th.[1]

We arrived here yesterday with all our cavalry and my regiment, to plan an ambush for the King of France, who is not far off, somewhere in the neighbourhood of Trelon and Chimay. We were in the saddle all this morning, hoping to capture some of the stragglers from his army, until we learned that he had retreated after demolishing the said Trelon and Chimay. There is a rumour that he is already over his own border. I do not know whether he means to give his men a little rest, which we hear that both foot and horse sadly need, as they are exhausted by the bad weather which they have encountered, and by the bad roads which they have had the greatest difficulty in passing, and in bringing their horses over. If he really retreats I will let you know. . . .

We shall depart to-morrow to rejoin the main army, and I have already sent my regiment on to le Quesnoy, whence they could return if it were necessary. I will not make this longer, as it is almost midnight;

[1] MS. Orange-Nassau family archives, The Hague. Printed in Groen, *Archives*, i., p. 8.

we have hardly slept for three days, and must be astir at daybreak.

CAMP AT DORLE, July 15th, 12 P.M.[1]

My wife: This is to advise you of our arrival at Arras yesterday. I delayed writing to you in the hope of having some definite information in regard to our plans. One day we think we are to make another journey, and the next it seems probable that we are to be quartered in some good city to refresh our men and ourselves, which I should consider the better. Brederode and I here, Hoogstraaten and the Marshal de Geldres at Douay, and the Duke of Aerschot at Cambray, are all waiting for the Queen to decide whether to disband us or retain us in service and put us in garrison, fearing lest the French king may attack Hesdin, if he knew our force were withdrawn. I am pretty sure we shall be disbanded, because I think funds are getting low, and another thing that inclines me to that opinion is that a review is ordered for day after to-morrow. I will not fail to advise you as soon as we hear from the Queen, who cannot delay much longer. If we are disbanded, I will take you, please God, the news myself, and I wish that could be to-day rather than to-morrow, for I cannot express in writing my longing to see you. I feel as if I were a year in arrears with you. (Nov. 13, Arras.)[2]

This fervent hope was fulfilled, and the Prince's troops were disbanded at Valenciennes, November 17th.

[1] MS. Orange-Nassau family archives, The Hague. Printed in Groen, *Archives*, i., p. 10.   [2] *Ibid.*, p. 12.

Meanwhile the Emperor advanced toward Metz, laid siege to the town for fifty-six days, and then abandoned it with the remark that Fortune was a woman who plainly preferred a young king to an old emperor. He spent the winter at Brussels in such close retirement that his death was rumoured. In the following spring the campaign was renewed with Emmanuel Philibert of Savoy in command of the imperial army, and under him Orange had his second year of active service. In 1554, just before he attained his twenty-first year, the Prince was promoted again. He says in his *Apology*[1]:

When I had not yet attained the age of twenty-one, when I was away from court at Buren, the Emperor chose me as general-in-chief during an absence of the Duke of Savoy, although the lords in council and the Queen suggested several other officers whose reputation was assured, as Counts Bossu and Lalaing, and Martin van Rossem, all veterans, and Aremberg, de Meghen, and Egmont who was twelve years my senior.

The pecuniary prospects were not, however, at all satisfactory.

My wife: As I am just on the point of departure, I must tell you of the arrangement the Emperor has made in consideration of my being captain-general. His Majesty has given me, as he gave the Prince of Orange, the Duke of Aerschot, and M. de Bossu, 500 florins a month and twelve halberdiers, each at

[1] *Apology*, Edition Lacroix, p. 76.

double pay, which will be my only income. I wish
you would find out from my lawyer, or from the accounts, whether the late Prince of Orange did not
have more, and let me know. As to your question
as to how much I shall need to spend a month, I
think it will amount to 2500 florins, and will be
obliged if you will take the trouble to get what
money I need. Hoping that some time I will be
able to deserve all the friendship you show me.[1]

A few days later Orange wrote again:

As to my generalship they have not yet decided
about the salary, and there was even some attempt
to persuade me to waive a salary altogether, but I
spoke to the Emperor yesterday who said he would
see to it. I beg you to see that we have some ready
money on hand, for out of the 3000 florins I received from Madame Culemberg I shall only have
a thousand to take with me to camp, as the other two
must be disbursed in this city for the debts incurred
here and for the 1500 florins that I owe my clerk.

BRUSSELS, July 31st.[2]

A note dated simply Aug. 2d seems to belong
here:

I am relieved at what you say of your illness. It
seems to me it would be better not to take any more
medicine for it may make you thin and weak. As
to the matter of the gallery I think it a good idea and
advise you to have it made. The 4000 florins were
received to-day. They were very "à propos."[3]

[1] Groen, *Archives*, i., 16.   [2] *Ibid.*
[3] MS. Orange-Nassau family archives, The Hague.

Charles V. had resolved to shift his burden to younger shoulders. During the summer of 1555 he was deeply absorbed in the arrangements for the proposed abdication. Orange was appointed to take part in the pompous formalities of the theatrical transference of sovereignty from father to son and he directs his wife to find out whether the Duchess of Aerschot[1] or "Madame Egmont" would not take her in for the short sojourn she would make at Brussels. As for him he would arrive by post on the very day of the ceremony and could not tell how long he would be free to remain in the capital. Anna evidently follows her husband's counsel and forwards her correspondence to him. On Oct. 4th he writes:

My wife: This morning I received through Varich your letter enclosing the Duchess's answer. I am much pleased at the latter which I consider a very suitable and courteous reply to your request. It only remains for me to get leave to see you, but you will already have heard that the Queen countermanded my movements, though only temporarily. So I think you had better write a polite letter to the Duchess of Aerschot and accept her invitation, awaiting further news from me.

On the 15th he writes again.

October 15, 1555.

I leave you to imagine the fine life I am leading in

[1] Anna of Lorraine, widow of René of Nassau, married Philip of Aerschot and was a widow for the second time in 1555. She was aunt to Mary Stuart.

this beautiful weather. I assure you my sole amusement is to go through the rain and mud from morn till night on our works. You may think whether, if it lay with me, I should make a long stay here. Further, in regard to the question as to what you ought to do now that all the principal ladies are going to court to take leave of the queens, it seems to me that as soon as you have certain information of the date when the said queens are going to depart, that then it would be well to take a trip to Brussels to take leave. But as you are still uncertain of the date of their departure and also as your train is rather small for your first visit to Brussels since the king's arrival there and that [the lack of state] might not be taken in good part, it would be as well to wait a little until you are more accurately informed of the queens' movements and then go to pay your respects.

Then came the abdication. It was a splendid spectacle and Orange had an honourable rôle in the pageant as he it was who supported the old Emperor when he took farewell of the world and delivered over his Netherland dominions to the tender mercies of Philip II. The little capital was gay with all the people assembled to see this ceremony, but Orange did not stay to take part in the festivities. On October 26th, the very morrow of the dramatic scene, he was back at his trenching.

The old problems—lack of funds, dearth of provisions, and consequent discontent among the troops—confronted the new sovereign as he mounted the throne. Philip's first letter to the Prince, written only four days after his accession, was encouraging, inasmuch as he promised to send twelve thousand crowns to the camp in a very short time.[1] The fulfilment of the promise was delayed; and the letters that passed between Prince and King during the autumn months were filled with complaints from the former and comforting assurances from the latter. The work on the forts progressed, however, in spite of all difficulties, and on December 29th, Orange christened one of them Philippeville, in honour of the young monarch.[2]

In November, Philip informed Orange that he had chosen him as councillor of state,[3] an honour that the Prince acknowledged very dryly.[4]

On the same date Orange writes pathetically to his wife that the condition of the camp would move any one to pity[5]: "For we are here without a penny, and the soldiers are dying of hunger and cold, yet they take no more notice of us at court than if we were already dead. I leave you to picture the amount of patience I am forced to have."

He adds, further, that it is impossible for him to know when he can return. The money, expected daily, might not arrive for a fortnight, and until that came the troops could not be dis-

---

[1] Gachard, *Cor.*, i., p. 165. [2] *Ibid.*, p. 281.
[3] *Ibid.*, p. 217. [4] *Ibid.*, p. 227.
[5] Groen, *Archives*, i., p. 23.

banded according to orders. The uncertainty makes writing difficult so that the Princess is worried at his silence:

My wife: I had already begged you in two letters to manage my affairs as though they were your own just as I had assured you that all mine is yours and therefore I had left all to you. Besides I am so worried that I can not attend properly to my own business.

For the rest, my wife, as to your last letter when you say you are in great trouble because I had not written for so long, and that you fear lest possibly I am angry with you, I should think that the friendship between us two was so sound that such suspicion would be dissipated and, too, that you would have given me credit for more sense than to be angry without reason. I delayed writing so long in order to be able to state absolutely what the king meant to do with this camp, and I assure you that I have no other desire than to be loved as I love you, for after God I think you are the dearest, and if I were not so sure of your love I would not be so much at my ease as I am, as the Creator knows. To Him I pray to give us grace to live out our life in friendship without dissimulation. Recommending myself from the bottom of my heart to your good graces, from camp near Escherenne. Dec. 5th.[1]

Your very good husband,
WILLIAM OF NASSAU.

To MADAME THE PRINCESS OF ORANGE.

[1] Groen, i., p. 21.

My wife: Two days ago I disbanded George von
Holl's regiment, who departed satisfied. Now I am
waiting for money for the regiment of Fernando
Lannoy.

If George von Holl stops at Breda, I think he will
give you a little hackney, and you would do well to
send a present to his wife, for you know we must
make friends with people.[1]

From Camp near Escherenne, Dec. 20th.

At the beginning of the new year the grumblings
among the soldiers in the Philippeville camp grew
louder and swelled into a murmur which insisted
on making itself heard at Brussels. Orange had
written time and time again to Philip narrating
in detail the difficulties that beset his path,
but not until a certain Hans Bernard, captain
of an independent company, sent an insistent
message, did Philip lend an ear. Then he coolly
gave permission to the soldiers to live off the land.
"A course of action that will injure your Majesty, and be the utter ruin of this poor country,"[2]
in vain remonstrated the unhappy lieutenant.

In February, a five-years' truce was signed at
Vaucelles, garrisons were left at Philippeville
and elsewhere, the remainder of the troops were
paid off and disbanded, and Orange was released
from his onerous duties. It can well be believed
that these dreary months had not served to
endear Philip to the Prince, who could not find his

[1] Groen, i., p. 22.
[2] (*Entière ruyne du povre plat pays.*)

grand prosperer en tout chose qui commence
Jusques à ceste heure a nous efforcer que
dieu nerrat pas de tout obé nous aydera
et peultestre qu'an nous pensserons que nous
serons en la plus gran necessité que nous
aurons secours

Vre bien bon mary
Guille de nassau

FRAGMENT OF A LETTER OF THE PRINCE OF ORANGE TO HIS WIFE, JUNE 29, 1552.

.... le Roy de

sovereign's plausible letters efficient substitutes for the necessary sinews of war.

But the truce lasted barely five months, and in January, 1557, Henry reopened hostilities and Philip found himself obliged to assume a defensive, which turned finally to the offensive. Egmont's success in taking the important town of St. Quentin suddenly placed the King in an unexpectedly good position toward France though he did not "march on to Paris" as his father might have done. On hearing the news the retired Emperor asked instantly, "Is Philip in Paris?"—only to be disappointed in the answer that his son was still far from the French capital.

Orange took part in the campaigns of this summer and wrote as follows to his wife, September 11th[1]:

My wife: This morning after a thousand cannon volleys, the castle of Han surrendered to the mercy of his Majesty, there being in the said château about 1000 or 1100 men. I think we shall hang some of them for having made his Majesty wait so long. I assure you this is the prettiest site for a château that could be desired, and there was, adjoining the said house, one of the most beautiful towns to be seen, but the French burned it on our arrival. I think we shall fortify both the town and château. I do not know what we shall do next; knowing, I will advise you immediately.

[1] Groen, *Archives*, i., p. 28.

The three companies of black hussars, who escorted us foragers, summoned the town of Chauny to surrender, and it promptly yielded. The French are finely embarrassed.

From Camp near Han, Sept. 11th.

During the winter of '57-'58, the Prince was frequently absent from home trying to find money for his impecunious master. It was hard work, but he finally succeeded in raising a loan from English merchants at Antwerp on very unfavourable terms as royal credit was low in spite of royal prerogative in two hemispheres.

In February, 1558, a Diet was held at Frankfort to which Orange went to fulfil his long-delayed commission (appointed in 1555) of transferring the crown of the empire to Ferdinand.[1] While in Frankfort the Prince became very anxious about the Princess's health and he hastened back to Breda where he arrived only in time to see her die.

He wrote to his father as follows on March 27th and April 14th:

Dear sir father: My saddened heart must not keep me from telling your Grace, that the weakness into which my amiable and beloved wife fell about a month ago, as you lately learned from me at Dillenburg, increased before and after my return,

[1] At one of the banquets that took place during this visit, Orange is said to have made slurring remarks about marriage as an institution—remarks which were quoted in after years as showing his low standard of morals at this period of his life.— MS. Orange-Nassau family archives.

until at last her life ceased. Thursday, the 24th of this present month, between six and seven o'clock, she departed, in a happy and Christian manner, to God the almighty, who will have mercy on her soul. . . . How heavy the loss is, which I and my young children have suffered, your Excellency may easily imagine. As, however, it cannot be changed, and as it is not proper to rebel against the ways of the Lord, I must leave all to the Eternal, and submit myself to His will, and console myself with the thought that she died in full consciousness and as a Christian.[1]

Philip wrote as follows:

My cousin: Having learned of the serious indisposition of my late cousin, your companion, and that, since your return to Breda from Frankfort you, too, had fallen seriously ill, I despatched the seignior de [Sombernon], bearer of this, to visit you both, and at the moment of his departure the news arrived, to my great sorrow, of the decease of my late cousin, which I feel keenly, both on account of her personal qualities, as well as for your sake, realising the loss you have suffered. . . .

Your letters have renewed the sorrow I felt for the death of the Princess, your companion . . . and there was no need for you to excuse yourself for not having yet reported your expedition to Frankfort, which can easily wait until your spirit is a little reposed.[2]

To the Bishop of Arras, Orange wrote[3]:

[1] Groen, i., p. 32.   [2] *Ibid.*, p. 33.   [3] Gachard *Cor.*, i., p. 397.

BREDA, March 28th, 1558.

Monsieur: I thank you warmly for the letter which you were pleased to write me by Monsieur de Chantonay,[1] your brother, in consolation, and as mitigation of the grief and unsupportable sadness by which I am surrounded, for which I am greatly obliged to you, knowing the good affection and friendship that you bear me.

But since it has so pleased God, and as in all things it is necessary to conform to His most holy will, I implore Him to give me strength that, following your advice, I can patiently bear it, and that He may give peace to the soul of the departed. As to what you desire to know of my malady, the beginning was, that on my arrival from Frankfort at Breda, the 20th of the month, I found that she had been already given up by the physicians, and was in great pain; on the 24th, death ensued, which caused me such perplexity and unspeakable grief, that I fell into a fever with convulsions. However (thank God) for the present I feel pretty well, only I still find myself weak.

The young children mentioned were Philip William, born December 17, 1554, and Marie, born February 7, 1556. Another child was born and died in 1553.

The formal phrases of these letters do not mean much, but the notes to Anna quoted above are sufficient proof that there was a pleasant relationship between the young pair. The Prince's letters are boyish and simple, written by his own hand, with an absence of etiquette and in great contrast

[1] Thomas Perrenot, Seignior de Chantonay.

to his ponderous, verbose communications of later date. They carry conviction that he trusted his wife, and certainly made her an active partner in their business affairs. Yet, even during the period of this fairly successful marriage, the Prince's warmest feelings seem to go out toward his brothers and sisters. Rarely was his household without some members of the Dillenburg family, trusted to the elder brother's care, in spite of certain apprehensions on Countess Juliana's part. At the time of Anna's death, Louis of Nassau and two of his sisters were at Breda. Juliana is very uneasy about their participation in the Catholic funeral rites. She writes to Louis that she is glad to hear that women are not expected to attend the ceremony, adding, "Thou canst find some excuse for absence. I wou'd be glad, indeed, if the Prince, too, could escape. Besides the fact that it is ungodly, I am sure it will only renew his grief."[1]

In all the family correspondence, it is very evident that the parents turn to their son for aid and counsel and that he responds to their demands warmly and affectionately.

Count William anxiously consults him about sending Louis and John to France, so as to acquire French, and Orange is quite willing to make arrangements and to pay a portion of the expenses. The Franco-Imperial war renders this project unadvisable, and the Count thinks that the ducal court at Cleves might be an excellent substitute

[1] Jacobs, p. 120.

for his boys' education. The Duke of Cleves insisted on French being the language of his household. To Cleves accordingly Count John was sent and there he chafed at his detention from the more exciting life led by Count Louis down in the Netherlands, to whom he writes as follows[1]:

Well born friendly dear brother: I have received and read your kind letter wherein you tell me that my lord, the Prince, means to return to the field with his Majesty. I hope that your affection will remind the Prince of my welfare, so that I, too, can go with him. If you can only effect this, I beg you earnestly and affectionately to let me know as quickly as possible, and tell me, too, with how many horses I should come, in your opinion. For I am longing to be in the business for a time. I do not doubt that if my lord, the Prince, would write in my behalf to the duke that his Grace would give me leave to go. My father and mother are perfectly satisfied and will add their sanction if the duke approves. I am counting on your affection to further the project as energetically as you can, and neglect nothing, and I will repay your kindness with right brotherly good will at every possible opportunity.

As to the mountain with lantern or light [here are untranslatable puns on *Leuchtenberg*, the family name of John's future wife], I will not hide from you—as indeed I never have concealed anything, though you have sometimes thought so—that I am working in that direction as well as I can in a short time, and I have succeeded so far that I have surrendered and it

[1] Rachfahl, i., p. 216. (From the Wiesbaden archives.)

has cost me hand and ring. I have not yet been at
the said berg—could not and would not go for I had
to take care of myself in the dog days. Further I will
not conceal from you that my sister Elizabeth has won
Count Conrad von Solms, and my sister Anna, Count
Albert of Nassau. The messenger of Count Schwarzburg came a short time ago to my father at Dillenburg about Count Günther's marriage to my sister
[Catherine] and soon there will be a great wedding
time [*Bräuterei*] there.

I have not anything more to send to you in haste for
we must get ready to ride out to meet Duke Ernest
von Grubenhagen, who is to spend the night with my
lord. I commend you affectionately to God in His
might. Mlle. Pallandt is our neighbour now. As
soon as I see her I will greet her in your behalf.

Your obedient brother,
JOHN, COUNT OF NASSAU.

From Düsseldorf,
July 5th, Anno '58.

Present my compliments to my lord, the Prince,
and give my affectionate regards to Counts Günther
and William von Schwarzburg, as well as to all the
Prince's young men and comrades whom I know.

Do try hard to get me permission to come to camp.
If it does not come soon, I shall die. I have been long
enough at court with maids of honour.

At last Louis is taken formally into his brother's
service.[1]

I wish thee much good luck [writes his mother] in
thy office. Now that thou art a regular official it is

---

[1] Rachfahl, i., p. 218.

high time thou hadst a wife so that thou mayst conduct thyself better, for she would keep thee from evil. I hope we shall soon see each other and herewith I recommend thee to Almighty God for all time.

HAARLEM MONEY

ORANGE MEDAL

CHAPTER IV

DIPLOMATIC EFFORTS
1558-1559

THE young widower was allowed brief respite from official duties. Nor was he allowed leave to attend the weddings in Nassau. Public affairs demanded all his attention. Even before the war closed, the part played by Orange was, however, diplomatic and confidential rather than military, as shown by his question whether it would not be useful for him, Orange, to sound Marshal St. André, a prisoner of war quartered at Breda on parole, before his guest had an opportunity to communicate with others. Would it not be expedient for him (Orange) to take *congé* from the camp on pretext of illness and discuss certain matters quietly with his visitor, etc. Then, very shortly after the Spanish victories of the summer, serious peace negotiations were begun at Lille and continued first at the Abbey of Cercamp, then at a château in the neutral territory of Cambray, by a commission of which the Prince was a member.

From the very beginning, when the degree of

the concessions each of the two parties might accept were warily angled for in private colloquies, to the final seal set on the treaty itself after six months' parley, the Prince was absorbed heart and soul in the proceedings.

The public joint conferences took place in the lodgings of the Duchess of Lorraine, the lady herself sitting

at the boarde's ende and on the one syde the French commissioners and we [the English] on th' other, the Duke d'Alva & his colleagues sitting together beneathe.[1]

Monseigneur: After dinner to-day we met [Orange writes to the Duke of Savoy, October 15th] and accomplished great things. There was some dispute before they agreed to our keeping Hesdinfert, as your Highness will see by our letter to his Majesty. We touched on other affairs and then adjourned until to-morrow. He is very firm about the sister as your Highness will see by our despatch.[2]

In case they agree to the restoration of Piedmont with the said sister, retaining certain places, which arrangement will, I think, be proposed, your Highness will have to decide about the marriage.[3]

The marriage here referred to was that of the

[1] Calendar State Papers, Foreign, 1553–'58, p. 402.
[2] The said sister was Margaret of Valois, whose marriage to the Duke of Savoy was made a condition of the restoration of his domains. There is an inaccurate version of this in Dumas's *The Duke's Page*. The fortress was named Hesdin*fert* in honour of the duke. The Savoy motto is indicated by the letters f e r t —*Fortitudo Ejus Rhodum Tenuit.*
[3] *Cor.*, i., p. 409.

Duke, a side issue; but another more important union became possible in the early stages of the parley. The English Queen, Mary Tudor, completed her unsatisfactory life on November 17, 1558, leaving her Spanish husband free to confirm his diplomatic promises by taking a French wife. When the treaty was finally signed at Cateau-Cambrésis on April 3, 1559,[1] it contained a provision that Philip II. was to marry Elizabeth of Valois, with a dowry of 400,000 crowns. This Elizabeth had once been intended as a bride for the Spanish Infante Don Carlos, but her hand was easily shifted from the son to the conveniently widowed and more important father.

Further, the treaty provided that all the places captured during the eight years of active hostilities should be restored to the *statu quo* of 1551. There was, moreover, a collateral item of immense value to France, as it definitely restored Calais to her after centuries of English occupation, a restoration accorded while Mary Tudor was still in life to be bitterly pained by the loss to England. The result of the general territorial provision as regards the two contestants was that they were really left about where they had begun, in spite of the heavy expenditure of life and treasure during seven long years. Only as in the early period the Emperor had suffered the greater losses, so now his son enjoyed the greater gain.

In his *Apology* the Prince takes great credit

[1] Dumont, *Corps universel diplomatique*, v., p. 34.

to himself for his skill in furthering this peace teeming with advantage to his sovereign.

As to this treaty, disastrous to France and honourable to Spain, if I may be allowed to speak of my part therein, the king cannot deny (had he a trace of gratitude) that I was one of the principal instruments in securing so advantageous a peace, for it was at his instance that I opened negotiations with the Constable and Marshal St. André. The king assured me that the greatest service in the world that I could render him would be to conclude this treaty, which he longed to obtain so that he might return to Spain.[1]

It is probable that the assertion is true and yet something more than the truth, for the Bishop of Arras (Granvelle) was an able diplomat and was not a man to relinquish authority to a stripling, but the Prince was certainly a factor in the proceedings. The final service asked of him was highly honourable, as he was appointed to act as one of the three hostages to Henry II. to assure the fulfilment of all the intricate and manifold provisions. With the Duke of Alva and Ruy Gomez, Orange proceeded to Paris in the early summer as the official guest of Henry II. The envoys carried their own baggage and kept up their own establishments during their obligatory detention in the French capital, as is shown by a little incident which Joseph de la Pise relates.[2]

[1] Dumont, *Corps universel diplomatique*, v., p. 384, etc.
[2] *Tableau des princes*, etc., p. 270.

The butler's pantry of the house occupied by the Prince of Orange looked out upon a lane and through the window an array of silver plate was plainly visible to passers-by. The sight tempted a clever thief who succeeded in drawing piece after piece through the protecting grating by means of a long hook. The loss was quickly discovered, the man arrested and condemned to death, all without the knowledge of the victim of the theft. Just as the execution was about to take place, the royal hunt rode by the place and the Prince, always alert to events about him, asked a bystander for what crime the culprit was to die. "For stealing the plate of the Prince of Orange," was the reply of the man, not knowing to whom he was speaking. At once the Prince begged his host to pardon the thief. Then he himself galloped up to the scaffold and stayed the proceedings until the more leisurely King arrived and gave his royal command to free the condemned, who was dismissed after a little gratuitous sermon from his deliverer as to the evil of his ways and the need of radical reform. "By this act," adds the appreciative historian, "the greater part of the silver was recovered which a more rigorous treatment would have lost to the owner."

There was a series of festivities before the celebration of the matrimonial alliance between the French Princess and the Spanish King, Alva being Philip's proxy, and also there was some bickering about the fulfilment of certain minor conditions of the treaty.

In this fashion the contract with exhibition of powers was concluded on Wednesday [writes Orange, June 24th] at about seven o'clock in the evening at the Louvre, where later the betrothal took place, and day before yesterday the marriage was solemnised in front of the great church by Cardinal de Bourbon.

The article respecting the first third of the said sum of 400,000 crowns was left with the words *de la consummation*. However, when it was read to the king at the time of registering it, the constable declared that payment should be prompt.

That, Monsieur d'Arras, is all that has passed up to now as regards my commission, without my having been able to obtain an answer from these people on the items of our joint charge that we submitted in advance. They have continually put me off with the assertion that they would do it. And seeing that they were so occupied with the festivities, I did not press them quite as much as would have been suitable. But if, now that the festivities are over, they still delay in answering me, I will not hesitate to force matters. I was worked so hard the day of the wedding that I was forced to stay in bed all day yesterday.

As to the wedding of the Duke of Savoy, that is postponed for a week—until eight days from to-morrow—with the excuse that his accoutrements will not be ready sooner, though it is said that the delay may be much longer. To-morrow the most Christian King will begin the tourneys. Please repeat this to his Catholic Majesty, and let me have frequent news of

your health. In recommending myself, M. d'Arras, etc.
From Paris, St. John the Baptist's Day, 1559.[1]

It is generally accepted that this Paris visit
marked the date when the young courtier, hitherto
loyal to his own sovereign, made a definite choice
of the line of conduct he meant, thenceforth,
to pursue. Among the popularly familiar illustrations of the life of the Founder of the Dutch
Republic is that of William of Nassau riding by
the side of Henry II. in the forest of Vincennes
on a summer day of 1559. The French monarch
took it for granted that this protégé of the late
Emperor, this trusted servant of the present King,
would be cognisant of all the purposes of Philip
and so casually referred to the concerted action
that he and his ex-foe were proposing to take
in order to uproot heresy effectually from their
respective domains. The Prince was taken completely by surprise. In these long months of
peace negotiations these particular measures had
never been mentioned to him as a part of the
international peace policy of the reconciled
neighbours. But he gave no signs of perturbation at the King's disclosure, and Henry was quite
unconscious of his companion's previous ignorance
of what he was divulging.

[1] *Cor.*, i., p. 416. The minute of the letter [Brussels archives]
is in the handwriting of Berty, secretary to the three hostages.
It is not signed, but Gachard considers that the writer was Orange
and the style seems like his of that period. Moreover his habit
of staying in bed when over-tired is well known.

Now it is possible that the hostage did learn from his royal host the fact that, in spite of his intimate association with the successive steps of the negotiations, there had still been secret conferences of which he had not been informed. The annoyance excited by this discovery rested in his memory to germinate later into a more definite criticism from a different point of view, more mature and highly coloured by intervening events. It is difficult wholly to reject the assertions of the *Apology*, supported as it is by Pontus Payen, while implicit trust in its being the perfect truth is equally difficult. There is the mingling of veracious and faulty statements in the document natural in retrospect when an individual has emerged into a later phase of existence, when an old order has given way to a new.

When I was in France [so runs the *Apology*][1] I heard out of King Henry's own mouth that the Duke of Alva had discussed with him the annihilation of all suspected of the religion in France, in the Netherlands, and in all Christendom. The king thought, since I was one of the plenipotentiaries in the peace negotiations, that I was informed of this important circumstance and that I belonged to the same party. So he revealed to me the secret schemes of the King of Spain and the Duke of Alva. In order not to fall into contempt with the king as if secrets were kept from me, I answered so that the king was not undeceived.

[1] There are, however, indications in other letters showing that his attention was turned to the persecutions at this time and that he strongly disapproved of them.

PHILIP II., AS PRINCE OF SPAIN, 1548
BY TITIAN

That led to a complete exposition on his part of the establishment of the inquisition. I confess that I was overwhelmed with pity and sympathy for so many worthy people dedicated to ruin and for this land to which I owed so much and in which an inquisition was to be introduced more terrible than the Spanish inquisition. Thus nets were to be spun in which the nobles and people of the land were destined to be entangled, so that the Spanish and their adherents should gain control over them, which they never could have acquired in any other way. Escape would have been impossible, for nothing more was needed than to look askance at an image to be condemned to the stake. Seeing these things as I say, I confess that from that moment I determined to aid in clearing these Spanish vermin out of the land and I have never repented my resolution.[1] ...

From the marvellous self-control maintained as he listened to the King's words the epithet of the silent one, of *le taciturne*, became attached for ever to this William of Nassau, at least such is the legend repeated by one pen after another until it has won a permanent place for itself.

If his antagonism to his chief were, indeed, aroused and formulated in that one flash, the Prince succeeded marvellously well in keeping up the show of his former loyalty and in proceeding along the general line of his official duty without any explosion in regard to the particular grievance. But relations between him and Philip were

---

[1] Dumont, v., p. 392.

strained at times in the last weeks of the latter's sojourn in the North.

The postponed marriage of the King's sister with the Duke of Savoy had to be celebrated in quite a different fashion from the splendour attending the nuptials of Elizabeth of Valois. On June 29th, the order of the entertainment was a magnificent tournament in the faubourg St. Antoine, in which the King received a wound in the eye. The court gaiety was instantly clouded by anxiety and apprehension, during the days that elapsed before the fatal termination of the wound. On July 10th, Henry II. died and the brief career of Francis II. and Mary Stuart followed.

The Duke of Alva was forced to stay on in the gloomy court, as Philip desired to have someone watch his own young wife under the changed circumstances, but Orange hastened back to Brussels as quickly as he could,[1] and then a series of important events, public and private, followed in rapid succession.

Margaret of Austria, Duchess of Parma, illegitimate daughter of the late Emperor, was appointed Regent of the Netherlands. Under her the Prince of Orange was made Stadtholder of Hol-

---

[1] He was urged to return by Count Egmont who wrote (July 8, 1559, Brussels): "Car il e(s)t question de fere quelques remonstrances au roy où que votre présence serviroit de beaucoup, se sont toutes choses quy vous emportent grandement comme des princhipaulx de pardecha." The holograph letter [2 pp. in fol.] was in the Rappard collection of MS. sold at Amsterdam, June 16–17, 1910.

land, Zealand, and Utrecht, as René and Henry of Nassau had been before him. Then he was immediately called upon to fulfil many delegated duties falling to the nobles' share, on account of the imminent departure of Philip II. for Spain. There were, moreover, important meetings of the Netherlanders to take the monarch's parting words. A chapter of the Order of the Golden Fleece[1] was held as well as an assembly of the States-General, and in both of these there was bitterness to temper the sweetness of the complimentary phrases addressed to the King. At the first, two of the vacant places were filled by the election of Hoogstraaten and Martigny directly against Philip's expressed wish. At the second, the provincial deputies respectfully and firmly demanded that the Netherlands should be cleared of all Spanish troops and refused to vote an *aide*[2] requested by the King, until this withdrawal were assured. Philip knew that Orange had been to the fore in both actions and naturally resented the opposition which he thought he could trace to its source. On his part the Prince had private grievances in addition to the suspicions that he had been played with in the treaty.

In common with all the nobles, Orange was

[1] The Prince had been taken into the Order in 1555.

[2] An *aide* was originally a pecuninary tribute paid on certain occasions by a vassal to his lord. In the Netherlands by Philip's time it had become a mere appropriation, but requested, not levied. If the deputies of the towns acceded to the sovereign's request they raised the money as they could.

displeased at the unexpected nomination of the King's half sister to the regency, and personally he felt that he had been undermined in certain advantageous marriage projects that had successively seemed almost within his grasp. But there was no open rupture between the two men although there is one frequently repeated story, resting on the testimony of a single witness, Louis Aubéry,[1] that Philip did give vent publicly to his irritation on one memorable occasion.

At the very moment when he was about to embark he began to reproach the Prince for the audacity of the States-General in daring to make conditions before granting him the *aide*. Orange replied that the States alone were responsible. "Not the States, but you, you, you," was the monarch's angry rejoinder, the last word of his ever heard by the Prince.

Then Philip turned his face homeward, and Margaret of Austria, Duchess of Parma, was left to carry on the intricate government of the aggregated provinces. Henceforth these Low Countries were to be administered as though they were a kind of colonial possession of Spain. The Netherland nobles were left in responsible individual positions as stadtholders of the various provinces and were, as a group, expected to be a support to the deputed ruler. As a matter of fact the balance of power was shifted at court in a way to effect the equilibrium.

[1] *Mémoires de Louis Aubéry, Seignior du Maurier*, p. 11.

The Prince of Orange had another change to meet in this year 1559, as the death of his father (October 6th) made him head of his family. He had not the usual gain of eldest sons, being already in possession of all that he was to inherit. The German estates fell to his brothers with John at the head, but the Prince never discarded the paternal titles he had a right to wear, and his position as actual chief of the Nassaus was never denied him by his brothers.

On October 15th he sent Count Louis a letter about the loss they had all suffered and filled with expressions of hope that the traditions of family unity would be faithfully preserved. "You who know my affection for my brothers can assure them of my sentiments. Try and assist Madame our mother according to our duty towards her. Serve her and please her in all that you can," etc., are the concluding phrases of the letter of "this very good brother to command." A postscript follows, less formal and less conventional in its phrases:

My brother: As to the journey which you were to make with the Count of Schwarzburg on the business you wot of, I beg you to tell me your plans and whether you expect to go or not so that I can arrange accordingly. I pray you to kiss for me the hands of the Count of Schwarzburg and of my sister Catherine and to assure her that I will be a good brother to her all my life as well as to Juliana and Magdalene. Though they have lost a father they shall find another in me. I beg you to let me know what the Count of Schwarzburg has resolved about his marriage and anything else going on there and present my most humble duty to our mother.

Your very good brother,
WILLIAM.

The purpose of the expedition mentioned introduces a new chapter in the Prince's career—which will be treated by itself later.

ORANGE MEDAL

CHAPTER V

THE PRINCE IN 1559

WITH Philip's departure and the death of William the Elder the Prince's terms of subordinate life may be counted as ended, and the mature man stands forth as the finished product of his inherited past and his acquired present, of his education and his training, of his experiences and his environment. What individual of twenty-six could be found in all Europe so singularly well prepared for his then opening career of public service as the younger William of Nassau? His early studies have been described. Undoubtedly they were good as far as they went and they went into languages, probably, rather than into mathematics or science. Later state documents, bearing the Prince's signature, show, indeed, a marvellous facility in classical and historical allusion; but some of that matter, occasionally the major part, ponderous as it is facile, was the work of secretaries trained to the use of compendia of knowledge. Still the Prince was never the blind follower of a scribe. His general information was sufficiently wide to enable him to know what suited his purpose in any line of knowledge; and, as time went on, his main desire was ability to handle human beings. In this age after the Renaissance, when many people of rank played with bits of learning, there was no trace of the *précieux* in this noble's amusements. He did not dip into the æsthetic pleasures affected by Italian potentates nor did he, like Philip of Hesse, revel in knotty theological problems as agreeable mental exercise. He was not a connoisseur in art though he indulged in an expensive household luxury that included art among its necessities, but it was distinctly as a patron, not as an amateur catering to his own sensitive æsthetic tastes. That little apocryphal glimpse of his dancing away merrily in Paris without keeping time to the music seems curiously possible as a true portrait of the young lieutenant at eighteen. At twenty-four his dignity would hardly have permitted him to dance for a prize, but he was no better skilled in music than Vieilleville made him in his picture. His ear was attuned to the human chord and the world of man was his orchestral instrument. At the court of Charles V., he was perfectly initiated into the mysteries of etiquette and into the usages of European society. He was completely at ease with people of rank, and when it came to conversing with his inferiors he adopted a genial tone without thought of his rank, too assured to be jeopardised. A pleasant way, a ready identification of faces, a cordial greeting to all comers, were habits as natural to him as breathing, and won him many adherents, with or without intention on his part. "Every time the Prince lifts his hat he wins a friend," was the statement of an opponent.

Then the practical training given to the youth after he passed on from the status of page and pupil was immensely valuable in developing his character and in enriching his resources. His military experience was one of exacting service, not that of a pampered courtier in a fancy regiment. He learned the kind of obedience which leads to a power of command. He was thoroughly disciplined by, and cognisant of, the sordid side of warfare, not stimulated by the strained excitement of a few brilliant battles. He acquired a field knowledge of the science of pitching camps and of building fortifications, and his letters show that he was well versed in the local conditions required for military construction. He gained a painful acquaintance with the results of short commons and of uncertain wages when dealing with grasping and restless mercenaries, and then, unlike most commanders, as a civil officer he had the equally painful experience of explaining financial needs to the non-combatant commercial and reluctant tax-payers or to their representatives, sitting solidly upon the covers of the civic money chests. When he was charged with the ungrateful task of urging Estates and towns to contribute liberally towards royal expenditure, he fulfilled his duty as long as he thought the requests of his master proper, and then he took sides with the opposition in open assembly of the States-General.

He had learned what was meant by the law's delays and by legal quips and quirks in the tedious Catzenellenbogen suit, in which his father was absorbed when he was born and which was communicated to him as an independent party before he was barely old enough to comprehend the intricacies of *meum* and *tuum*. All his early experiences were far in advance of the usual age for responsibility. While his own children were still in their nurse's arms, it has been shown how Orange was consulted by his father regarding the details of the education and training of his younger brothers and sisters, who all accepted his fraternal advice gratefully and were his adoring admirers and faithful followers to the end of their days.

The Prince's missions to Germany both at behest of his sovereign and in behalf of Nassau affairs, possibly one journey to England, the important part he played in the Cateau-Cambrésis treaty, the official sojourn in Paris with its disillusionments and annoyances,—all these experiences alike were wonderful training for a mind like his. He was very young when he came under the influence of the Bishop of Arras, Anthony Perrenot, and was thoroughly schooled in the skilful methods of that astute churchman when he was rudely turned from a natural boyish admiration for the man's high degree of cultivated cleverness by the discovery that Orange himself had been treated with the same smooth duplicity that he had seen diplomatically employed towards others, with the same pretended frankness combined with actual deception. Yet the outer relations between prelate and prince were unchanged for some time, because the latter had learned worldly wisdom and self-control from the former.

The fact that his experiences in affairs, as in theology, were international was one element that differentiated William of Nassau from the majority of his German, Italian, French, and English contemporaries. As said before, it would be strange if a man living contentedly in one set of daily associations with loving memories of and intercourse with another quite alien, in respect to the standards of religious life, possessed the same intensity of conviction regarding any local standard as a home-keeping youth. Family links certainly formed a strong chain to keep the Prince from floating away in the court atmosphere. There was always one anchor that tugged at his heart-strings while he was sailing close to a Spanish-Austrian wind.

As regards the Prince's outward appearance there is the portrait given as frontispiece, painted about this time. That shows an agreeable, forceful face. In addition there is the following contemporary (1562) description of him: "Now twenty-five years old, his stature is well developed, his figure distinguished. He is strong and manly, skilled in military science, a great favourite among the people whose affection he gains by open-handed generosity. He is a prince of the greatest promise."[1]

From a material point of view at the first glance, his position appears as favourable as that of a private individual could be, especially after 1559 when the Franco-Spanish peace restored, to a partial degree, the enjoyment of the Orange-Chalons estates. His property consisted of several distinct portions, besides his interest in the German heritage of his House. The smallest fraction of the whole was the German part. That was confined to certain liens upon the Nassau heritage and upon one-half of the Catzenellenbogen portion adjudged to the plaintiffs. The principality of Orange was not very large. The Prince referred to it as about one-sixth of his whole property.[2] But it was a dominant sixth— as its sovereign held by the gift of God, subject to no king. To be sure this nominal independence was somewhat shadowy, although the princes were enabled by it to address kings as "cousin." The enjoyment *de facto* depended on the good will of the French monarch in whose realm the tiny statelet was embedded, bordering on Languedoc, Provence, Dauphiné, and the papal Avignon. The capital was the city of the same name, the seat

---

[1] *Cor.*, Marg. d'Autriche, Reiffenberg, p. 368.
[2] La Pise, *Tableau de l'histoire des princes et principauté d'Orange*, p. 261. See also Rachfahl, i., p. 141.

of a university founded in 1536 and of a parliament (not established, however, until 1571) the highest court of the diminutive land. The town lies east of the Rhone, at the foot of a hill crowned with a citadel. It is further noted for a theatre built into the green hillside and for other remains of Roman occupation. Besides the town of Orange there were, within the principality, three unwalled towns, various villages and hamlets, castles and fiefs in the hands of noble vassals. It is a lovely spot, a garden of France, the northern edge of the olive region. But there had been few periods in its history when the enjoyment of the line of petty sovereigns of Orange had not been hampered. These seigniors had usually adhered to the Emperor in the long series of Franco-imperialist hostilities, at the outbreak of which the principality was regularly confiscated by the French King to be as regularly returned when peace was made. The loss suffered by William of Nassau was simply a repetition of the experience of his predecessors. In 1552, as a compensation for the deprivation of his lands in France, Charles V. assigned to him the temporary usufruct of certain Netherland estates confiscated from Anthony of Bourbon.

In the heritage as it fell to René of Nassau from Philibert of Orange, there were also various estates in the duchy and Franche-Comté of Burgundy and, in addition to what the legal possessor could be actually invested with, a number of claims and titles of one kind and another all so shadowy that it could be truly said that the major part of this fair sounding wealth consisted of castles in the air rather than on earthly foundations. For instance, as legatee of the three families of Orange, Beaux, and Chalons, William of Nassau had pretensions to one kingdom, Arles, to one duchy, Gramine, to three principalities, sixteen countships, two margraveships, two viscountships, and to more than fifty baronies, and three hundred lordships! If he could have made good his claims on French soil he would have been the richest peer in France, but his actual usufruct was fragmentary in spite of intermittent prospects of better times. In the treaty of 1559, all the estates in Dauphiné were ordered to be restored to the Prince but the restoration was never effected.

The exact scope of the estates he was ever actually permitted to control in France is not known. Those in the Franche-Comté yielded about 27,000 livres excluding the dower right of René's sometime widow, the Duchess of Aerschot. But this was not clear revenue. Litigation respecting other portions was a continual drain and there were other leakages that diminished the current flowing into the Prince's private treasury.

In other sections the value of the property can be more precisely estimated. The profits from the countship of Brabant and the viscountship of Antwerp amounted to 65,500 livres. There were

VIEW OF BREDA.

a few holdings in Brabant which finally lapsed to the Prince after the demise of the Duchess of Aerschot and some fairly profitable estates in Luxemburg and Flanders, to which were added all the disposable property of Anna of Egmont whose will was in her husband's favour, so far as she was free to make it. The estimated income was in total about 200,000 livres, which implied a capital of about 4,000,000 livres. In order to obtain the comparative significance of this revenue, it may be stated that the net return of the royal domain in the Netherlands was about one-third more.

Unfortunately for the Prince, much of what revenue he did receive was spent long before it fell due. The estate was terribly encumbered at his accession. In 1549 his guardians had difficulty in saving 12,000 livres for the cash income. The years of minority were well employed in nursing the estate, and some relief was afforded when certain moneys came in on the death of the Duchess of Aerschot and when a large quantity of timber was felled in Luxemburg and sold at a good profit. But the whole debt was not liquidated and new burdens came. Every charge accepted by the Prince, military and diplomatic, entailed heavy outlays for which the allotted honoraria were insufficient. Granvelle estimated the Prince's debts (1560) at more than 900,000 guilders, his available income at 25,000, and his household expenses at 90,000. This estimate was probably not mere guess-work, as Jerome Perrenot was at one time chamberlain of the Prince's household and might have given his brother definite information as to the state of affairs.

The administration of this encumbered estate was a veritable business in itself and was carried on at Breda by several officials retained for the purpose.

Meantime the maintenance of the ordinary routines of the households at Breda and in Brussels was very lavish and very extravagant. An open buffet laden with good things invited not only the passing friend but the chance acquaintance to make good cheer, and the invitation was easily accepted. Perhaps the years of the most reckless expenditure were those of the Prince's widowerhood, as they were also the most self-indulgent. There are frequent references in the intimate letters which show that his standard of life and morals was by no means puritanic at this period.

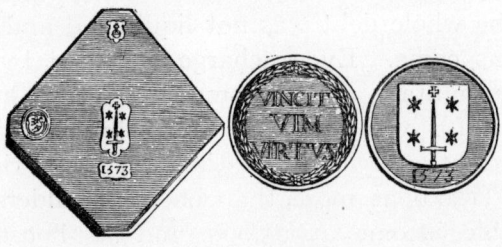

SIEGE MONEY

CHAPTER VI

THE SECOND MARRIAGE

1560–1561

IN the postscript to the Prince's letter of October 15, 1559, occurs a reference to a personal matter that, in the end, took on large proportions and shadowed his actions for nearly two years. The Nassau family circle was at one in the desire to see this important member enter into a second marriage. The question before them all was what eligible *partie* in the matrimonial market offered the highest degree of advantage to an ambitious man. Worldly motives, such as had invariably affected the choice of a consort among the Prince's forbears, were paramount in his own case in a perfectly undisguised manner.

Two separate schemes for a French alliance had failed in a fashion to convince Orange that there had been underhand machinations on the part of Philip, instigated by Anthony Perrenot.[1]

---

[1] Orange had proposed for Renée of Lorraine, Philip's cousin german. It is said that her widowed mother, Christine, intimated that she herself would be a more suitable match for the Prince than her daughter. Another version of the rupture of negotiations was that the widow stipulated that her daughter's

Therefore, when he turned to Germany to pursue his quest, he kept his own counsel strictly within a small group of intimates until the negotiations were fairly launched, so that the project should escape the risk of being stifled at the outset. The "business you wot of" mentioned in the October letter quoted in an earlier chapter was nothing less than preliminary steps towards a proposal for the hand of Anne of Saxony, daughter of the late Duke Maurice and niece of the reigning Elector of Saxony. Many advantages were apparent in this match. No other person, available at the moment, was equally well connected with various quasi-independent German princes whose friendship was peculiarly tempting to the Netherlander. This significance of the bride's kinsmen compensated for the fact that her actual dowry was not very large. Still that too was no insignificant sum for the times. It amounted in all to

---

possible offspring should take precedence of the Prince's children by Anna of Egmont. Still another was that Philip and Perrenot feared Christine's intrusion into Netherland politics through a powerful son-in-law.

The Prince's second choice in France was the widow of the Duc d'Enghien, a daughter of the Count of St. Pol. This time it was, apparently, the French king who put in a veto.

Meantime Orange was not enhancing his own reputation for good morals. A certain Eve Elivir who bore him a son (September, 1559), Justin of Nassau, was, apparently, only one of several mistresses with whom he amused himself. This is proven by various passages in familiar letters. Justin was acknowledged and educated by the Prince. Later he became Admiral of Holland and a good right hand to his half-brother Maurice whom he served faithfully.

100,000 thalers.[1] There were, however, potent reasons why this particular selection of a German bride should have been peculiarly repugnant to the Prince's royal master. Anne's father, Maurice of Saxony, had inflicted notorious humiliation upon Philip's father; and not only had the girl herself been nurtured in the Protestant faith, but another bitter opponent of the late Emperor and of the Catholic Church, Philip, Landgrave of Hesse, was her maternal grandfather and possessed equal control with her paternal uncle over the disposition of her hand. The Landgrave, on his part, was not pleased at the proposed match and had many sententious opinions to utter on the impropriety of sacrificing an innocent young girl by mating her with an irreligious courtier who attended popish rites regularly, albeit with the careless heart of an indifferent worshipper.

The Elector was the main promoter of the matrimonial alliance. Private reasons made him find the suitor quite to his taste. Had his niece been a boy, Augustus could not have filled his brother's electoral shoes, and he was far from feeling perfectly secure in his footing until it was certain upon what manner of man Anne's hand was to be bestowed. With an ambitious German princeling or baron as her husband an inconvenient claim

[1] Of this 25,000 came from Anne's mother, 10,000 from her father in accordance with an informal memorandum written on his death-bed but duly recognised by his heir Augustus, who moreover increased the legacy by 35,000 thalers. Thirty thousand thalers came to Anne after the death of her step-father.

upon her paternal heritage might be urged. The suit of the Prince of Orange offered an excellent opportunity of sending the late Duke's heiress safely out of the empire with an honourable husband possessing a dignified sufficiency of titles and offices of his own. The prospect was tempting enough to make the Elector willing to shut his eyes to the diversity of religious interests, and this willingness was fully shared by the Electress who found her husband's niece no agreeable member of her household and was desirous of being freed from an uncongenial guardianship of a difficult ward.

Anne was born in 1544 and was, therefore, in her seventeenth year in 1560, when the negotiations for her hand were well under way. Thus she possessed youth but little else of the charm associated with her tender years. Not only were her features without positive beauty but her figure was actually slightly misshapen, a fact that induced her uncle to add, when stating his reasons for accepting the Prince's proposal, that if this opportune chance of matrimony missed fire, Anne might be left unwedded for good and all. Her disposition was apparently in harmony with her figure,—slightly distorted out of the normal. There was early indication that she was extremely self-willed and headstrong. Both tenacity and obstinacy were traits to be expected in Anne's composition. Her own father and her mother's father were two of the most determined and least conciliatory men of their generation, and it was not astonishing that a child of their joint race should fail to be a gentle and amenable Griselda. The very qualities that, at their best, made the Landgrave a kind of intellectual force and stamped the Elector as a masterful soldier, at their worst rendered poor untrained, immature Anne restless and jealous at her failure to be first, and unable to see that fate had not united capacity to her ambitions. At an early stage in the proceedings her imagination was fired by stories of the stately court at Brussels, and when at last the Prince, a shining ornament of that gay court, came (December, 1560) in person to Dresden to further his own wooing, she was completely captivated by his manner, polished beyond the wont of the ordinary German noble. His graceful speeches carried more meaning to her inexperienced mind than they would have to a woman of fashion. They were sweet music to an ear unaccustomed to the mere commonplaces of social life. This agreeable gentleman had said, too, that he would rather have her amuse herself with gay romances than be bored with treatises. It all sounded very pleasant. Thenceforth Anne was bent upon the alliance with all the dogged force of a mind intense as it was limited, meagre as it was undisciplined.

Her consent was, however, a very small item in the affair; and it was many months after Count Louis and the Count of Schwarzburg had carried the Prince's overtures to Dresden, before the

nuptial contract was concluded. The interests
involved were contradictory, and Orange had to
feel his way very carefully before the Catholic
Philip's countenance was obtained and before
the Protestant Philip's prohibition was removed.
Only a man with the innate qualities of a com-
promiser could have steered through so many
shoals without losing the ballast of his personal
integrity, without actual deterioration and a loss
of self-respect. One author calls the incident
of the Saxon marriage a black spot on the Prince's
character.[1] It may be urged, however, that the
procedure showed capacity for sophistry rather
than moral turpitude. The man had determined
to act according to his own judgment, and he let
fly plausible versions of his motives here and there
with the evident intention of silencing rather than
with any hope of converting his critics. He went
as far as possible on his way before his itinerary
was published and he did this with deliberate
purpose. He meant that it should be too late
to retrace steps, the right to which he intended
to have taken for granted, as belonging to himself
alone. His first formal announcement to his own
government was made not to the Regent, who might
be too well informed about the Saxon family, but
to the distant King, to whom vague and general

---

[1] "For his fanatical admirers as well as for the enemies of
Orange, the caution is not superfluous that they must remember
it is not charged that his whole character consists of these two
blemishes."—Ritter, *Hist. Zeitschrift.*, lviii., p. 410.

terms could be used, veiling the exact identity of the maiden. The Prince's undated letter to Philip advising that monarch of his proposed marriage with "a niece of the Elector of Saxony," was probably written in February, 1560.[1] He is definite in his assertion that due regard will be paid to the interests of the Catholic religion. Philip replies in non-committal terms. His sister "would be a more competent judge of the matter," etc.[2] During the subsequent months when the ultimate maturity of the plan was often doubtful, Anthony Perrenot seized every occasion to refer to the project incidentally in his letters to the King, always adding that he earnestly hoped for its failure.[3] "The Prince had indeed every appearance of being a Catholic yet one never could tell what would be the results of alien influence," etc. When Orange returned from Dresden and again mentioned the marriage in more definite terms, Philip in his turn wrote to Perrenot expressing his great disappointment, although at the same time he directed his sister to give her consent if there were no means of stopping the proceedings, adding in plaintive rather than authoritative phrases: "Really, I do not understand how the Prince *can* mate himself with the daughter of a man who acted towards his sainted Majesty as Duke Maurice did."[4]

[1] *Cor.*, i., p. 430.   [2] *Ibid.*, p. 345.
[3] *Papiers d'état du Cardinal Granvelle*, vi., p. 29, etc.
[4] *Ibid.*, p. 175.

The Prince's expedition to Dresden and back was made the occasion of much merry-making. Orange appears entirely in the light of a man relaxing from the tension of public affairs and ready to amuse himself in social converse with the friends who were interested in his projects and in furthering his wishes. And they lightened their labours by sparing neither wine nor beer as they journeyed along. In his letter to Augustus, to thank him for his agreeable visit at Dresden, Orange says that he and his comrades have quaffed so many glasses to the Elector's health on the homeward journey that they are still suffering from the ill effects. From Breda he writes to Schwarzburg, now husband of Catherine of Nassau, that his party made disturbance enough on their way home (*assez de désordre sur le chemin*), and then adds:

I assure you I feel very solitary here and cannot forget the excellent cheer we have had together. I long to be with you, not only for your own sake but because I should be near *fraielle Anne*. I have not yet been at court as I am obliged to make a trip to Holland, so that I have no fresh news to tell you.[1]

The business that demanded Orange's presence in Holland was to urge the Estates to grant the supplies needed by the Regent. This trip was a contrast to the other. There was no joyous companionship. The alternation of frost and

[1] Groen, i., p. 68.

thaw increased the difficulties of travelling, and the Prince's errand was an extremely ungrateful one. The Estates steadily refused to make an appropriation except upon conditions which the Regent declined accepting, and the stadtholder found reconciliation of the two points of view fully as difficult a task as that of satisfying the opposing opinions in relation to his own plans.

For, to return to the Prince's private affairs, antagonism to the Saxon alliance remained rampant long after the principals in the bargain, the guardian, the suitor, and the maiden, were firmly resolved to guard against possible shipwreck of their intentions when once launched upon the current. All the projectiles of argument hurled against the bark rebounded, fell, and made little futile whirlpools without imperilling the channel.

In March, a polite and ponderous epistle came from the Landgrave to Orange explaining why it was absolutely impossible to allow his granddaughter to give him her hand. Having stated his objections on the score of religion, Philip of Hesse adds that even if that insurmountable barrier did not exist, never could he permit an alliance when the very name of the possible offspring was uncertain. Necessarily, Orange's children by his first wife had the right of primogeniture, and it was not suitable for the grandchildren of the great Elector Maurice to take second rank, etc.[1]

[1] Groen, i., p. 81.

There is a story, gravely repeated with an appearance of credibility, that the old Landgrave was less punctilious in regard to the consciences of his own offspring than to that of his ward's, and that he was willing, rather than countenance an incongruous mismating of Protestant and Catholic, to permit one of his daughters — there were several still flourishing on the parent stem—turn Catholic outright and marry the papist Prince.[1] Undoubtedly, this assertion, strange in this Philip's mouth, was a mere figure of speech, a *reductio ad absurdum* of the argument, not an offer expected to be taken seriously by any one.

The following letter from Orange to Count Louis, written about a fortnight after the receipt of the Landgrave's futile ultimatum, was as follows:

I have decided to send someone to the duke to make a verbal statement concerning my intentions [evidently *in re* religion] and certain other things of which my German secretary will inform you. I am thinking of begging you to do this service for me and of asking you affectionately to take this trouble and to go to the said duke and discuss the subject with him confidentially, taking as your guide the enclosed memorandum and the advices of my secretary. . . .

Pray press the maiden's hand on my behalf and tell her how I envy your good fortune in being able to see her when I cannot. Thank her for the warm affection toward me that her letter shows and say further that I implore her, as our wedding day is fixed and

[1] Bakhuizen van den Brink, *Het Huwelijk, etc.* p. 145.

WILLIAM OF NASSAU, PRINCE OF ORANGE, 1561

the arrangements so advanced, to continue in the same attitude of mind and not to let herself be persuaded into indefinite postponements. If anyone tries to make her believe the existence of obstacles regarding religion or anything else, tell her to rest assured that for my part I will try my best to live with her so that she may be content. If they attempt to put any notion in her head to increase the difficulties, I think the answer best calculated to silence everybody would be, "If God has willed this we will agree together,"—which ought to stop idle talk. I beg you to make this plain to her, for you know very well the result of incessant chatter. I regret troubling you and am sorry, too, to lose your company for so long but it need not be a matter of more than a fortnight.

As to the chase of Holland my license is come from Spain and the King has also appointed me to the government of Burgundy.

I have had a present of the prettiest hunting dog in the world, white as snow. I took a heron yesterday on a very long flight which lasted a quarter of an hour in steady ascent.

Your affectionate and obedient brother,

WILLIAM OF NASSAU.

BRUSSELS, March 23, 1561.[1]

On the younger brother's part ready obedience was, indeed, always to be counted on when the Prince's behests were to be fulfilled. In this case he proved a faithful emissary to Dresden, certainly as far as Anne was concerned. A letter written

[1] Groen. i., p. 93.

by her to the Prince a little later contains assurances of her steadfastness and of her determination not to be overruled by her grandfather's prejudices. "My feelings towards your Highness are the same as when I last wrote and I mean to bide by them, for I firmly believe that what God has decreed the devil himself cannot hinder,"[1]—a phrase suggestive of a sweet and docile maiden! The commission to press Anne's hand in behalf of his brother was a side issue in Louis's mission. The main point was to convince the Elector by word of mouth that the Prince would protect his wife in the exercise of her religion. Louis was less successful with the uncle than with the niece. Augustus insisted on his taking charge of a certain "little document," characterised by the Count as "rather strange, diffuse and hairsplitting" ("*etwas seltsam, weitläufig und spitzfindig*")."[2] This contained stipulations that Anne should enjoy Protestant services, and be assured of Evangelical baptism for her children and of a better dower house than Hadamar. In forwarding this paper to the Prince, Louis advised him to have nothing to do with it.

As he then stood with the King and Church it would have been impossible for Orange to have set his signature to such a document, whose existence would speedily have been reported to Spain. He confined himself to verbal assurances that his wife should be treated as befitted her

[1] Groen, i., p. 94.   [2] *Ibid.*, p. 101.

lineage and her upbringing, while she must conform publicly to court usage, and with such statements the not over-solicitous uncle was obliged to be content. Signature to the "little document" was not made a *sine qua non* at that moment and the preparation for the nuptials went gaily on in spite of the frowns from Spain and the prohibitions from Hesse.

My brother [wrote Orange to Louis], now that the wedding day is appointed, please inquire particularly of Count Schwarzburg, if you see him, about the arrangements that will be necessary for my journey to Dresden, whether I should take a large escort from here, what presents I ought to give the bride and the bridesmaids, whether a wedding journey be needful or not, what Germans should be invited, and many other items which you think it would be well for me to know. Pray find out how the bride will be dressed and what colours the princess considers hers.[1]

The date settled on was August 24th,—a date that might have been considered one of ill omen a dozen years later when the name of St. Bartholomew became associated with the terrible massacre at Paris,—and the preparations were energetically rushed on to completion.

The old Landgrave, finding his protests quite unavailing, submitted to the inevitable with the words, "Since it must and will be, God the Almighty grant that it goes well with the fräulein

[1] Groen, i., p. 103.

in soul, in honour, and in weal of body and of estate." This chary blessing was all that could be wrung from him, and he steadily declined the invitations to ceremony and to festival for himself and his sons. Still, in lieu of better, his grudging words were gratifying to Augustus and to the Prince's mother, Juliana of Stolberg, who congratulated her son (June 21st) on the withdrawal of the opposition of the one man who was "so set against the marriage." Piously and affectionately she expresses a hope that henceforth Almighty God will have the couple in his keeping.

The Spanish Philip, too, bowed assent to the inevitable. In spite of dissatisfaction his outward yielding was fairly graceful. He commanded Martigny to be his proxy at the wedding, and he sent his sister a draft of 3000 crowns wherewith to purchase a ring for the bride. Undoubtedly the formal sanction on the part of the King was advised by Granvelle as the wisest measure under the circumstances, but the prelate still continued to utter deprecatory phrases.

I am in no wise satisfied. *Perhaps* it will not be wholly disastrous to the Lord's service, but if He does not work a miracle it is to be feared that the Prince, instead of enhancing the reputation of his House which he publishes as his aim, may find himself involved in serious calamity—a result we have prophesied repeatedly.[1]

[1] Granvelle, *Papiers d'etat*, vi., pp. 288, 333.

Orange was obliged to content himself with
the scanty marks of royal courtesy thus accorded
him. There were disappointments, however, as
the chief nobles in the Netherlands were not
allowed to grace his wedding, finally appointed for
Leipsic instead of Dresden.

The Prynse of Orange is departyd for Docheland
to be maryed to the daughter of Duke Marysse with a
small company [writes an Englishman]. For whereas
he thought to have had dyvers nobellmen of thys
countrie with him there ys commandment given by
the King that no man in all thys Lowe Countrie bearing
any offys shall go with him on payne of losing his
offys and the King's displeasure besydes with ex-
presse words because they shall not be infected with
any of the heresies that are rife in that countrie.
What matter it ys thought that the Duchess will not
take in good part; which in the end may fall out ill:
for the Prynse is now waxing grette by this marriage
and presently his offyssers do sell most of the land
that he hath in thys country.[1]

The bridegroom's German friends and kinsmen
made up in number for the enforced absence of
official colleagues. The Elector's list of guests[2]
mentions 5500 persons entertained at his expense,
and the lists of provisions show that there was
no scarcity. The lesser Netherland nobles who
were free to follow their own devices came with
ninety-three horse. Orange himself brought an

[1] Richard Clough, in *Life of Sir T. Gresham*, i., p. 390.
[2] Arnoldi's *Historische Denkwürdigkeiten*, p. 131.

escort of sixty, while another cavalcade mentioned as "forty nobles and courtiers of the Prince," was composed of 117 horse. Naturally there were some regrets besides those from the Hesse family, —the King of Denmark, the Elector of Brandenburg, the Prince of Anhalt, and the Archbishop of Magdeburg could not come. But the wedding party was sufficiently large to prove the importance of the event and to tax the resources of Leipsic to the utmost. Every guest was requested to bring his own cooks and butlers, tableware and kitchen utensils, but all were assured that good cheer should be provided at the host's expense. The chief guests were entertained at dinner daily in the town-hall, the electoral residence being under repairs, and at these banquets the service was furnished by a corps of gentlemen and noble pages who had been requested to report at Leipsic on August 22nd.

Careful regulations were made for the benefit of the junior members of this volunteer band. There was a special injunction to abstain from drinking and from riotous conduct of every nature while the state dinners were in progress. "It would be a shameful impropriety if the foreign quality when at table found themselves unable to hear their own voices on account of the screaming of the attendants," seems an incontrovertible statement. Other precautions were taken, too, to ensure safety. Eight extra constables were sworn in to aid the two policemen in ordinary. A special force of fifty arquebusiers was provided for the town-hall, and a burgher guard of six hundred was distributed throughout the city to watch for fire.

The Elector, accompanied by four thousand followers, met the bridegroom outside the city, and the whole party—almost a royal cavalcade—rode in pompous procession to the town-hall, where Anne stood at the top of the staircase to greet her future spouse, and then she retired with her women to be arrayed for the nuptial ceremony.

That was to take place at five o'clock. Just before the appointed hour, the bridal pair together with the Elector and his wife, John of Nassau and Henry of Wiltberg, Sophia von Miltitz and the councillors Hans von Ponika and Ulrich Woltersdorff were assembled.[1] In the presence of the above named witnesses and the public notary, Wolf Seidel, Woltersdorff read aloud the unsigned document drawn up by Augustus on April 14th and sent to Orange by Louis, and the bridegroom was asked whether he would give a verbal promise to fulfil all the stipulations therein contained. They were that the Princess should be allowed to read evangelical books, and receive communion across the frontier and in her chamber in case of imminent death. The Prince answered: "Gracious Elector: I remember this document and all the

[1] Preserved in Dresden archives. See Motley, i., p. 312 *et seq.*

items read by Doctor Woltersdorff were contained therein. I promise your Grace herewith that I will keep all as becomes a prince." To enforce his words he gave the Elector his hand. The notary drew up a formal instrument containing this statement which was preserved in strictest secrecy, but undoubtedly the Elector was left free to mention the transaction to Philip of Hesse or to any of his niece's kith and kin inclined to blame a guardian for sending his ward into a papist household. Such was the end of the long-pending discussion. As said before, the Prince had behaved very diplomatically during the eighteen months of his international courtship. When he visited Dresden he went "diligently to church,"—a procedure not without parallel in many humbler circles of life, if a young man were anxious to propitiate family prejudices for the sake of the girl he was wooing. It is not probable that Augustus was deceived into thinking that Orange was satisfying his own soul, starved in the Catholic atmosphere of the Netherlands by drinking in the discourse of the German pastor. He treated the matter with the Prince as between two men of the world. The Electress, indeed took the pains to write on her own behalf to the suitor to ask some definite assurance of what Anne's religious future would be.[1] His answer was rather flippant. "There is no need of troubling a young girl with melancholy topics. Let her read *Amadis de*

[1] Böttiger in Von Raumer's *Taschenbuch*, 1st series, p. 100, etc.

Gaule and other romances rather than the Bible
and learn to dance a galliard instead of sitting over
her knitting and sewing." Naturally, to Philip of
Spain, Orange did not indulge in this light tone.
He certainly gave him to understand that his
own devotion to the ancient Church was perfect,
and asserted that his wife should live as a Catholic, *catholically*. Undoubtedly he dwelt more
on his own unhappiness at any other state
of affairs than was in accordance with his
convictions.

After the Elector had eased his conscience and
set himself right in case of inquiry by this little
private formality, all the guests assembled in state
in the great chamber of the town-hall to witness
the marriage ceremony performed by the Lutheran
Doctor Pfeffinger. At its conclusion, comfits and
spiced drinks were served to the newly wedded
pair, placed together upon a magnificent gilded
state couch, and their healths were drunk by the
assembled company. Margrave Hans of Brandenburg, speaking for the Elector, solemnly
committed the young wife to her husband's
charge, exhorting him to cherish her and to leave
her undisturbed in her fidelity to the gospel and
to the right use of the sacraments. After this
the Prince and Princess retired to their respective
apartments to dress for the banquet, during which
a program of the merriest, most ingenious music
was played, and after the tables were removed
dancing followed.

On the following day at seven o'clock a procession was formed to escort the young couple to the church of St. Nicholas to receive a blessing on the marriage already solemnised. Thus both ceremony and benediction followed Lutheran usages and there was no pretence of anything else. This was strictly in accordance with the law as it then stood in the empire. The ruler's theology was all dominant within his territory, and it was accepted that Augustus should send his niece away with a Lutheran blessing just as it was that she should consent to live "catholically" in the Netherlands, where King Philip was overlord.

In the three days' festival that followed, there was "no room for sorrow" in Leipsic.[1] Then the Prince and his wife started out on their homeward journey. The Landgrave permitted them to pass through his territory, but still nursed his displeasure sufficiently to refrain from inviting the travellers to come to his house. Little by little, however, he seems to have allowed himself to be pacified. In January he sends a special messenger to Breda bearing a gold chain for Anne and a gracious letter to the Prince. "A thousand good nights," in recognition of his gift are sent back to him by his granddaughter with assurance that she is happy as a queen and treated like one. A few months later comes another grandfatherly letter anxiously solicitous to know if Anne were true

[1] Poem on the wedding, Hague Library.

to the religious teachings of her father's house. To this she answers respectfully but in general terms, reiterating assurances of her complete contentment with her lot.[1]

[1] Groen., i., 118, 123.

BEGGARS' MEDAL

SIEGE MONEY

CHAPTER VII

THE NOBLES AND THE CARDINAL

1561–1564

WHILE the future still concealed the defects of the Prince's much-talked-of matrimonial bargain, he plunged into a second contest where again to outward appearances he was the victor and again the victory carried him to a field that he had not surveyed.

The Regent of the Netherlands, Margaret of Parma, was an industrious, painstaking person but far inferior to her predecessor, Marie of Hungary, in originality and in mental calibre. She was not really strong enough to stand alone and, though jealous of patent control, she was bound to be under the domination of some energetic will. Nay more, she was undoubtedly selected by her brother for the regency because he counted on this very quality of dependence. The person whom Philip intended to be his executive deputy *de facto* was Anthony Perrenot, Bishop of Arras, afterwards Cardinal Granvelle, and the politically minded prelate was both willing and able to keep in his hands all the threads within his reach as well as to stand behind the Regent's chair and dictate her actions. But neither he nor Philip, satisfied on his departure with this arrangement, took into consideration Margaret's own resentment of this policy as it ultimately manifested itself, nor the strength of the nobles' objections to an extraneous element being dominant in national councils. The double opposition speedily limited the extended operations of the ambitious prime-minister. The first reasons for the rise of antagonism against him were elemental in their simplicity. No human beings like to be deprived of authority nominally vested in themselves, and such deprivation was the grievance of the nobles.

As far back as 1531, Charles V. had established a Council of State in addition to a Privy Council and a Council of Finance, all three ostensibly designed to aid the existing Regent of the Netherlands in administration during his absence. The Council of State was composed of the most prominent native nobles and was represented as a bulwark for national interests. It proved to be nothing more than a showy ornament to display to the people as a sign that they were not governed by aliens; for Marie soon found that this new body might prove an inconvenient limitation to her own authority if it were permitted to stretch its wings. Accordingly nothing of importance was ever referred to it. "Councillor of State" became simply an honorary title. It seemed, therefore, a mark of great political liberality on Philip's part when he evinced his intention of revivifying this council, and of endowing its members with actual power in the administration of public affairs. Indeed it was only under pledges that the change should be wrought that Orange, Egmont, and the others were persuaded to accept seats. They were assured that, instead of being figure-heads, they were to represent their respective provinces in the open discussion of policy and of proposed legislation, and to have due voice in all decisions. Philip was, moreover, very courteous in his request to them to support his sister and to aid her with their local knowledge and their valuable advice. But even between the Emperor's departure and the King's, friction had arisen in regard to this branch of government. During the brief administration of the Duke of Savoy, a committee of nobles, with Lalaing at the head, had declared to the Regent their intention of resigning unless they were treated with more confidence. Their complaints seemed to bear fruit; some changes were made at once and there was a brief period when Granvelle, in his turn, asserted that important national interests were sacrificed to the nobles' procrastination. Then Philip gave no particular heed. His pressing need of funds forced him to humour those who might help to open the purse-strings of the Estates. Thus the nobles' weight went up and down in the balance, and there were criticisms and counter criticisms between the King's officials and the provincial functionaries.

But after Philip was gone, little time elapsed before it became evident that his henchmen were completely in the ascendant, and that Margaret was transacting state business much as her aunt had done, discussing details with three confidential advisers alone, Granvelle, Viglius, and Berlaymont, who formed an informal secret council, a *camarilla* or *consulta*. The titular councillors were again reduced to mere figure-heads. The method of procedure opened up a breach between the nobles and Granvelle. The latter was regarded as the chief instrument in the government concert, as the real factor in their discomfiture. Viglius and Berlaymont were rated as negligible quantities. It was natural enough that the native councillors should refuse to shoulder responsibility for decisions upon which they had never been consulted; yet many months passed by before the Prince's old friendship with the increasingly unpopular minister lost its outward guise. From August, 1559, to September, 1561, amicable relations were ostensibly maintained between the two, although Granvelle's correspondence with Philip teems with insidious intimations to the Prince's discredit. Orange might be loyal to King and Church, but he had his doubts. Iago's aside, nicely calculated to strike Othello's ear unpleasantly, "I like not that," was exactly on a par with Granvelle's references to his former protégé, even while he praises his general zeal.

But after Orange was settled in Brabant, with his German wife not converted to Catholicism, entertaining his German kinsfolk openly devoted to Protestantism, this outward harmony vanished. There was no further pretence of the intimacy that formerly led the Prince to drop in at the prelate's house on his return from a journey, to visit him in his bedroom, and to show all the marks of affectionate familiarity natural from a younger to an older man. It was war, if not to the knife, at least to the point of gratuitous insult. The development of the Prince's character is shadowed by the circumstances attendant on this alienation with his old friend, and the main events affecting it must be touched on although the condensation necessary here renders the story imperfect.

Long before the accession of Philip II., his father had planned a reorganisation of ecclesiastical jurisdiction in the provinces. As Charles had erected the territory into a circle of the empire (1548) for better political administration, so he deemed it wise to bring them into a compact group for the more convenient ordering of all religious matters. Primarily this was a simple affair of regulating church machinery.[1] The

[1] Fruin, "Het voorspel van den tachtigjarigen oorlog." *Verspreidegeschriften*, I., p. 267. "De oprichting der nieuwe bisdommen in Nederland in 1559." *Ibid.*, viii., p. 298.

existing dioceses were over-large and were, moreover, under the ultimate authority of the German and French archbishops of Cologne and Rheims. The step was not even initiated by Charles V. after the Protestant revolt had so disturbed the ancient foundations that new props were needed to shore up the ancient structure. The plan had been conceived by the Burgundian dukes far back in the fifteenth century, and naturally enough. It was a self-evident measure in the progress of nationalisation. If the Netherlands were to be an independent circle of the Roman Empire it was proper that French and German archbishops should be deprived of power to interfere in local church affairs.

On Philip's accession he lost little time in taking up this question and needed no instigation from the bishop to make him appeal to Rome for authority to work the changes. Granvelle, indeed, was not primarily in sympathy with the plan. He said that he preferred being one of four rather than of seventeen. He furthered the scheme only in obedience to the King's will, possibly, too,

---

It is curious to note that the enumeration of the bishoprics is by no means a fixed and simple one. Fruin mentions four old sees: Cambray, Utrecht, Arras, Tournay, and fourteen in the new list: Arras, Tournay, St. Omer, to be comprised within the Walloon archbishopric of Cambray; Antwerp, Ghent, Bruges, Ypres, Bois le Duc, Roermond, within the Flemish archbishopric of Mechlin; Haarlem, Deventer, Leeuwarden, Groningen, Middelburg, within the archbishopric of Utrecht."

Pirenne says—six sees originally: Liège, Tournay, Cambray, Arras, Terouanne, Utrecht.

being reconciled by prospect of preferment for himself in the proposed creation of new dignities. The result of the negotiations[1] was a bull issued by Paul IV., May, 1559, and confirmed by his successor in later bulls, which ordered the erection of three Netherland archbishoprics at Cambray, at Utrecht, and at Mechlin, with fourteen new sees under them to add to the four ancient sees hitherto dependent on the archbishops of Cologne and Rheims. This for a population of 3,000,000 people was not, perhaps, too large a quota, if the Church of Rome were still to be counted as intact, as alone responsible for the spiritual welfare of mankind irrespective of their individual proclivities, and if the new congregations with their protestations against compulsory conformity to the orthodox creed were to be regarded as simply malignant growths on the body politic. Hence, though the newer heresy and its dangers were technically ignored, Philip's desire of multiplying the shepherds was, undoubtedly, coupled with the need of keeping a sharper outlook for schism, a need that also stimulated the new monarch to hasten on the work of reorganisation.

[1] It was long before the bulls were published. Granvelle writes that the delay is all due to Rome's avarice, and again (Feb. 7, 1561) that they will not publish the edict at Rome for less than 12,000 ducats and there is not sufficient money in the Netherland treasury even to pay a courier. Apostolic authority ought to be supported *gratis*. He adds that the Spanish troops have at last departed after much discomfort. It was a great pity they could not have been kept, but the Estates had been very obstinate.—*Cor. de Philippe II.*, i., p. 193.

After the tardy publication of the bulls, a commission of five was appointed to execute their provisions. Granvelle and Viglius were the executives *de facto*, and they completed the arrangements as rapidly as they could. The way of procedure was not smoother than that of the path towards the Prince's marriage, and the lines of the two negotiations were about contemporaneous. In both, the principals were equally anxious to publish an achievement to the world without letting the public see the difficulties and the means of removing the same. The problem of providing a suitable endowment for the new lords spiritual was solved as follows: Certain abbeys and rich monastic establishments were to be incorporated into the new sees, certain ancient revenues in various localities were to be appropriated for the *mensa episcopalis* of that locality, and the bishops were to be the titular abbots of the foundations. This would imply the appointment by the lord bishop of deputies—priors or provosts—to administer monastic affairs, while they took the seats in the Estates assigned to the resident lord-abbots and enjoyed all the worldly advantages hitherto belonging to those gentlemen. It was a measure that carried with it a change of political equilibrium. The old abbots were elected by the brothers, the priors would be selected by the bishops, who, in their turn, would be the appointees of the King. This was regarded by the brothers as an unwelcome "novelty," but Granvelle so far supported Philip's policy that he argued that bishop-abbots had been frequent in the history of the Church. It was, he urged, by no means essential that the non-resident abbots be entirely dissevered from their conventual charges. It would be easy and helpful to the bishops to use the abbeys from time to time as retreats where they could take spiritual refreshment and come in touch with the brothers.

For instance, as an example of the methods to be used, the old abbey of Egmont was to be incorporated into the new diocese of Haarlem. The revenues were rated at 30,000 florins. Deducting the expenses of the monastery and certain taxes, the remainder was to be considered henceforth as the *mensa episcopalis* for the bishop of Haarlem, who would have his deputy and his retreat at Egmont, while his ordinary official residence would be Haarlem, the headquarters of diocesan business. Similar adjustments were proposed for divers localities, all changes to take effect as the old abbots died off. In some instances, pending this release of certain funds, Philip II. provided that Spanish revenue should be applied to this purpose,[1] remarking it was only right for one church to help another.

It was the incorporation of the monastic foundations into the sees together with the political

[1] *Cor. de Philippe II.*, i., p. 190.

questions involved in the change of representation in the Estates—native abbots giving way to prelates of royal nomination—that roused the first storm of opposition to the new bishops in the Netherlands.[1] And it must be noted that in this

---

[1] Granvelle states certain difficulties so clearly that a glance at his words is worth while.

"The greatest difficulty in relation to the new sees will be to obtain their acceptance in the provinces in which they are situated. There are particular difficulties in Friesland and Groningen and the city of Deventer in Over Yssel. Ruremonde can also be considered a doubtful quantity, considering that it is part of Guelderland. These territories, recently conquered, whose inhabitants were promised that their laws and peculiar customs should be protected, fancy they see in this establishment the introduction of a new jurisdiction. The fears are the more active in proportion as the remedy is needed, on account of their vicinity to lands infected by heresy. Moreover, the ill thinkers will do their best to avoid this jurisdiction, persuading the faithful that it . . . is established to molest the entire province and that in suffering the first innovation soon various kinds will be introduced." [Need of a firm hand on part of provincial governors. Difficulty of permitting free discussion in the consistories *in re* the endowments of new sees and dismemberment of abbeys. Secret cannot be guarded, etc., etc. Serious lack of funds prevents needful measures.]

"A preacher, exiled from England, lives on a boat near Antwerp with his wife and his books and preaches in the conventicles. He may escape arrest because the Council of Holland could not command enough money to ensure his arrest. It is to be hoped that no agitation break out within or without the land. In that case, your Majesty may be sure that every kind of remedy would come too late, even if all the treasure of the Indies and Spain together were sent here. I do not dare dilate further on this subject because your Majesty is perfectly well acquainted with our difficulties, etc., etc. . . . Some of the nobles of this land are still grumbling about the erection of these sees, alleging that the object is to exclude from the episcopate their sons and

chorus of opposition there was no note of the reformed faith. It was a cry from the orthodox and the nobles. Petitions were showered upon the curia urging the illegality of infringing the ancient charters of the religious foundations. Envoys from the abbeys hurried down to Rome and waited patiently at the doors of those high in authority with the new Pope to beseech their intercession in persuading the holy father to revoke the edict of his predecessor. The abbots were aghast at the idea of the loss of political prestige for their foundations. The nobles sympathised with that point of view for national reasons, and they also had a grievance of their own. The bull contained a clause providing that no candidate for high ecclesiastical honour should

---

relations in only admitting doctors, because a large number of people of birth, who otherwise possess all the necessary education, do not care to strain themselves to take the degree. They are answered that the condition was imposed by Paul IV. and that the measure had as end to incite gentlemen to study, and if there be some difficulties solely pertaining to the doctorate they can be obviated in time. It will be well to write from Spain an answer to the same effect because if the first appointees are doctors in conformity with the bull, so that the thing be established little by little the former course can be resumed and the opposition will die away."[1]

In a letter to the ambassador, Vargas, September 14, 1561, Granvelle writes (*Papiers d' état*, vi., p. 341): "Pardon this long letter, but I do not say the hundredth part of what I think. Would to God there had never been any idea of erecting these sees."

---

[1] Granvelle to Philip II., Jan. 5, 1561. (*Papiers d'état*, vi., p. 240.)

be counted eligible without an university degree. This eminently suitable measure toward a reform in the quality of the clergy was deeply resented by the aristocracy, who had long been accustomed to see the younger members of noble families provided with good incomes and convenient sinecures unhampered by academical requirements. To their mind the introduction of academic standards was inconvenient and unnecessary pedantry.

The main issue was, however, the subordination of the independent monastic establishments to a higher authority which might be alien, and it was a severe disappointment to the Netherlanders that the measure was not blocked. In spite of special protest and general dissatisfaction, the bull was allowed to stand and its provisions were executed wherever immediate action was demanded. As already said, the revised regulations were to bide the expiration of the life terms of all existing incumbents.

As a reward for his waiving his own opinions the Bishop of Arras received one of the best of the new appointments in the royal gift. Anthony Perrenot was made Archbishop of Mechlin and his office carried with it the primacy of the Netherlands. This new dignity was further crowned by a cardinal's hat obtained from the Pope by Margaret's exertions, so that the churchman, hitherto yielding social precedence to Orange and Egmont, was elevated over their heads as Cardinal Granvelle. Therein lay one

cause for the nobles' strenuous objections to the
prelate's good fortune. Moreover, they attributed to him more weight in the matter of the
new sees than belonged to him. They did not
know his opposition to them and to other antinationalistic measures.

During the Prince's absence in Leipsic in 1561,
the new Archbishop was formally installed at
Mechlin, assumed the pompous scarlet robes of
his office, and prepared to enjoy all its dignity.
He was not of a nature to abrogate one jot or
tittle of any personal privileges falling to his lot.
There was really much that was petty and trivial
in the dissensions and heart-burnings clouding the
court atmosphere from 1561 to 1564. Anne of
Saxony may be reckoned as a factor in part of it,
but not because of her Protestant convictions or
of high-minded religious fervour on her part. She
was not the patient helpmate, the domestic administrator that the first Princess of Orange seems
to have been. Anna of Egmont came to Brussels
only at her lord's behest and was content with her
station. Anne of Saxony, on the other hand, was
attracted thither by the glamour of the life she
had heard of. When within the magic circle she
became very tenacious of her rights. She felt that
much was owed her personally as being the great
Elector's daughter. So in the midst of the incidents of court life, her naturally discontented and
ill-regulated nature was always on the alert to
be sure that due recognition was accorded her,

ANNE OF SAXONY
PRINCESS OF ORANGE

The very first time she went to wait on the Regent, she was indignant at not being received instantly, and after that her suspicion was ever ready to be aroused by fancied slights, and her small nature betrayed itself constantly. The Countess of Egmont and she had various tiffs about precedence, and occasionally the two ladies squeezed through a narrow door side by side rather than yield the one to the other. With this watchfulness, undoubtedly Anne also had her fling about the insolence of the Franche-Comté priest in pushing himself before the Prince of Orange, the husband of the great Elector's daughter. Her own Protestantism was not profound, nor was her religion, but this was probably a point on which her conviction was quite clear. Legitimate reasons certainly existed in abundance to justify the nobles' efforts to dislodge Granvelle, but there can be little doubt that there was a small side to the quarrel.

At the same time the Cardinal's manner of life was such as to justify criticism. Nor were his extravagances confined to ecclesiastical pomp. He amused himself as a self-indulgent worldling, and he permitted the continuance of many of the flagrant abuses within the Church that had led in the first instance to the great Protestant revolt. Provost Morillon, Granvelle's creature and devoted adherent, was called *the double ABC*, because he had more benefices than there were letters in the alphabet, and he was not the only prelate to enjoy far more than he deserved.[1]

A few letters may serve to show what was demanding the Prince's attention in various directions during the three years 1561–64.

On November 2, 1561, Orange writes to Pius IV., who has sent him piteous plaints about the Protestants in his little principality.[2] It is addressed, *Beatissime pater post sanctorum pedum oscula*, and contains the express assurance that the writer is in sympathy with the papal admonitions and that there is nothing he desires so fervently as to be obedient to them.

> Indeed I could wish that the heretical pest which crept into Orange from France, taking me unawares, could be removed with the same facility with which it entered. . . . I have written to the officers of my principality and have ordered that they, in my behalf, protect, in the churches of my principality, the doctrine of our orthodox and catholic religion as we have received it from our ancestors—that it be taught diligently and my people kept within its bounds. All those acting contrary to this order and teaching otherwise, either openly or secretly, should be thrown into prison and their property confiscated with no respect to persons.

Orange adds that he speaks on the basis of "my Catholic faith which alone I have always observed and cherished."

[1] *Cor. de Philippe II.*, i., p. 320.
[2] Groen, i., p. 169.

These plain and unequivocal phrases do not chime in well with the Prince's attitude toward a new university founded a few months later by Philip at Douay,[1] one intended "to do away with the need for students to go abroad, notably to learn French." The Brabançons grumbled about it and the Prince of Orange remarked that papal seminaries ought not to be established in the province. Possibly he only wanted to please the Estates of Brabant, not desirous of seeing a rival to Louvain.

If the old Landgrave, watching European politics from his fireside in Hesse, heard of the interchange of friendly letters between the Pope and his grandson-in-law, no wonder that he felt concerned about Anne.

Friendly dear daughter [he writes], . . . we cannot refrain from asking how your health is and whether you are steadfast in the religion in which you have been educated. . . . Zapffenburg, January 11th.[2]

Her answer is prompt but hardly satisfactory to the old man.

Dear sir father: I am grateful to your Excellency for your friendly greeting sent by your councillor. . . . If I can serve your Grace in any way I gladly will do so and so would my dear master. As regards religion I will bear myself so that I can defend my-

[1] Groen, i., p. 138. Granvelle, *Papiers d'état*, vi., p. 503. The King thought that a number of universities might be founded in the Netherland cities to good advantage.

[2] Groen, i., p. 123.

self to the Almighty and to the world. Your Grace need not doubt that. Herewith I wish to your Grace and to your sons all good fortune, etc.[1]

The young wife evidently desired her grandfather to understand that marriage had given her her majority and that she was not accountable to her German kinsmen. He is not content with her vague assertions and writes again to suggest that if she fails to hear a weekly sermon and to be diligent in reading pious books, the wiles of Satan might turn her from godly truth, or at least dim her vision.

In response Anne begs her grandfather not to doubt her devotion to the Christian religion, concerning which she has incurred no criticism. She closes with assurances that her husband's treatment leaves nothing to be wished for. When her first baby is born, the Prince is away at Frankfort assisting at the election of the King of the Romans. All responsibility falls upon Gaspar Schetz and his wife. Although the latter feels that it is an honour beyond her rank she takes upon herself to see the poor little mortal baptised with Catholic rites by the curé of Ste. Gudule before the feeble life flickered out.[2]

Another family interest that appears in various

[1] Groen, i., p. 124.
[2] *Ibid.*, p. 139. *Cor. de Philippe II.*, i., p. 22. Philip had been much preoccupied about the birth of this baby, anxious lest Orange should make the baptism a grand affair. The King orders the Regent to forbid invitations to the electors of Saxony and Brandenburg.

letters of this epoch is the question of Count Louis's marriage. There is a certain Mlle. de Rytberg who seems like a desirable *partie*. Louis discusses the plan in a letter to the Prince[1] (January 20, 1563), and then slips in a little picture of old Philip of Hesse, ever anxious to keep in touch with the world which is closing around him.

The young landgrave has written to me more than three times, begging me to mention the post [established by the landgrave] to you . . . he also wants me to beg you to write oftener to his father—once a week at least—even if you have no news. The old man said, "Methinks I put in that post for nothing. They are slow to write to me." Could not you send him Italian news if there is nothing from France? . . . Orders ought to be given at Cologne about forwarding letters to Brunswick. Messengers are dear at Cologne. It makes me quite ill, Monsieur, when I read about your daily enjoyment of falconry at the thought that I cannot be with you. I am hastening to come as soon as possible. We have little enough pastime here; we rise before six o'clock to work before and after dinner. I trust that you will accustom me so well to work that you will be better served in everything that you desire to entrust to me and I will spare no pains. . . .

Louis de Nassau.

Dillenburg, January 20th.

Then comes a postscript delightfully characteristic of Nassau prudence, ever anxious to make friends.

[1] Groen, i., p. 145.

A gentleman of the Emperor's bedchamber is on his way to Brussels. You supped with him once in his lodgings at Frankfort. It would be worth while to show him courtesy as the Emperor is very fond of him. He wants to see everything in the Netherlands, in which you can surely help him. The Emperor spoke very warmly of him to me.

The Nassau financial embarrassments were many and complicated. March 10th[1] finds Louis still regretting that he cannot get off to the Netherlands. The debts amount to 300,000 florins and had they not been taken in hand just then, they might have augmented so as to burden the estate for fifty years. It was serious enough as it was. Some of the Nassau employees were completely discouraged at the prospect and had asked for dismissal because they thought there were no chances of improvement. "What words these were for me to hear, you can imagine." The brothers spared themselves no pains and their exertions were rewarded inasmuch as they reduced the debt by 60,000 florins before Whitsuntide. Thus far the letter was in French, then Louis drops into familiar German.

I see little amusement in prospect. We meet at five o'clock every morning except Sunday, and we certainly still have three weeks' work before us and then I will be free to assist your Excellency as far as I can with my very ordinary capacity and the aid of God.

[1] Groen, i., p. 149.

BEGGARS' MEDAL

Meanwhile in the Netherlands the quarrel with Granvelle became more and more bitter. The nobles despatched Baron Montigny to Spain to explain the state of public opinion to Philip and to urge him to come north and take matters into his own hands. The messenger was pleasantly received by the Spanish King, but obtained no satisfaction whatsoever in regard to his errand. Finally on March 11th a decisive step was taken in the Netherlands. Orange, Egmont, and Horne joined in writing a clear statement to the King setting forth their grievances specifically in terms as plain and unvarnished as epistolary etiquette permitted.[1] Painful as their duty is they cannot feel justified in keeping silent about Granvelle's mismanagement which is alienating the hearts of Philip's faithful subjects. They assure Philip that not only his royal interests but those of religion are endangered. "And lest your Majesty may be inclined to think that we make this remonstrance for our personal advantage, we request to be dismissed from the Council of State where we deem our presence useless."

The sentiment here expressed, that a stern sense of their obligation forced the nobles to open the King's eyes, is curiously echoed by Granvelle in a letter that followed close on the heels of the above on its way to Spain. On March 12th the Cardinal writes that he feels in duty

[1] *Cor.*, ii., p. 35.

bound to inform Philip of his dissatisfaction at the state of affairs.[1] Should vassals of the King make secret league against their sovereign? Possibly Philip did not think it important, but it vexed him to see his master's authority ignored as it was daily. Would it not be the part of wisdom to appoint the Netherland nobles to good posts in Italy or Spain? Sicily would be an excellent field for the Prince's activities if the Duke of Medina Cœli could be transferred elsewhere to make room for Orange.

Never were cleverer letters penned than those of Granvelle, none better calculated to breed a deep-seated distrust in such a mind as Philip's— a distrust which no argument or reassurance could ever eradicate.[2] For a time the Regent espoused Granvelle's cause.

Cardinal Granvelle [she wrote to her brother] is devoted to your Majesty's service. I am glad to give him perfect confidence for he is too sharpsighted not to give me the best advice. I cannot say the same of

---

[1] Granvelle, *Papiers d'état*, vi., p. 528.

[2] For instance he writes (May 13, 1562, *ibid.*, vi., p. 551): "As to the Prince of Orange, I do not assert that he is ruined in religion, as I have heard nothing exactly to justify such an opinion, but I do not see that he is much concerned about instructing his wife in the doctrines of the Catholic Church. The prince's brothers and sisters living under his roof, and some of the brothers of Count Schwarzburg, who hardly ever leave him, form his usual society and I fear the effect of such associations. Certain persons report that he means to send Count Louis . . . to Burgundy as governor. . . . A step sufficient to imperil the cause of religion there."

the Prince of Orange and Count Egmont, for they are incited by ambition. They have their own interests in view and only want to satisfy their passions and give vent to their personal hate for Granvelle.

And further she says:

I cannot conceal from your Majesty that it lies little in our interest nor does it become our honour to have every one informed of everything that happens, and if the dangers and anxiety in which I am suspended came to the ears of certain persons, they would assuredly make capital of them for their own advantage and to the injury of state and empire. . . I write all this to you to prove that if they [Orange and Egmont] were entrusted with state secrets it could easily happen that they would use their knowledge to cross our intentions and to cause the most important enterprises to fail. . . . Give me your opinion on all these items and I will do my best to act according to your Majesty's wish.[1]

On the very same March day that Granvelle's letter was despatched to Spain, Louis, still at Dillenburg, writes as follows to the Landgrave:[2]

. . . That the inquisition in Spain should be reformed would be more than a good thing. For with its rascality and hideous tyranny it has sinned far more against God than France. The Count of Feria is an excellent man for the purpose [reform] for as he is entrusted with all the king's secrets and has a quick

[1] *Cor. de Philippe II.*, i., p. 258 *et passim*.
[2] *Cor. de Lodewijk van Nassau*, Blok, p. 6.

mind, he could take up the matter prudently. May the Almighty prosper him. The Netherlands are in the same state as they were; I think that there may be outbreaks soon.

It was long before Louis was released from the drudgery of the business at Dillenburg and was free to join his brother in Brabant, but wherever he was, his brother was always sure of his interest in his affairs.

It was marvellously inconvenient that the Jew failed us with the 20,000 florins [writes Orange to Louis] for the reason you know. I sent my German secretary at once to the said Jew to see if he would not waive his condition that my brother John and the rest of you should give him a mortgage on a certain estate, making the subjects and officers swear to let it be executed in default of payment.[1]

The Jew was as stiff as Shylock and the pressing need of funds necessitated compliance with the usurer's exactions.

Certainly the conditions are hard [writes the Prince to Louis in November] and I am sorry enough to put you to inconvenience on my account, but the times are such that one must make use of friends. Of this thing I can assure you that I will take care you do not suffer damage or annoyance, for I do not intend that the mortgage shall run over a year as the terms are so hard. I have reason to hope that I can soon recover

---

[1] Groen, *Archives*, i., p. 173.

a good sum of money. I will not say much about thanks, either to you or John, for your great kindness in giving me this bond. Between brothers there is no need of compliments, especially as I am sure that you know how glad I shall be to serve you when I can.[1]

After referring to a summons to Brussels to meet the States-General and to the trouble in Orange, he adds: "We celebrated St. Martin's here very jovially, for there was good company. Mons. de Brederode was like to die one day but he is better now. . ."

The meeting mentioned above took place informally; the Cardinal was present but hurried off to Mechlin on the same day, while Aerschot held himself aloof from his peers, paid no visits, and departed without leave-taking as though the nobles had the pestilence and might contaminate him. So says an anonymous despatch which continues:

O happy are the poor in spirit, *propter ipsius affirmare et negare nihil mutatur rerum natura*. Berlaymont says nothing and goes round like a cat around the porridge. Aremberg sticks close to his precious cardinal and yet will not let himself be convinced by him nor by the others and is a free lance.[2]

Louis, when in the Netherlands, makes constant

[1] Groen, *Archives*, i., p. 184.
[2] *Nova* sent anonymously Dec. 11, 1563, to Louis. *Cor. de Lodewijk van Nassau*, p. 21.

reports to the Landgrave, sometimes desiring the letter to be burned and again wishing it to be sent to other Germans. His epistles are always lively, often incautious. Gradually two younger Nassau brothers, Adolph and Henry, come to the fore, the first humbly anxious to be admitted to some service under the Prince for which he is old enough, while the latter is still writing stiff letters from the University of Louvain under a tutor's direction. The second brother, John, writes very freely. He indulges in quaint bits of humour and picturesque colloquialisms such as are wholly lacking in the Prince's letters, but the style is ponderous and sententious. He often retails items of local interest to Louis, boundary quarrels, wooings, marriages, deaths, births, etc. He gives advice about Louis's own conduct and counsels him in one instance not to take many attendants when he goes to see the mother of a possible bride. She has lived so long as a widow that she is accustomed to quiet and parsimony. "You will ruin your cause if you don't go peaceably and will simply be told that the maiden is too young and not yet come to her understanding," etc. The writer's pen runs on over so many lengthy pages that it is not surprising that he has no time for a fair copy.[1]

As to the debts [writes Orange to Louis, January, 1564[2]] we are still about where you left us. I am con-

[1] *Cor. de Lodewijk*, p. 22.
[2] Groen, i., 196.

tinually hampered in fulfilling my estate and can well say *sicut erat in principio et nunc et semper, et in sæcula sæculorum.* I believe it is a family characteristic that we are bad managers in our youth but improve as we grow older like Mons. our father. My greatest difficulty is the falconers, although I have reduced them so that they only cost me 1200 florins. If this point were gained I would be free from debt but I hope, since only 1500 a year remain, that we really shall speedily be in better condition. When you come we will speak more fully. . . . I wish you were here now just for my amusement. There is good company assembled to take a hand at tennis and falconry, to which last I am going now in this fine weather.

They were undoubtedly gregarious, those noble Netherlanders, and spared no occasion to eat, drink, and be merry together, and in the midst of the merriment they often gave vent to their increasing dislike of the Cardinal. In December, 1563, one of the frequent festivities took place at the home of Gaspar Schetz, Seignior[1] de Grobbendonck. As the wine went round the conversation turned naturally on their *bête noire* and the epithets heaped upon him waxed in vehemence as the night grew older. The seigniors were especially severe about Granvelle's luxury and pomp, and it was finally suggested that they should show their contempt for the gorgeous array of his

[1] Schetz was Philip's financial agent and intimate with the Prince, as shown by his taking the initiative in the baptism of Anne's baby.

retinue by adopting a severely simple livery for their own followers. Dice were thrown to determine who should design the proposed dress, and the lot fell on Egmont. In a few days his designs were carried out and his retainers were the first to display the new livery, which consisted of a plain doublet and hose of coarse grey frieze with long hanging sleeves on which was embroidered an ornament described now as a fool's cap and bells, now as a monk's cowl. Possibly some liveries had one and some the other, or perhaps, owing to the diminutive size, the outlines were ill-defined. As a matter of fact this design was soon replaced by a bundle of arrows, typifying the union of the nobles in the cause.[1]

Party spirit ran high and it was well known what were the sentiments of every person. In a letter of August 2nd to the Landgrave, Count Louis adds a postscript:[2]

I send your princely grace a memorandum showing what nobles stick together and who are against the cardinal.

Prince of Orange, stadtholder in Burgundy, Holland, Zealand, and Utrecht.

Count of Egmont, stadtholder in Flanders and Artois.

[1] At first Margaret thought that the nobles "had no ill intention" in adopting the livery, but the people did not understand, so the thing did great harm. Two thousand sleeves had already been made and all that she had achieved in her remonstrances was to have the fool's-caps removed.

[2] *Cor. de Lodewijk*, etc., p. 14.

Margrave of Bergen, stadtholder of Hainault.
Count of Mansfeld, stadtholder of Luxemburg.
Count of Megem, stadtholder of Guelderland, Lord of Montigny, stadtholder of Tournay.
Count of Hoogstraaten, member of the Order.
Count of Lengen, member of the Order.
There are in addition various other nobles who have declared themselves on this side, notably the governors of the cities.

Cardinalists:
    Duke of Aerschot.
    Margrave of Rentin.
    Count of Aremberg, stadtholder of Friesland.
    Lord of Berlaymont, stadtholder of Namur.
    Lord of Glajon.

The opinion of the opposition is also expressed. The point of view of the Cardinalists was simple.

Every time I see the despatches of these three Flemish seigniors I am moved to anger so that if I did not control it your Majesty would think me a madman [wrote Alva[1]]. They must be punished. But as that is not practicable now, divide them and separate Egmont from the others. As to those who are to lose their heads, it is necessary to dissemble.

The prince is a dangerous man, astute, *rusé*, affecting to sustain the people and to share their interests even against the Estates, seeking only popular favour, appearing now Catholic, now Calvinist or Lutheran. He is capable of undertaking secretly everything that a vast ambition and an extreme jealousy can inspire. It would be well not to leave him in Flanders. He

[1] Groen, i., p. 175.

could be honourably withdrawn on pretext of some
embassy or some vice-royalty. You could even call
him to your court. The count simply lets himself
be seduced [by the prince]. It would be easy to win
him back by making him think that he was the
favourite.

As time wore on the Regent lost her boasted
confidence in the Cardinal. She became aware
that he was making her appear as his tool and
she hotly resented the implication that she had no
will of her own. Terror of the effect of the nobles' disaffection seized upon her. Unless means
were found to free the government from the
weight of debt, the King would be left in a very
embarrassing position.[1] He was dependent upon
the nobles for their intercession in their various
Estates. He did not dare alienate them. At
the same time he was not willing openly to yield.
He assures the nobles that he cannot consider
any vague complaints against the Cardinal, and
finds their action strange.[2] Yet before these
words were read the prelate had already received
a private letter from the King suggesting that it
would be an excellent plan for him to visit his
mother.[3] Margaret was advised to grant this
request so that all might pass smoothly and

[1] Among Philip's creditors were certain German cities whose
citizens suffered seriously. They were frequently arrested for
the debts they had incurred in his behalf.
[2] Gachard, *Cor.*, ii., p. 67.
[3] *Cor. de Philippe II.*, i., p. 285.

naturally without giving the nobles ground for flattering themselves that their remonstrance had been effective. The secret was ill guarded and vague rumours were afloat in the city long before there was any definite knowledge of the Cardinal's departure. In a letter of March 5th from Orange to Louis occur these words: "It is a sure thing that our man is going. God grant that he go so far that he will never return."[1]

The reports caused a fresh crop of pasquinades and pamphlets in Brussels, and street wit ran high without fear of punishment, as it could not have done had the rumours been baseless.[2] On March 13th, wild joy spread through the city hand in hand with information that Granvelle had actually left Brussels.

My gracious prince has written to the Landgrave William [writes one Lorich,[3] the prince's secretary, to Count Louis] and mentioned among other things how it was with the Cardinal's hasty journey. When he received the king's order, he growled like a bear, shut himself up in one room for a time, and then took himself off as quickly as possible. He has given out that he is called away on the king's business and will be back in two months, but many people think it will be two long months and like the Jew's interest will expire and renew themselves automatically.

[1] Orange-Nassau family archives.
[2] In February Granvelle uses the phrase to Philip, "this wicked beast, the people." *Cor. de Ph. II.*, i., 290.
[3] Groen, i., p. 228. The writer was a confidential secretary of Orange and in charge of young Henry of Nassau at Louvain.

Immediately after the Cardinal's departure the regent requested the seigniors to come again to the Council and they agreed but with the understanding that should the Cardinal return they would again absent themselves. There is universal surprise at the sudden move and a certain suspicion that it is a mere blind. It will be well for the seigniors to look to their defence so that they may not be taken unawares. Otherwise it is quiet here . . . and everything stands in a good peaceful fashion and every one is satisfied now that the Cardinal is out from under their feet.

The party of the opposition had triumphed and their triumph proved to have firmer basis than they had dared to hope. Never again did Granvelle set foot within the Netherland province. Naturally the nobles were elated at their victory, but it must be conceded that local and personal jealousy played a larger part in the whole quarrel than any zeal for religious toleration at this crisis. This was pre-eminently the case with the Prince of Orange. His relations to Protestantism in his own principality already mentioned show it. And, perhaps, nothing reveals his character, as it then was, better than his attitude towards the education and career of his youngest brother, Henry. He regarded the Established Church as something into which it was perfectly legitimate for a man with Protestant leanings to enter for the sake of an assured income, and, once in possession of a post, to steer deftly between difficulties of theological opinions without a qualm of conscience. The elder brother endeavoured to procure a fat benefice for the younger, a dignity as high as the bishopric of Liège being mentioned in that connection, and he felt perfectly justified in so doing. This easygoing standard was not, however, acceptable to Henry's other guardians, in spite of their loving devotion to the man adopting it. Juliana and John of Nassau were genuinely alarmed lest Henry should be perverted. They were apprehensive about the influence of Louvain teaching upon the home-nurtured lad and endeavoured to keep him from contact with the rites they considered idolatrous.

In reply to some such suggestion, Lorich writes to Count Louis that it would be impossible for the lad to study at Louvain if he did not attend mass, and that the Prince had desired him to be diligent in all formal church observances. But Orange evidently is not able to direct the boy's course exactly as he desired. Home prejudices have to be considered. In August, 1565, he writes to Count Louis:[1]

I am vexed about Henry and am not at all satisfied with the plan made by my mother and brother. It is not suitable to send him to France on account of other reasons than "Hueguenotterie." Nor am I better pleased at the idea of his going direct from Germany to Italy with a German gentleman who has been with the Count Palatine and his son. Believe me by such measures we will lose every chance of

[1] Groen, i., p. 417. Henry had returned to Dillenburg.

obtaining advantageous offices or dignities for him. There is already talk about it and those who were willing to help him draw back suspicious that we are going to let him be educated in the other religion. I enclose a passage from a letter from the Bishop of Utrecht showing how this rumour has spread. Therefore I advise that he shall be sent here for four or five months and go to Italy from here with some suitable gentleman. By that time too, everything will be clearer.

There is another opening, too, and I think if God is willing to help us we ought to help ourselves. Count William of Schauenburg . . . out of affection to us and especially to me, offers to make Henry coadjutor in his provostship of Hildesheim. This is a place a count can honestly hold and be free from obligation. He can do as he wishes in regard to religion, provided a little discretion be shown and no constraint be exercised over the people. He [Count William] thinks, too, that the brother of Count Königstein, Count Christopher, provost of Halberstadt, would also make my brother coadjutor. This provostship yields sufficient to support twenty horse with their equipment and the places [the two provostships] are only five leagues apart. Since such gifts are within our grasp we ought not to sleep but to follow up the matter. It will be necessary to have the pope's consent and that can only be asked if my brother be here. Otherwise it is labour lost.

I only suggest this for a time—say for five or six months, so that you can lend a hand to sending him for that time. Repeat all this to my brother so that he can speak as if at his own instance to Mme. my mother about her brother's provostship, advising her

to sound her brother about nominating my brother
Henry as his coadjutor. I do not doubt that she will
approve for she must know that her brother has no
trouble in living as he pleases. I told Count Schauenburg that he should have my decision in three weeks.
. . . I send you a letter from the governor of
Orange, which I opened, thinking it might contain
more details than mine but it is all one. You see
what is going on. I wish that we could exchange it
[Orange] for Enghien, retaining name and arms. For
I see no prospect of being clear. The King of France
has made some overtures towards me through his resident ambassador. . . . I will tell you everything on
your coming, which I beg you to hasten as speedily
as your health permits.

It is evident that the Prince's attitude towards
the Catholic Church and its faithful adherents is
still that of an opportunist. He is frankly disappointed that his mother's objections prevent
his executing his plans for Henry. He is perfectly willing to place his young daughter in the
Regent's court as maid of honour (July, 1565),
and he is still far from any desire to separate
violently his interests from the court and its
opinion. His course of action, his opinions were,
moreover, in line with those of the majority of
the nobles. As said before, they were mainly
conformists. There was no such party of declared Protestants as that of Coligny in France.
There was still a deep cleft between the Netherlanders of the ruling class and the people, stirred
heart and soul by the reformed religious ideas.

CHAPTER VIII

THE GROWTH OF POPULAR DISCONTENT

1564–1566

IN 1564 the nobles were fairly satisfied with the prospect they saw before them of exercising a degree of home rule and of local autonomy. They brought their families to Brussels and exerted themselves to obtain certain amendments in the administration, confident that they were supporting, not opposing the Regent. Orange had three important measures at heart. The first two were the assembly of the States-General and the augmentation of the powers of the Council of State.[1] He urged that this latter should be the chief of all councils. He had a clear conception of an executive cabinet government, the responsibility resting on Netherlanders, mere ratification being expected from Regent and King. Thirdly, he demanded a modification of the edicts concerning religious conformity. The question of persecution of Protestants comes, therefore, definitely

[1] The grievances on this point are fully set forth in the *Justification* (1568). Lacroix, *Apologie de Guillaume de Nassau, Justification*, etc.

to the fore, as it had not done hitherto. It is really only in the light of later events that it appears as a dominant element in the early active opposition to the institution of the new episcopal sees and to Cardinal Granvelle.[1]

After 1564, when the appointment of local inquisitors followed the erection of the new bishoprics, then freedom of conscience became, indeed, an issue. The edicts contained in the placards referred to were framed under and issued by Charles V. in the early years of the Protestant Revolt. Designed to check anarchy within the Church, they contained stringent requirements of conformity, provided methods of investigating individual opinions, and set penalties for any form of heterodoxy or any tendency towards the adoption of tenets stamped as heretical by Rome. There had been spasmodic waves of conviction for heresy and a few executions during the Emperor's time. But that monarch's connection with Germany was such that political motives restrained him from any widespread attacks upon the new sects; moreover in his contracts with German mercenaries he was obliged to agree to concessions for the Protestant troops. The Regent's Erasmian tendencies also had a subduing effect on over-zealous inclinations on the part of Netherland officials, and the edicts remained inoperative, mere dead letters, except

[1] There is similarity between its political status and that of slavery in the United States before 1860.

where some isolated magistrate was roused to enforce them, either from real devotion to the Church or because they offered convenient tools to his hand for personal revenge. In the King's reorganisation of the ecclesiastical machinery in the Netherlands, Philip was, undoubtedly, anxious to increase the number of eyes watching for the infringement of these long-existing laws which he was fully resolved should henceforth make themselves felt, but the intention was not immediately revealed in the general plan of the new sees.

For many years, orthodox people of Erasmian proclivities, indifferent to minor doctrinal points, but placidly convinced that a state church was a wise and needful institution, hoped for good results from the ecclesiastical council sitting at Trent, and engaged in deciding upon and sifting out the fundamental truths of orthodox faith. The sessions of this council, convened for the first time in 1545, had been broken and intermittent, and it was not until December, 1563, that their labours ended and their conclusions, pronounced infallible in advance, were published to the world.[1]

---

[1] In France the end of the Trent deliberations had been looked for anxiously. The political situation there was serious. In 1562 the Protestants, already known as Huguenots, were a formidable element that could not be ignored. During the minority of Charles IX. there was a constant struggle for supremacy between the Catholic Guises and the Huguenot nobles led by Condé, Coligny, and, for a time, by Anthony of Bourbon. A long letter from the Duke of Guise to the Duke of Würtemberg reveals his point of view in plausible terms. Not unnaturally the orthodox Guise declares that the arms assumed by the "reformed

The result was a blow to Erasmian ideals. No concession was shown to the demand of the Protestants, there was no bending to reform ideas. Orthodox tenets were fixed irrevocably, the doctrines concerning the sacraments reasserted without elasticity, and the absolute jurisdiction of the one Church universal over all people reaffirmed. The document ended with anathema to all heretics, anathema, anathema.

A definite yardstick of orthodoxy was thus furnished to the faithful, which Philip II. was rejoiced to seize upon and to have his subjects measured therewith, but it was not until past midsummer, 1564, the epoch when the Netherland nobles were most hopeful in regard to territorial administration, that he wrote to his sister directing her to have the ancient placards republished throughout the provinces and to insure civil

must be opposed by arms to prevent the imposition of an intolerable yoke upon the Catholics" and "to maintain our religion which is that of our king, bequeathed to us by our ancestors . . . the Faith in which we were baptised and nurtured and to which we conscientiously adhere. In all places where they [the Huguenots] have been stronger they have so ruined our churches as to deprive us of the means of worshipping God. . . . To counteract this we have tried to replace all officials not holding the Faith by others above suspicion. . . . Such is the obstinacy and malice of men that it is easier to long for unity and reform in the Church than to see that longing realised. However I am not ready to lose hope that some day God will evince his pity and give us by means of His good and legitimate council some alleviation to the ills we suffer," etc. *Documents inédits relatifs à l'hist. du XVI. siècle*, Kervyn de Lettenhove, i., p. 3.

support of Church officers in their inquiry into individual consciences.

It must again be remembered that to attain the desired end, Philip needed not one iota of fresh legislation. He simply took the occasion of the Church's own decision, made by her Council of Trent, as to orthodoxy, to declare his purpose of reviving statutes long existing and continuously ignored. The King was not left in ignorance of the difficulty to be expected in executing his orders. The Duchess of Parma explained to him in painstaking phrases that non-conformity was terribly widespread and deeply rooted and that whole villages could not be penalised without ruin to the population, to commerce, and to the fisheries. She implored her brother to come to the Netherlands and see the situation for himself, and the nobles added their entreaties to hers, assuring the King that literal obedience to his orders was beyond their capacity.[1]

Among Philip's officials there were, naturally, some of Granvelle's friends, who thought that the nobles were taking too much on themselves.

They are clamouring for a council [writes Viglius to the Cardinal] which will have sovereign superintendence of everything. I do not see how this could be consistent with the authority of Mme. the Regent, or whether, indeed, his Majesty himself would not be restrained by it. . . . Certainly I have no desire to belong to the new régime. . . . [I believe] they

[1] *Cor. de Philippe II.*, i., p. 326 *et passim*.

will go far, as she who has the most at stake voluntarily seconds those ill advisers and there is not the slightest hope of the king's coming. . . . The bishop and others convened here to consider the question of religion have decided very wisely to my mind.[1]

The decision referred to was an important stage in the course of events. The nobles had cherished a hope that the Netherland theologians appointed to discuss the decrees of the Council of Trent would take local conditions into consideration and would recommend a decided moderation in the edicts for the territory of their jurisdiction. The divines gave much time to the matter, while the nobles watched their proceedings with the keenest interest. "I fancy affairs are not in such a state as to leave you much leisure for pleasure walks," writes Brederode to Orange. Undoubtedly the Prince foresaw the probable brief duration of the nobles' satisfaction and did not relax his vigilance. At this time Louis of Nassau was at Spa recuperating from an illness, though probably he was not in a serious condition, as may be inferred from a note of Brederode's written with delightful indifference to any standard of spelling.[2]

[1] *Cor. de Philippe*, i., p. 360. *Cor. de Granvelle*, i., p. 26. It is worth noting that Viglius himself was accused of intercourse with heretics.
[2] Groen, i., p. 397. Count Henry Brederode was a picturesque character. Descended from the ancient Counts of Holland he retained many of the lawless traits of his ancestors. Groen

I should have more confidence in good wine helping you than the springs. At least I am convinced that if I had given up wine in my last illness here among these abominable dykes, I should have quitted my bones too, for I assure you I never was so near it. I rather think I was not good enough to die and that the good God would not have known what to do with me, which is why I do not worry about you. Take care not to drink too much water. That is the way people drown.

To Louis the Prince suggests that the enforced leisure of semi-invalidism might be made useful by talking over the "affairs we were speaking of" with the Marquis de Bergues and other fellow-visitors at the springs.[1] It is phrases like the above that force the conviction that Orange was very wary in relation to his brother at the time. There was evidently no want of confidence between them; but the elder was more than willing not to be informed of all the projects in which the younger was involved. He gives him cautions and then lets him go his own way.

As to writing to George von Holl [Orange to Louis], I would not do it. The fewer letters to strangers on such matters the better. Even if they are at present

---

rates him as a mere drunken roysterer and boon companion of better men. Bakhuizen van den Brink gives him greater credit.

[1] Spa was often used as a convenient neutral ground as other watering places have been since. Granvelle mentions Egmont's presence there to Philip: "As he is reported perfectly well, probably he has *altras cosas* on hand."

friends, after their death, letters may fall into the hands of those who would try to make capital from them.[1]

For five months Margaret of Parma was left in doubt as to whether Philip II. was going to yield to her persuasions and refrain from forcing the oppressive edicts of the Council of Trent upon the Netherlanders, dissenters and faithful alike. Meantime, the Regent's son, Alexander Farnese, was preparing to be married to Maria of Portugal at his mother's court in Brussels. In the very midst of the magnificent wedding festivities a royal courier arrived from Spain with despatches

[1] Groen, i., p. 398. Egmont went to Spain in the winter of 1565 to plead with Philip about the enforcement of the edict. His mission with its hopes and disappointments is not described here. The Count returned to Brussels in April reporting that Philip was ready to meet the wishes of the nobles. When he was proved wrong then "began the old song" (*Cor. de Philippe II.*, i., pp. 355, 385, etc.) Margaret's instructions to Egmont contained the following passage (*Cor. de Marguerite*, iii., p. 544): "There are daily reports that people from Valenciennes, Tournay, and neighbouring places desert their homes and go to France and other countries of the new religion, transporting their business and manufactures with them, together with their property, merchandise, and riches, and that others will follow, preferring emigration to being burned or otherwise publicly executed. There are quarters where the Anabaptists are very numerous, especially in North Holland, Friesland, and elsewhere, and there are a great number of Calvinists, especially in lower Flanders, and in addition there is a great infection of Lutheranism and their hangers-on [*sequaces*], and others, vacillating in the Catholic faith and cold to holy traditions and to ceremonies of the Church, hating priests, monks, and ecclesiastics. And the magistrates will not enforce the placards."

for Margaret. Philip's orders were plain and
unequivocal. His sister was to pay no attention
whatsoever to popular remonstrance. The pre-
valence of heresy was no reason why it should be
respected, and she was, therefore, to enforce every
regulation regarding conformity to the Catholic
Church. The decrees of the Church were to be
scrupulously maintained.

Margaret was terribly disconcerted by the orders, but did not reveal the cause of her depression until a council meeting in December, when
the despatches were read. After a few minutes
of silence the discussion began. Viglius advised
a fresh appeal to Philip with a further explanation
of the unpopularity of the proposed measures.
The Prince of Orange took a different point of
view. He declared that any further application
to the King was futile. His Majesty had been
fully informed and his commands were perfectly
plain. It would now be wise to execute the orders
promptly and to have the placards posted in every
market-place. And his motion to this effect was
carried. After its acceptance by the other councillors, Orange whispered to one, who reported it
later, "Now we shall see the beginning of a fine
tragedy."[1] His manner was almost insolently ju-
bilant. The incident has been made much of by
certain Catholic writers as indicative of a kind of

---

[1] "Hac conclusione accepta princeps Auriacensis cuidem in
aurem dixit, qui post id retulit, quasi lætus gloria bundusque;
visuros nos brevi egregiæ tragediæ initium." *Vita Viglii*, p. 45.

Satanic quality in the Prince's mind, as though he were ready to exult over a hideous prospect whose possibilities he perfectly grasped. Surely another meaning may be read into the incident. All the representations made to Philip had been vain. Now if he persisted in ignoring the mighty strength of the Protestant movement, the Prince was glad that his orders were perfectly explicit. Events would now take their course and the inevitable result would at last prove the political acumen of the King's advisers.

A letter from Morillon to Granvelle[1] (December 9th) is filled with reports current about this particular council meeting. The nobles drew a long face when the King's autograph letters in Spanish were read. The Duchess laid aside her embroidery,[2] rested her head on her hand, and gave all her attention to the discussion. "No one believed that the King would really come," etc.

Shortly after this, instructions were sent to prelates, to universities, and to cities providing for the rigorous enforcement of the ancient edicts. An outcry arose at once in Brabant, protesting that the provincial privileges were infringed by this order and that no inquisition could legally be introduced. The answer to this was that *there was no inquisition, no novelty, nothing* except

---

[1] *Cor. de Granvelle*, i., p. 44. The Cardinal is asked to "burn this letter."

[2] Delightful suggestion of her feminine habits, even in political life.

perfectly commonplace and ordinary adherence to perfectly self-evident, commonplace regulations against anarchy in the state of God's own religion. It is curious to note the surprise in various letters of Granvelle and his informants that any one should think of coupling the term *Spanish inquisition* with these simple, conservative measures!

Here they are talking of nothing else but the inquisition [writes Morillon to Cardinal Granvelle, Feb. 10, 1566[1]]. At Tournay the notice herein enclosed has been posted from the same shop as the others. It is impossible that the author of such an unhappy work should not be discovered. God knows what efforts are daily made to seduce the people and the part played by Montigny in it. There is little pleasure in many places at the creation of the pope but I trust that God's will was expressed. The four cities of Brabant petition the council that no inquisition shall be proclaimed there. The council have reduced their grievances to writing and I hear that the deputies of the said city are now repenting their action because the said council has forwarded the remonstrance to his Highness, without affixing any seal and ordinance—and I believe the answer will be that it is not new but that since the time of the late Madame Marie inquisitors general were appointed in Brabant and [here follows list] many culprits have been apprehended and punished. Nevertheless it is reiterated that the inquisition has never been in vogue and all the blame is put on your Seigniorship. . . .

[1] *Cor. de Granvelle*, i., p. 111.

I told the dowager duchess that you would be the first to oppose the inquisition of Spain and that you were very zealous in guarding the privileges of the land, and I also pointed out that they were giving the name of the *inquisition* to the placards made by the late emperor and by his Majesty on the topic of religion in which no innovation was to be introduced. Simply the observation of these was to be enforced. To the great prejudice of religion the semi-annual publication of these had been omitted and they were never less observed than at present. . . .

The Duke of Aerschot thinks that there is an attempt to make the king odious. He speaks very devotedly of you. . . .

. . . I have heard from good quarters that in the college of Mechlin, van der Aa, the sheriff, dared grumble openly at the said publication, the others did not agree with him. He declared that there were more than fifty thousand men waiting to see what was going to be done. I begged Weyns [Augustus Weyns, sheriff of Mechlin] to take notice and to mark the day and those who were present.

They have commenced to take the images out of the churches and to roll them in the mud, with other insolences. When del Canto spoke of this to Mme. de Parma she said what would he say if the priests themselves did it to bring discredit on the people? I believe that this suggestion came from the officer who ought to be more energetic in discovering the authors, priest or otherwise.

If your seigniory would give me a distinct assurance about this point of the Spanish inquisition of which he [Philip] is accused, I would be glad, so that I could pass it around among friends. Certainly things are going ill and we are in greater danger than appears on the surface. If there should be any excitement the poor people who are starving would ally themselves with the heretics and the latter would reap the benefit,—especially if the ecclesiastics should fall prey to them. I am astonished how little the abbés of Brabant understand the situation. They may easily be called on to pay the piper any day. As the world is now going, if I had nothing here but my own business I would not stay long. But I shall hold on to the end.

I am sorry that you have so much furniture here and wish that a part were in a safer place, for I do not see how it could be protected if anything were to happen.

This letter, too, closes with the words *Lecta comburatur*. Curious how many letters exist bearing that injunction to the recipient to burn them!

In another epistle Morillon mentions that the service at Mechlin was never so beautiful as at this moment and the music never better.

I have heard [writes another correspondent, Pero Lopez, March 2d] that it was said in Count Egmont's presence, that these territories, fiefs of the empire, are at liberty to choose the religion they desire—the Confession of Augsburg or the Ancient Faith—and that they are resolved to accept the former. Verily sometimes I am afraid they may take us unawares by a *coup d'état*. At the same time there is a show of checking the calamity and Orange has actually forbidden the son of M. de Toulouse to remain on an estate within his jurisdiction.

charles de cecin

guittame de
Bergues Mons

Jan d' pstonē me

Charly le
fyle de marbays
de Lomrnal

[illegible signatures]

de Bernes

vandenbouvh
conulle de Ghysselle
A const va Burgtonhouvg
[illegible] de Calunbo
A de Bauqver

H. de Brederode

Louys de nassau

Florent de Pallant

Jean de Marnix

franuoys de Haeffen

bvert de boehsler ... d'aspy

...ger de Mierde

...de Koneckm

... Saumans

Renes...

... Renesso ...

1

die hie ein hertz gibet bitten
und dem barmhertzigen ...
und bitten das ...
... werk der ...

2

... Et vous voij ...
... Je voudrois que ... p...
de vous faire prendre resolution

3

a Brouxelle le 29 ...

Margarita

FAC-SIMILES OF SIGNATURES: JULIANA OF S

...... h l fom rH ßhicken.
wollest yf allen tag beden
deinen sachen an richten
ßen begeinen wol vnd
es ist
inhauer griffien zu naßew
witwe

lre an Roy vng prie denn ou
fme vns pais des frimrs aufpres
its les points les plus neueßairs

nnes de naßaw

...... fant par Roy stey
e 1565 aout päßymd

That kind of thing I do not consider at all serious.
It is done simply to deceive the king and throw him
off his guard. How could they [the nobles] pretend
they were expelling the wretched sacramentaries
when they pack their houses full of them (M. d'Egmont does this more than any one else) and de
Hames is the inspiration of all. . . . Certainly if
his Majesty does not come soon things will take such
a turn that he will hardly be able to come when he
wishes, so impudent have the people become. There
is no more question of maintaining the placards than
if we were at Geneva. . . .

I believe that Madame is more and more confused every day and with reason. She renders an
ill account of her charge.[1]

I am extremely displeased that the publication of
the edicts has been delayed [writes Granvelle[2]]. It
is manifest calumny that his majesty is thinking of
introducing the Spanish inquisition. He has been
precise on that point. I am aghast at the impudence
of the pasquils. I had not at first understood their
virulence, as the attacks on me were softened in the
reports.

To Philip, the Cardinal writes that the rumour
of the introduction of the Spanish inquisition was a

slander spread abroad to alienate your subjects
from your Majesty. . . . If I did not assume that
your Majesty were already in possession of the pasquils scattered by the rascals, I would send you
what I have. . . . It would be well to have Courte-

[1] *Cor. de Granvelle*, i., p. 139.   [2] *Ibid.*, p. 142.

ville translate them from Flemish into French, so as to enable your Majesty to see whether the course of events be in the interest of your Majesty or the reverse.

I pardon these perverse nobles all their calumny of me, but I will never consent to assist them in acts prejudicial to the service of God and your Majesty, even should they kill me. I fear that everything may be precipitated towards a complete disaster, etc.

Much advice follows, always preceded by the deprecatory "*sauf meilleur avis.*" Above all, the Cardinal is convinced that an assembly of the States-General *without* the King's presence would be a serious political blunder. The result might be (this in a postscript) that Mme. de Parma's government would be overthrown and a new one set in its place.

It is perfectly evident from all this correspondence—and there is much more to the same effect—that there was a singularly clear prevision of the real significance of the issue on the part of the King's advisers—while the abundant crop of pasquils and caricatures springing to life in all Netherland cities show, too, that the populace was intelligent enough to take a hand in the game. The ephemeral literature assumed serious proportions. The anonymous writers hit out in every direction and no one was spared. The Prince of Orange was only half trusted and his house was often plastered over with appeals to him to take measures to prevent the inquisition coming to the Netherlands—appeals that often took the form of threats.

In addition to these irregular and unrestrained efforts to direct action, an orderly combined protest known as the *Compromise of Nobles* came into being. Possibly this grew out of the conference at Spa, possibly it was a spontaneous movement not premeditated before a certain day (December 1 or 2, 1565) when some young nobles, feasting together with Count Culemburg as host, signed a paper, drafted possibly by one Francis Junius, possibly by Philip Marnix, Sr. of Ste. Aldegonde. The document was a vigorous arraignment of all inquisitorial measures, "bound in a land accustomed to liberty to result in a horrible confusion," followed by a pledge of mutual support among the subscribers to resist the said measures.

The original draft has only three signatures, Charles Mansfeld, Henry Brederode, and Louis of Nassau.[1] Several copies of this *Compromise of the Nobles* were immediately circulated through the province and in a brief time a thousand names lent their weight to its substance.

Orange, as well as the other chief nobles, kept ostensibly aloof from this organised movement. But the Prince was not out of sympathy with it. He could have checked it, had he wished. Certainly he could have kept Louis out of it. Like other leaders on the eve of a revolution, Orange was perfectly willing that his brother should go

[1] Royal archives, The Hague.

as far as he could, ready himself to espouse action
or portions of action at a later date, were they successful.
Meanwhile he was part of the administration,
sometimes willingly blind and sometimes
seeing.

My brother, I am waiting [writes Orange in January,
1566] impatiently for news of you and would give a
thousand crowns if you were here for there is an affair
affecting you which is making a great stir. You are
accused of writing a broadside which has been found
in Antwerp, together with several other things which
I have not time to write you about. . . . I beg you
do not do things like this. I will send you other news
at the first opportunity. Do you let me know the
progress of your negotiations and what the chances of
success.[1]

But, nevertheless, the Prince's opinions are not
veiled. On January 24th he writes a perfectly
fair exposition of his own position to the Regent.[2]
As he did not possess the gift of condensed expression
his letter is too verbose to be given in
full, though it is an important chapter in his
biography. After stating that he is aware that he
is giving advice unasked, but that he feels that,
as Philip's loyal servitor, he is morally bound to
try to avert ruin from the land, he continues:

As to the reformation of the priests and in regard
to ecclesiastical ordinances . . . I refer these to
the proper authorities and will obey his Majesty's

[1] Groen, ii., p. 10.   [2] *Ibid.*, p. 16.

commands when I can. As to the second point, viz., that governors and other civil officers should aid the inquisitors . . . and maintain the human and divine authority belonging to them, your Highness must recall the fact that the opposition to the new sees was wholly caused by the fear lest, under this guise, some form of the inquisition might be introduced; moreover, your Highness must remember that his imperial Majesty and Queen Marie repeatedly assured the Netherland people verbally and in proclamations that *the said inquisition should never be introduced.* It was such assurances that have enabled commerce to prosper here, etc.

The third point is that his Majesty has ordered that . . . all the placards successively issued by emperor and king shall be rigorously and literally carried out. Madame, this seems to me very hard. The placards are numerous and diverse and have never been enforced, even when there was not such widespread misery as at present. Their execution now would be unbearable and inexpedient.

Orange proceeds to say that the toleration obtaining in the neighbouring lands would make any oppression seem very unfair and that it would be the height of folly "to rouse popular passion now when the populace are already suffering from the wheat famine," and he hopes that all rigorous measures will be deferred till Philip comes "to set all right by his presence,"— that ever fallacious will-o'-the-wisp! Orange concludes his epistle by saying that if the King persists in his orders he prefers resigning all his offices rather than to "incur the blame which would attach to me and mine if misfortune falls on the lands under my charge." "The Prince's answer to the Regent will give her something to bite if she has good teeth," was Hoogstraaten's comment on this letter.[1]

In February a number of the nobles were again assembled at Breda. Nicholas de Hames writes thence to Count Louis:

> At the last meeting there were present Sr. de Waron, the admiral's lieutenant, Mons. Dolhain, Mons. de Louwreval, Mons. de Thoulouse, Mons. de Leefdael, and myself. A plan was decided on which seemed better than anything else suggested and which was approved by M. de Brederode, *to whom we confided the details, while we only gave a general outline to the prince.*
>
> M. de Brederode was heartily in favour of the proposed enterprise, but the prince did not approve the outline, deeming it utterly impracticable. Moreover he does not think the time ripe for arms and without force action would be impossible.[2]

Before the famous petition was decided on there were other meetings at Hoogstraaten's château and at Breda. Hoogstraaten remained at home after the first and missed his friends sorely. In a letter to Count Louis, March 15th, suggesting some changes in the draft, he desires him to press the gentlemen's hands 100,000,000 times.[3]

---

[1] Groen, ii., p. 54.   [2] *Ibid.*, p. 35.
[3] *Ibid.* p. 46. The château is now the town poor-house.

In the further negotiations between the government and the nobles about the details of the presentation of the petition, Orange is entirely identified with the former. He does not, to be sure, seem over-eager to go to Brussels, pleading his wife's illness and other private affairs, as reasons for remaining at Breda, but when at the capital his advice at the council is good, and he uses his influence with Louis to keep things smooth.

April 5, 1566, was the momentous day when about three hundred petitioners, with Brederode at the rear, marched up the hill to the palace in Brussels with the petition for moderation and for respect to nationality.[1] As Brederode read it aloud, Margaret grew more and more agitated. At its conclusion tears were running down her cheeks. As soon as she was calm enough to speak she said that an answer should be given after consultation with her advisers.

A long animated debate followed. Orange tried to calm the Regent by assuring her that the petitioners were no wild conspirators but sober, earnest, well-meaning, well-born gentlemen, who knew the temper of the land and whose protest deserved honourable consideration. Egmont shrugged his shoulders in the Italian fashion and remarked that his leg was beginning to trouble

---

[1] The canvass for signatures was almost house-to-house. Louis had assumed charge of Zealand, Friesland, and the "city"; Brederode of Holland. Protestant ministers everywhere did good service. See Pontus Payen, i., p. 136, etc.

him again, and he thought he would have to go to Aix for treatment. Then it is said that Berlaymont put in his word and said, "How, Madame, can it be that your Highness is afraid of these beggars? By the living God, if my advice were taken, their petition should have a bastinado as sole commentary and they should be made to go down the palace steps faster than they came up."[1] Meghen and Aremberg agreed with Berlaymont.

It was the moderate counsel of the Prince that prevailed so far that Margaret's *apostille* on the petition was at least civil. She agreed to refer the matter to the King and meanwhile she would recommend gentleness and discretion to the officers. So decision was postponed until a messenger could travel to Spain and back again.[2]

On the 8th, Brederode brought back an answer to Margaret's *apostille* which assumed that she would give orders that all persecution should cease until the King's word came. The petitioners promised to keep the public peace and asked that their petition should be officially printed. Satisfaction that all had passed so well found expression at a banquet given by Brederode in Culemburg's house, on the evening of June 8th. In the midst of the talk over the incident, Ber-

---

[1] See Gachard, *Études et notices historiques*, i., p. 130. This story is discussed and weighed. Also see *Apologie van Lodewijk van Nassau, Bijd. van het Hist. Gen. van Utrecht*, 1885, p. 216.

[2] Groen, ii., p. 84.

laymont's term of "beggar" was referred to and there was unanimous consent to assuming the appellation as their own.

By the salt, by the bread, by the wallet yet,
The beggars will not change, no matter how they fret,[1]

was the doggerel they chanted as they adopted the derogatory term for their chosen title. And furthermore it was resolved to wear a dress and a device that would show their intentions to assume the name as an honourable badge, while they meant no disrespect to the sovereign. It was "faithful to the king even to a beggar's wallet."[2]

At a late hour Orange, Egmont, and Horne, who had supped with the Count of Mansfeld, dropped in at this banquet and drank one health to the company, who shouted out noisily, "Long live the King, health to the Beggars." A party name was born. The opponents of Spanish rule in the Netherlands were henceforth to be known as *Gueux* or Beggars. Their shaven chins and long mustaches soon became familiar sights on land and sea.

[1] "*Par le sel, par le pain, par le besache,
Les gueulx ne changeront quoy qu'on se fache.*"
[2] The device was "*fidèles au roy jusques à la besace.*"

CHAPTER IX

THE PARTING OF THE WAYS

1566-1567

THE younger confederates were full of jubilation over their recognition by the Regent and separated for their homes highly delighted with their achievement. From this same moment, however, the more astute Prince of Orange apparently abandoned all hope of modifying the King's policy. His correspondence with the Germans, which had never flagged, took on a more specific tone. He began to make definite preparations for other contingencies.

The sectaries had been greatly impressed by the reception of the petition and they exaggerated their success. They felt that the tide had turned in their favour and the boldest of anti-orthodox sentiments were voiced in the pulpits by sometime priests who had changed their faith, as well as by the unlearned, unlicensed preachers who preached indoors and out wherever they could find a foothold.[1]

[1] The term *Haagpreek*, hedge preaching, seems to mean nothing more than non-legalised sermons. *Haag* is used as in *Haag-weduwe*, equivalent to grass-widow. Fruin viii., p. 307.

When reluctant consent was wrung from Margaret that the placards[1] should be modified, she had not the slightest idea of granting a license for free preaching, and was aghast when she found that this liberty was being regarded by the reformers as their natural right and that the nobles were apparently fostering this idea. She was soon convinced that Orange was one of the chief culprits in this regard.

It must be conceded that Orange was curiously inconsistent at this time. He was continually referring to Germany as an example of a land where toleration worked well, but there the principle had always been that the princes could dictate within their territories, and a logical conclusion to the argument would have supported Philip's pretensions in the Netherlands as long as he was sovereign. The Regent was filled with terror, and very doubtful about her best procedure. In the fear of unchaining a war of religion she did not dare trust wholly to the purely Catholic party, as represented by Mansfeld, Aerschot, Berlaymont, Aremberg, Meghen, and Noircarmes. The confidence she had once felt in Orange, Egmont, and Horne was gradually undermined, but she continued to cling to them because she felt that they understood the people as no one else did.

In July, 1566, the infection of insurrection reached Antwerp and it was Orange who was sent

[1] This word is used continually in the sense of the provisions contained in them.

thither to pacify the restless spirits and Orange, too, from whom help was hoped in relation to the confederates, who had arranged a new convention for July 14th at St. Trond in the territory of the Bishop of Liège. The confederates, on the Prince's advice, still declared themselves faithful to the King, but they took care to be fully informed of everything going on in Madrid and to be on their guard. To their fresh demands, formal and informal, Margaret answered that she would ask the advice of the Knights of the Fleece in an assembly appointed for August 28th. Before that date Margaret's anxiety as to her brother's wrath was somewhat relieved by advices from Philip approving the temporary suppression of the inquisition, the moderation of the placards, and a general pardon for all the doubtful deeds hitherto committed.[1]

To return to Antwerp, where the progress of affairs gives the best picture of the temper and methods of the Prince of Orange. This Brabant seaport was by no means a homogeneous city of Flemish burghers. It contained a very mixed population. Merchants from all the chief trading centres of Europe kept offices or houses there for the benefit of their fellow-townsmen visiting Antwerp on commercial, financial, or diplomatic errands. These travellers were incidentally the

[1] In a commission given the nobles to treat with the insurgents, Margaret inserted the words, "*consideré la force, necessité inevitable.*"

bearers of new thoughts. Unlike the westerly towns open chiefly to French influences, Antwerp had, moreover, large numbers of Lutherans and Anabaptists as well as Calvinists.

As the rumours of increasing audacity among all these sectarians rendered Margaret more and more uneasy she begged the Prince—hereditary Burgrave of Antwerp[1]—to try his strength at pacifying the seething elements. In considering his part two points must be borne in mind, first, that Orange had already tendered to Philip his resignation from all his offices, and second, that he had plainly told the Regent that he knew the free exercise of religion could not be checked. *"Universæ fæces Antwerpæ inciderunt,"* says Strada and the Prince found it true.

On his arrival he wrote as follows:

ANTWERP, July 14th.

Madame: I only reached here at seven o'clock because I was delayed by various affairs, and left Brussels late. When I came near Berchem, half a league from here, M. de Brederode met me with a goodly number of gentlemen, who gave me a salvo with their pistols, and then a few bourgeois in the troop shouted *" Vivent les Gueux,"* and this continued from time to time, all the way into the city. I should judge that there were, in all, about 30,000 men.

The citizens greeted me warmly, and when I

[1] Engelbert, Henry, and René of Nassau had all held this office before William.

expressed the great desire of your Highness to aid
them, they presented certain articles, or ordinances,
designed to establish quiet in this city, which we
shall carefully examine to-day. They report that
preaching took place to-day outside the walls, and
that many of the large congregations went armed to
protect the others, because they had heard that the
Drossart of Brabant was commissioned to disperse
their gathering. As soon as possible, I had an interview with the chief dissenters and urged them to de-
sist from large assemblies. I fear, however, that this
will have no effect, but I hope that they will not try
preaching within the walls.

Whatever happens shall be straightway reported
to your Highness.[1]

Then Orange proceeded to act according to
what he deemed the needs of the moment. He
decided not to prohibit the sermons but to control
their unruliness with a firm hand. Under the
reassuring influences of his methods the foreign
merchants consented to abandon the idea of
immediate departure and to hope for better
things.

The early part of August was employed by
Orange in pacificatory efforts. Then the Regent
insisted on his return to Brussels for the appointed
assembly of the Knights of the Golden Fleece, and
refused to take his word that he could not answer
for the peace of Antwerp if he left the city. August 18th was then and still is a favourite festival

[1] Gachard, *Cor.*, ii., pp. 136–138.

in the holiday-loving town. It was called the day of the *Ommegang*, from the custom of carrying a certain little image of the Virgin in solemn procession through the city. Apprehensive of the danger of any kind of crowd and excitement in the highly wrought state of feeling, Orange delayed his departure for Brussels until the morrow of this festival. Accompanied by his wife and Louis, he watched the procession from a window in the town-hall. The poor little image, decked out in the rich gifts that had been showered upon her in the past, did not command the reverence that had been her wont. "Mayken, Mayken, thine hour has struck. This is thy last walk abroad. The city is tired of thee," were the cries with which she was greeted. Her guardians were glad to hurry her back into safety behind the iron railings in the choir, without permitting her to remain at the west door for a time to receive homage on her fête. Hoping that immediate danger of rioting was past, Orange set out for Brussels at an early hour on the 19th. Before he could have reached his destination, little Mayken had been discovered in her hiding place of the Cathedral choir and an unruly mob had begun to attack her with jeers and insults. It is not likely that there was any deliberate intention at the outset. A Flemish mob is inflammable material. The mocking word of a ragamuffin who dared to parody a sermon from the pulpit proved a torch to combustible stuff, but the priests at last succeeded in clearing the

church on that day and in closing the door. On
the 20th, the crowd, still excited, flocked to the
edifice again and the best efforts of the town
officers in a body only resulted in stilling the
tumult momentarily. The crowd finally broke
all bonds of decency and the sacred building
became the scene of wanton destruction. There
was utter contempt for sacred property. All the
accumulated hatred for what was disliked in the
ancient establishment found vent and those who
were actuated by religious fanaticism were aided
by riffraff without any serious opinions joining
the mêlée from mere love of excitement.

Orange was not allowed to return to Antwerp
immediately. It was rumoured in Brussels that
the image breakers, the iconoclasts, as they began
to be called, were to repeat these scenes in all the
churches of the capital. Margaret clung to the
Prince as a bulwark against the mob. On August
25th, she yielded to advice, gave way to the demands of the populace, and sorely against her
will, signed articles providing that the dissenters
should be permitted to enjoy their public sermons
in all places where preaching had taken place
before this date. Formal articles were also exchanged between the Regent and Louis of Nassau,
attended by fifteen confederates. These latter
pledged themselves to consider their league dissolved and to maintain the King's authority as
long as the Duchess held to her promises. The
so-called Accord further declared the inquisition

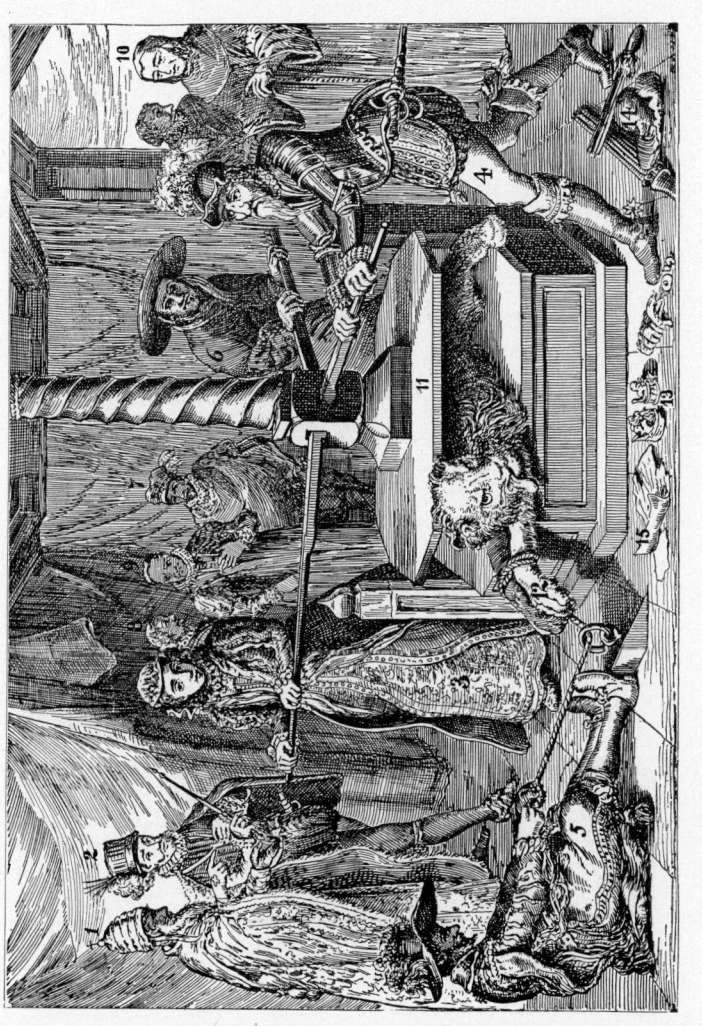

ALLEGORY, REPRESENTING NETHERLAND LION CRUSHED BY SPAIN. (Redrawn from an old print.)
1. The Pope. 2. Philip II. 3. Margaret of Parma. 4. The Duke of Alva. 5. Don Frederic. 6. Cardinal Granvelle. 7. Vergas, 8. Delrio (Spanish officers). 10. Brother Cornelius. 11. The Press of Tyranny. 12. The Belgian Lion. 13. The Lion's Broken Crown. 14. Injured Liberty. 15. Violated Privileges of the Land.

The Parting of the Ways

in abeyance, and pledged the King to protect the nobles from any punishment for past transactions and to accept of their elegibility for royal service.

When the letters patent containing this Accord were published in the various cities, the Netherlanders thought a new day was dawning. In Antwerp the Prince left no stone unturned to give all citizens their due, while he continued to urge that the government simply betrayed its own weakness by making laws that could not be enforced. The intelligent English observer at Antwerp, Sir Thomas Gresham, wrote as follows to Lord Cecil, September 8th:

On the fourth of this present, the Prince of Orendge sent for me to dine with him, who gave me verie great entertainment; and as he demanded of the helth of the Quene's Majestie, he of himself discoursed unto me all the proceedings of this toun, and what a dangerous piece of worke it was, and that now he had agreed with the Protestants; which, agreement he caused to be reade unto me by the recorder of this toune, Weasingbeck (he which came into England for the license of corn) being the same daie proclaimed at the toune-house: the copie thereof I send you here inclosed. But in all this discourse he said: "The Kinge wold not be content with this, oure doings"; which causeth me to think this matter is not yet ended, but like to come to great mischief; and specially if the Kinge of Spaine maie get the upper hande. He also asked me "whether our nation was minded to depart this toun or not." I showed him, I heard of no such matter. . . . In all his talk he said unto me, "I know this will nothing content the king"; and at dinner he carved me, himself, all the dinner time; and in the midst of dinner, he drank a carouse to the Queen's Majestie, which carouse the princess, his wief, and withal the borde did the like.[1]

Twelve days after the ruthless desecration of the Antwerp Cathedral, it was solemnly restored to its original purpose and almost entirely by the exertion of the man whose title later became the synonym for aggressive Protestantism. His report to the Regent was as follows:

Madame: Yesterday, thank God, there was again preaching in the great church at Nôtre Dame, owing to my exertions. Mass was also celebrated publicly as usual, in the presence of a goodly assembly.

Your Highness may rest assured that in a short time, with God's aid, I will execute the orders that divine service be re-established everywhere. The opposition, however, in this city is very strong, even among people of good standing.[2]

At about the same date the Prince writes to William of Hesse, and to other Germans, giving a slightly different colour to the same events (August, 1566). The postscript is freer in tone than the letter, and meant only for the Landgrave's eyes.

We do not doubt . . . that things will turn out well and come to no open outbreak. For we have in

[1] Burgon, ii., p. 160, etc.
[2] Gachard, *Cor.*, ii., p. 208.

this city now three churches [three church organisations] of which the first is Catholic. The honourable council allotted one church [edifice] to the Augsburg Confession. The Calvinists preach at three places in the city, but all in the open air. The Anabaptists, too, have their meetings but in secret and they never show themselves. And thus the four religions exist side by side. But we hope that when the Estates meet they will hit upon a means—with God's help—to heal up this cleft, so that *the right one may be planted* and the weeds uprooted.[1]

Had not the Landgrave the right to infer that *das rechte* was the Lutheran faith? The italics are not in the original.

Three months later (November), Orange goes further and asks the Landgrave's opinion about the advisability of writing confidentially to Philip, who already suspects him of heresy, and telling him plainly that he is indeed faithful to the Augsburg Confession, in which he was "born and educated," but that he will pledge himself never to try to convert any one else to his way of thinking.[2]

The old Landgrave Philip is greatly rejoiced that Orange is turning towards truth and writes hopefully of the aid that Lutheran princes will be sure to give the Netherlands if matters be pushed to an issue. Nevertheless, the winter proved a period of hesitation. Egmont and Horne could not agree with Orange that the time had come to

---

[1] Groen, ii., p. 261.   [2] *Ibid.*, p. 495.

"unite their counsels rather than to sell their lives cheaply." Had they done so "we could have employed every means in our power, our money and blood, to prevent Alva and the Spanish from getting a foothold in the land" (*Apology*).

Meantime what had taken place in Antwerp was repeated in Holland. The sectaries wished the sermons, the Regent wished them stopped, and the Prince was determined to assure the reformers the privileges he considered as legalised by the Accord of August 25th. There was much wrangling over the exact dates when preaching *had* taken place in the various localities, and often the question was not easy to decide, as the sole witnesses were interested parties. On January 24, 1567, Orange sends the Regent a copy of his final accord with the citizens of Amsterdam.[1] He had excluded the dissenters from the church of the Minorites, but had decided to permit them to hold their assemblies inside the city until they could build an auditorium outside in the spring. That is in complete conformity with his whole habit of mind—he checked religious excesses, but planned proper outlets for religious zeal, and in so doing claimed that he took the best means of preserving the King's authority even when he went a little beyond the letter of his instructions. For instance, the environs of Amsterdam, the Venice of the North, offered no convenient fields for

[1] Gachard, *Cor.*, ii., p. 341.

assemblies, there being hardly a dry foothold without her gates. So Orange insisted that certain concessions be made, refusing to have the eager worshippers forced into boats for their services, as Margaret suggested.

Margaret was irritably sure that he was wrong in his liberality, but had to accept his measures for the time. She insisted on his personal direction, and permitted him to employ no lieutenant, even while out of sympathy with him. Her feeble representations to her brother were, meanwhile, just of a kind to nag the King into complete distrust. After meditation, Philip arrived at the conviction that with so much disaffection in the air the only effective means of separating the sheep from the goats would be to demand a new oath of allegiance from every royal functionary, officer, and servant in his Netherland service. Whoever refused this test was to be rated as a traitor and Margaret was ordered to apply it at once. In answer to her directions to give this test to his own troops, Orange said rather nonchalantly that it would not be convenient for him to do so in person. His companies were in Brussels—some one might take the oaths there if she wished it.

It was not until March that the formula of the required oath for his own signature was sent to the Prince. He let no grass grow under his feet but returned it instantly to the Duchess with the following note[1]:

[1] Groen, iii., p. 46. Condensed.

Madame: As you desire me to take a new oath, according to a prescribed form you send me, I must at once advise your Highness that, though I am devoted heart and soul to his Majesty's service, as evinced by my whole career, I find great difficulty in consenting to this. If I swear fealty again, it might appear that I had neglected, or forsworn my previous vows.

The form of this new oath, too, is somewhat strange, and seems to imply that I either meditate excusing myself from loyal exertions in the king's service, or that I am to receive orders that I could not conscientiously execute, as I have also sworn to protect the privileges of the provinces.

As his Majesty now writes that all officers and servants, with no exception, must subscribe to this oath, or be discharged from his service, I must consider myself of the latter number, and will retire for a time, until his Majesty comes to these provinces himself, to obtain a true judgment of affairs. . . .

Therefore, I pray your Highness, send some gentleman to me with proper papers of dismissal, to whom I may deliver my commission, assuring you at the same time that I will never fail in my service to his Majesty for the good of this land.

That the Regent refused to accept the resignation was her affair, not the Prince's. Yet in spite of his separation from her interests, his part in a transaction *subsequent* to this correspondence showed that he kept his standard of official responsibility to the end of his service.

Some portions of the confederates became

COUNT JOHN OF NASSAU.
(Reproduced from an old engraving.)

impatient and a premature, ill-advised attempt was made to open active hostilities in Brabant by a small body under the unskilled leadership of an ardent young Calvinist, Jean de Marnix, Sr. de Tholouse. He was attacked, March 13th, at Ostrawell, just outside Antwerp, by Philip de Lannoy and his little force was practically cut to pieces. The Antwerp Calvinists saw the encounter and were eager to rush out and take part. Orange resolutely held them back and was loaded with obloquy in consequence. The sight of the Catholic soldiers ordered by him into the Place de Meir filled the insurgent sympathisers with intense indignation. Orange was called "foul traitor," "Papist," and "servant of Anti-Christ," "pleasant little epithets habitual to the Huguenots," remarks Pontus Payen.[1]

The angry throng spent the whole night on the Place de Meir, whither they had, in defiance of orders, dragged seventeen pieces of artillery. Like people out of their heads they surged from church to church, from monastery to monastery, pillaging as they went. The crowd was strictly Calvinist and was as hostile to Lutherans, "demi-papists," and to Anabaptists as to Catholics. It was a very critical situation, and Orange alone acted with firmness and decision. He obtained the co-operation of the merchants whose property was in jeopardy as well as of various worthy citizens and finally forced a convention upon all

[1] *Mémoires*, i., p. 304, etc.

factions and the menacing tumult was stilled without confusion.

Many praise the prince highly for this act, crediting him with preserving the city from pillage by his presence. They claim he alone saved the lives of the Catholics, to whom the Lutherans too gave timely assistance. As for me [continues the Catholic royalist Payen[1]], I should be sorry to deny honour to the prince but I consider that the Calvinists owed him far more gratitude than the Catholics and Lutherans, because the compromise he made was for the advantage of the weakest body, who were moreover on the point of receiving condign punishment for the thefts, sacrileges, and impieties they had committed.

Four days long three hostile parties thus, armed with rude but dangerous weapons, glowered at each other within the narrow walls of Antwerp. On March 17th the Calvinists finally subscribed to the convention and the immediate danger of terrible disorder was averted.[2]

Now, Sir, howe the Regent and the court will take this business that the Prince and this towne have done, it is to be doubted [writes Gresham to Cecil], not well; for that I am crediblie informed that the Regent hathe no greate trust in the Prince's doings in this town. Yet, I will assure your honnor the Prince verie nobly hathe traveled both night and daie, to kepe this towne from manne slaughter, and from

[1] *Mémoires*, i, p. 310.   [2] Gachard, *Cor.*, ii., cxxxviii.

despoile: whiche doubtless had taken place, if he had not been,—to the losse of XX thowsand men: for that I sawe never men so desperate willing to fight: and speciallie the Valloons who joyned all with the Calvinists.[1]

There was bitter feeling among the Calvinists that the Prince had forsaken them and that to his defection was due the disaster to Tholouse. In his speech defending the articles of convention, Orange pointed out that the calamity was a warning against pitting weak, untrained volunteers with experienced soldiers. His terms implied sympathy with the vanquished, but he ended his speech with "God save the King." And, perhaps, it was not surprising that caricatures were published, showing Orange with two faces and his hand stretched in two directions. For the accusation was also made that he took money from both sides.

"Although this was wrought with . . . danger to life and limb, we may be sure that the service will not gain much thanks at court," writes the Prince to a German friend. He fully appreciated that there was no more place for him in connection with that court.

April 10th is the date of the last of several letters written by Orange to Philip, reiterating his intention of resigning. It is verbose but on the whole it is a remarkably honest transition

---

[1] Burgon, ii., p. 207.

from loyalty to rebellion. On the 11th Orange left Antwerp, returned to Breda, and spent eleven days in preparations to withdraw to Dillenburg. His son Philip William took a brief holiday to come from Louvain to receive what proved to be his father's last words to him and to take leave of the family.

Formal letters of farewell were written to various people, Egmont and Horne among them, and all passed in a deliberate, leisurely fashion. The Prince shows pretty plainly in his talk with Elbertus Leoninus two hours before he set forth, that he fully understood his position, yet he continued to play with gracious loyal words to the very end in his last letter to Margaret, useless words which deceived no one. He took his daughter from the court, alleging that Countess Juliana wished to see her, but his son was allowed to return to Louvain, as an ostensible hostage for his father. Noircarmes says that Orange took a hasty departure followed by a single equerry.[1] As a matter of fact there seems nothing hasty in the circumstances. He may have gone as far as Cleves alone. There his wife and household joined him. Then with a train swelled by an ever-increasing number of fugitives, the Prince made his way up the Rhine valley, stayed a month at Siegen, and finally established himself at Dillenburg, which was to be his headquarters for four years.

[1] *Lettres missives*, Brussels archives.

CHAPTER X

THE EXILE

1568–1570

IT was a great change from the troubled atmosphere of the Netherlands to the quiet Nassau castle, perched on its hill-top, remote from courts and even from the great highways of travel. It did not remain quiet, however, as Orange was one of those people who bring bustle and activity with them wherever they are. His claim to the house where he was born was by courtesy only, as he had definitely ceded his rights to his brothers, with Count John as the legal head, but there is no doubt that the best was offered ungrudgingly to the honoured eldest brother, although this visit must have entailed serious inconvenience upon the household, already a patriarchal one. John and his wife Elizabeth, the Landgravine of Leuchtenberg, had several children. Juliana of Stolberg with her unmarried daughters continued to make Dillenburg her chief residence, receiving from the inmates, one and all, reverence and affection. The younger sons, Adolph and Henry, who fluttered ordinarily around the Prince like moths about a candle, attracted first by the possible emoluments and later by the sure excitement of the Netherlands, enjoyed the freedom of the German castle as homing-ground, and the married daughters and their husbands were frequent guests. But when the Prince came, the provision for his large suite—at least one hundred and fifty persons—was probably a light burden to the castle hostess in comparison with that of entertaining the Princess of Orange herself.[1] Anne was no easy member of a household when she was the head and the first person for consideration and certainly was not an agreeable visitor, under the present untoward circumstances. The happiness that the young wife had boasted of in the first months of her married life had been of very brief duration. References to the Prince's domestic difficulties are frequent in Granvelle's, as well as in the Nassau correspondence, showing how notorious was the uncomfortable state of affairs. Indeed, Anne's behaviour could hardly have been concealed from public view, as her eccentricities showed themselves at home and abroad alike. At the end of his own resources her husband at last appealed to her relations, and much debate ensued in regard to remedies.

As I was prevented from speaking to the Duke of

[1] The account of Anne is taken mainly from an article by Böttiger in von Raumer's *Historiches Taschenbuch*, vii., p. 98, etc., and *Het Huwelijk*, etc., Bakhuizen. Groen prints some letters, iii., p. 327, and others are in the Orange-Nassau family archives, The Hague.

Saxony's gentleman [wrote Orange to Louis, June 22, 1565[1]], both this morning and after dinner, I think it would be well for you to see him and say that although my wife promised to behave better, she has acted in exactly the same manner again. In order that my statements may not seem like fabrications, I should like him to get testimony about her behaviour from the steward, van der Eike, and from the other servants, especially from her own maid, the little German girl. After hearing all sides the duke will, perhaps, be able to make some suggestions. What my wife has said to him she has reiterated to me and to others a hundred times, so that I fear it will be the same old story as soon as the messenger is gone. In case that he cannot find any remedy, let this report reach the ears of the elector, so that he may think out something and write to my wife.

Anne was, evidently, a thoroughly uncomfortable person; her moods and vagaries being, perhaps, half explained by the continued ill health incident to successive disappointments in childbearing. Before 1567 she had become more and more critical of every person and thing in the Netherlands. She was loud in her indignation against her husband for not standing up more sturdily for his rights and her precedence. "He let every one ride over him," etc. As already mentioned, this discontent of hers has been rated as a factor in the Prince's revolt. But it was not. It was only a thorn in his flesh—not a spur to

[1] Groen, i., p. 386.

action. He soon learned to take her at her worth.

When the actual proposition came to abandon the hated land, Anne suddenly saw matters in a different aspect and opposed the project violently. She did not, however, refuse to follow her husband, and there may have been some special cause for apprehension that frightened her into quitting Breda on April 22nd. No sooner was she lodged safely at Dillenburg, however, than her discontent took on a bitterer tone. Everything was uncomfortable to her mind. The house was crowded. The service was inadequate. Her sisters-in-law did not give her the respect due to her birth and rank. They were not inclined always to remember that she was the great Elector's daughter, and hence infinitely superior to small nobles like themselves. She looked back to the Netherlands with longing eyes, and spent all her days in deploring the emigration her husband had forced upon her.

On his part, the Prince showed no regret for his decisive step. His time of hesitation and compromise was over. He was convinced that the cleft between Philip and his subjects was to increase; and he began to prepare in a characteristic fashion for leadership which would knit him more closely to the Germans whose alliance he desired. Within a very few days after his arrival at Dillenburg, he writes, June 13th, to William of Hesse, asking for the loan of a Lutheran

preacher, Nicholas Zell, from Treysa, to give him
religious instruction.[1] "We are heartily desirous
of using the time we are to stay here out of the
Netherlands for strengthening our character and
for studying the Holy Scriptures." The Landgrave was delighted to give his aid. Possibly ab-
sorption in this new idea afforded Orange some
relief from the nagging tongue of the Princess,
which probably continued its reproaches in spite
of speedy proof that the Prince had shown wisdom
in his action.

The hegira had indeed been none too soon.
Scarcely a month after the departure from Breda,
the Duke of Alva left Carthagena, at the head of
a picked army and further armed with definite
instructions to accomplish with an iron hand
what the Duchess had failed to do, viz., to crush
all popular movements and to restore among all
alike complete conformity to the Church of Rome.
Almost up to the moment of Alva's embarkation,
Margaret had cherished the hope of her brother's
peaceful coming to approve her conciliatory efforts. She had even made plans for receiving
him in Zealand. After all the threatening trouble
and laboured pacification in which she felt that
good work had been done, she was filled with consternation at the thought of the alien army and
the policy it implied, and she tried to convince
Alva with letters sent to various points on his
line of march that he had better leave his troops

[1] Orange-Nassau family archives, The Hague.

at a distance and come on alone to survey the situation. Of course her words were unheeded. Alva had no doubts of his ability to settle difficulties that had baffled a mere woman. "I have tamed men of iron, and shall I now not be able to tame these men of butter?" is one of the phrases credited to his mouth. It is also said that when the Catholic Count Egmont, who had chosen the part of faithful royalist, came to greet him, he said contemptuously, "There is the great heretic," in a voice loud enough to reach Egmont's ears. But face to face with him, Alva's manner changed and he greeted the Count cordially and put his arm around the neck he had already dedicated to the block. As he passed through Louvain, Philip William of Nassau, accompanied by his tutor, Henry von Wiltberg, came out of his lodgings "to kiss his hand, and M. de Buren was well received and caressed by the Duke," and invited to another interview on the morrow, when the young student was completely captivated by the veteran. Wiltberg, thinking that some good might ensue from pleasant relations between the new Regent and young Nassau, suggested the present of a horse on the boy's part to the Prior of St. John, Alva's illegitimate son.[1]

One effect of the receipt at Dillenburg of the news of Alva's arrival in the Netherlands was singular and exactly contrary to what might have been expected. Anne became more and more

[1] Groen, iii., p. 120. Henry von Wiltberg to Orange.

restive and begged permission to go back to Breda to see about her property. Assured by her husband's relations that such return was impossible, she appealed to her uncle, the Elector, asking him to help her leave the Nassau house. When Orange heard of this indirectly, he sent a special messenger, Volbrecht Riedsel, post haste to Dresden, to explain his own motives in keeping his wife with him. His statement was as follows: The Princess had not liked the Netherlands and had repeatedly desired to leave the land, "because she would not stay any longer with such godless and faithless people." Now she desired to return when she would imperil not only herself but her unborn child. Besides that reason, he was unwilling to permit the separation because it might lay him and his brothers open to the charge of ill-treating her at Dillenburg, and because she might incur danger on account of her religion or be forced into perversion from the true knowledge of Christ (although she formerly had such a warm inclination for religion) "to popish horrors or to other errors most painful to you," etc. In addition to the above reasons, Orange adds a very pointed intimation that he cannot afford two households under the existing circumstances.

Augustus was quite willing to agree with his nephew-in-law and obediently repeated his lesson to his niece and bade her be patient.

On November 14th, Anne gave birth to a son who was to perpetuate the qualities of the boasted great Elector in his name, Maurice. He was the first of the Prince's children to be publicly baptised with full Protestant rites.

The events in the Netherlands ought to have convinced Anne of her husband's wisdom in bringing her and her children to a safe refuge. The treacherous arrest of Egmont and Horne was followed by the swift measures on the part of Alva towards obtaining "perfect obedience." He ordered that all culprits alike should be tried before a newly instituted arbitrary tribunal, called the Council of Troubles and speedily nicknamed, from its sanguinary sentences, the Council of Blood. There was complete disregard of all the cherished ancient privileges of the provinces. Persecution of heresy was determined and pitiless. Possibly the numbers of executions have been exaggerated, but certain it is that the suffering was intense and widespread, that many suffered death for their convictions and many emigrated to England rather than renounce their faith.

The Prince's inborn disposition to throw out anchors in two directions brought one heavy penalty upon himself. There can be little doubt that his object in leaving his eldest son at Louvain was to conciliate the new Regent and to protect, if possible, the Netherland property. For the boy's personal safety he depended on the protection of the University privileges. The result was the loss of the boy as well as the land.

I am very sorry to have to send your Grace grievous news [writes some unknown friend to Orange, Antwerp, February 12, 1562], but as it has come to my knowledge, I must not leave your Grace uninformed. It is that the old Countess of Horne wrote to me yesterday that her mounted messenger saw your Grace's son in a pony waggon with his chamberlain, von Wiltberg, riding from Louvain towards Antwerp, and the plan was that he should proceed to Zealand and be sent to Spain with the first wind. Those of the University of Louvain protested, but nothing helped.[1]

The rumour was speedily confirmed, for the Seignior de Chassy, attended by four officers and twelve archers, had, indeed, waited upon the young Count of Buren at Louvain and invited him to go to Spain to be educated for the King's service. De Chassy asserted that his duty was to escort, not arrest the youth, and that he might be accompanied by two valets, two pages, a cook, and a bookkeeper. Alva's pleasant note, written *manu propria*, signed "your friend, the Duke of Alva," offered Philip William of Nassau an opportunity "to serve the King as his forbears had served Philip's ancestors." The youth seems to have walked into the trap with actual pleasure, accompanied his captors to Antwerp, enjoyed his stay with Count Lodron, accepted festivities given in his honour, embarked at Flushing unprotestingly, and sailed away for the land where he was destined to spend twenty years.

[1] Orange-Nassau family archives, The Hague.

The protests of "those of the University" at this base violation of its immunities were answered by Vargas in the same barbarous Latin phrases that he addressed to the municipalities, probably less critical of his Latinity: "*Non curamos vestros privilegios*"—"We do not care for your privileges." The Prince's negligence in leaving his son exposed is the more surprising and unjustifiable, because the kidnapping did not happen until at least a fortnight after Philip had published his specific arraignment of the Prince of Orange, leaving nothing to be inferred even from the treatment already accorded to Egmont and Horne. On January 28th, a herald, escorted by six trumpeters, stood in the great square at Brussels and read aloud a summons requiring William of Nassau, Prince of Orange, etc., to appear before the Council of Troubles within three fortnights and there respond to the charge of being chief leader, promoter, and favourer of the rebels, while his brother, Louis, Hoogstraaten, and their adherents were also summoned as disturbers of the public peace. If the summons were disregarded, all those cited were condemned to perpetual banishment and confiscation of their estates. Orange was named as the real instigator of the confederates, as the responsible party for every action hostile to the King. At Antwerp, when acting ostensibly in the King's behalf, he had deliberately encouraged heresy and schism, etc., etc.

The justification of himself that Orange set about preparing and which he finally published on April 6th, is singularly like a modern letter to the press in tone.[1] Translated into German, Latin, Dutch, English and Spanish, it was spread broadcast over Europe. Forty-four pages long, the statement is a trifle more verbose than was needful to express the meaning. Repudiating all accusations of personal ambition, and still more of disloyalty, the Prince justifies every step he has taken, while he acknowledges that he had disapproved the rigour of his monarch's instructions and had considered enforcement of the placards unpolitic and tending to excite the reformers, religious persecution in all ages having had a stimulating effect. He had never been a confederate, he had discountenanced all excesses of the Beggars, but at the same time he had approved their petitions. He had certainly desired the assembly of the States-General, a measure that the late Emperor had often considered expedient. Whenever he had differed from the Regent as to policy he had supported his views by arguments that seemed to him convincing. After defending certain other points, specifically, Orange sums up his attack on Alva's present procedure as follows:

All of which is . . . directly to the prejudice of his Majesty, as all his promises, obligations, contracts,

[1] *Apologie de Guillaume de Nassau—Justification*, etc. Editor, A. Lacroix.

and oaths are disregarded, and such extraordinary, exorbitant, and odious things are done, that it is impossible that the results will not be felt some day. We pray God to illumine his Majesty with divine light, and make him understand aright the actions of his good and loyal servitors and subjects, now calumniated, persecuted, and afflicted, so that the world may at last know that all that has happened does not proceed from his Majesty himself, but is due to the reports, defamations, and calumnies of those who up to now have concealed the truth from him.

There are several noteworthy things about this document. In a literary sense it is not well written, but it is to the point, and restates what the Prince had said in his letters for the previous two years. He separates Philip, as far as possible, from the acts that have been committed in his name, and there are few of the superfluous protestations of fidelity to the person of the monarch which occur in all the Prince's earlier letters. But he does not yet throw off allegiance to his sovereign, nominally, at least. He blames the royal servants, and the easy credence given by Philip to misrepresentations of his officials. For the first time in addressing the most Catholic King, there is no mention, whatsoever, of "*our* true and ancient religion."

The note with which Orange sends this document to the Landgrave of Hesse is delightfully characteristic. Desiring him to tell the bearer, Dr. John Meixnern, his views, he adds[1]:

> Especially I would ask your Excellency to let me or my councillor know whether he finds anything to criticise in the document concerning the Spaniards, for I am a little afraid that it is too ungracious. . . . Would your Excellency perhaps think it more advisable to direct the pamphlet entirely against the Duke of Alva? Also I am not quite sure of that little word "*kriegsrüstung,*"—(war preparation.) Is that perhaps too hard and sharp, and likely to be understood as though we meant to undertake a war from wanton pleasure rather than for simple defence?

By the spring of 1568, plans seemed fairly ripe for actual attack upon the Netherland provinces. The long processes of alliance with the Huguenots and of making friends in Germany—dating back to the time when a little present to George von Holl's wife was conceived as a tactful measure—had been so far successful that sufficient troops were levied to justify the opening of hostilities in a more definite form than was done by the futile and deplorable effort of the Seignior of Tholouse. Levies were made in Germany with no concealment of the destination, and funds began to flow in from various sources. Orange sold jewels, plate, and furniture to get together his own contribution, which amounted to many thousand florins, while his brothers were generous to the

[1] Groen, iii., p. 209.

best of their means, John raising considerable sums by mortgages and Louis contributing 10,000 florins.

Three simultaneous attacks upon the Netherlands were planned from the French and German frontiers. Two failed entirely and there was no sympathetic rising within, to compensate for the failure outside, the provinces. Count Louis and his followers alone met with some success. On April 24th he invaded Friesland with three thousand foot and three hundred horse, surprising the Duke of Aremberg, sent by Alva to defend the north from invasion. For nearly a month Louis held his own in Friesland, while he increased his small army by enrolling stragglers. Then he engaged with Aremberg's forces near the convent of Heiligerlee. It was a valiant fight and resulted not only in the complete defeat of Alva's troops, but in the death of the leader. On Louis's side there was one heavy loss. Count Adolph of Nassau met his death—at Aremberg's hand, it was said—and thus the first human sacrifice to the Netherland cause was offered on the part of the Nassau family.[1]

---

[1] Adolph, fourth son of William the elder, was born at Dillenburg, July 16, 1540. His academic studies were completed at Wittenberg under Melanchthon, his first military campaigns were under the direction of the experienced George von Holl, then serving the King of Denmark, who took a great fancy to Adolph. Later the young Count was captain in the Emperor's service so that he had had considerable military experience and had seen something of life. In the Nassau family archives is to be found

MONUMENT TO COUNT ADOLPH OF NASSAU ON HEILIGERLEE BATTLEFIELD

For the moment it looked as though the libation brought a fairer prospect. Louis finds himself with twenty-five ensign of foot soldiers, fairly well equipped, and two hundred horse, while captains and men-at-arms are flocking to his standard daily.[1] "As for money, that comes in too, but not in great abundance." He had special cause for congratulation from his capture of field pieces, among which were six famous cannon called *ut, re, mi, fa, sol, la*.

Alva was furious that his tried veterans should have been routed by untrained men under a stripling. He was resolved to trust no more to subordinates, but to take the field in person and wipe out this iniquitous rebellion with a firm hand. In order to clear the decks for action he first ordered the trials of Counts Egmont and Horne to take place immediately. "Trial" is a perhaps too euphemistic word, for the proceedings

---

a brief account of him entitled "*Descriptio vitæ comitis Adolphi Nassovii.*" There is also a suggestion that he, too, was hospitable, in the shape of an itemised bill for a banquet which Adolph gave in 1562, Barbara Mutzhagen furnishing the supplies. Twenty-one pounds of lamb do not seem dear at one thaler three and a half alb, though a little out of proportion for one and a half thaler, three alb for the sugar. Butter is cheap, six pounds for twenty-one alb. The bread consumed came to one thaler. Eighty quarts of wine sound abundant, to say the least. Its cost was six thalers, forty-eight alb. A *thaler* is about four shillings, while an *alb* is a penny. The exact value is difficult to appraise for any given time.

[1] Memorandum, Louis to Orange, May, 1568. Groen, iii., p. 227.

were conducted in an arbitrary fashion with no
regard to precedent. The enormous mass of
documents was never properly examined, though
Alva solemnly (June 4th) declared that it was
on the basis of this testimony that he pronounced
judgment on the prisoners as accomplices of the
arch traitor Orange, and as renegades from the
true religion.[1] As a matter of fact the sentence
of death that the Duke sent to the Council had
been duly signed by Philip before Alva's departure from Spain. On June 5th, the Duke actually
assured the Countess of Egmont that her husband
should go free on the morrow, thus enjoying his
little private joke (*en dreef er zyn spot mêe*), as
Hooft says. And on the morrow he kept his word
by sending out Egmont's soul into the freedom
of eternity. On the great square of Brussels the
two men who had refused exile and tried to be
faithful to their monarch, even while disapproving
of his measures, were beheaded as base traitors,
to the indignation of all Europe.

In Louis's camp the first glow of success soon
paled before the difficulty of providing for troops
without funds. The voluntary contributions fell
off and he had to resort to threats to increase the
gifts, each one more unwilling than the preceding.

[1] The accusations against Horne consisted of 63, against
Egmont, of 88 articles. "The whole process is handled more
clumsily than if a village judge had conducted it and no one
pays any attention to the usual rules of procedure."—Morillon
to Granvelle. v. Raumer, *Hist. of the Sixteenth and Seventeenth
Centuries*, Documents, i., p. 182.

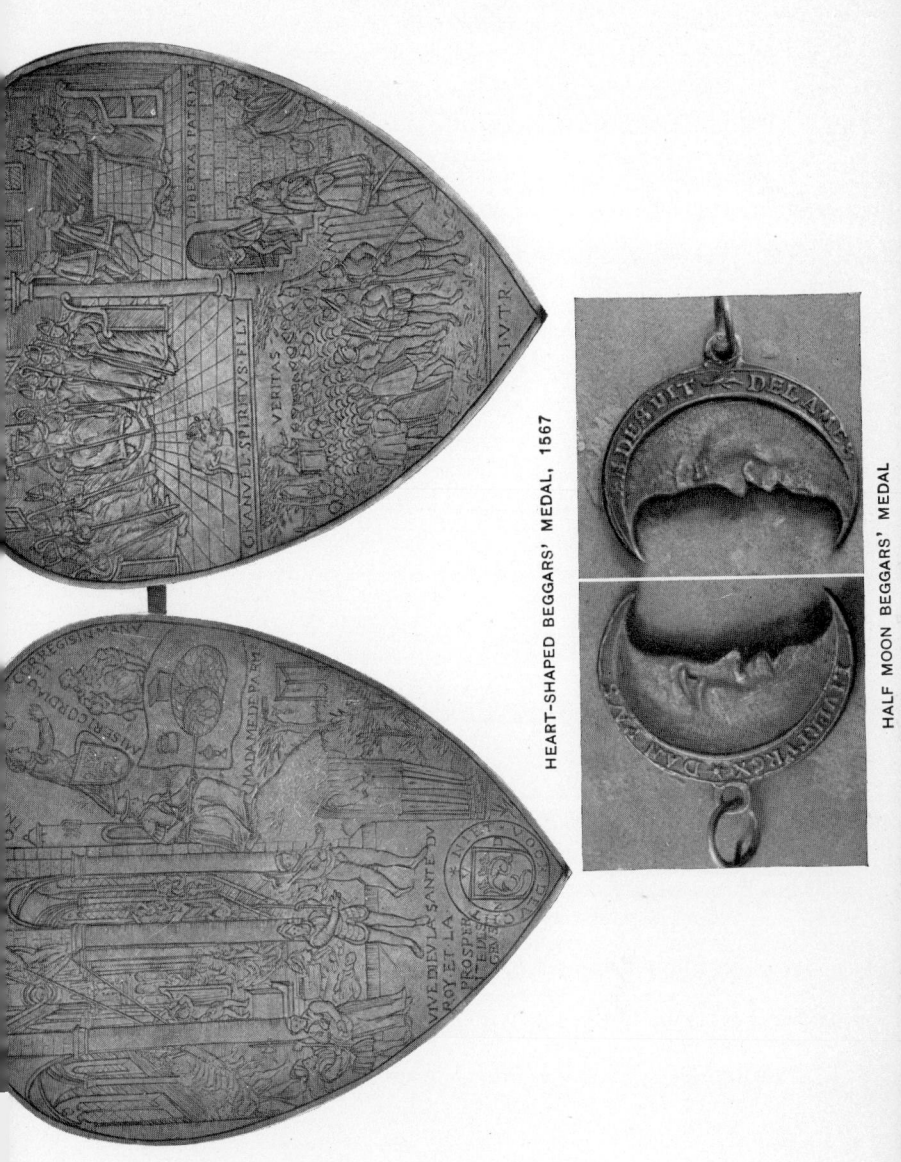

HEART-SHAPED BEGGARS' MEDAL, 1567

HALF MOON BEGGARS' MEDAL

The people knew that Alva was coming to avenge Aremberg and they were frightened by the proclamations affixed to the church doors, declaring that whoso gave to the rebels must pay twice as much to the Spaniards.

The story cannot be followed. Its end was a foregone conclusion and the crushing defeat suffered was rather tamely described by Louis in a letter to one Taffin, a minister of the Reformed Church.[1] He acknowledges that his army is repulsed and dissipated but is thankful that the Prince is active with five thousand horse and eight thousand foot, and begs Taffin to hasten his business so that they might get ships upon the sea. The Prince wrote to his brother as follows[2]:

July 31st.

My brother: To-day I received your letter by Godfrey and have also heard what you commissioned him to say. As to the first point, be assured that I have never felt anything more than the pitiable success which you met on the 21st of the month, for many reasons which you can easily understand. This defeat increases the difficulty of the levy we have on foot, and has greatly chilled the hearts of those who might otherwise have given us aid. . . . With God's help I have determined to push ahead, and hope on the 8th of August to be on the spot for muster, at the place you agreed on with Ste. Aldegonde. I have written to the same effect to Count Joost de

---

[1] Groen, iii., p. 272.   [2] *Ibid.*, p. 276.

Schauenburg, desiring him to report there with his thousand horse, although I do not know exactly where he is at present, and fear, after what has happened, that he cannot easily arrive so soon. In case you know his whereabouts, tell him of this plan as soon as possible, since delay affects us all. As the report is current that the Duke of Alva wishes to keep us from our muster, I pray you remember to advise me whether he be still in Friesland, and what are his forces. In case you hear that he is going to the said place, please at once advise Balthasar von Wolffven, whose house is not far from the Lippe, and also Otho of Maulsburgh, and this you may always do with any advices, for by sending me word first, intelligence might reach them too late. I cannot counsel you about your own plans, as I am ignorant of your resources and your information, and what naval forces the enemy may have. . . . I can only say if you think you can achieve anything *why do it in God's name*, but I cannot heartily appprove your risking your person on the water. . . .

This postscript follows:

My brother, as I said above, watch the Duke of Alva closely. If he means, peradventure, to descend on the muster, you would do well to turn on Duke Eric of Brunswick. In case you find it possible to come to the said place of muster I should be very glad. We could then talk freely over affairs together. In case you cannot come, which [coming] I greatly desire, let me have daily news and keep in correspondence with the Count of Emden, and know from him what is going on there.

There was wonderful restraint and patience in these phrases, considering how every plan, every future movement was hampered by Louis's misfortune and that the incipient sympathy of the Germans had been chilled. The Emperor ordered Orange to cease his levies, while the lesser princes begged him to "sit still" and were unmoved by the continued letters and explanations which he addressed to one after another, reiterating his statements in his *Justification*. In France he found more efficient sympathy, and a fresh gage was thrown down in the shape of a joint proclamation issued in the names of Gaspar de Coligny, Admiral of France, and William of Nassau, Prince of Orange.[1] They declared that they joined forces to defend the liberty of conscience, attacked in France and the Netherlands, while they were still true to their respective sovereigns, "led astray by bad advisers."

On August 31, 1568, the Prince issued a proclamation of his own as head of the army of about thirty thousand men which his herculean efforts had brought together. Some of his standards were decorated by a pelican feeding its young, others with the words, "*Pro lege, grege, rege.*" These words may have been conceived as direct answer

---

[1] Groen, iii., p. 282. The French Protestants feared that Alva was executing only a part of a campaign against their religion recently decided upon with Catherine de' Medici at Bayonne, and that the next step would be suppression of the Huguenots by France and Spain together.

to Margaret's assertion that the people were "*sans loi, sans foi, sans roi.*" They were certainly staunch to Orange's uniform policy of protesting loyalty to the King, against whom he was raising the standard of revolt. Was it quixotic or purely sophistical?

The army was raised, but there was terrible uncertainty as to its support. Urgent appeals for aid were scattered through the Netherlands, bearing Scripture verses at their head.[1] Orange made his way to the neighbourhood of Cologne and then on to the Meuse near Stochem. Alva was on the other side of the river, but in spite of his vigilance the Prince succeeded in getting his men over unmolested. To stem the force of the current he had the cavalry stand in the stream and form a kind of dam to give protection to the men as they forded the river—an old device used by Cæsar himself.

Alva was completely taken by surprise, as he had declared that only a flock of wild geese could possibly cross the unbridged stream. But when he found that he was mistaken he changed his tactics. His skill lay in his ability to grasp a situation as it stood and never to be hampered by military formulas. In July, an engagement was absolutely necessary to him to retrieve the Spanish prestige, injured by the affair of Heiligerlee. In October everything was different. The Duke

[1] "The righteous shall never be removed but the expectation of the wicked shall perish."

had adequate shelter at his service, Orange had not a single city to fall back upon as winter quarters. Therefore Alva avoided any pitting of strength but used a Fabian policy with the deliberate intention of holding the rebels at bay until cold, snow, ice, and dearth of provisions forced the troops without a base to yield their ground and seek shelter elsewhere. The Prince realised that an engagement was essential to him in order that confidence should be assured and enthusiasm aroused in the cause of the patriots—make his army patriots, indeed, instead of irresponsible rebels. But his efforts were in vain. The Duke succeeded in holding the exasperated invaders on tenterhooks and in forcing the Prince to change his camp twenty-nine times. He had, moreover, all the sails and stones removed from the mills and destroyed houses and even whole hamlets that might afford shelter. There was one little pitched battle near Waveren, when the Huguenot allies under Genlis tried to make a juncture with the Prince, but failed. Don Frederic, Alva's son, succeeded in destroying three thousand men under Hoogstraaten.

The Prince penetrated Brabant to within a few leagues of Brussels, but nothing came of his presence there. The towns were terrorised and even failed to furnish the three hundred thousand florins they had once promised. The Prince was left without the walls at the mercy of his unfed, unpaid mercenaries, who would not disband

without their pay, even though they had no
shelter. Over the French border the Prince went,
and made his way to Strasburg; and the reports
went out that his fortunes were so impaired that
they never could be mended. "The major part
of his army are broken, starved, and cut to
pieces," wrote Alva to Philip.

Wretched years of wandering and uncertainty
followed this fruitless and expensive expedition.
Orange stayed on French soil for the most part
and continued to write lengthy explanatory
epistles to the German princes. In July, 1869, he
is at Conflans almost within view of the sea, as he
says, and resolved to throw in his lot with the
Huguenots, having definitely decided that the
issue between the Netherlanders and their Spanish
monarch was religious and of a nature that made
a bond between anti-Catholics a natural alliance.
It was an odd chance that kept Orange out of
the pitched battles of his allies, as well as out of
the actual important engagements of his own
cause. On March 13th, occurred the battle of
Jarnac, in which Louis of Nassau won the affection
of the Huguenots for all time, while they did
not win the victory. But the Prince himself
played no part, not from the cowardice imputed
to him, but because he was busied elsewhere in the
harder task of trying to raise funds for his unpaid
soldiers.

They were terrible years for Orange out in the
open, and trying years for the Nassau women, shut

up in Dillenburg castle, sometimes alone and sometimes with Count John, all watching anxiously for the couriers who brought little good news, but many warnings to see to it that Dillenburg was well guarded, suggestions as to making saltpetre mines, etc., and requests, sometimes pitiful in their humble quality.

I beg you to send [wrote Orange to John, Jan., 1570][1] by the bearer of this, the little hackney given me by the Admiral, in case he is in good condition. Send me also two pairs of silk trunk hose. Your tailor has one that Nuenar gave him to mend; the other pair please have taken from the things I recently used at Dillenburg, which are on the table with my accoutrements. If the little hackney is out of condition, please send me the grey drudge with the cropped ears. You may have noticed that Afferstein begged me for a horse. Do look around and see if some good horse cannot be found and send it to me with the price and I will forward the money to you. Since he is so amiable, something ought to be done for him. Pray forgive me for troubling you with my affairs. I hope to repay you some time.

Much of the Prince's correspondence during this period, 1568–72, was in cipher or half cipher. In certain letters between him and his confidential agent Wesembeck, the names of metals are used to designate the provinces, those of Greek deities

[1] Groen, iii., p. 342.

and demigods to represent the cities. Rotterdam was Triton, Brill, Pollux, etc. None of the elaborate plans lurking under these veils were, however, carried out.

In all these schemes the Prince found not the slightest sympathy from his wife, whose story may be finished here. "*Non deest principi Xantippe vel deferior,*" Cardinal Granvelle had written in 1664. As a wife, Anne proved to be worse than the Greek scold. After months of unhappiness at Dillenburg she actually succeeded in raising sufficient funds to betake herself to Cologne and to set up an independent household there, where she found fresh cause for complaints to be shared with any relative who would hear her. One Volmar von Berlepsch came to her from the Elector and reports what she has said to him.[1] She had always warned her husband against being involved in war with Spain, but he had turned a deaf ear to her counsels and now was nicely caught in the net woven for him by others, notably Louis of Nassau, whom she could not abide. Her husband and his brothers had spent all their ready money and sacrificed plate and jewels for the maintenance of soldiers who would never accomplish anything and were now clamouring for wages and threatening to hold the Prince prisoner until they were paid. She was poor enough. Orange had only given her two hundred

[1] Dresden archives, quoted by Böttiger. *Hist. Taschenbuch,* vii., p. 130.

and fifty crowns in nearly two years. She would
be quite willing to live with him as count, as
noble, or as plain citizen, but really it was unbearable to have absolutely nothing in the world, to
be expected to subsist on wind and to eat one's
own hands and feet. She was just on the eve of
her confinement and that was why she had come
to Cologne. All the ladies in Dillenburg neglected
her. Often she could not get a glass of common
wine or beer, and sometimes days would pass
without their coming to visit her in her apartments. She simply could not endure the thought
of another six weeks' illness there. But there was
still another reason that had caused her sudden
journey. An epidemic had broken out at Dillenburg and there was not one barber surgeon to be
found in the whole Westerwald. How could she
stay there? At Cologne there were a hundred
and fifty Netherland gentlewomen with whom
she could amuse herself during the ennui of her
confinement. She had moreover taken care to
provide herself with a learned pious preacher, a
Netherland refugee, and she had nothing to fear
from Spanish interference. She meant to live so
that no ill reports of her could arise. She had not
a stuiver and was overwhelmed with debt, but
poverty-stricken as she was, she simply would
not go back to Dillenburg without her husband.
She would die first. Why could not the house at
Dietz be repaired, etc., etc? All her plaints might
have been those of any selfish wife to any husband

engaged in a cause which the wife considered already lost.

Berlepsch testifies that her table was not extravagant, although forty-three persons were fed at it. His advice is that Anne should return to her husband's family. Shortly after this Emilie was born—the last child of Anne and the Prince. Then a long discussion ensues between Anne's various relatives. Recriminations fly back and forth but Anne receives little sympathy. As her uncle mentions to her John's remark that she is "stiff-necked," his counsel to return to Dillenburg naturally does not meet Anne's approval, and at Cologne she remains. In desperation over her poverty she finally determines to recover her confiscated property at any price and she appeals to Philip himself, pleading that, by her husband's refusal to answer the summons of his monarch, the Prince of Orange has suffered civil death. In the eyes of the Netherland law he was a dead man; *ergo* on Netherland soil she was a widow, *ergo* the Netherland estates were hers, etc. The answer from Spain to this astounding plea was that she was no widow, but the aider and abettor of rebels. She had sold her plate to help her husband and was thus a culprit under the law.[1]

---

[1] v. Rommel, *Philipp der Grossmüthige*, ii., p. 660, states that this plea that Orange was legally dead—*civiliter mortuum*—was made. Böttiger could not find the document but considers the statement true.

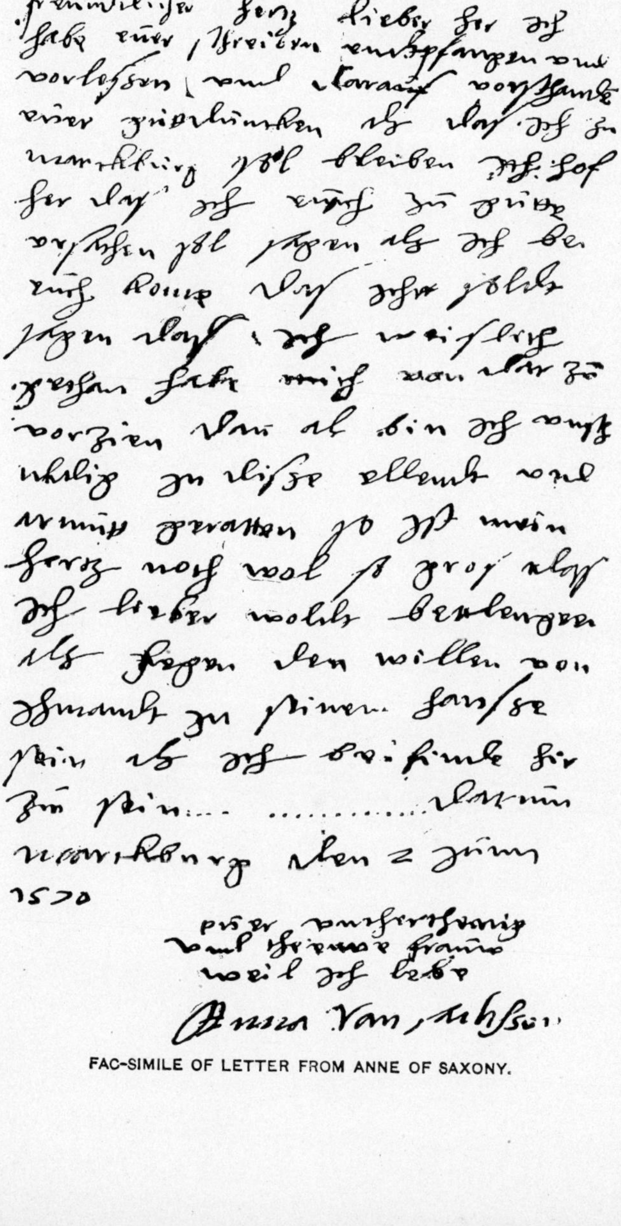

[handwritten letter in old German script]

FAC-SIMILE OF LETTER FROM ANNE OF SAXONY.

In November, 1569, Orange sent the following letter to Anne:

My wife: I have seen by your letters, and heard from our secretary, the reasons why you have not come to meet me, and I do not find them sufficient, considering the duty and obligations a wife owes her husband, in case she bears him the slightest affection. When you say that you have promised yourself never again to be found in this land, you ought to consider that you promised before God and his Church to abandon everything in the world to cleave to your husband, and I think you should have this more at heart than all other trifles and frivolities, if you have any idea of your responsibility. These words are not intended to persuade you to come hither. Since you dislike that, I will not press it, but they are to remind you of your obligation, as I am in duty bound to do.

When a man is immersed in difficulties, there is nothing in the world that would give him greater refreshment of spirit than to be comforted by his wife, and see her bear her cross with patience, especially when her husband is suffering for his efforts to advance the glory of God, and win the liberty of his country. Then, too, there are so many things to say to you which are unsafe to write, without endangering my life and honour. It seems to me that if you felt the slightest friendship for me, you would be governed more by your heart than by frivolous pretexts. I will not lay further stress on the fact that we are giving every one an opportunity to talk about our private affairs, but will leave you to judge whether

such publicity is pleasing to me. I promise you that if
you had asked me to meet you at Frankfort instead of
Siburg, which is in the very midst of my enemies,
nothing would have kept me from acceding to your
proposition, so anxious am I to see you, though all
my officers and friends implore me to avoid cities,
because of the great danger to which I expose myself.

Do you not see, my wife, that you who are my
spouse, leave me to find consolation in trouble from
others who are not so near me? I notice, too, that
you advise me to go to France or England. I wish,
indeed, that French affairs were in a state to warrant
our going thither safely, for then the unfortunate
Christians would be better off than they are now.
But you may be sure that if God in his mercy does not
give some remedy, the poor Christians in France will
be worse off than those in the Netherlands. If the
King treats his subjects so harshly, what would he do
to strangers? So you see what prospect there is of a
retreat there.

In regard to England, there are reasons which I
cannot write, but I assure you, when you hear them,
you will lose your desire to go thither. Our affairs
are in such a state that it is no longer a question of our
deciding upon a place of residence, the point is rather
who will receive us. In both towns and republics I
imagine that they will think more than twice before
giving me shelter, as would the Queen of England,
Kings of Denmark and Poland, and all the German
princes. I do not speak here of *you*, but of *myself*,
because I am out of favour with the Emperor.

After all, there would have been little to say about
this particular point, even if I had seen you, and in
the most secret way, for all my gentlemen and friends

agree in this opinion, that, since my movements commence to be a public matter, it is better for me not to stop in any one place, but be here to-day, tomorrow there. . . .

I would have been glad enough of the relief of seeing you, if only for a few days. . . . I am off tomorrow. Concerning my return, or when I can see you, on my honour I can now tell you nothing for certain. . . . You may be sure that your affairs will never go so well that better cannot be desired, and nothing would please me more than to see you contented.[1]

In February, 1570, Anne writes[2]:

Friendly dear sir: The reason why I did not answer yours of Dec. 14th, your secretary will tell you, together with other things that I commissioned him to report. In answer to your request that I should appoint some place where we could meet, since you do not wish to come in the neighbourhood of the Netherlands, I do not know any better place than Leipsic. I meant to visit the Elector about this time anyway, as I have not seen him for nine years. I will take my way to Leipsic, which ought to be convenient for you, as I hear that you are not far from there. Or if you like it better, come to Braubach with Landgrave Philip. I know of no better and more convenient places than in the lands of my two cousins, and I believe you will be perfectly safe. Let me know which of these two places you prefer, so I can write to the Landgrave Philip and ask him to

[1] This letter is slightly condensed. Groen, iii., pp. 327, 352.
[2] *Ibid.*, p. 354.

lend us his house, for I never again will go near any of *your* friends. If you go on urging me to do so, I shall consider it a proof that you wish my death.

Again, on April 6th, she writes[1]:

Friendly dear sir: I have received your letter and message from T'Serraets—I cannot believe what you write concerning your desire to see me, for you have not acted at all in accordance with your words. In respect to the place that you wish me to come to, which I am to reach in three days, it is not at all convenient for me, and I do not know how to get the means of travelling to join my lord and relations. You write that you are unable to send me money, but I have noticed that you do not care much about helping me. You know better than I whether you could or not. As I cannot get what belongs to me from you and your relations, I must appeal to my friends to get means of sustenance. For I see I need not expect any good from you and I do not wish to be called a disgrace to, and ruin of, the House of Nassau, which I can rightfully call *my* disgrace and ruin. As to your saying that when I come to you I had better leave my anger at Cologne, I have never been angry at you or yours, except with just cause. Our meeting will probably be the cause of increasing my just anger instead of diminishing it, if you expect to go on in your old way. As it does not please you to come to any of the four places I have named, I must bear it patiently. For my part I cannot go to the place you appoint, so I commend you to God's pro-

[1] Groen, iii., p. 367.

tection, and hope He will treat you better than you have me.

The meeting between the two is continually delayed. The Prince seems to try to be patient, and in a letter written in May he still addresses this trying helpmate as "*Ma mie*," and at last they meet at Siegen. Probably the meeting was their last.

Anne had found other amusement in Cologne besides the conversation of the one hundred and fifty Dutch gentlewomen. Dr. John Rubens, father of the painter, a lawyer from the Netherlands, had pleased her fancy and responded to her flattering advances. Though he had a very high-minded and devoted wife of his own, he actually followed the Princess to Siegen and there in March, 1571, Orange forced him to confess his intimacy with Anne. According to the existing laws of the land, the Nassaus had perfect right to put Rubens to death. For a time Anne protests her innocence. On March 22nd she writes to Orange declaring that Rubens — already arrested — had perjured himself and had said that he was her lover simply out of fear of torture. She continues:

If you fell into the hands of the Duke of Alva, which God forbid, you, too, would confess that white were black. So he cannot be too severely blamed for what he said nor should my honour be suspected from it [his confession], for usually unfair questions receive false answers, as has just happened to you. . . . Secondly as to the aforesaid doctor's statement that you will be convinced by letters,—that cannot be, for it can never be shown that I have written other than as becomes an honourable woman. Thirdly, you assert that you have witnesses of my fault in my servants. God in Heaven! What falsehood it would be to testify what I never thought of! Any one could see the falsity, for if I had so far forgotten myself,—which God forbid,—I think I would hardly have called in witnesses. How one sometimes admits into one's house beasts worse than dragons or lions! . . . I would like to know the names of such witnesses. I could easily answer them. . . . I have examined my conscience closely and find myself innocent of all the dishonour you accuse me of and my children will suffer no contempt on my account.[1]

The matter has, however, gone too far to be hushed up. Three days later Anne is convinced of this and writes to Rubens in quite a different spirit[2]:

. . . I am rejoiced to hear from your letter that you have acknowledged the great sin that we have committed and that you have thrown yourself on God's mercy for death or life. I have been troubled lest you would not realise that this was best and that I would be responsible for your ruin, body and soul, but God has relieved me of this anxiety. As to me, I have confessed to-day before God and the world and do not doubt that God in his mercy will forgive me. I have also confessed to my lord and spouse that I have grossly and deeply sinned and implored

[1] Groen, iii., 387.   [2] *Ibid.*, p. 391.

his forgiveness for God's sake and I do not doubt that
he, in accordance with his innate goodness, will not
make full use of his power. He has already given
evidence of this to you and me. For had he proceeded according to his rights he would not have
treated with you or me as he has already done, so I
hope that Almighty God will inspire him further with
His holy spirit and induce him to evince more mercy
and to grant you your life, which I heartily desire, so
that you may join your wife and children. My
conscience is not a little heavy that I have given your
wife such ill reward for the services she has rendered
me. Herewith I commend you to God whom I implore to comfort you with His spirit and to keep us
from such sins as we have committed.

ANNA VON SACHSEN.

SIEGEN, March 25, 1571.

Rubens ventured to beg for no further mercy
than that his death should be by the sword. This
was contemptuously denied him, but he was
allowed to linger on in confinement. The fact
is, it was probably clear to the Nassaus that Anne
was the guilty one, and that it would have been
impossible for any one of Rubens's rank to have
approached her had not she made all the overtures herself, when he was managing her legal
affair.

At this time Orange was at Dillenburg. He
wrote to John, April 9th, upon the subject,
expressing a fervent hope that the mortifying
affair might be kept quiet. That was his main
concern. On May 13th Anne humbled herself

so far as to appeal once more to John, whom she had disliked so long and so fervently.

Well-born dear brother: I cannot refrain from applying to your Excellency about the well-known matter and asking what has been decided, as I am most anxious for a decision. I sit here in pain worse than the torments of hell and my one anxiety is to know certainly what is to be done, in order that I may act accordingly and try whether in the other world there be as little pity for me as in this. For I find none from God or man. Your Excellency writes me in your last letter that the decision rests with my lord and my friends. It is evident that it depends on my lord and not on my friends, for I am sure the Landgrave will not assume any responsibility because I would not follow the advice of my blessed grandfather in regard to my marriage. He will not be in a hurry to punish me for my folly, when he was so slow in helping me in my need. As to the Elector, if he is to be told, I am lost, and shall then ask no further grace than that I shall not have more trouble in this world as I hope soon to be in another. So I implore as earnestly as I can that this affair may not be brought to the Elector and that my honour may be saved . . . and that I may not have reason to complain at the last judgment that entering into a marriage with the Prince of Orange was the reason for losing property, honour, body and soul. [She implores in various phrases that the matter be kept secret] . . . I have confessed all to you, although I might have concealed it and the witnesses would have to be sought far and if they were there I could easily prove that they were not trustworthy [*und die dar waren das soldt ich leichtlich haben keonnen beiweiszen das sie zu keinem rechte recevabel waren*], but I wanted to confess my sins, hoping that my lord, when he heard that I had poured out all from the bottom of my heart without finesse, would be merciful, and I beg your Excellency to lend a hand to this forgiveness and I hope that your Excellency and my lord too will remember that we are all human beings and that such experiences might have happened and might still happen to his Excellency and to your Excellency. I commend your Excellency to God's protection and beg a speedy answer for I am worried to death. *Dutum* Siegen. May 13, 1571.[1]

Your Ex. well-wishing sister,
ANNA G. H. z. SACHSEN,
Princessin zu Uranien.

À Monsieur Monsieur le
    COMTE JAN DE NASSAU.

The letter is not pleasant reading, with its frightened, grudging humility, but the poor Princess was in sorry straits. She did not care for the public affairs, to which she felt that she had been sacrificed. That no one cared for her, she thought was due to the world's injustice, and not to her own delinquencies.

For three years she remained in Nassau, dwelling at Beilstein, a living disgrace and heavy burden to her husband's family. Her children were removed from her charge and brought up by Count John, who watched over the details of their

---

[1] Groen, iii., p. 397.

education with loving, parental care, so that they grew to have a more familiar affection for him than for their less known, absent father. Many letters passed between Anne's uncle and brother-in-law regarding the unfortunate mother. On February 26, 1572, William of Hesse wrote in a paper of instructions:

Whenever men forget God and follow the Devil nothing else is to be expected than is taught by the Old and New Testaments and confirmed by heathen writings and daily experience. My niece knows how we begged her, not only as an uncle, but as a father, to refrain from speaking contemptuously of God, the Master, and to be diligent in prayer and in reading of the Holy Writ. We also advised her to show due respect to her husband, who was not forced upon her, but whom she took voluntarily, against the wish of our father of blessed memory. We urged her, moreover, to conduct herself with the honour and dignity behooving a princess, according to good old German usage; we warned her to beware of light, foreign customs with their idle show, and to hold fast to praiseworthy German manners, and especially to be very chary of entertaining strangers in her own apartments. Had she followed this counsel she would not now be under so heavy a cloud.[1]

The Elector of Saxony attempted no defence of his niece. He had been too well informed of her eccentricities to be surprised that Anne's character had gone from bad to worse. But he stoutly

[1] Bakhuizen, p. 129.

asserted that the Prince was far more at fault than the Princess. Orange had not entered upon the marriage in the right spirit, but had said flippantly that he would rather have his wife read romances than the Bible. Now he was reaping his reward for such light-mindedness. Anne was a modest, well brought up young girl when entrusted to him. He had not taken proper care of her. No wonder that she had gone wrong, etc.

It was natural that Anne's uncle should blame some one for the deterioration of the girl's character, but her fantastic, undisciplined behaviour during ten years had been too notorious for the Prince to be touched by these words of condemnation. Anne's mind was unbalanced from her girlhood, an unrestrained habit of wine-drinking at all hours of the day increased her peculiarities, and insanity was the not unnatural result.

During the years that she remained under the care of Count John, it became increasingly difficult to find any servants to stay with her, no matter at what wages. Her conduct was so violent that her maids were often in danger of their lives, while in her quieter moments she, poor thing, often wished herself dead, a wish that was probably echoed by all her relatives and connections. So little real sympathy did the Elector evince for her that, in 1572, he proposed to the Landgrave William to have her locked up alone in a room where her only communication

with the world should be by a grated window,
through which her daily food could be given her,
and a preacher could offer her spiritual consolation. Meanwhile the report could go abroad that
she was dead and no denial need be made.[1]

This inhuman proposition was not carried out
at the time, and the Princess dragged on her
existence at Beilstein.

In 1575, the correspondence about her was
renewed. The Elector and Landgrave finally consented to resume the ungrateful charge of her
person. Anne was taken to Dresden, and her
uncle actually put into execution the plan he had
formerly suggested to the Landgrave. She was
incarcerated in a dungeon, fed through a slit, and
a preacher expounded the true doctrine to her
daily. As her mind was entirely gone by that
time, it may be assumed that his were but idle
words. Life lasted long after all else was gone,
and the poor Princess lived for two years in a
dreary state of living death. At last, on December 18, 1577, in the thirty-third year of her age,
Anne of Saxony died, raging mad. On the following day this most wretched "Great Elector's
daughter" was buried at Meissen, in the tomb of
her ancestors, followed thither by a long procession of "school children, clergy, magistrates, nobility, and citizens."

[1] Groen, v., p. 195.

CHAPTER XI

THE CAPTURE OF THE BRILL AND AFTER
1572–1573

THE wretched incidents of Anne's disloyalty probably did not affect the Prince's affections very deeply, but they must have been unpleasant blurs in the midst of years already full of one disappointment after another before there came a happy turn in public affairs.

By virtue of his independent principality held "by grace of God," Orange had assumed the sovereign right to establish a navy and to issue letters of marque to Dutch vessels manned by men, some discontented with Spanish rule, some only at odds with their lot in life. Known as "Beggars of the sea" these sailors speedily made the term synonymous with pirates, from their lawless behaviour. Rules of conduct to be observed on the little fleet, as issued by the Prince, were excellent, but unfortunately they were regulations only honoured in the breach, and the behaviour of the wild sea-rovers became more and more disgraceful with every

day of their sailing, and with each descent they
made on the coast. In April, 1570, Coligny's
elder brother wrote to Orange, advising him
entirely to suspend all "commissions" hitherto
issued by himself and Count Louis, so serious
were the many charges against the vessels that
carried his flag.[1] The Prince followed the advice.
When he issued fresh commissions and made his
new appointments he endeavoured to institute
rigid reforms. The code of conduct was re-
enacted, and every craft was ordered to carry a
minister of the gospel, but still the discipline continued to fall short of the standard; the new
regimen was disregarded as the old one had been,
and each individual vessel dodged along the coast
much at its own sweet will.

In October, 1571, Orange appointed William
de Lumey, Baron de la Marck, as "admiral." It
was the Prince's third appointment to that office,
the first two incumbents having retired with fair
fortunes of their own after contributing nothing
to the general cause but a share of their own
questionable reputation. Some aid had been
given the "Beggars" by Protestants and anti-
Spaniards along the Netherland coasts, but as a
matter of fact, their coming had been dreaded in
the seaboard villages even by the Prince's
sympathisers, and the rigorous efforts of Alva to
suppress their depredations and piratical raids
were fully justified.

[1] Groen, iii., 373.

The harbourage enjoyed more or less openly by his rebel Netherlanders in English ports was greatly resented by Philip. As early as July 17, 1568, his ambassador to England, Guzman de Silva, wrote:

I thought well to speak to the Queen and tell her clearly what was passing. I did this and said that it was two months since I had told her that the rebels were taking refuge here and at that time I had not cared to say anything about the way in which they were sheltered, thinking it best to leave to her *as a friend* to determine what was her most fitting course.[1]

Probably at the bottom of his heart the Spaniard knew that this alleged confidence in the lady was resting on shaky foundations. Rumours of Spanish intrigue in favour of Mary Stuart were indeed quite sufficient to turn Elizabeth from fraternal interest in her "brother of Spain" to hospitable concern for his revolted subjects' welfare. Then again certain considerations of policy would arouse conscientious scruples in her breast about the validity of a nobleman's sovereign rights to commission ships of war, and she would order all craft carrying the flag of the Prince of Orange to be treated as unlicensed pirates. This was less hampering to the rebels than it might have been because the merchants in the English seaports cheerfully evaded the royal prohibition to furnish

[1] *Calendar of State Papers* (Spanish), 1568–1579, p. 54.

supplies, and the cruising "Beggars" found no difficulty in spending the money dropped into their wallets as contributions to the cause of revolt or as accumulations from the "reprisals" on Spanish merchantmen.[1]

In the course of these years Anglo-Spanish relations were often very strained. Philip's ambassador, De Silva, was replaced by Guereau de Spes. "Lies are afloat everywhere in regard to Flanders," wrote the new envoy to the King when he paused at Paris *en route* to his post.[2] On his arrival in London he finds continued difficulty in separating truth from falsehood, so he reports all he hears to let the King make his own deductions. His lengthy, gossippy budgets are filled with rumours. In these voluminous despatches there are frequent mentions of the piratical "Beggars," of their infamous theology with its dangerous tendency towards recognising even Mohammedanism, of their nefarious plots, together with details of their resources and their allies, with many insinuations of England's bad faith. "If the Queen has the understanding you claim she has with the princes of Germany to induce them to

---

[1] "The pirates are better supplied than ever before. A man of mine has come back from France where they are and says that M. de Lumbres went to France mainly to beg Count Ludovic [Louis of Nassau] not to allow M. de Lumey to take the first place as there was great division among the gentlemen now at Dover upon the subject."—Oct. 31, 1571, Guereau de Spes to Alva, *Calendar of State Papers* (Spanish), p. 347.

[2] *Calendar of State Papers* (Spanish), p. 68.

arm and co-operate in an attack on my Netherlands, it will be a decided proof that she is my enemy," comments Philip sagely on some of this information.[1] He adds: "Watch and write to me and to Alva, as you see how important it is to the interests of the States." One of these letters from England bears the endorsement in the King's writing: "It is not well to express an opinion about any one or to put more in a letter than is necessary. They or the cipher might be lost."

Philip found it good to dismiss the English ambassador in Spain, John Mars. After some little lapse of time Elizabeth decided to take that as a grievance, and De Spes was informed that he was no longer a *persona grata* at her court.

I cannot stay longer [he writes Dec. 21, 1571] as I am ordered to Canterbury there to await the return of my servant [sent to get travelling expenses from Alva] on the excuse that John Mars was served in that way in Spain, for they are very unfortunately harping on that business.

No successor was appointed. Thus in March, 1572, when Lumey sailed away from England, there was a definite breach in the Anglo-Spanish diplomatic relations and it certainly was not to please Philip that Elizabeth ordered her ports cleared of Netherland ships, as has been frequently stated, when the story of later events is recounted.

[1] Feb. 28, 1569, *Calendar*, etc., pp. 122 and 113.

The Beggars' fleet was making for the north when a head wind decided them to take shelter in the mouth of the Maas. Then, favoured by some chance advantage they made a successful descent on the little town of Brill on the island of Voorne and wrested it from the Spanish garrison. "The Guese have taken the Brill in Holland, which is the best haven in that coast: they took in the towen with force, but use no force that we here," is one simple despatch sent to England.[1]

Now undoubtedly there had been many projects to capture some Netherland seaboard town. The rebels sorely needed a base such as La Rochelle was for the Huguenots before they could extend their operations. One eligible place after another had been discussed as weak enough to be captured or as having citizens who would connive at a forced change of allegiance. Designs on Sluis are referred to in one of the ambassador's letters,[2] of October 15, 1571, and on April 15th he states that he had foreseen the assault on the Brill. No scheme of attack was, however, actually perfected and at the moment of the capture there was certainly an element of chance in the success of the venture and then circumstances favoured what had long been thought desirable. The tide was taken at the flood.

[1] *Rel. pol. des Pays-bas et d'Angleterre*, vi., p. 365.
[2] *Calendar of State Papers* (Spanish), pp. 348, 380. Mr. Hume lays more stress on the intention than seems fully justified from any authorities given. See his *Philip II*.

The news of Lumey's attack was carried to the town council of the Brill, who summoned Koppelstock, the ferryman, to give them information on the strength of the invaders. This man was sufficiently in sympathy with the rebels to exaggerate the force on the ships. The corporation, impressed with its own weakness in comparison with the strength imputed to the assailants, decided that discretion was the better part of valour and the city keys were forthwith delivered to Lumey in behalf of the Prince of Orange. The rebels then had a solid tower on which to float the standard of revolt and the Orange flag was raised with jubilation. This was April 1, 1572.

Meanwhile, within the Netherlands, certain administration measures had prepared the way for a change of allegiance not only in the Brill but elsewhere. Alva had not liked his post. Several times he had asked to be relieved and just so often had Philip refused his request. In 1570, the Duke had tried to make peace with the Netherlanders by virtue of a general pardon. The document was read aloud in the Grande Place in Brussels, rejoicings were ordered and actually participated in by the obedient and careless populace before it was realised that the phrases really signified nothing, that no one was pardoned except those who had not sinned openly against Church or Spanish authority, and that there was still no place, whatsoever, within the provinces for any one of Protestant faith. There was no general agitation, however, until the beginning of this year of 1572, when the Duke took steps to enforce the collection of certain taxes instituted in 1569, but never actually levied. In his legislation Alva disregarded the dearest provincial privilege—that of controlling its own financial grants. Granvelle had assured Philip in 1559 that any attempt to impose a tax like the *Alcabala* of Spain would be deeply resented in the Netherlands. But it was an imitation of that same arbitrary tax, the *Alcabala*, that the Duke adopted. Instead of the *aides* furnished by the town to the sovereign, *aides* which always preserved the colour of being voluntary contributions, even when given most reluctantly, Alva's proposition provided that the following regular taxes should be raised in behalf of the central government:

1. A tax of one per cent.—the hundredth penny—on all property, real and personal, for immediate collection.

2. A tax of five per cent. on every real estate transfer.

3. A tax of ten per cent.—the tenth penny—on every article of merchandise every time it changed hands.[1]

---

[1] In Spain there was so little buying and selling that this so-called *Alcabala* levied on exchange was endured. With the frequent exchange of a commercial nation it would have been unendurable. If an article changed hands seven times, the tax would be sevenfold upon it.

ROYAL MEDAL

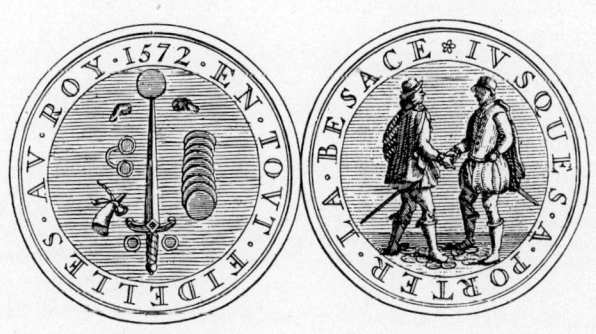

BEGGARS' MEDAL

ALLEGORY, REPRESENTING THE COMING
The Netherlands personified as Andromeda. The Prince of Orange appears as Per
and others are in the foreground. At th

RINCE OF ORANGE. (From an engraving of 1572.)

cue her from the monster who wears the Spanish arms. The heads of Egmont, Horn, the individual provinces with their arms.

The first tax was bad enough because the land was poor, but the second and third aroused bitterer antagonism because the ultimate effect was dreaded. Petition after petition was presented and the whole matter was postponed from month to month and it was not until the year of 1572 that the Duke determined to permit no further delay, but to insist on the fulfilment of the orders.

The result of the attempt to execute his commands was an intense indignation that turned public sentiment at last towards the exiles who had been vainly begging for co-operation for four years. "If we only had funds now," wrote Orange, February 17, 1572, "we could, with God's aid, accomplish something."[1] Watching as he did from a distant vantage ground with many eyes at his service, the Prince perceived that this determined attack on the traffic of a commercial people might be a potent factor in driving them on to the just rebellion he had desired for five years. It was in the midst of this agitation that the capture of the Brill took place, and the Prince's standard was raised in his name as *stadtholder* of Holland and Zealand. It was a very illogical proceeding but the fiction fulfilled its purpose.

"*No es nada*" "It is nothing," said Alva, when the events at the Brill were reported to him. "*Ah,*

[1] Groen, iii., p. 411. A terrible flood, too, in West Friesland caused great misery in this year. It is described in a quaint little pamphlet in The Hague Collection.

les sots, ils se sont trop hâtés," "The fools, they were too hasty," exclaimed Louis of Nassau; while Orange himself does not seem to have been perfectly satisfied. But the Prince speedily accepted the advantage won, opportunist as he was, and used every means in his power to cloak the spreading disaffection with a decent show of legitimacy. Town after town, roused as the people were by the burning injustice of the unpopular tax—declared in favour of the ex-stadtholder. Orange showered letters upon each and every one, and used specific arguments to secure their allegiance. Louis, too, forgave the haste he had criticised, and Alva found that it was by no means a circumstance to be annihilated by a phrase. "For despite he teareth the heires of his hedd," is another report of his sentiments.

The shifting of authority in the Brill did not pass without serious blots on the good name of the patriots. Reprisals were made and revenge was taken for the actions of the Council of Blood. The story of Lumey's treatment of certain devoted priests and monks of Gorcum who remained faithful to their Church and their King, shows how little the theory of persecution was confined to the one side. The Gorcum victims of the Beggars' cruelty reached the last stage of canonisation as martyred saints in 1867 and have been commemorated with an appreciative hand by a Dutch historian.[1]

[1] Their memories are still warmly cherished to-day. Their bones have been transferred to Brussels and rest in a shrine

There were several other instances of the invaders' barbarous retaliation for Alva's long series of judicial murders[1] but when the Prince asserted his authority the most rigorous efforts were made to enforce fair treatment. And there was no great delay before Orange resumed the office of Stadtholder of Holland, Zealand, and Utrecht that he had formally resigned five years previously, calmly ignoring the fact that his liege lord of Spain had taken him at his word and had placed Maximilian de Hennin, Count van Bossu, in the legally vacated chair. There is really a

---

in the church of St. Nicholas honoured with ever-burning candles (1910), while the ancient Holy Well just outside of the Brill at whose edge the execution is said to have taken place, is identified with their miracles and there is a constant stream of pilgrims thither. See Fruin, *De Gorcumsche martelaren*, *Verspreide Geschriften*, ii., p. 277.

[1] For instance William de la Marck assured six captains that he would treat them as gentlemen, not as the Huguenots were treated in France. So he gave them time to make their peace and then beheaded three for Count Egmont and three for Count Horne. That was in the course of warfare. Other more innocent victims suffered cruelly, simply because they were steadfast to their faith.

In regard to a rhyme rendered into English as
  "In April on All Fools' Day
    Duke Alva's specs were stole away,"
Fruin has pointed out that this and similar rhymes made on Alva and his *Brill*—the latter being understood as *spectacles*, rest on a misconception of the first jokes about it. He takes "Brill" as meaning a kind of yoke or bridle. On the first of April Duke Alva had a bridle set on his nose,—"Brill" being a piece of wood used to tame a bull. Lumey had a picture of such a yoke on his standard. *Alva's Brill*, *ibid*. viii., p. 373.

ludicrous element in the action and in the show of legality assumed by the exile and by an assembly of the disaffected nobles and cities which met, successively at Dordrecht, Rotterdam, and Delft in July.[1] The theory that these deputies, convened as a kind of committee of safety, were the Estates of Holland, proved a good working hypothesis; and certain decisions were adopted which formed a practical basis for the executive conduct of affairs without reference to the legitimate governor of the Netherlands, Alva. The self-convened deputies were in session and had already had some discussion when Marnix appeared before them on July 19th, as the Prince's commissioner, and made a clear, eloquent statement in his behalf. The result was that on the following day the Estates resolved that they recognised his princely Grace, the Prince of Orange, as lieutenant of the King over Holland, Zealand, West Friesland, and Utrecht, just as his Excellency had been previously appointed thereto legally by his royal Majesty, without prejudice to any of the customs and rights of the land.

Further, it was declared that as one of the chief members of the States-General of the Netherlands, Orange was the natural person to resist

[1] The status of this assembly has been discussed by Kluit, Bakhuizen van den Brink and Muller. The conclusion reached by the last two that it was, in spite of its legitimate claim, revolutionary in character, seems the most tenable theory. But its novel feature was in the *method* of convention rather than in its being when in session.

oppression and to protect the land in the absence of the sovereign and under the stress of *Albanian* oppression. The Prince was, moreover, entrusted with the appointment of a deputy lieutenant for himself and with the work of reorganising the high court (Hof van Holland),[1] because, with the dispersion of the council and other officers, "justice stands still and great confusion will be caused." The Prince was to take no final action without consulting the Estates; and they on their part were to exert themselves to bring other members of the generality to their way of thinking.[2]

[1] The Hof of Holland objected strongly to the first placards issued by the Prince of Orange which emanated from himself. Only when he replaced the name of King Philip was the tender conscience of the judicial mind able to approve the revolutionary proceedings.—See Fruin, *Staats instellingen*, p. 62.

[2] The cities represented were in the first instance Dordrecht, Haarlem, Leiden, Gouda, Gorcum, Alkmaar, Oudewater, Enkhuisen, Edam, and Monnekendam,—some small as well as the six great cities. Before the conclusion of proceedings, Delft too was included.

The action, offensive and defensive, legislative and reconstructive, taken in 1572, was undoubtedly instigated by the Prince himself, but a certain memorandum emanating six years previously (December, 1566) from the consistories of the Reformed Church is worth noting here as it suggests that concerted resistance to Philip might have taken place without a Nassau hand at the helm:

[Original in French]. "Question. If His Maj. fail to observe the privileges, etc., may a portion of his vassals and subjects resist his authority? Resolved that it would be right and that means must be found to execute it. Needs;—a leader or leaders, money and troops. As to leaders, the most fitting would be the Prince of Orange, if he would promise to preserve the public

The deputies regarded themselves as the successors of the previous Estates of Holland, and did not ostensibly act as a constituent assembly, directing an extraordinary situation. Nevertheless the body assumed the right to confer upon the Prince powers over which its predecessors had had no jurisdiction, and its history shows him in turn conferring powers on the congress never before assumed in Holland by the representatives of cities convened together.

Not until August did the guarantee of supplies from the "Estates" enable Orange to proceed actively in his campaign. Towards the end of the month he crossed the Meuse and passed through Diest, Tirlemont, Louvain, Mechlin, and other places. Mechlin accepted his garrison and money began to pour in from various quarters so that he was greatly encouraged.

I must not fail to tell you [he writes, August 11, to John[1]] that to-day I received letters from the Admiral [Coligny] informing me that notwithstanding the late French defeat, he was levying 12,000 arquebusiers and 3000 horse, intending to join me. . . . He advises me to defer an engagement until we can join forces by the grace of God. I shall follow his advice only so far as it seems advantageous.

---

exercise of the reformed religion according to the confession of the churches of the Low Countries. In default of the Prince, Mons. de Horne and Mons. de Brederode or one of them."—Groen, ii., p. 515.

[1] Groen, iii., p. 488.

The elation of these early months of the summer of '72 was followed by a crushing disappointment that stunned all Protestants throughout Europe. Poor Count Louis, especially, suffered untold misery at the terrible blow struck at his friends the Huguenots. He had had the good luck to wrest the important town of Mons from the Spaniards and was within it, standing a siege well and confident of reinforcements from France, when the shocking massacre occurred at Paris on St. Bartholomew's Day. No juncture between the Beggars and the Huguenots was ever to be effected. Poor Louis, shut up within the beleaguered town, conceived such bitter sorrow over the deed of Paris that he was ill for three months (says La Huguerye[1]). The Prince wrote to John that not only he but every one in Europe had been totally unprepared for the sanguinary event. It had struck him like a thunderbolt. "Usually wiseacres declare that they foresaw what was in the wind, but who would dare to say so now?"[2] The letter

[1] Michel de la Huguerye, *Mémoires*, i., p. 130. The writer is not always reliable.

[2] Groen, iii., p. 501. The reason for the massacre of the Protestants on Aug. 24th cannot be discussed here. Possibly the fear lest Coligny would give aid to the Netherland rebels was one factor in hastening the attack, but much is still obscure in its regard and the subject demands more space than can be afforded. A wholesale murder of all the Protestants in Paris at the very moment of the wished-for alliance between Henry of Navarre and Margaret of Valois was the terrible fact—whatever the reasons. Hopes had been high that Catherine de' Medici would espouse Protestantism for political reasons.

is partially in cipher. It was not a time to trust any man's honesty.

Under the heavy cloud of discouragement, Orange pressed on slowly towards Mons to relieve Louis, and finally pitched his camp in early September at Hermigny, about half a league from Mons. Don Frederic, Alva's son, held his army in the village of St. Florin, close to one of the gates. On the night of September 11th, the Spaniard, Julian Romero, fell upon Hermigny with a small force of six hundred men, all wearing white shirts over their armour to enable them to distinguish each other in the darkness. Silent as falling snow they surprised the sentinels, cutting them down like grass, and then made their way into the sleeping camp. The Prince was aroused from his sleep by a little spaniel which was lying at his feet. Not content with barking, the devoted creature had the sagacity to lick his master's face. Awakened at last, the Prince sprang out of bed, seized a horse that was ready saddled, and rode off in the darkness. His men were less fortunate. Several hundred at least perished, many who escaped the sword being driven back into a stream. The Spanish loss was insignificant.

This news was a fresh blow to Count Louis. He decided to give up Mons, obtained extraordinarily good terms from Alva and permission to march out with honour. Then he went to Dillenburg, where he arrived at the end of October.

"After a little rest [says La Huguerye], and careful nursing from his mother, who loved him tenderly, Louis was able to attend to business in which Count John of Nassau was unskilled and unable to dispense with the assistance of the said Count."[1]

Orange waited to say good-bye to Louis as he passed, and then turned towards Holland and wrote from Zwolle on October 18th:

Owing to the fall of Mons and the necessary dismissal of my German mercenaries, cities on all sides have lost heart, and I perceive a great change everywhere, even the warmest sympathisers are discouraged, not because they have less affection for the cause than formerly, but because they are terrified to death, and I fear that in the end I shall find myself alone, abandoned by every one, unless God performs a miracle. . . . One place after another has ceased resisting the Spaniards. No sooner was I out of Roermond than the soliders abandoned it. . . . I am determined to go to Holland and Zealand to maintain affairs or to find my sepulture there.[2]

By this date the Prince was already called the Father of his Country. The confidence felt in him by his adherents is a strong proof of what his personality must have been. *The Wilhelmuslied*[3] had already proved its power to animate the rebels and to make them forget the persistent ill luck of their chief. For it is singular how very little

[1] *Mémoires*, i., p. 138, etc.   [2] Groen, iv., p. 2.
[3] The words of this song are attributed to Philip Marnix. The music is an old French air according to Fruin.

achievement there was to his credit, how little
effective skill the Prince had shown thus far!
His own military operations had failed utterly
from the hour when he crossed the Meuse in 1568
until he was surprised at Mons, in September,
1572. The gains actually made for the rebels had
been, to a large measure, without his knowledge
and in a fashion that he did not wholly approve.
Yet the potent forces of life seem to be over and
above minor accidents. His adherents believed
in Orange for his aims and did not abandon him
for his failures. His enemies continued to fear
him more than any other hostile force even while
they declared that he was impotent to harm
them.

The siege of Haarlem occupied the thoughts of
all during the winter of '72–'73. Heroic endurance was manifested by the citizens and Orange
exerted himself to the utmost to relieve the city,
but it was in vain. Don Frederic had the
resources of Amsterdam at his back; with that
base he was finally successful in reducing Haarlem
and making it pay a heavy penalty for its resistance. Orange hovered in the neighbourhood of
the besieged town and from his post on the Haarlem lake he sent out volumes of appeals for
pecuniary assistance. But the answers received
were discouraging. Elizabeth was very vaguely
sympathetic, the French were dazed completely
after St. Bartholomew, and the Germans advised
that the revolt should be abandoned as futile and

that reconciliation with Philip be sued for, and even John and Louis of Nassau were disposed to agree to that counsel.

On February 5th, Orange writes thanking the brothers for their warm interest in his affairs and specifying the terms upon which alone he would make peace with Spain,—liberty of conscience and of worship to all men, restoration of all ancient privileges, and expulsion of all Spanish garrisons. Also Orange thought that it would be only just for Philip II. to assume the expense of the rebel troops. (Such a wise and practical thought on the rebel's part!) With all these items adjusted, the King would speedily see that public peace was the Prince's desire and "that I am not opinionated against what is reasonable. But here is our difficulty. Can we trust these assurances when we know . . . that they hold that promises to heretics can be absolved by the Pope?" etc., etc.[1]

That seems a far more candid expression of opinion than the phrase in another letter of March to Count Louis[2]:

In your last letter you speak of my shortly receiving good news. Not knowing what it may be and suspecting that it may concern the peace negotiations, I beg you to give me full information . . . so that I may know how to act. To my mind . . .

[1] Groen, iv., p. 49.
[2] *Ibid.*, p. 72. This paragraph is in German, the rest of the letter in French.

it seems very important to consider whether in proposing conditions, . . . on which to base an accord, *we may not expose ourselves to the charge of wishing to lay down the law to our superiors.* Even the form used by the Admiral in France does not seem to me quite proper from a subject, a vassal, towards his liege. Would it not be better to let them propose conditions which we can accept or reject? Then besides the fact that we would remain entirely within our rights, we would gain credit for our modesty. Pray ponder these points. As to affairs here, the Haarlemers hold out valiantly, although provisions are short and the people so weary of war that they are lax in their duty. It will be difficult to prolong their efforts. For my part, I see no prospect of raising the siege, so I beg you to see what you can do, either by a grand levy or by persuading the princes to act in unison. It would be a shame to let worthy people perish so and if they fall after such staunch resistance the effect on the other towns will be very bad. . . . Use your discretion and take care of your person. All the country is longing for you like the *Angel Gabriel.*

Under the circumstances the apparent sophistry —hardly worth while between these men—seems strange, but there may have been some other meaning to the phrases. At this moment, Orange distrusted any alliance with France, which his brother was still disposed to make.

I must tell you frankly [writes Orange to Louis in May, 1573] that the Estates individually and collectively have a deep-rooted distrust of the king [of France] on account of his late enormity. If we are to be under any tyrant it is surely better to be tyrannised over by one's natural prince than by a stranger. This is the universal conviction.[1]

The fall of Haarlem (July 12, 1573), was followed by the splendid and successful defence of Alkmaar, which Don Frederic had besieged with the expectation of speedily reducing it as a mere bagatelle. Four hours of assault and seven weeks of siege convinced him that the town was not ripe to fall like a plum into his mouth. But it was not only the vehemence of the resistance within the walls that caused the enemy to retreat. At the Prince's suggestion the sluices were opened and the Spanish forces found the water rising above their feet. That was the argument to which Don Frederic finally yielded, and on October 8th he drew off his troops from Alkmaar's gates and marched south. Counting the capture of Brill as the first, this release of the North Holland city was the second milestone on the road towards the ultimate success of the rebellion.

This autumn of 1573 marks too, another milestone in the Prince's personal life. He came to the conclusion that the Calvinistic form of theology was better adapted to the needs of the Netherlands than the Lutheran tenets which he had commenced to study seriously under the instructions of Nicholas Zell. The former fur-

[1] Groen, iv., p. 113.

nished political theories excellently adapted to the regeneration of a state such as was taking place. It was a not unnatural decision to one of the Prince's temperament.

On October 23d, Bartholdus Wilhelmi, a Dordrecht minister, wrote to one of the Leiden churches:

> Brethren, I must hasten to inform you that the Prince of Orange, our pious stadtholder, has joined the congregation, broken the Master's bread with the faithful, and submitted to discipline.[1]

In 1567, when union would have meant national strength, the Prince's earnest counsel to the sects was in substance what Hooft expresses in the phrase: *"Het geschil is te kleen om gesplijt te blijven,"* "The difference is too slight to separate you the one from the other." There is no reason to think that the man's profound conviction of this belief had changed in '73, when he thus allied himself with the Calvinists instead of standing aloof from all the sects alike with neutral kindness toward each one. To his ideas of political leadership it seemed the act of wisdom to identify himself with the strongest political body and from one vantage ground to protect the devotees of other theological creeds. Expediency, not dishonesty, was the main spring of his action. After writing himself down a Calvinist, the Prince

[1] Groen, iv., p. 226.

PHILIP MARNIX, SEIGNEUR OF STE. ALDEGONDE

did not change his nature so as to lose, in any
degree, his sense of toleration. Indeed, his liberality often prevented his stricter brethren in the
faith from wholly trusting him, after his enrollment
among the faithful, as before.

It was a surprisingly brief period, considering the
provocation, before Count Louis's belief in aid from
the French court began to revive. He thought
that the desire to erase the blot of St. Bartholomew
would induce Catherine de' Medici and her son to
show kindness to other Protestants. There is a
very interesting letter from him to Charles IX.,
in which the writer expatiates on the chance
offered the King to rehabilitate himself.[1] The
young German certainly does not gloss terms.
He declares that the King's reputation had suffered terribly from the massacre, as was proven
by caricatures, by libels, etc. An alliance with
Protestant princes was the one thing that could
clear Charles from the accusation of having
deliberately planned an act of horrible treachery
towards people he had cherished. "How did
your Majesty deal with the Admiral—pretending
to be alarmed about his wounds and promising
vengeance on his assassins two days before your
Majesty took vengeance indeed, but in rather ill

---

[1] Groen, iv., p. 81. Michelet says, x., p. 28. "History has preserved nothing more bitter than this cry of Louis of Nassau. . . .
This terrible piece of frankness is oblivious to all the diplomacy
of the period." Again, p. 45, "The bold words of Louis of
Nassau proved to be a message from a man on the eve of death
to a dying man."

fashion!" The writer urges that Charles must retrieve himself if he wished his word to be trusted again, and that he could do best by furthering the Protestant religion, which was far from being exterminated.

Apparently this plain speaking did not bring Louis into disfavour with the French court. Commissioned by the Elector Palatine to greet the newly elected King of Poland *en route* to his new realm[1] Louis determined to see if something good could not be concluded to aid both Count Frederick and the Netherlands. He was so far successful that he was able to write[2]:

In sum the King of France has pledged himself to espouse the cause of the said Netherlands in the same way that the Protestant princes espouse it, however that may be, openly or secretly, and *without counting the money he has already given us*. You may be assured, Monsieur, that your affairs go better in Germany than ever before and that my brother and I will not lose a single minute in advancing them. As to the bishop of Cologne, he is in good train, thank God. . . . We have arranged that the King of France shall give him 16,000 livres pension and that he shall have one year's income . . . in advance, on consideration of breaking from the Spanish entirely from this time forth. . . . As to the money you need we will try to send it to you as secretly as possible.

[1] The French King's brother, Henry, Duke of Anjou, had been elected King of Poland. Later he was Henry III. of France.
[2] Louis to Orange, Groen, iv., p. 278.

... As soon as this journey be over, Monsieur, I shall join you with a large or a small company. I had an interview with the Duke of Alençon[1] who whispered to me as he pressed my hand that if he had the government there [the Netherlands] as his brother that of Poland, he would second you to the utmost. I know how to use his fidelity, which would be of no slight service to us. If God grant that France and Poland work together, as I think they promise to do, I believe our affairs will be marvellously furthered.

In spite of the shortness of the time since Orange had stated his opinion that it was sheer folly to trust in French assistance, he let himself be convinced and adopted the policy which continued to dangle before his eyes until his dying day—French protection for the provinces, reinforced by the Protestant German princes, and by the Archbishop of Cologne, who dreamed of changing his faith and taking his see with him as a lay principality.

In Holland the Prince was beset with other dangers than that of open warfare. He was, legally, an outlaw. Granvelle himself had advised that he and his brothers should be disposed of "like Turks." Philip was quite ready to take this advice and there were plenty of assassins ready to please him. On February 3, 1573, Juan de Albornoz, Alva's private secretary, wrote to Philip's chief secretary[2]: "The man who brought

---

[1] This was the fourth son of Catherine de' Medici. He became Duke of Anjou on his brother's accession to the French crown.
[2] Gachard, vi., p. 1.

Coligny's head has offered to strike off the head of another who has injured Christianity as much as the scamp now in hell."

Gabriel de Cayas showed this letter to the King, who wrote on the margin, "I do not understand this, because I do not know where the Admiral's head was taken or whose this other head is, although it seems to be that of Orange. Certainly they have shown little pluck in not killing him, for that would be the best remedy."

There is plenty of evidence to prove that assassins were willing. One hireling had to renounce his project because his ignorance of Flemish prevented his gaining the entry to the little court then established at Delft. The Prince was on his guard and as he had his own spies, even, it is said, in Philip's cabinet, he was usually sufficiently informed in advance to frustrate the plots against his life. Many of Alva's "trusty people" met their death as they were on their way to rid the land of the rebel leader.

Meantime the two governments *de facto* went on side by side in the Netherlands. Alva convened the Estates at Brussels and Orange found means to send his own statement of affairs to the assembly. It was a fervent call to co-operation with the rebels. "Did not Alva obtain the sinews of war from them? Why should they continue to furnish means to pursue these oppressive hostilities? Former princes of the Netherlands lived on the soil and had *never had a stuiver not expressly granted to them.* Why should this foreigner usurp privileges in a manner a native count had never dreamed of? Holland had taken her stand and meant to abide by it, even though Amsterdam remained out of the new bond. If there were but union among all the provinces, what could not be done?[1]

This appeal was followed by an "Epistle to the King of Spain," which was scattered broadcast over Europe. A picture of the misery in the land was drawn with a strong hand, the futility of the "pardons" offered by Philip was characterised in scathing terms, and the declaration was made that arms would never be laid down while there was a hand within the disaffected provinces to wield a sword.

In 1573, the Duke of Alva was finally relieved from his charge, not by Medina Cœli, as had once been determined, but by Don Luis de Requesens y Cuniga, Grand Commander of Castile. The arrival of the new lieutenant-governor at Brussels on November 17, 1573, was most welcome to Philip's regent. The task of taming "men of butter" had proved as disagreeable as it was difficult. He was completely at the end of his resources and blamed old royalist Netherlanders like Viglius for his failure. They were too lukewarm. Alva wrote to Philip that he could do nothing with the "ancient set of dogmatisers.[2] Till all are gone, together with Viglius, who teaches

[1] Bor, i., p. 459, etc.   [2] *Cor. de Philippe II.*, ii., p. 359.

them their lessons, nothing will go right. One or two Spaniards are like pouring a flask of good wine into a hogshead of vinegar. All is soon vinegar."

Broken in fortunes and discouraged, Alva sailed off to Spain, managing to escape the crowd of his private creditors at Amsterdam by departing before the date set. He left his reputation behind him together with his repudiated debts. And thus far no apologist has written his biography and tried to show his virtues.

Alva leaves Belgium [writes Hubert Languet to Philip Sidney, December 21, 1573]. I believe nothing vexes him more than that he has left any survivors of his cruelty. His successor is pretending the greatest moderation. He has just given a beautiful instance of his wisdom for he has taken a motto for his colours, *Debellare superbos*. It is the mountain in labour. The threads of his net are too coarse and he will not catch many birds. He promises immunity to all who shall give themselves up to be tortured. Orange's affairs are not altogether unpromising, for Holland and Zealand make so much of him that they consider their well-being to depend on his safety and therefore they do not allow him to encounter the risks of war but will have him preside at their councils and let others execute his commands.[1]

Before the change of governors, Don Frederic

[1] *Cor. of Philip Sidney and Hubert Languet*, p. 14.

had shifted the base of offensive operations from Alkmaar to Leiden.[1] In Holland, Haarlem and Amsterdam, in Zealand, Middelburg, were the only cities in the Spaniards' hands. Prior to fresh operations conciliatory measures were tried. Julian Romero, one of Alva's veterans, actually opened a correspondence with his former colleague, Orange, in evident desire to bring him as far as peace negotiations. Possibly among the Prince's partisans the wish for peace spread. Certainly one of his most devoted friends, Philip Marnix, chose the moment to urge submission. Marnix, captured at Maaslandsluis, was in the hands of the foe and had evidently lost heart when he wrote[2]:

I think it would be far better to forsake all conveniences of the fatherland, all this world's goods, and live in a strange country, possessing one's soul in patience, rather than to continue a war, which can result in nothing but misery. . . .

Consider too that Alva is retiring and that the King is free to exercise his own natural clemency. Even if he does not, surely a rigorous government would be more endurable than the burdens of this war. . . . I would like to have three words with your Excellency and you would understand how this proceeds from my heart. Your Excellency can have the opportunity if he wishes, of speaking to the master of this camp, who leaves for Spain on Monday and who has expressed a desire to meet you.

[1] De Valdez succeeded as commander of this enterprise when Don Frederic departed for Spain with his father.
[2] Groen, iv., p. 285.

With his customary deliberation Orange communicated this proposition to the Estates and received prompt and decisive assurance that there would be no use in making an accord sure to be broken.

The Prince's old acquaintance, Noircarmes, also opened a correspondence with him, urging him to reconciliation. To him Orange replied in a cool and dignified fashion and finally showed him some confiscated letters which had fully convinced the Prince that there had been no change of heart in the Spanish quarter.

From Germany, instead of the hoped for subsidies, there came advice of similar tenor. "It is a losing game you are playing [wrote Landgrave William]. Give it up while you have anything to save."[1] Louis of Nassau, however, was not among the doubters. He had high hopes from Germany and he continued to believe that the French King would finally redeem his damaged reputation by some great deed. At least one hundred thousand crowns had been given to Louis at Blamont, and he wrote glowingly of his plans for his expedition to Holland, in which Duke Casimir of the Palatine was to aid him.

[1] The Landgrave was full of schemes for evangelising all Germany but he was very wary and often warned his friends to beware of snakes in the grass,—"*anguis in herba latitaret.*" Groen, iv., p. 349.

CHAPTER XII

THE BATTLE OF MOOK HEATH

1574

IN December the Prince changed his headquarters from Delft to Zierikzee, so that he might be nearer to Middelburg, faithful to Spain and closely besieged by the Netherland troops. Within the walls, Spaniards and royalists subsisted on rats and cats as bravely as the Haarlem people had done, and were quite as determined not to yield.

Then Orange moved on to Flushing where he writes to his brothers (January 6th)[1]:

My letter from Zierikzee of the 23d ultimo, of which I enclose the duplicate, will inform you how troubled I am at hearing nothing from you since November 6th. Pray relieve my anxiety. . . . Tell me whether I can surely count on aid from you, tell me *everything* without concealment, that I may take measures accordingly and prevent here the repetition of Haarlem's fate. The worst may be expected from the foe, because since the surrender of Haarlem they have met

---

[1] Groen, iv., p. 320. Addressed to John, Louis, and Henry of Nassau. Condensed.

contempt, shame, and humiliation in Waterland and
Zealand. You know their nature,—not only ambitious and vindictive, but almost devoid of humanity.

I do not say this from distrust of your zeal, being
assured by several letters that you are working unceasingly, but because several excellent measures
which you have initiated are so long deferred and any
delay entails irreparable injuries at this moment . . .
as the enemy's forces are discouraged at odds and
scattered in several directions. Again I beg you to
let me have definite news from you and through two
or three channels.

Before this letter was despatched, advices of
November 21st arrived with the encouraging news
of the interview between Louis and Anjou and of
the promise of French assistance. The Prince
continues his letter:

As to your difficulty in reading my cipher, I hope
by this time you have received the duplicates and are
in possession of my plans. . . . Middelburg is in
such extremity that we trust it must soon fall into
our hands. . . . And as the enemy are making strenuous efforts to revictual it, I beg you to have general
prayers offered, imploring God to take pity on our
misery and to prevent too great a sacrifice of blood.

On January 29th, an engagement took place on
sea in which Boisot, the Prince's Admiral, lost an
eye and won a splendid victory. Julian Romero
was in command for the Spanish, although quite
ignorant of naval warfare. The ships were locked

together and a hand-to-hand conflict ensued, from which the royalists retreated with the loss of at least 1200 (some Spanish authorities say 7000) men and seven ships. Romero was forced to save himself by swimming, and he joined the Grand Commander, who stood watching the conflict from the top of a dyke in a drenching rain, and said nonchalantly: "I told your Excellency I was a hard fighter and no sailor. Had I had a hundred ships I doubt if I would have done better." With this philosophical resignation to his defeat, Romero accompanied Requesens to Brussels, and within Middelburg Mondragon was left to his own resources, which were insufficient to sustain him beyond mid-February[1] when he capitulated. The articles of surrender signed by him and Orange on February 18th implied a certain recognition of the Prince's position *de facto*. This was a third milestone and a distinct stage in the great rebel's career. In the northern cities of his sometime government, Orange had been named stadtholder by citizens in open revolt.[2] At Middelburg the resumed dignity was acknowledged by Mondragon, Philip's defeated general,

---

[1] Hooft, ix., p. 323.

[2] Prior to his departure, Alva had inaugurated a new plan of campaign. "I am busy [he writes] in so distributing the troops that they may be able to prevent the Beggars from obtaining supplies from the open country. . . . In this wise the rebels will be hemmed into the cities and must perish of hunger. And on some winter-night when the ditches are solid, it may be possible to surprise them."—*Cor. de Philippe II.*, p. 112.

in delivering up a city that had heroically endeavoured to remain loyal. Orange reorganised the magistracy, received oaths of allegiance from the burghers, and swore to maintain ancient local privileges. Further, in consideration of the hardships that the city had endured, he waived two thirds of the indemnity promised him.

In Germany, the Nassau brothers assuredly were strenuous in their efforts "to be diligent." The ingenious activity of Louis in this winter, that proved his last, was extraordinary. In addition to his cautious parleying with France, which grew more and more definite, he busied himself with plans for converting the Rhenish bishops into Protestant leaders. He was convinced that they were on the eve of the desired transformation, and were quite ready to enter into matrimony and to turn the bishoprics into perpetual holdings. "He converted the Bishop of Spires," says his devoted La Huguerye, "who had his wife already found. They have good hopes of the incumbent of Mayence, while counting little on him of Trèves." The Count's most strenuous endeavours were exerted in regard to the chief prelates at Cologne and Liège.[1] To the latter he suggested one Charlotte of Bourbon as a wife.[2] He might then restore the castle of Bouillon to her kinsman, who would, as a recognition for obtaining his own

[1] *Mémoires*, i., p. 202.
[2] Daughter of the Duke of Montpensier, whose story comes later.

rights, surely dower the Bishop's wife. Louis did not, indeed, find these princes of the Church wholly amenable to his advice, though the negotiations with Cologne certainly went far and permitted his hopes to rise high.

This person [the archbishop] cares nothing at all for the pope, for his council, for absolution, for prohibition of matrimony [writes the Chancellor Ehem to William of Hesse] nor for the execution of the edicts of the Council of Trent. . . . He is anti-Spanish and hates priests, especially the Jesuits. He is ambitious and avaricious on account of poverty and means shortly to take a wife. He poses as having a German heart and as being a warrior by nature, as your Grace can see from his extraordinary statements, which I could hardly listen to without laughing.

After diagnosing the case, remedies must be applied suitable to win over his electoral Grace, etc., etc.[1]

The idea of an alliance with this man was looked on somewhat askance by the canny Landgrave, who had a touch of his father's shrewdness and vigour of utterance. "I doubt the man. That one who was of contrary mind should suddenly turn around without any such miracle as converted Paul does not seem very plausible to me." And in the end the Landgrave proved right, although the Archbishop so far aided the rebels as to permit Cologne to be used as a base of supplies.

[1] Groen, iv., p. 337.

In February, 1574, John, Louis, and Henry of Nassau, accompanied by Duke Christopher, son of Frederick, Elector Palatine, set out for the Netherlands at the head of a small army. By the end of the month they reached the Meuse and camped on the German side of the river near Maestricht, which the Prince had suggested their taking *en route*.

Requesens had prepared to confront them with fresh mercenaries, levied in Germany, added to the Spanish collected from the garrisons of all the towns where he dared weaken the defence. The immediate command was entrusted to Sancho d'Avila, whose efforts were centred on preventing a junction between the Prince and his brothers.

The catastrophe that followed all these preparations was overwhelming for the Nassaus. Everything went wrong. More than a thousand men deserted from the invading army before they reached the frontier. The ice was too broken to allow crossing and too thick for the passage of boats. An unexpected descent upon d'Avila's camp might have given the invaders a chance of success, but their delay enabled Mendoza to march his troops up and to cross the Meuse, where he was joined by d'Avila, Mondragon, and others. On April 13th, Louis reached the little village of Mook, near the borders of Cleves. After d'Avila's crossing, the Count found his men inconveniently hemmed in in a narrow space between the Meuse and the Waal, with no defence but a trench hastily dug before Mook and with no space in which to use his cavalry, his best strength.

In the Spanish council of war there was a lively discussion as to whether it would be politic to force an immediate engagement. Extra reinforcements were at hand, and it was urged that at Heiligerlee, Aremberg had shown error of judgment in opening hostilities prematurely when he might have had greater strength, later on. At the same time, it was recognised that they had to do with a commander remarkably fertile in resources. If the Spaniards held off, Louis might manage to slip by them in the night, and if he effected the desired junction with the Prince, affairs would speedily take on a different aspect. The skirmishes over the trench grew fiercer. Louis made a desperate charge upon the Spanish horse under which they gave way. Those who ran away as far as Grave spread reports of a victory won by the patriots. Unfortunately for the Prince, it was a baseless report. The repulse was insignificant, and fresh Spanish lancers and German troopers were close at hand to fill the space. A short sanguinary engagement ensued. Louis, Henry of Nassau, and Duke Christopher rallied a few men about them after the first rout of their forces and led on a charge. It was their last. None knew what became of any one of the three.

When the three hundredth anniversaries of Heiligerlee and Mook Heath came around, the celebrations were made the occasion for violent criticism of Louis of Nassau and of his efforts to further the Netherland cause. Many contumelious epithets were heaped upon his memory—that of an irresponsible adventurer being the most plausible, inasmuch as he was a foreigner engaged in a struggle that was not his. But was there ever a war when some such adventurous spirits were not attracted to its field? And in such cases the most laudable motives cannot be completely cleared from a certain percentage of the spirit of adventure, pure and simple. Sharing certain traits with all young men who wander afield in search of a wider career than they could find at home, Louis of Nassau was also animated by fraternal affection, attested in every line of the voluminous family correspondence. This affection, as well as the opportunities for more life, drew the younger brother naturally into the concerns of the elder, and the former eagerly identified himself with the latter's interests as they branched out from those of Philip.

Louis of Nassau was in his thirty-sixth year when he met his death. In spite of his rather roving experience of life a nimbus of youthfulness hangs about him and his every word to the last. Perhaps that is the natural result of his continual association with two elder brothers, for it is not unnatural that fraternal relations should preserve the hierarchy of childhood. Enterprising as he was, his projects do not invariably show good

COUNT LOUIS OF NASSAU.
(From an old print.)

judgment, even as he advanced to the age of maturity. His scheme of capturing Requesens in 1573 showed that he had not changed essentially since he pasted incendiary papers on the walls at Antwerp in 1565, or feigned illness at La Rochelle in the hope of obtaining a private visit from the Queen. His ruses seem boyish rather than hypocritical.[1]

His early education was at Dillenburg, with a group of contemporaries under the supervision of his mother. It chances that there is very little extant touching on his training, and Arnoldi's statement that he studied at the universities of Strasburg and Geneva, instead of at the Lutheran Wittenberg, where John and Adolph went, seems open to doubt. Count William the Elder was certainly Lutheran in sympathy and the choice of a Calvinistic environment for his third son would have been peculiar. Louis's student career was, however, short wherever passed, for by his eighteenth year he was at Brussels, a regularly appointed official of Philip's government, in spite of his declared Protestantism. He says himself that Philip sent de Bergues and Horne to him for the express purpose of urging him to adopt the ancient Catholic religion because the King feared his pernicious influence upon the nobles with whom he associated. His answer to the King's

[1] See Blok, *Lodewijk van Nassau. Correspondence de Lodewijk van Nassau. Apologie.* MS. in Nassau family archives, The Hague.

emissaries was that he could not desert the tenets in which he had been educated by his parents, his preceptors, and by theologians; but that he certainly did not possess sufficient skill or learning to convert his friends and in their sports and amusements their talk naturally fell on other topics. This statement occurs in his *Apology* written in 1568, after Louis was formally cited to appear at Brussels to answer the charges against him. The document was never completed nor disseminated abroad as were the Prince's *Justification* and *Apology*. Possibly the preparations for his expedition into Friesland caused Louis to lay it aside for the time, and he never found leisure to prepare it for publication. Perhaps, too, after the execution of Egmont and Horne he would have desired to change his tone somewhat. At the time of writing, they were in custody and Louis would, naturally, have been very careful to avoid incriminating them.

The first part of the document touching on events prior to the presentation of the petition cannot be considered as very candid, in the light of Louis's other correspondence. It was natural, however, that in response to a citation which implied his being at the root of the Netherland troubles, accused him of meddling in affairs that did not concern him, as a foreigner, he should answer hotly and attempt to give the best colour to his motives. As a literary piece of work the document is open to criticism, being ill put together and verbose, but certain impetuous individual expressions, however, give the imperfect draft a distinct character, though naturally less vivid than the personality that pervades the Count's correspondence, private and semi-official alike.

Even in his formal and respectful letters to Orange, boyish phrases often creep in, while few communications to his intimates are without jokes and light-heartedness in the midst of weighty subjects. In 1571, when in France, Louis writes to Dr. Schwarz that he believes the latter wants to prove himself worthy of his name, "gruff Westerwalder," because he is so remiss in his epistolary duty, "or perhaps," he adds, "you think I have forgotten my German in the society of French ladies." Then he asks news of his "zoological garden," by which term he means to designate his friends.[1]

I wish you knew the man [wrote Walsingham to Leicester, Aug. 12, 1571[2]]. They talk of him as the arm and the head, as if he were a second Coligny. He is eloquent and mellow in his words but the chief point is that as regards religion he is as honest in his morals as he is frank and of good faith in negotiation.

It does not appear just when Louis passed over from the Lutheranism of his father to the theologi-

[1] *Cor. de Lodewijk van Nassau*, p. 86.
[2] A letter to Burghley on the same date describing an interview with Louis of Nassau is the corroborating evidence that this refers to Count Louis.

cal creed of his French allies. In 1565 he seems
to have been antagonistic to the Calvinists and
especially to their sermons, unlicensed and unregulated as these were. His final identification with
the doctrines of Geneva was due, undoubtedly,
to political convenience of the theories and still
more to the fact that the Huguenots, who proved
to be the most durable allies, were of that faith.

Ardent as the young Count's Protestantism
was, it never prevented his enjoying madcap
freaks proposed by Brederode or any other comrade. Many of his impulsive acts menaced the
success of important plans. Undoubtedly in the
early days, the prudent Prince preferred not to
know what the younger brother had afoot, while
willing, probably, to reap advantage from actions
if they proved successful, even if the deeds were
not wholly to his taste. Not of a temperament to
see both sides of a question, Louis cannot be
accused of hypocrisy, as Orange frequently is.
In his attitude towards religion he was always
direct, and always put Protestantism first. When
he was governor of the principality of Orange, in
behalf of his brother, he reorganised the university upon a Protestant basis.

After failing in his suit for the Rytberg heiress
Louis does not seem to have been very anxious for
matrimony. Possibly Charlotte de Bourbon was
thought of but there seems no positive evidence
in that regard. Rumour did not leave his character quite unsullied. In his *Apology*, Orange

says: "As to their slurs on my brother Louis, they would do better to leave so good a chevalier in peace. They cannot compare to him and he was a better Christian."

Certainly there can be no doubt of his personal popularity among those who did like him. The French Huguenots were anxious to adopt him as their own leader; the Hollanders longed for him as for the "Angel Gabriel"; and he was called the German Bayard. His loss was irreparable to the Prince.

Henry, who perished at the same time, had been at his brother's side during the French campaigns, but there is little record of his career of twenty-four years except the references to his education and the anxiety that his young life should not be wasted, expressed by his mother and brothers.

The Prince waited on the Isle of Bommel for tidings, tidings curiously slow in coming. On April 15th, the day after the battle, he moved to Gorcum to be nearer the place where he expected his brothers to cross the Meuse. Thence he wrote to Louis, still in ignorance of the calamity:

Monsieur my brother: Returning to-day from Delft, I received in Dort, yours of the 12th, and learn where you are. I am sorry to have received your last too late to collect soldiers to send for your escort. However, I hope by to-morrow we shall have thirty-five or six companies and a fair number of vessels. And to arrange better, I came to-day to this city.

Let me know when you plan to cross the river, so that I can meet you.

Written at Gorcum, April 15, 1574.[1]

As to your crossing, I do not know a better place than the environs of Tiel, at Wammel ford, Wamel, or Varick, or near there. It is narrow, however, for the cavalry, but you must make a virtue of necessity.[1]

Two days later he wrote from Bommel[2]:

My brothers: Since my last, I have heard that your foot and some horse have deserted and are already across the Rhine. If this be true, it is to be feared that the rest will soon follow, and that if you temporise a little, you will find yourself alone. My advice, subject to your correction, would be, if it be true that many of your people have abandoned you, *and that I can find no means of coming to you*, your best expedient would be to pick out 3000 or 4000 foot and 1000 of your best horse, go down to Emden and cross there. Otherwise it is to be feared, that since I have to do with a people who get easily frightened, as easily rejoiced and frightened again, all courage might ooze away at this retreat.

But if I can keep holding out the prospect of your coming, it is to be hoped that the people will continue in the good-will that they have shown up to this moment. In any event, it will be best to put an end to the affair of England, which Dathenus has mentioned to you, having received a letter two days ago to that effect. They are very keen on the league with Germany, offering, if that can be com-

[1] Groen, iv., p. 368   [2] *Ibid.*, 369.

passed, to declare open war on the King of Spain. You might exert a little pressure there, for, in truth, the German delays are slow death to us.

BOMMEL, April 17th.

Messieurs my brothers: You will recall what I wrote you on the 13th of this month, concerning the enemy's overtures to peace. As I am daily expecting news of their intention, I wish you could temporise a little, and delay on the frontiers, pretending always to be coming to join us. You could write to the Estates of Holland and Zealand not to be disheartened, that you do not retreat to abandon them, but only temporarily, during which you wish to fortify yourself, that they may be effectually aided. I beg you let me know who of yours are left on the field [euphemism for dead] or wounded, and whether they are people of rank. Mention, too, the enemy's loss, and say whether you have any distinguished prisoners, as is rumoured. My regards tó the Duke Christopher, my brothers, and others in your company.

April 18th.[1]

My brothers: Being in the greatest trouble in the world at having had no answer from you to the seven letters I have written since the 10th—the last being on the 18th—I have decided to send you this messenger. . . . I do not know whether you have received mine of the 18th. If not, the bearer will tell you the contents. Only let me hear your condition.

April 21st.[2]

[1] Groen, iv., p. 371. [2] *Ibid.*, 373.

Count John's wife sends word to the Landgravine of Hesse on April 21st that both brothers are living but Henry is wounded in the arm, so slow is the final news in reaching Dillenburg, and apparently it is as late as April 22nd before Orange even knows of the engagement and then he writes to Count John, who had luckily gone to Cologne on the 11th, begging for news. The Prince still cherishes hope and makes plans for his brothers, "if they be still in life." It seems impossible for him to accept the fact that the silence is never again to be broken. The persistence with which he continued to arrange details for the dead brothers' advance was evidently a mental protest against acknowledging an unwelcome truth.

The great advantage gained by the Spaniards at Mook Heath was diminished by a mutiny on the day after the battle. Three years' pay was in arrears; and the moment of victory won by the soldiers' exertions was utilised to put in their claims. Requesens finally succeeded in raising a loan of 400,000 florins from the Council of Antwerp by giving a mortgage on the crown domains. After this agreement was effected, the mutineers came to Antwerp and were paid in corn or cloth. Then they proceeded to celebrate in the Place de Meir, arrayed like children in the cloth and velvet given them in lieu of wages, and their revels were at a great height when word came that the Prince's Admiral, Boisot, had seized the opportunity to advance up the Scheldt. The call to arms was obeyed by the crowd, just as they were, arrayed in motley, but they were too late to prevent Boisot from capturing or sinking fourteen Spanish ships and taking one Spanish admiral prisoner. Thus again the rebels found fortune kinder on the sea than on land.

The one slight success was insufficient, however, to restore heart to the Prince. He was terribly cast down. In his lonely despondency, he turned with pathetic persistency to his one surviving brother. "I have sent you ten messengers [he wrote, April 22d] but can obtain no news."[1] Indeed the majority of his despatches never reached their destination. In 1593 an intercepted letter of May 7, 1574, fell into the hands of William Louis of Nassau, one of Count John's sons, who returned it to Count Maurice. It is written after Orange has at last reluctantly accepted the fact of Louis's death and shows his desire to bring John into close touch with him as a substitute for his vanished right hand.

And, Monsieur my brother, that you may have a clear idea of our ordinary expenses simply for soldiery and ships, without including extraordinary things like artillery, ammunition, scouts, fortifications, governors' salaries, messengers, spies, commissioners that have to be sent here and there, expenses of the people in foreign courts, and such like things, I send herewith a summary of the men-at-arms and

[1] Groen, iv., p. 378.

the boats we have. 1st. In South Holland, 71 companies—French, English, Scotch, Walloons, and Flemish. In Zealand, 14 companies. In Waterland, 20 companies. As to boats, we have in Holland, 6 sloops and 20 other ships, both *drommelers* and ships of transport. In Waterland, 8 big ships, 6 galleys, 5 catboats, 10 *boeyers*, and others called water scows *schepen*, which make in all, counting the galleys, 102 bottoms. This is all I can write you at present on the state of our affairs and the necessity we are under of being aided, hoping shortly to send you some one to explain matters more fully.[1]

[1] Hague archives. Groen, iv., 378.

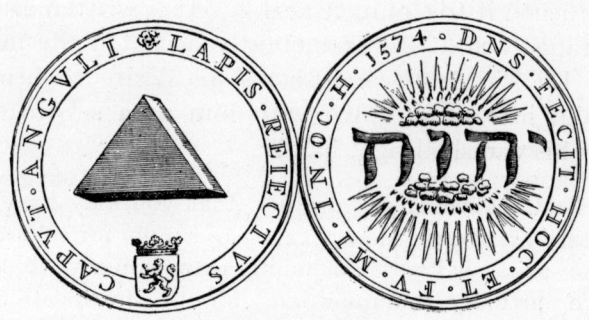

ORANGE MEDAL

CHAPTER XIII

THE SIEGE OF LEIDEN

1574

THE mutiny disposed of, the Spanish leaders resumed the blockade before Leiden, begun in the winter and interrupted by the Nassau invasion. The burghers ought to have profited by the interval to prepare for the contingency of a new attempt, but all precautionary measures had been neglected and Leiden was in no better state to withstand a siege than it had been when Don Frederic first took steps towards possessing himself of the city.

By the end of May, the foe, under De Valdez, had gone so far as to cut off the approaches from south, east, and west.[1] Within the walls, not only was the insufficient provision fraught with danger to the citizens, but also the lack of solid cohesion among themselves. The majority were, indeed, Protestant, but there were many shades in the colour of their zeal for the cause of the rebellion against Philip. Some were devoted heart and soul to the Prince and willing to live or die with him.

[1] Fruin, *Het beleg en ontzet der stad Leiden in 1574*, ii., 381.

Others would have stopped short of dying, finding their own life sweet and disposed to adhere to the rebel leader only if too much were not at stake. Then there was a small minority vigorously and conscientiously opposed to the new order and anxious to see a united land return to passive obedience to King and to Church. These were called "papists," not Catholics,—a name meant to imply fidelity to the Pope rather than to their country. In all these parties, the lowest classes were the most zealous. In the ascending social scale, there was a corresponding increase in indifferentism. Among the well-to-do, many were to be found who were disinclined to sacrifice themselves for either party but were willing to accept any authority under which their property might not only be safe, but where it might possibly increase. Such is the estimate of public opinion as given by a clever contemporary, one Jan van der Does, or Janus Douza, Seignior of Noordwyck, and probably it is a faithful picture. He is especially severe upon the manufacturers and the captains of the gilds who urged accommodation with the foe before it was too late, and also, upon the city officials who at first were as lukewarm in the defensive measures as they had been in their declaration for the Prince in 1572. Luckily for the nationalist cause a new member was added to the town council who finally succeeded in infusing a spirit of tenacious resistance into all the wavering elements of that body. He was one Pieter Adriansz Vermeer, better known as Adrian van der Werff, from the calling of weaver which he had followed before his participation in the protests of 1566 had obliged him to leave Leiden. During the years of exile he had come under the personal influence of the Prince, and had also forged strong links of friendship with other refugees. In 1573 he was one of the burgomasters of Leiden. During the second blockade he was at the head of affairs as presiding burgomaster. His appointment was especially fortunate, as his three colleagues, Cornelius van Zwieten, Cornelius van Noorden, and Jan Halfleiden, were all insignificant, selfish characters. The city secretary, Jan van Hout, was of better stuff and did valiant service. The third staying element among the besieged was embodied in a man not a resident of Leiden and not a local official whose name is closely identified with the events, the above mentioned Jan van der Does. When in the city he enjoyed the privilege of a seat in the assembly of town councillors and notables (*vroedschap*) from his membership in the Estates of Holland, and his unswerving personal devotion to the Prince and to the cause of revolt inspired him to urge cohesion among the divers constituents of the population.

Possibly one reason why there was so much delay and negligence at Leiden in preparation to withstand a siege and why the more timid counsels prevailed, was the strenuous effort to conciliate the citizens made by Requesens. A pardon was offered which the royalists within Leiden were especially anxious should be accepted. Moreover the new governor had abolished the Council of Troubles, remitted the tenth penny, permitted Alva's statue to be destroyed, and showed many more evidences of a desire to inaugurate a new era in the administration of the provinces and to propitiate the people. Many of the anti-war citizens actually ensconced themselves within Spanish lines whence they sent back fervent entreaties to their friends to be wise and accept the King's generous proffers of forgiveness. Probably it was Douza with his literary turn of mind who suggested the trenchant answer to these "Glippers," as they were termed: *Fistula dulce canit volucrem dum decipit anceps*,"—"Sweetly sounds the pipe as the bird catcher snares the bird." [1] A less pedantic but equally definite answer was given to the "Glippers" by the requisition of a new oath of allegiance to the Prince and to the States-General, which many were quite as unwilling to refuse as to accept.

The pardon not proving acceptable, the Spanish lines were drawn close and the memorable siege began. A terrible pest stalked through the ranks of besiegers and garrison alike and made its way unchallenged into the city; the troops mutinied, provisions gave out, the half-hearted swelled the

[1] A favourite phrase of warning at this time. Dr. Wotton uses it in reference to the Peace of Cateau-Cambrésis.

ranks of the seceded Glippers or at least echoed their protests at the useless sacrifice of life. Nevertheless the stout-hearted made the others hold out even though they felt that the efforts of their friends without the walls were criminally slow.

These latter were not idle indeed, but the plan of rescue finally adopted was on so large a scale that it was dependent on divers elements and some could not be hastened. For it was resolved to pierce the dikes, overflow the land, and sail a relief fleet up toward the city so that the Spanish camp could be assailed from the west! It was on July 30th, after the siege had lasted two months, that the States-General passed the formal resolutions providing "that Rynland, Delftland, Schieland, and adjacent districts should be flooded . . . in order to dislodge the foe . . . and to relieve Leiden by ships. . . ."

Difficulties of engineering, of finance, of private ownership, were all set aside. We know some of the objections urged and the answers given: "Leiden was higher than the meadows." "Then a greater volume of water must be obtained." "Crops would be destroyed." "Better a drowned land than a lost land." "There was no money." "Holland had already paid for defence ten times the sums refused in taxes to Philip II. and funds would be forthcoming to make that sacrificed already, valid, etc." A placard of August 1st enjoined the inhabitants of the doomed region to place their cattle and families in safety under penalty of confiscation of their property. There were some natural delays and then the dike was formally pierced in the Prince's presence at Capelle, a few miles east of Rotterdam. Louis de Boisot was called from Zealand to take command of the novel expedition and a large fleet of flatboats with light draft was brought together. The measures adopted were all sound and eminently practical,—only terribly slow to the hungry, waiting Leideners.

Then a great misfortune happened which almost blocked the whole project. The Prince of Orange fell ill and his condition became so serious that his recovery was despaired of. The illness to which he succumbed was an acute culmination of recurrent accesses of intermittent fever from which he had suffered during the winter of 1573-'74. In a low state of health as he was, his condition was aggravated by the protracted anxiety about his brothers, and by the final sorrow at their fate. Thus miasmas that might have lurked along the dikes found a fertile soil for their poison. The fever remained doubly intermittent rather than continuous, but one access followed very quickly on the other. Dr. Pieter van Foreest was the doctor invited to consult with the Prince's regular medical attendant, when the latter failed to inspire confidence as the situation became grave.

When I was called to the Prince your father [writes

van Foreest in a dedication of his *Observations* to Count Maurice[1]] his recovery was despaired of by others. In the first instance, I told his Excellency the nature and cause of his malady and stated the treatment I intended to pursue. He then remarked to his friends: "This doctor understands my constitution, condition, and the nature of my malady. Next to God, my hope is fixed on him. I give myself entirely into his hands." And his confidence was not misplaced. With the help of God, to whom I am willing to accord the honour of the recovery, I restored to the fatherland the most excellent Prince, to you the beloved father. . . .

It is not surprising that the doctor is a trifle vainglorious in recounting his achievement. There was grave reason for the despair of the others.

Every conceivable treatment had been employed,— cupping, aloe, pills. These remedies applied to a body exhausted by previous fevers, by anxiety, and by overwork, only served to increase the bilious symptoms, instead of relieving them, and to cause diminution of strength under the steadily rising temperature. When I was called in, on the advice of John Philip van der Aa, I found the patient very low and noticed, in addition to the persistent fever, other disturbing symptoms, to wit, a bilious discharge that drained his strength, high temperature, and inextinguishable thirst, allied with such exhaustion that the patient could not sit up to have his bed made without becoming faint. Once his secre-

---

[1] Fruin, *Over eenige ziekten van Prinz Willen*, *Verspreide geschriften*, iii., p. 40.

taries made use of an occasion when he was sitting up to obtain his signature to various documents that had long been waiting and he fainted away so completely that the nobles attending him thought he was dead, but luckily he came to when I had him rubbed and sprinkled his face with water. After he was assisted back to bed, he drew breath again.

As soon as I saw the patient's regimen, I considered it inevitable that he should have grown worse. He was taking warm food and heating drinks, as for example, red wine. . . . After I had made my diagnosis, I had the diet changed and especially forbade French wine. His Exc. heard my orders and asked, "But what shall I drink while I am so consumed by thirst?" and I answered modestly, "Your Excellency is suffering from a violent fever of a serious nature, not yet dangerous, but possible to become so if it be fed by wine." I advised barley water or cinnamon water, if he preferred it, as he did. The change of treatment had not been followed more than a week before certain alarming symptoms disappeared and the accesses of fever abated, although the temperature still continued high. . . . Every time the patient took nourishment, even a sirup or julep, the fever increased instantly, sometimes with a chill and sometimes with the fingers growing cold, just as in hectic fever, a feature of the case that alarmed me greatly, considering the invalid's constitution and the manner in which it had been undermined. The diet was kept very low for some time,—an egg, a little blanc-mange, and some confitures,—just enough to keep the spirit in the body, but insufficient to increase vitality.

In order further to make sure that he was doing the best for his illustrious patient, van Foreest held a consultation together with Hadrian Junius, a learned physician, and the Prince's house-doctor in ordinary. They all three agreed that a plaster on the stomach might be beneficial at that crisis. Unfortunately Junius caught the fever at the consultation and carried it back to Middelburg with him, and was himself too ill to be summoned, while the house-doctor lost all hope and all initiative; thus in spite of the consultation, the final responsibility rested on van Foreest, who showed great ingenuity and readiness not only in altering his prescriptions with every minute change of condition but in alleviating discomfort.

For instance, the weather turned hot and the shooting gallery in which the invalid lay opened upon a garden exposed to the sun on all sides. Moreover it was on the first story, floored with wood, and very hot on that account. There was no other convenient room at hand and the patient was too weak to be carried far. "We had to cool the room as best we could, with sprinkling water and strewing green boughs and leaves.. . ."

On September 2d, Brunynck writes to Count John:

Until yesterday the malady increased steadily, but since then, thanks to God, his Excellency has begun to feel some relief. Yesterday there was no access of fever. His Excellency rested well all last night and consequently we have hopes that his Excellency is now out of danger.

The improvement continued steadily, the most alarming symptoms slowly yielding to gentle remedies such as confiture of roses, lemon and quince sirups. Thirst was assuaged with cherry or currant juice, sleep was lured by barley drink. When the fever slackened and was followed by a wholesome perspiration, we stopped the cinnamon water and gave instead thin beer mixed with wine and vinegar to support strength. This was to his taste. Little by little more solid food was administered in order to build up the depleted system as rapidly as possible. This was prepared with the juice of unripe grapes, lemons, bouillon of capucines, and confitures of pistachio nuts. The result of the care was that his Excellency recovered completely, contrary to universal expectation and to the disappointment of his foes, who had reported that he had succumbed to the pest. The death of the Prince's body physician followed shortly on this illness, and henceforth, whenever he was ill in Holland, the Prince invariably asked my advice [adds the doctor].[1]

By September 7th, Orange was able to write to his brother, giving little space to his illness, from which he still feels very weak, and much to the cares that oppress him.[2] He never had head-

---

[1] Groen, v., p. 50. It is worthy of notice that van Foreest's statements tally with the letters written from the Prince's household.

[2] Groen, v., p. 52.

ache in the fever attacks[1] so that his brain was fairly clear to think during the illness. Acute mental depression was the natural result of this feverish contemplation of difficulties. A tendency to worry pervades the whole letter. The convalescent has by no means recovered his normal tone. He worries about expenses. He is afraid of German aid. Agreeable as it would be to have the company of several nobles with whom John is negotiating, especially Count Albert of Hohenlohe, the Prince does not see any possible way of maintaining them. "I assure you no matter how closely I calculate, still we come out short every month in what we need and at the same time we do not cease doing our best to keep hold of every one now in office by promises for the future." The reports of large treasure taken at Middelburg are false. "There was barely enough to satisfy the soldiers and sailors, etc."

As soon as his strength permitted, the Prince wrote to Leiden, begging the people to persist in their resistance. The tiny letter, tied around a pigeon's neck,[2] reached its destination and aided van der Werff and van der Does to keep the counsel of the weak-hearted from prevailing. It was three weeks later before Orange was allowed to be rowed out to the fleet and consult with Boisot and his officers as to their plans.

The difficulties of bringing relief to Leiden had

[1] Maurice inherited the characteristic of fever without headache, rare among the Netherlanders.

[2] It is still preserved.

by no means been solved by the piercing of the dikes, and calling in the friendly sea as an ally. The twenty-mile cruise across the meadows did not prove easy sailing. The wind was counted as an important factor in causing the water to rise to the depth required even for the meagre draught of the flat-bottomed craft and that proved a fickle friend. It was a north-west wind that was needed to force the water inland. The prevailing wind in that region is westerly, as is testified by the long rows of trees bending as in homage towards the rising sun, but in those September days of 1574 a land breeze blew persistently and the water refused to rise in the teeth of the east wind. It was on September 11th that the fleet, sixteen galleys with a number of transports, started in at Nootdorp. They succeeded in crossing the *Landscheiding* at the place proposed, but were stopped at another dike on the 17th, retraced the course, made a circuit around the village of Segwaert, held by the Spaniards, and pushed slowly on. There was some fighting from time to time and the noise of the firing was always most encouraging to the besieged, to whom the delays seemed interminable.

In the city the food supplies dwindled and the pest increased, and the despairing Leideners had no idea that the foe were in a state of terror and trepidation quite equal to theirs within the walls. Valdez sent despatches to his chief with piteous accounts of the rising water, especially

after the 18th, when the wind was north-west.
This intruding flood, creeping noiselessly up to
their tents, was infinitely more disquieting to the
Spanish than it would have been to Hollanders
with their hereditary familiarity with the sea
and its invasions. For them the flood was unconscionably slow. When the Prince visited the
fleet, on the 28th, it had lain a whole week at
Noord Aa, helpless. On the 29th, the east wind
had repelled the water until it was only nine
inches high on the flooded land and at least
eighteen inches were necessary for movement.
On the 29th the fine weather which had permitted
the Prince to make the expedition from Delft
changed, the sky darkened, the water rose and
carried the Netherlanders on their cruise over
the slime up to the foe. Then ensued the first
naval engagement fought on land. This was
between the first and second of October and was
so far to the advantage of the Netherlanders that
dawn found the whole fleet advanced beyond
Zoeterwoude with the wide waterway called the
Vliet conveniently at hand to bear the rescuers
henceforth with less difficulty towards Leiden.
Poles had been more efficient than sails and oars
in bringing the boats over the slimy ground
upon which they actually rested in most cases.
Then the water again began to rise and rose
steadily, to the infinite discomfort of the foe, who
were more unnerved by the silent, cold invader
than by any cannonading. Zoeterwoude was

abandoned, the garrison wading away knee-deep in water. This left the second line of the blockade broken.

The strong Spanish fort of Lammen still barred the invaders from their goal and its capture was necessary before Boisot felt that his advance was secure. How easy the way was to be made for him he could not know. At Zoeterwoude Valdez had seen for himself the strength of a union of Beggars and water, and his own course of action was promptly decided. The commander at Lammen was ordered to withdraw to Leiderdorp without waiting for any attack and from Leiderdorp the whole Spanish force quietly slipped off *en masse* to The Hague. Valdez took care to leave a note on his table in his deserted quarters to excuse his retreat: "Farewell city, farewell little forts, abandoned on account of the water, not because of the force of the enemy," [1] an explanation that must have been highly satisfactory to all concerned.

The plans Boisot spent the night in making proved quite unnecessary. Within Leiden there was fresh anxiety. They anxiously listened to hear the sound of the attack of whose imminence a pigeon had brought them tidings. The silence was hard to bear. But it was not long before the first boats of the fleet, looming out of the October mist, proved conclusively that the strange

[1] "*Vale civitas, valete castelli parvi, qui relicti estis propter aquam et non per vim inimicorum.*"

hush in the air was friendly, not inimical to them.
At nine o'clock on the morning of October 3d,
the first relief party sprang ashore on the Vliet-
bridge and the siege of Leiden was at an end with
triumph for the burghers. Pitiable however was
their condition and Boisot found the task on his
hands of restoring the city to itself as hard as
that of reaching its gates.

October the third was a Sunday and the Prince
was sitting quietly in the great church at Delft,
when a letter was delivered to him describing
the above events. Possibly his thoughts were
already more occupied with Leiden than with
the discourse that was in progress. As soon as
that sermon came to an end, Orange sent the
despatch to the preacher to be read from the
pulpit and the concluding prayer was a glad
thanksgiving for the victory.

On the following day Orange hastened to Leiden
in the face of protests that there was especial
danger for a convalescent in the poisoned air.
Before leaving Delft he began a letter to Count
John which he finished the same day at Leiden.[1]
"I cannot tell you how great joy there is among
the citizens at the relief. We hope that henceforth there will be more prudence and that this
God-given victory will bear fresh fruit."

For ten days Orange stayed in the wounded
city, using as his headquarters the house of Dirk
Jacobusz. van Montfort, a citizen of standing,

[1] Groen, v., p. 66.

not in the government. He at once proceeded to install an efficient garrison and to see that Leiden was adequately provisioned for two years; and then he assumed the charge of reorganising the government, an action that must be regarded as a war measure, for he certainly set aside privileges cherished by Leiden as by all these petty city-states.

Two gifts were bestowed on the city by the States-General and the Prince,—permission to hold an annual fair, scot-free, and the erection of the university,—the first Protestant school on Netherland soil. In this last there was wonderful expedition. On February 5, 1575, only four months and two days after the raising of the siege, a corps of professors were established in a vacated convent, and the new seat of learning was opened with the elaborate ceremonies and allegorical representations so dear to the hearts of the Netherlanders.

The preamble to the university charter is noteworthy, inasmuch as the fiction of Philip's sovereignty is steadfastly maintained, and the most Catholic monarch is represented as erecting the Protestant academy as a signal reward to Leiden for her persistency in keeping his faithful general out of her gates.

Considering [so runs the preamble of the charter] that during these present wearisome wars within our provinces of Holland and Zealand, all good instruction of youth in the sciences and liberal arts seems threatened with oblivion . . . considering the differences of religion; considering that we are inclined to gratify our city of Leiden . . . on account of the heavy burdens sustained by her citizens with such faithfulness during the war, we have resolved after ripely deliberating with *our dear cousin*, William, Prince of Orange, Stadtholder, etc., to erect a free academy and university, etc.[1]

Then this royal benefactor is made, by the articles of this grant, to entrust "his dear cousin" of Orange with all power needful to regulate the details and policy of the infant institution.

[1] Bor, vii., p. 593.

RELIEF OF LEIDEN

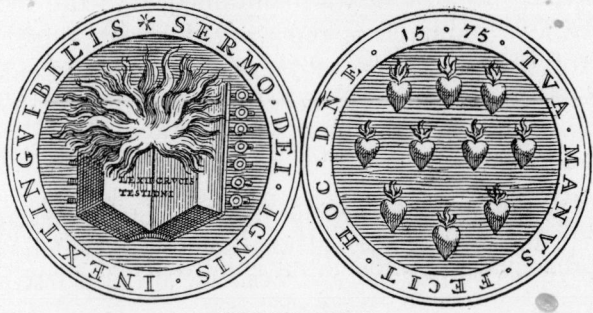

HOLLAND MEDAL

CHAPTER XIV

NEW ALLIANCES

1574–1575

WHEN the strain of the siege of Leiden was relieved the Prince took certain measures to define his own status both in public and private affairs. It was as though his convalescence were a new birth and fresh equipment became necessary for his revived energies.

The form of administration for the transaction of official business without the countenance of the hereditary sovereign, as adopted by the Estates of Holland in 1572, had furnished, to be sure, a working basis for the time being, but, naturally from its provisional origin, when the outcome of the revolt of the group of cities was totally uncertain, this basis proved a defective platform for a long period, when the conduct of a war was at stake. Orange had refrained from accepting the degree of supremacy the "Estates" had been inclined to intrust him with, not because that body was anomalous, as it was, but because his political creed taught that more vital and widespread participation in national defence would be best secured if a sense of common responsibility were felt. It was at his instance that the executive control was lodged, nominally at least, in the Estates, while he kept himself somewhat in the background, playing the rôle of moderator between the various selfish interests present in that assembly of deputies. He was determined to enlist the sympathies of every class of Hollanders in the cause that had to be common property if success were to be won. Orange wanted to see attained for the chaotic government the greatest measure of militant power mathematically possible as the sum resultant from the meeting of cross currents and he neglected nothing that might contribute to that end.

Two years of trial proved the inherent weakness of the system. The burden of endeavouring to steer with the clumsy barnacle-covered rudder grew intolerable and Orange determined to demand reorganisation. On October 20, 1574, he appeared in person before the Estates of Holland and presented a plain statement of the difficulties that were clogging their course. One of his personal grievances was the popular conception of his own relation to public concerns. People seemed to think that he was battling for his private interests, and, further, they were criticising him for failures while he was left without adequate resources to avert a repetition of similar calamities. Therefore he proposed that the Estates should assume the entire administration, civil and military alike, and let him withdraw from the scene of action, or that they should now strengthen his hands so that he could wield the helm effectively in their behalf and at their behest.

This address was considered until November 19th and the reply to it was definite, consisting of an official request that "his Excellency should assume, under the title of governor or regent, the superintendence, supremacy, and rule of Holland with the co-operation of the Estates, vassals, inhabitants, etc., to this end there being conferred upon his Excellency absolute power, authority, and sovereign control in the conduct of the common affairs of the land without exception."

Before accepting this apparently liberal proposition the Prince further stipulated that a monthly allowance of 45,000 florins must accompany the delegated authority. He absolutely refused the compromise of 30,000 florins proposed on November 25th, declaring that rather than attempt the impossible, he would leave the country and let who would follow him. Then affairs could be managed as cheaply as the burghers desired. The deputies took alarm at his displeasure and voted the 45,000 florins that very day without further bickering.[1]

It chances that there is a sketch of the Prince's methods of handling public business while the

[1] Muller, *De Staat der vereenigde Nederlanden*, p. 122, etc.; Groen, v., p. 90, etc.; Blok, iii., p. 151; Kluit i., p. 95.

1. ~~Jexaminerad~~ tous mes actions j~~e~~
   ~~Je vous asseure~~
   qu'n j'ay tousjours porté au bien
   ~~que L'executtions~~ Je ~~vous~~
   l'eur auoir esté importun pour
   a mon particulier que
   estez llmié es charges jen ay
   ~~esté by patrie et la gin~~
   ne le désir ancores
   ~~et commande~~

2. Tres humble et tres obeis-
   sant filz
   P. Guillaume de Nassau

6. Matthias

4. L. L. ...

   Yhilips ...

m̃ en et finire
eux heureurent sont envir affection
 sest saint
 de nr̃e patrie sans
 que en regard
affaires particuliers ny pretendre

 comme dieu le scait que ie
plus a ceur et peur

reshumble et obeissante sœur et
 a Jamais vous complaire

Juliana de Nassau

re bien affectione cousin

Françoys

division of authority between him and the Estates was vague and ill-defined. It occurs incidentally in the *Mémoires* of Count Louis's former secretary, who had passed over to the service of the young Duke of Condé after the disaster of Mook Heath. The leadership of the French Protestants was divided at this time between Henry of Navarre and Condé, and it was the latter who was anxious that a fresh alliance, offensive and defensive, should be struck between the Huguenots and the Beggars. In the autumn of 1574 Michel de la Huguerye was despatched with letters from his master to Orange urging a union of interests, and on November 29th arrived at Dordrecht, the Prince's headquarters for the moment, and was admitted to a private interview.[1] Orange is very friendly in giving ear to all that the confidential messenger can tell him over and above the contents of the letters. In order to avoid interruption by going to supper the Prince even orders a tray of refreshments brought into his cabinet and the tête-à-tête conversation is continued over the evening meal and far into the night, to the infinite satisfaction of the envoy, highly encouraged by the intimate character of his reception by the great man. At a late hour La Huguerye sought his lodgings confident that he had convinced the Prince of the futility of expecting any assistance from France

[1] La Huguerye, *Mémoires*, i., p. 276; see also Blok, *Lodewijk van Nassau*, p. 3.

except at the hands of the French Protestants, the
natural allies of the *Gueux*. He was over-san-
guine. Before he was accorded a second interview with Orange, another French messenger rode
into Dordrecht, this time from the Catholic court,
and the fresh batch of letters brought by him to
the Prince contained more or less definite offers
of pecuniary aid against Spain. The Valois who
thus took the initiative had the revenues of the
realm at their disposal. To be sure La Huguerye
was not alone in his conviction of the folly of
taking any such offers seriously when it was but
two years since Catherine de' Medici and her son
had proven their capacity for treachery by the
Massacre of St. Bartholomew. This was the
argument he had reiterated in his talk with Orange.
The Prince's reasoning was, however, that, though
anti-Protestant, the French King had ample
grounds to be anti-Spanish. Further, Henry III.
might find it politic to whiten the reputation of
the French court; and finally if he were disposed
to furnish money to a cause, he was in a position
to open his purse-strings, while young Condé
and Henry of Navarre, with all their good will,
were pitifully poor and their followers were no
richer than their brothers in the Faith across
the border. So the mere suggestion of an alliance with the court party, whatever might be the
Valois reasons for their conciliatory step, made
Orange very unwilling to jeopardise the chance
of cementing the pact by involving himself with

the Huguenots. When La Huguerye was again summoned to the Prince's presence he found the atmosphere changed. Orange told him that he himself was not competent to give any answer to Condé's propositions. All that was in his power was to lay the matter before the Estates, which he pledged himself to do.

This shattered my hopes [continues the writer] for I knew by experience that when he [the Prince] was favourable to a measure he adopted it readily on his own initiative in order to have all the credit for its success, but if he were opposed to a proposition he referred it to the Estates and threw on them the odium of the refusal so as to avoid incurring unfriendly criticism for himself.

If Orange did, indeed, conceive the expedient of letting a numerous body bear the onus of the blame for an unpopular decision, he simply relieved his own shoulders as many an administrator has done since. It must be remembered, however, that La Huguerye is not an accurate reporter nor was he among the Prince's ardent admirers. He is often inclined to give an unfavourable colour to the leader's action.

In the winter months of 1574-5, overtures were made towards an accommodation between the insurgents and their sovereign in which a recognition of the Prince's more assured position was implied if not acknowledged. Philip was urged to make peace by the Emperor and it was through the mediation of the latter that a formal conference was arranged at Breda. The discussions lasted for three months although the outcome was a foregone conclusion from the opening day, March 6th. The Spanish deputies were able men and the hostages were of as high rank as Julian Romero, so that the safety of the rebels' deputies entrusting themselves within Spanish lines was amply secured by the presence of the royalist guarantees sojourning at Delft. Breda, the Prince's own town, was in Brabant and still held as a Spanish garrison.

Undoubtedly Philip felt that he was making wonderful concessions in his appointments and in the liberal conditions proposed to induce the insurgents to lay down their arms. Long periods were offered to the Protestants to gather up their goods and to leave the Netherlands if they would not return to the Church. They were to be free to appoint trustees among their Catholic friends to care for their estates until sold. Confiscation and persecution were thus to be abandoned for pacific methods of separating the sheep from the goats, but the two were not to be allowed within one fold. Philip could not stretch his conscience to countenancing heresy under his jurisdiction. He had changed somewhat from his tone of 1566, but he still refused to recognise the impossibility of extirpating the creeds that had sunk tenacious roots into the soil. Hence accommodation was utterly impossible even had there been no fear of "Spanish honey" and if the negotiations could have been taken in good faith to the extent of the inadequate provisions offered. And grave doubt was felt in that regard.

On July 13, 1575, the Breda conferences were concluded and the truce called into being to permit them, expired. Yet the event left permanent results.

It was during the negotiations and after their speedy collapse was evident to all, that a closer union between Holland and Zealand, with the Prince as joint ruler, was resolved upon.[1] Before setting his own seal to the contract Orange insisted on an important change in the draft. In so doing he was perfectly consistent with his uniform policy in relation to the burning questions of religious freedom. One article provided that Orange, as chief executive, was to protect the exercise of the reformed and suppress the exercise of the *Roman religion*. The words here italicised were changed at his instance to *religion at variance with the gospel*. Such was the limited degree of toleration which the sectaries suffered him to phrase ambiguously.

[1] In the discussions as to the more formal installation of Orange into the duties of his sometime stadtholdership, there were many opinions embodying various shades of confidence in and dependence upon him. One proposition emanating from the Zealand contingent distinctly forshadowed the hereditary status later enjoyed by the Nassaus. It was suggested that the six-year-old Maurice should be brought from Dillenburg to Holland and recognised as successor, under guardianship, to his father in case of the latter's sudden death. Orange rejected the proposal unhesitatingly.

Thus at the beginning of the summer of 1575 the Prince was sheltered by a cloak of authority conferred upon him by an assembly, partly constituent, into which he had himself infused a prerogative,—authority that he could, *de facto*, have assumed two years previously. His headship in the one province of Holland had been first established and defined. Then a "generality" was obtained by the union and the Breda conferences lent a dignity to the party of revolt. Orange was placed in a quasi-legal position, as a revolutionary leader forced into an assumption of executive power by the popular needs of the hour. In all the methods employed there was no anarchy. Laws and ancient usage were simply bent to fit new contingencies.

The next steps taken by the Prince were towards the reconstruction of a new household for himself. The last vestiges of the Saxon marriage were to be wiped away as completely as the links between provinces and sovereign were to be severed. His sometime wife had passed entirely out of her husband's life. He considered himself a widower *de facto*, perfectly free to marry again. The unfortunate Anne of Saxony, steeped in the misery she had brought upon herself, remained under the protection of the Nassaus until 1575, when Orange insisted that her own relatives should resume her charge. He shows no remnants of affection for the mother of Anne,

Maurice, and Emilie and says very plainly in his
letters to Count John that he does not object
to the Elector's plan of incarcerating his niece[1]
and letting a report of her death go abroad, only
he stipulates that the Saxon family must bear
the full onus for such procedure. There is not
the slightest hesitancy or double dealing on the
Prince's part now. His methods are different
from those he used in 1560 to reconcile his divers
critics. Again there are opposing forces among
those concerned in the suit that preceded his
proposed marriage but the suitor does not try to
appease them. He declares that he alone is the
judge of his actions and ignores all dissuading
voices. The story of the woman whom he selected
to be his wife is a curious one and typical of the
changing order in France.

Charlotte de Bourbon was the fourth of five
daughters born to Louis de Bourbon, Duke of
Montpensier, and his wife Jacqueline de Long-vic.
François, known as the prince dauphin, was the
only son. The eldest daughter, Françoise, married Henry Robert de la Marck, Duke of Bouillon,[2]
two others made less notable but honourable
alliances; while the remaining two were provided
for in religious foundations. Charlotte was dedicated to a celibate career almost at her
birth, as there was a fine opening for her in prospect. Louise de Long-vic, Jacqueline's sister, the

[1] Groen, v., p. 195.
[2] He was the grandson of Diane de Poitiers.

abbess of Jouarre, agreed to bequeath the dignities
and emoluments of that rich convent to her
niece. Born in 1546 or '47, Charlotte was delivered over to her aunt's care at a tender age
and was brought up at Jouarre. In 1559 the lady
abbess fell ill and became anxious that the desired
succession should be absolutely assured. At the
urgent request of the dying woman seconded by
the Duke and Duchess, the little girl was induced
to take the veil. As witnesses to the ceremony
there were Dame Jeanne Chabot, prioress, Dame
Cécile Crue, destined to succeed to that place
when Jouarre's prioress rose to be abbess of
Paraclet, besides all the nuns in chapter assembled.
Claude Bonnard, *avocat au parlement*, bailiff and
legal adviser of the abbey, was also present, as
well as M. Ruzé, also *avocat au parlement*, counsellor and special representative of the candidate's
parents. The abbess of Paraclet came from the
neighbouring convent to receive her young cousin's vows made before the assembly in the chapel.
How repugnant the novice's acceptance of the
articles of faith were, a few nuns knew well,
for, on March 16th, they had been witnesses to a
formal declaration of the candidate that she was
about to take her vows under compulsion, against
her will and at the command of her parents, whom
she feared to disobey.[1] This seems an extraor-

---

[1] Jeanne d'Albret was but twelve years old when she made
(1540) a secret protest against her proposed marriage with the
Duke of Cleves, witnessed by three officers of her household.

dinary proceeding for a minor whose career would naturally have been at her parents' disposal, but the statement of its occurrence was made under oath and is thus no idle gossip. The prime reason for the compulsion was to keep the revenues of Jouarre in the family and to enable Charlotte to renounce her share of her own inheritance in favour of her brother. The Duke thought it an excellent arrangement. To his mind silly scruples on the part of a child like Charlotte were easily brushed aside. Surely her parents knew better than she what was for her ultimate advantage. At any rate they were in a position to make good their desires. It only seems strange that such attention was paid to the girl's reluctance that two sets of articles were drawn up, one couched in mild terms, *paroles douces et fort legères*, the other containing the ordinary legal vows which alone would have bound the novice irrevocably to the religious profession. Yet the accusation is made that this double set were used with deliberate intention to deceive the candidate and were juggled with by the abbess of Paraclet.

Six years passed and the little girl came to years of discretion. She had the training for, and fulfilled the duties of, convent-head, but she was not happy in her high estate. Some consideration

---

"All I may say hereafter . . . will be forcibly extorted against my will from dread of my father and of my mother who have threatened to have me whipped by . . . my governess." This protest was considered when the marriage was annulled.

moved her when she was eighteen or nineteen to make a formal deposition before a notary of the circumstances attending her reception into the order. It chanced that a provincial synod of the reformed churches in France was held on April 27, 1564, at La Ferté sous Jouarre. This gathering of Huguenots at her very gates may have had its influence on the young abbess. She may have thought that the new faith was about to receive official recognition and that it would be well to begin to take steps to range herself with the anti-Catholic party. There were examples of such procedure within her ken. Charlotte's father belonged to the younger branch of the Bourbons and was strongly Catholic. In the elder branch, however, were the most notable of the Huguenots. Anthony de Bourbon, King of Navarre to be sure, wavered between Protestantism and the Church and finally threw in his fortunes if not his faith with the latter. But his brother Louis, Prince of Condé, and his wife, Jeanne d'Albret, never wavered and the Queen of Navarre was keenly alert to the legal position of her co-religionists. Direct evidence is not forthcoming but as she was warmly attached to Charlotte and interested in her affairs, the surmise seems fair that it was she who advised certain legal steps as preliminary to Charlotte's renouncing her profession and that her counsel was seconded by the Duchess of Bouillon. At this date the Duchess of Montpensier was dead and

so was her abbess sister. The former prioress
of Jouarre was abbess of Paraclet; the Duke's
counsellor, M. Ruzé, was bishop in the comfortable see of Angers. Possibly Charlotte had just
attained an acknowledged majority. At any rate
on August 25, 1565, the young abbess gathered
about her the little group of sisters who had
heard her protests in March, 1559, and obtained from them formal notarial statements [1]
about her profession of faith. This document
furnishes the details given above. "Against her
own inclination, Dame Charlotte de Bourbon,
at present abbess of the abbey Nôtre Dame de
Jouarre, was forced to take her vows by her father
and by Madame Jaquette de Longwy his spouse."
The witnesses remembered distinctly how unhappy the girl had been, how she had protested
on March 16th, how she had wept before the
ceremony on the 17th and had continued her
protestations after all had assembled in the chapel.
The sworn testimony concluded with the statement that Charlotte had had it drawn up before
the undersigned notaries "to serve her in such time
and place as she may require." The subscribers
were Dames Jeanne Chabot and Cécile Crue and
the sisters Michelle de Lafontaine, Jeanne de
Vassery, Anne du Molinet, Jeanne de Mouson,

---

[1] Delaborde, *Charlotte de Bourbon*, pp. 7 and 9. It is quoted
from MSS. Bibl. Nat., vol. 3182, p. 82; Collect. Clérambault,
vol. 1114, p. 182; Coustereau, *Vie du duc de Montpensier*, p.
217.

Antoinette de Fleury, and Louise d'Alouville. Still another important witness acknowledged the truth of this declaration seven months later.

And I, the undersigned, who am mentioned in the above act and who was not present when the signatures were given, certify that the contents of the said act, all, the profession, declaration, protestations, and tears, were true and that I was a witness thereof. In testimony of which I have signed the present certificate, March 21, 1566, according to the ordinance of the king. (Signed) JEAN RUZÉ.

In nearly all the testimony given at this period and later, Jacqueline de Long-Vic is charged with the main responsibility in the arrangements for Charlotte. She seems to have been the active parent. "The Duke of Montpensier does not mingle in affairs but his wife does it for him. She is the Queen's gouvernante (Catherine de' Medici) and very intimate with her and able to obtain all she wants.[1] So says the Venetian J. Michiel." It is certainly doubtful whether

[1] *Relazioni*, i., p. 433. De Thou narrates that the Duchess implored the Qeen-mother to form a strong party of nobles to counteract the Guises. A chancellor was needed to replace Oliver. The Duchess of Montpensier, the Queen's favourite, persuaded her to select a firm and courageous man to withstand their (the Guises') designs. In other words, Michel de l'Hôpital, and to him the seals were given. (*Hist. Univ.*, iii., p. 498). De Thou asserts further that the Duchess intended Charlotte to marry the young Duc de Longueville, a friend of Calvin. This does not chime in well with the assertion of the sisters that Charlotte was forced into her profession by her mother, the Duke not caring much about it.

this "queen's favourite" were indeed Huguenot as is frequently stated, but it is quite certain that her daughter, the Duchess of Bouillon, was in the advance guard of the reformed party. In 1562 her husband declared that "in a brief time he and his wife would eradicate the mass and priests from their lands and that this could not be prevented because it depended upon God and himself alone." At Sedan and Jannetz free asylum was offered to Huguenot refugees. Thus Françoise towards the east and Jeanne towards the west were friends ready to sympathise with Charlotte when she began to find her position irksome, but several years elapsed before she abandoned it for good and all.

In 1570 the Duke of Montpensier, then fifty-five years of age, took a second wife, selecting the eighteen-year-old Catherine of Lorraine, sister of the Duke of Guise, first cousin to Mary Stuart. This alliance naturally brought the Duke closer to the ultra-Catholic party and undoubtedly was a factor towards influencing Charlotte to declare her own opinions and to resume a station in the world. Jeanne d'Albret answered an appeal for aid as follows[1]:

My cousin: I have received your letter and am infinitely sorry that I cannot serve you as I wish and I

[1] Copies of these letters of Jeanne d'Albret to Charlotte labelled *Copies des lettres de le feue Reyne de Navarre* are in the British Museum (MSS. Harley, 1582, f. 367). The handwriting is crabbed

beg you not to doubt my affection on that account. But your affair is so important that it must not be marred by the least fault, and since the bearer of this assures me that he can deliver my letter in safety I can tell you that we find no better expedient for you than what we have already suggested—to go to your sister Mme. de Bouillon and thence to Germany. And if you wish me to write again to the gentleman in question let me know and I will arrange your journey by my letters. I do not doubt that M. your father knowing that you are in a foreign land will prefer to have you with me in order to withdraw you from there, and this I desire infinitely so as to show you the affection which I bear you and to have you with me as my daughter. If I can attain that I will fulfil the office of mother in all that pertains to your grandeur and satisfaction. Everything, my cousin, must be managed wisely and secretly. Pray let me know through M. de Teligny who will deliver your letter to me safely what you wish me to do and make use of my friendship.

On this assurance I will pray, my cousin, that God may grant you increase of His holy grace.

Your very good cousin and perpetual friend,

JEHANNE.

From La Rochelle, July 28, 1571.

Here were definite suggestions. The large-hearted Jeanne d'Albret was delighted to give her kinswoman all that she could. She was not in a position to act openly. The negotiations

---

and almost illegible. Careful comparison with the text printed by Delaborde shows some discrepancies but they are not important for the actual meaning.

for the marriage of her son Henry with Margaret
de Valois were well under way. The alliance was
not perhaps wholly desired by the Queen of
Navarre in 1571, but she was nevertheless unwilling to jeopardise her son's interests in any way
by alienating the court party. She hoped for
more freedom later on.

The young abbess proceeded to follow this
advice though a few more months passed before
her plan of escape could be completely matured.
In February, 1572, Charlotte left Jouarre accompanied by two nuns and François and George
d'Averly besides a small escort of abbey soldiers.
It was believed that she was going to pay a simple
visit to the abbess of Paraclet.

When the illustrious princess your mother [wrote
Jacques Couet in the dedication of a treatise on predestination to Louise Juliana of Nassau, Electress
Palatine[1]] withdrew from superstition and popish
idolatry and sped away from France as from the
climate in which all men and women who desired to
serve God purely were grievously persecuted without distinction of sex, age, or condition, princes and
princesses of the blood royal such as she not being
excepted any more than the common people, I know
as eye-witness that she took the route for Sedan—
to her sister—but she received advice and counsel,
based on various notable considerations, not to go
thither but to proceed farther if she desired to live
in full tranquillity. As there was question of making

[1] Delaborde, p. 27.

for some safe port where she might count on shelter secure from the tempests threatening elsewhere, prudently and happily she applied to that phœnix of princes of his time, the very puissant elector Frederick III., count palatine of the Rhine, as to one who being the paragon of piety and virtue received willingly all deserving applicants.

The Elector was, indeed, a wonderful benefactor to all and especially to the persecuted Huguenots. At this time a chapel at Heidelberg was devoted to Protestant services in French and the great castle itself gave harbourage to a moving train of fugitives pausing for shelter, *en route* to permanent homes in foreign lands. Early in March, 1572, Charlotte reached Heidelberg where she was cordially welcomed by the Electress, once widow of Henry de Brederode, and the Elector, who hastened to inform the French King, the Queen-mother, and the Duke of Montpensier of his guest's arrival and of the reasons for her flight. His letter to the latter is a model of exquisite courtesy.

I do not doubt that their royal dignities will be pleased and satisfied, as I am persuaded that you too, knowing that it is only the force of conscience—chiefly in regard to religion, that influenced her, will not disapprove the departure of my cousin, your daughter, but will take it all in good part as debonair father, showing your accustomed prudence and kindness—and will permit her liberty of conscience to serve God, obey you, and enjoy her property, etc., etc.

From Heidelberg, March 15, 1572.

The Elector's real hopes of placating the father may have been much less than his conciliatory words implied. The Duke lost no time in expressing his sentiments roundly. His reply bears the date of March 28th and is the letter of an infuriated man who does not gloze his anger that his own daughter, Charlotte, had spread abroad complaints that ought to have come to his ears first.

If she had only told me herself of her distaste for the convent, I would have looked about for honest means to take her out and to place her with the least scandal in a position she preferred. But who could have dreamed that she disliked her office after she had lived in her abbey thirteen or fourteen years, invested with the quality and title of abbess, giving the habit to and receiving the vows from many in my presence and out of it, fulfilling all the duties of her charge?

I cannot agree with you that she was moved to this step by zeal for God's service. It was rather the intrigues of others that tempted her to a liberty void of sanctity, and tainted by the world and the flesh, as is shown by the fact that her sole escort consisted of two or three coquins, vicious and bad people, notorious for their scandalous lives.

I have never heard that God's glory was advanced by violating an oath and vows offered to him voluntarily and frankly, nor that kings, queens, princes, and princesses of this crown acquired the name of Most Christian by any such extraordinary and damnable methods. She is the first of her race to desert the holy faith of her ancestors, the first who was willing to wear a religious garb for eighteen or more years, live under vows, enjoying the title and emoluments of an abbess for thirteen or fourteen years, and then, all of a sudden, without confiding in father, brother, sister, or kinsfolk, to abandon everything, king and fatherland, to flee to Germany.

To remove any idea she may have given you that she was forced into her profession I assure you that neither I nor my late wife was present when she took her vows, we being more than eighty leagues distant. No one represented me except M. Ruzé, at present Bishop of Angers and then my son's tutor. ... The alleged compulsion is nothing but a masque to cover her duplicity.

The Duke then dilates on the liberality to all opinion prevailing within the realm of France, on Charlotte's ingratitude, and last but not least on the impossibility of her receiving any property that she had once renounced in favour of her brother, etc. He ends his letter with the words:

Being sure that Frederick will not wrong me by harbouring her and that you will act like a relation and friend, I finish this large and tiresome epistle.
Your humble and obedient cousin,
LOUIS DE BOURBON.
At Aigue perse the 28th day of March, 1572.[1]

Frederick's letter was not the earliest announcement of Charlotte's flight received by the Duke, though it gave the first information of her exact

[1] Delaborde, p. 320.

whereabouts. Louis de Bourbon was already hot when it arrived from the tidings that the abbess of Jouarre had disappeared, brought to him at Auvergne, by his daughter Louise, the abbess of Farmoutiers; the irate father declared that his recreant child should be returned dead or alive.[1] He filled the court with his complaints. After the interchange of letters with the Elector, the Duke sent a commission to Jouarre to make a formal investigation of the reason "why the lady had discarded her habit worn for thirteen or fourteen years without a murmur, and an inquiry into who had suborned her to such action." The commission comprised:

Nicolas de Gaulnes, lieut.-gen. of *M. le bailly* de Juere, Pierre Desmolins, registrar of the bailiwick, and M. Pierre André sieur de la Garde, advocate in the court of the *parlement de Paris*, and superintendent of the affairs of Monseigneur the Duke of Montpensier. Joined thereto was the procureur of the said nuns and convent.[2]

The substance of the testimony given under oath is that the nuns had had no idea that their abbess was not coming back when she departed ostensibly for Paraclet. There are six depositions, all very naïve and simple, each differing a little

[1] Letter to the abbess of Farmoutiers, Delaborde, p. 36; Bibl. Nat. MSS., f. fr., vol. 3182, folio 5.

[2] Delaborde, p. 37. The report is endorsed *Par Commandement de MM. le premier président et Boissonnet, conseiller ceste information faicte par les officiers de Jouerre.*

from the others.[1] All agree that the d'Averly brothers and others of the "pretended reformed religion" probably influenced Charlotte, as they had haunted the abbey, and that no one had the least suspicion of her purpose until the return of the soldiers.[2] All agree too that Charlotte had assumed the veil very reluctantly at her mother's command and at an uncanonical age. Radegonde Sarrot mentioned the serious illness of Louise de Long-vic as the immediate reason for forcing the child to take her vows. Marie Brette names Jeanne Mousson and Jehanne Varrettz as the sisters who might have been in the lady's confidence and who certainly shared her flight. The two forms of the articles to which the novice subscribed are mentioned as being a fraudulent device to blind her. All throw the blame of coercion on the mother rather than the father,—Marie Beauclerc stating that the Duchess even threatened to send her disobedient daughter to Fontevrault if she persisted in her refusal. Catherine de Perthuis does indeed suggest a recent breach between the father and daughter in her statement that when the Duke of Montpensier came to Jouarre and "forced the baptism of several

---

[1] The signatures of the nuns vary in form: Richement, C. de Perthuis, Marie Brette, R. Sarrot, Marie Beaucler, Marie Soeur de Mery. The ages of the deponents vary from 40 to 80. All had entered Jouarre at 12 or 13.

[2] The soldiers were Jehan Petit, Jehan Parent, Loys Lambinot, Gilles Leroy, and Jacques de Couches. "One named Roubichion had remained with my lady" besides the d'Averly brothers.

Huguenot children, my lady declared that since her father had played her that trick she would play him another and prove that she had no vocation for the convent but had been forced into her profession." There is a curious simplicity about it all, as though it were quite natural that the abbess should have received the Seignior de Minay, François d'Averly and his brother on terms of intimacy and that her own reluctance cast a shadow of illegality over her vows. Again there was doubt as to whether the abbess of Paraclet who had administered the oath to the young novice was ordained and thus legally equipped for the act of consecration. Thus it seems that four items were alleged why Charlotte de Bourbon was not bound to the profession: Immaturity at the time of making the vows, ineligibility of the abbess who received them, fraud in the presentation of the articles of faith, and undue constraint.

In reply to the first of these charges it might have been urged that all the testifying witnesses had apparently taken the veil at about the same age—twelve or thirteen,—so that childish vows were not unheard of. Moreover, it often seemed to be the case that the heads of both convents and monasteries were in somewhat ambiguous position between the world and the cloister, and assuredly in the sixteenth century young people were expected to accept their parents' plans for their establishment in life. The position at stake, that of abbess of Jouarre, was certainly a highly honourable one besides being richly endowed. Two charges seemed serious, first that a pretended (*simulé*) profession had been shown to the candidate instead of the real articles ordinarily sworn to by the nuns. The substitution implied deliberate fraud. Secondly, there was the ineligibility of the abbess of Paraclet to receive such vows.

But if Charlotte were Protestant and discarding the rules of the ancient Church, what difference did these points make?

President de Thou and the Sieur d'Aumont, commanded by the Duke to go to Heidelberg to bring Charlotte back to France, were told politely but firmly by Frederick III. that his guest should not leave his castle without assurance of permission to exercise her chosen religion freely.[1] Her father preferred to leave her where she was rather than to give any such promises. It made little difference. St. Bartholomew's Day in that summer of 1572 proved the quality of any pledges from the court of Charles IX. One who had trusted her own son to the King and his mother wrote two more sympathetic letters to Charlotte:

My cousin: Having heard what happened in Germany I wrote to M. the Count Palatine and to M. the Duke Casimir, his son, to announce the good news of the convention of the marriage of Madame and my son. I thanked them by the same means

[1] Aubéry du Maurier, *Mémoires*, p. 97.

for the kind reception they have given you. Moreover, I believe this alliance will help you for I shall have better credit, from which you shall profit as from the best of your relations. I have begun to talk of your affairs but M. de Montpensier is still very bitter. I will not fail to intercede for you and to use every means which God has given me. In the midst of my rejoicing over the marriage of my son God has afflicted me with the illness of my daughter, a second pleurisy which has returned four days in succession. She has been bled. I hope in God that the issue will be happy. She is in His hands. I implore Him to give her what He deems needful for her, and you, my cousin, what you desire
 Your good cousin and perfect friend,
 JEHANNE.[1]
From Blois this 5th day of April, 1572.

My cousin: I think you must have now received my letter and M. the Count, my thanks for his kindness to you. My son will add to this when he comes. As to your affairs, I have shown the queen-mother the count's letter and told her what I thought would help you but I have not had the answer I hoped for. You have many sympathisers but few dare say anything on account of the bitterness felt by M. de Montpensier towards all of this court.

However, nothing will make me hold my tongue. I will work with all my heart and leave nothing untried that occurs to me and you shall be informed when I have a chance. Both my children have been seriously ill. God has preserved them for His glory.

My cousin, make use of my friendship, my resources,

[1] British Museum, MSS. Harl. 1582, f. 367.

and my property, and thereupon I pray God my cousin to give you His holy grace and assistance in all this weighty matter.

Your good cousin and perfect friend,

JEHANNE.

From Vendôme this 5th of May, 1572.

Jeanne was at Vendôme for the obsequies of a Huguenot leader. "La da Vendoma[1] set out for Vendôme. Count Louis the Admiral and all his troop are there for the funeral of the Prince of Condé and to lay him in the church among others of his blood."

A month later and the death of the Queen of Navarre brought bitter disappointment to Charlotte. The "perfect friend" was not to adopt Charlotte, the late abbess, as her daughter. Then came the terrible massacre of St. Bartholomew which annihilated all the hoped for improvement in the condition of French Protestants as a result of the alliance between Henry of Navarre and Margaret of Valois. The temporary hospitality offered by the Elector to the escaped abbess had to be extended for it was evident that there was no safety for her in France. The guest was treated with affectionate consideration and the slightest disrespect to her was resented. Michel de la Huguerye says that the Elector would never have invited the Duke of Anjou to visit

[1] Such was the appellation given to the Queen of Navarre by the Spaniards. Pedro de Aguila to the Duke of Alva, Blois, May 5, 1572. Charlotte de Bourbon, p. 49.

Heidelberg *en route* for his new kingdom of Poland had he dreamed that he would be so rude to Charlotte.

During her sojourn at this hospitable castle there were frequent suggestions of an eligible *parti* for her, among which was one of the Rhine bishops whom it was proposed to convert. The name of Louis of Nassau too was, occasionally, coupled with hers, sometimes honourably, sometimes with a disagreeable sneer as though it had been he who tempted the abbess to discard her chosen calling. Letters and memoirs of the time were as full of gossip as the modern press, and the moral character of no one was safe in the hands of a political or theological enemy. Charlotte's character stood the calumny, however.

No negotiations for Charlotte's establishment went very far until the Prince of Orange made a definite offer of marriage in the winter of 1575. What led him to charge Philip Marnix to be his "courtly messenger" during his convenient stay at Heidelberg where the learned man was selecting professors from the Heidelberg faculty to fill chairs at the new University of Leiden? Had the Prince ever seen the lady? It is more than possible. During 1568–72 Orange was often in France. Charlotte might have met him when visiting the Queen of Navarre, for abbesses were not chained to their convents and Charlotte's high birth undoubtedly gave her freedom of movement in spite of her nun's habit. Then in the summer of 1572 Dillenburg was the exile's headquarters. Orange was constantly on the wing. It would only have been natural for him to break one of his many journeys at Heidelberg to discuss political events with the sympathetic Elector. After he was once within the Netherlands in the autumn of that year the Prince never crossed the boundaries again. But, prior to that date, many opportunities for a meeting between the future pair are well within the bounds of possibility. The memory of a pleasant, calm personality, trained for a career, disciplined by adversity, might have haunted the wanderer's memory in agreeable contrast to the disagreeable, selfish stormy capriciousness of Anne of Saxony. It seems as though he must have been influenced by a personal attraction to account for his selection of a woman whose past history and position showed so many arguments why an alliance with her at that moment was peculiarly hazardous for the advancement of his political projects.

The prudential arguments against the match were patent. Orange needed friends in Germany. A marriage in Anne's lifetime meant a public repudiation of her that would alienate Saxons and Hessians, still her kinsmen, even though they might recognise that the judicial decision of Count John as to Anne's guilt was just enough. Orange needed friends in France. But assuredly there was no prospect that this particular French bride would cement his friendship with her royal cousin whose authority she braved, both in rejecting her profession and in abandoning the solemn vows of celibacy which her father considered legal. In spite of Catherine von Bora's example the thought of a renegade nun entering into matrimony was not wholly agreeable even to Protestants, while it seemed a peculiarly heinous action to Catholics. It gave renewed ground for the grave charges against Charlotte's integrity of purpose, charges that continued to flutter in the air long after her dignified and noble bearing as consort to the struggling revolutionary leader had refuted the accusations completely.

Her first letter is as follows:

To Monsieur the Prince of Orange:

I have received the letter you were pleased to write me and have heard your message from the gentleman who brought it. It is something that I can only answer by the advice and command of M. the Elector and of Mme. the Electress to whom I have confided all. For as I consider them in the place of father and mother and as I receive from their Excellencies paternal kindness, it is only reasonable that I should render them filial duty.

As far as my own will goes, I can only express my esteem and honour for you with desire to serve you as far as God will give me the means which I am going to beseech Him to give you after my humble recommendations, etc.

Your humble and ready to serve you
CHARLOTTE DE BOURBON.

At Heidelberg, Jan. 28, 1575.[1]

[1] In the family archives of the Duc de la Trémoille. Delaborde, p. 86.

The following report to Orange continues the story:

Monseigneur and most illustrious Prince:
The seignior has returned from France bringing the answer from the King and Queen-mother. . . . The King does not wish to mix himself up in this affair, as being against his religion. Nevertheless he thinks that Mlle. is fortunate at meeting so good a *parti*, and the Queen-mother is of the same opinion. In short, *they will not take in ill part what Mlle. does by the advice of the Count Palatine*, and what seems to her advantage, provided it is not against the service of the King. Nevertheless, they advised announcing the matter to the Duke of Montpensier. It has, however, been decided in the presence of the Count Palatine, Chancellor Ehem, and myself, that there is no use in waiting for the consent of the Duke of Montpensier, because the same answer is to be expected from him as from the King, being of the same religion, and she, having attained her majority, is perfectly content to obey the Count Palatine in all that he advises. In this affair she considers him her father. As the Count Palatine approves, and declares that he would not advise her against so desirable a match with one of her own religion, Mademoiselle has roundly declared that she will obey him, and is willing to give her consent, and this is what the Count Palatine has commanded me to write to your Excellency.

As to the other point, namely, the explanation to be made to the other party's relatives, that will be left by the Palatine to your Excellency, though he will do all that is suitable to appease the said relatives, and to guard the honour of your Excellency and of Mademoiselle.

As to the dowry, the Count Palatine and Mademoiselle have heard what your Excellency has resolved about the house at Middelburg, and as Mademoiselle asks nothing better than to share with your Excellency what God may please to send to your joint lot, so she and the Count Palatine do not doubt that your Excellency will have consideration for her sex, and will make some disposition of the property which your Excellency has in France, either in Burgundy or Orange, if these estates be not pledged to your older children.

If she may have something on which she can live suitably she will be content, but she would be unwilling to inconvenience either you or your brother, and lays absolutely no stress on the point, leaving everything to your discretion. Nothing remains but your Excellency's declaration, and for your Excellency to arrange what you wish Mademoiselle to do. For it seems superfluous to send again to the King, as the enclosed answer is sufficient. The Count Palatine waits from one day to another the answer of the King's brother, and of the King of Navarre, to whom the count has written to ask their consent to this marriage, and to soften the heart of the Duke of Montpensier, her father.

Frankfort, March 31st.[1]

A little later in the spring, Count Hohenlohe[2] is

[1] Groen, v., 165.
[2] Wolfgang, Count Hohenlohe, married Madeleine of Nassau, and was brother-in-law to Orange.

sent by the Prince to Germany with messages to Count John, to the Elector Palatine, and to "Mlle. de Bourbon."

The memoranda of instructions contained the Prince's directions:

Hohenlohe will show my brother the correspondence with Zuléger, and declare my intention of proceeding in the matter, provided only that Mlle. de Bourbon gives her consent.

After discussing with my brother the best route for her to take,—by Emden, or straight down the river, which I prefer, as she would thus avoid expense, delay, and other inconveniences,—advise with my brother what means are available for the journey. This done, my brother [Count Hohenlohe] will take his way towards Heidelberg, where, having given my letters to the elector and his wife, and presented my humble salutations, he will proceed to declare his charge.

M. Zuléger advised me, by his of March 31st, of the declaration of the consent given by Mademoiselle in presence of his Excellency, and I now beg him to arrange the necessary details for the fulfilment of this promise. M. de Ste. Aldegonde will have explained my situation, and now my brother will give more ample declaration, so that his Excellency will be fully informed and know what advice to give. He will let him understand that my intention is to *march roundly*, without attempting to deceive her, or to give ground for reproach. He will explain what is the condition of affairs with my former wife, and will add the opinion expressed by her relatives, so that he can see that no hindrance, or even delay, is to be feared from that quarter.

Secondly, he will point out that nearly all my property must fall to my older children, so that I am not now able to assign to Mademoiselle any dower, but I mean to do the best I can in that respect, according to the means it may please God to give me in the future. The house I have bought at Middelburg, and the one I am building at Gertruidenberg, are nothing to boast of, but if she will accept them as a beginning, and as a testimony of my good will, there will be no difficulty. She must bear in mind, moreover, that we are in the midst of a war whose issue is uncertain, and that I am deep in debt for this cause, to princes and other gentlemen, captains, and men-at-arms. She must remember, too, that I am beginning to grow old, being forty-two years of age. Having stated these items, my brother will pray his Excellency and Madame, on my part, considering their friendship, etc., for me and her, to decide whether they approve. If, after all is well weighed, Mlle. agrees to proceed in the matter, he [Hohenlohe] will give a promise on my part, and receive one from her, and then consult about the best arrangements for the journey to complete what is begun to the glory of the Lord.

WILLIAM OF NASSAU.

At Dordrecht, April 24, 1575.[1]

When the Count realised that his brother was on the very eve of matrimony, he was deeply

[1] Groen, v., 189.

concerned and his dismay was shared by all the family at Dillenburg. John had been ill and was still so weak that writing was a weariness to him, but he hastened to send off a letter to Ste. Aldegonde, in the hopes of delaying the fatal step:

Dear Aldegonde [no ceremony this time]: If you have any love for the Prince and for the welfare of the elector, and if you do not want to run into danger yourself, *do let this thing be delayed for a time;* at least, until we can be sure of the foundation of the other friendship, so that we can see our way clear to act conscientiously and honourably, and until we know how matters are to be settled with the Princess; especially and most important of all, just wait until the coming meeting of the electoral college and Reichstag—appointed for about July 29th at Frankfort—shall be over. . . . If you have already started, which I hope is not the case, let her wait at Emden or Bremen, for a time, as though she were going to England. . . .

It is a shame to put all friendship in jeopardy. There is an old and true proverb, *præcipitis consilii pœnitentia comes*. The matter is surely worthy of consideration. But of what use is endless writing? Any one can get advice for what he wants to do. If there is no hope, I and other good hearts must look on sadly and let it go as it will, because it cannot be otherwise, but I cannot help telling you, that if this matter be pushed on so roughly you will not be safe in Germany.

JOHN, COUNT OF NASSAU, etc.

DILLENBURG, May 20th.

I enclose Hesse's opinion so that you can see that the matter will not be allowed to drop: as the tree does not fall at one blow, I would be hopeful if the affair were conducted with prudence and modesty and not rushed through so thoughtlessly.[1]

This particular enclosure is not preserved, but Hesse's opinion on the matter is well known. He had written to Dr. Schwartz that he simply could not believe that the Prince was in earnest. No divorce had been granted that would permit remarriage and if Orange persisted in this course, Anne's position would be altered and the judges would declare that there was mutual delinquency and grant compensation accordingly.[2]

The Prince's formal announcement to John of his coming marriage is dated May 21st. He treats his purpose simply as a foregone conclusion and requests that all the papers relating to Anne's case should be given to the Elector Palatine. If the documents were not forthcoming, the scandal to the House of Saxony would be greater.

I should find it only good, if you made the culprit [Rubens] again confess his misdeed before some gentlemen and people of quality, so that you and I should be more at our ease, and be sure of him for our greater security if any one should hereafter malign us, and accuse us of illegal imprisonment. . . . For other news, the peace conference is not yet at an end, etc.[3]

---

[1] Groen, v., 201.
[2] *Ad mutuam parium delictorum compensationem.*
[3] Groen, v., 205.

It is a singularly quiet, unmoved letter, as though the contemplated step was the most natural one possible.

John, however, could not take the matter lightly. He wrote to the Landgrave that it was not his fault, and William of Hesse replied that he could well believe that such a marriage did not meet with the Count's approval, or with that of any person in his right senses. He continues in Latin, that the Prince must be distracted by his troubles, even to dream of such a mad, insensate action. When John receives his brother's letter of May 21st, he writes, on June 3d, a long, careful, affectionate, brotherly, though very respectful letter, begging Orange not to complete this alliance. He ventures to use the word "geliebte" in the midst of his letter, having begun "Honoured Prince," and says modestly: "Although it does not become me to prescribe measures to your Highness, I must confess that the unseemly haste in this important matter shocks me, and certainly cannot further your public affairs." It was not a time when Orange ought to follow his private inclinations. The "other party's" relatives will be furious; her dowry will be demanded, which will be very inconvenient to pay back, as it amounts to 12,500 thalers a year. A *notorious fact* does not always admit of documentary evidence, etc.

Then the matter was discussed by Calvinistic ministers in France and the Netherlands. MM.

Feugheran and Capet of France gave their opinion in writing, that the new marriage was legitimate—their chief argument being that Anne's conduct released her husband from all obligations towards her. Finally, on June 11th, a formal act, by which the marriage of the Prince of Orange was declared legal, was drawn up at Brill by five of the most eminent ministers in the Netherlands. They were Gaspar van der Heiden, John Taffin, Jacob Michael, Thomas Tylius, and Jan Miggrodus. After reviewing all the circumstances, the document concludes with these words: "whereby it follows, that Monseigneur the Prince is free according to human and divine law to marry, and that she whom he espouses will be, before God and man, his lawful wife." [1]

This Orange accepted as the legal justification of his freedom to marry. Yet he had hardly awaited the decision before committing himself to make the alliance. When this dictum was pronounced, Charlotte had already entered the Brill under the escort of Ste. Aldegonde, who had not "let the grass grow under his feet." He was not disposed to criticise his chief. Orange wanted to be married. Aldegonde had been asked to fetch him his bride and he fetched her as fast as roads and weather would permit.

The bride was formally received by the deputies of Dordrecht, Alkmaar, Flushing, and Brill and

[1] Groen, v., p. 223.

presented with a gift of six thousand pounds. On June 12th the wedding ceremony was performed and the pair proceeded to Dordrecht, where they were received with every token of joy, but "no dancing."[1]

The Landgrave's emphatic expressions on the subject of this alliance may be taken as voicing the widespread disapproval.

I cannot understand what the Prince is thinking of, let alone that wiseacre, Aldegonde, or whoever else has helped in the matter. *Nam si pietatem respicias.* If you consider piety, you must remember that she is French, and a nun, a runaway nun at that, about whom all kinds of stories are told of the way she kept her cloister vows, before the Prince wanted to put himself out of the mud into the sea.

Si formam. If it is beauty he is after, you can hardly believe he was charmed by that, since, undoubtedly, no one can look at the bride without being rather frightened than pleased.

Si spem prolis. The prince has, indeed, already too many children for his circumstances, and ought rather to wish, if he were in his senses, that he had neither wife nor child.

Si amicitiam. If it is friendship, we do not believe he will get it. Her own father is so incensed against her, that the Prince cannot expect much gratitude from him and her relatives.

So we cannot imagine what has led him into this business, which will estrange many of his friends

[1] *Komst van Charlotte van Bourbon te Dordrecht.* Poem in Schotel's Dordrecht, p. 50.

whose friendship had not stood him in ill-stead. Then everything is in a muddle, and it looks to us as if Holland and Zealand, in seeking *protection*, were going to bring themselves into subjection. They had better look to it that it does not go as it did with the Admiral at his Paris wedding, for the gentlemen do not pardon such injuries without *mercury and sublimated arsenic*.[1]

However, the marriage was not stayed and soon was an accomplished fact. The Nassau family had to swallow their dismay, and make the best of it. On June 24th, Charlotte wrote a pleasant, respectful note to Juliana, her new mother-in-law, evidently hoping that she is to be well received in the family. On July 7th, Orange despatches a very long, characteristic letter to John in answer to his remonstrance upon his marriage. First he regrets that the documents asked for were not sent to him. Then he expresses his sorrow that John had taken his alliance so keenly to heart and refers to his objection to the celebration before the meeting of the Diet at Frankfort.

To which I reply, my brother, that my method has always been . . . not to trouble myself about objections to anything I could conscientiously do without wrong to my neighbours. If I had heeded the remonstrances of princes and others, would I ever have embarked on the enterprise I have undertaken? As soon as I was convinced that neither prayers nor exhortations would have any effect,

[1] Groen, v., p. 226.

I saw that active resistance was the sole course open.

It is the same thing now with my marriage. It is something I do with a clear conscience before God and without just cause for reproach from men. Indeed I consider that I am bound to this procedure by God's holy ordinance and that there is really no need to answer men, because the matter is so clear. [He expatiates on the uselessness of further delay.] There is nothing that checks evil suspicions so quickly or that is in such good taste as a quiet and rapid mode of procedure, as though one's self were the most competent judge of one's own behaviour, rather than to blazon matters abroad with the sound of the trumpet and then to invite criticism from those who must necessarily be only partially informed as to details.

In regard to the difficulties you raise, of dowry and of provision for children who may be born to me, pray consider that no delay till the next Diet, or the next century, so to say, would have solved them. . . . I have made a frank statement about my duties to my older children . . . and there was no further reason for my being longer in the state of widowerhood to which I have been condemned for so long. . . . I firmly believe that I have taken the right course, not only for myself, but for the public weal.[1]

The letter is dignified and yet brotherly. There is a ring of truth in every word and between the lines which shows the writer on a far higher moral

---

[1] Groen, v., p. 244.

plane than ever before. The skilful "diplomacy" of the Prince's earlier years, the ability to give two completely different views of the same action, do not appear in this episode. Honesty of purpose and honesty of expression have at last united, and the man lets his own conviction stand out clearly; as regards his personal conduct his own standard was attained even though he was running counter to accepted standards.

The apprehensions entertained by the Prince's friends that the event would excite criticism proved fully justified. Orange begged the Elector of Saxony to take his marriage in good part. But no words were powerful enough to work that end; and the terms in which Augustus expressed his disapproval were vigorous rather than polite. Nor was the Elector alone in his opinions. The Prince's agent in France, Gaspar Schomberg, wrote that the disapproval there was very strong, and when the Diet met at Ratisbon in October, comments were freely expressed on the matter. The Elector Palatine bent to the wind and finally asserted that the match was none of his doing.

In Charlotte's family it is rather strange that the orthodox Louise de Bourbon, abbess of Farmoutiers, the first to inform the Duke of her sister's flight, showed herself very gracious to the unexpected brother-in-law. Possibly the fact that the vacated dignities of Jouarre were presented to her made her more lenient to Charlotte's resignation as abbess.¹ Two months after the wedding she writes to the Prince of Orange:

> Monsieur: I cannot tell you how much I appreciate the esteemed favour you have been pleased to show me by your letter, recognising me for what I have the honour to be to you now. Pray believe that, for my part, I prize as I should, the honour that is done our house by my sister's marriage with you. I count her very happy to be sought by a prince as virtuous and sage as your reputation makes you. Do me the honour to believe that I should consider myself very pleased to receive your commands so that you might judge by the execution thereof how I desire a place in your good graces. Beseeching God to give you, Monsieur, etc.
>
> Your very humble and obedient sister to do you service,
>
> LOYSE DE BOURBON.
>
> At Jouarre, Aug. 21, 1575.²

François de Bourbon, too, did not repulse the advances of his sister and her husband. The exchange of letters that began in the early summer of 1575 continued throughout Charlotte's life. Orange implores this brother-in-law to use his "singular courtesy and honesty" in persuading the Duke "to take back my wife into his good

---

¹ A third sister, Anne de Bourbon, Duchess of Nevers, died in this same year. Although "of the religion," the Duke of Montpensier insisted that her obsequies should be celebrated with Catholic rites. Delaborde, p. 107.

² Groen, supplement, p. 174.*

graces, recognising her as one who has the honour to be his daughter."

Still in spite of the friendliness of these French kinsfolk, it was only very gradually that the cloud of criticism hanging over the new marriage was dissipated. Perhaps no one suffered more from its presence than Count John of Nassau—loyal to his brother but critical of his course. Indeed it often happens that an interested person at a distance from the scene of action feels a blow for a longer period than the active participants, speedily absorbed in fresh events.

Before his marriage, Orange had told his brother to make out a statement of the indebtedness of the insurgent provinces to him. Count John has done this and begins to feel that settlement is in order if the Prince feels justified in assuming new burdens of private expenditure. This again is a natural sentiment. Money is still scarce, however, and the answer to John's legitimate request made by Orange is (July 21st) that, as yet, any payment is a simple impossibility. In the face of this rebuff and in spite of his grieved disapproval of the Prince, John does not drop his affectionate tone when he touches on his own household cares.

My children and yours [he writes, October 13th] are, thank God, pretty well, in spite of the disease ravaging this neighbourhood, where more than a hundred deaths of the plague have occurred in some villages. Within three months four persons have died in my household of this disease, though we did not know about it until afterwards.

The young people are all at Siegen. My mother, your Excellency's daughter, my wife and sister, insist however on staying here with me, as I cannot get away.[1]

This "daughter" was Marie, whose devotion to her Uncle John makes one of the prettiest pictures of the Nassau gallery. The Count feels it his duty to point out to her father that something should be done towards finding her a husband. Orange replies that he would be glad to see her settled but he cannot do much by way of a dot.

Then there are problems of education. John's sons are destined for Heidelberg University soon. "It is the best school in Germany." What shall be done with Maurice? The plague increases. By December 4th two hundred more deaths have occurred, including several of the little court. The family have escaped, though Countess Juliana and John's wife were ill for a few days.

[1] MS. Orange-Nassau family archives, The Hague.

ORANGE MEDAL

CHAPTER XV

THE PACIFICATION OF GHENT

1577

AFTER the rupture of the peace negotiations at Breda, the disappointed Grand Commander turned his attention to vigorous offensive operations. An exploit in Zealand that brought some renown to the close of his rather colourless career was a curious contrast to the relief of Leiden by floating a fleet overland to the city walls, for his men succeeded in marching to an island!

In Zealand, the Spaniards held the island of Tholen alone and that had been won by Mondragon's men wading at low tide to its shores. Requesens ordered a repetition of this experiment and it succeeded though the conditions were more dangerous. The Netherland garrison in Duiveland was as much surprised by 1500 Spaniards suddenly rising out of the sea as Valdez's troops had been by the entry of the sea into their tents before Leiden. Between the ebb and flow, in the night of September 27th, the Spaniards had made the six miles from Tholen to Duiveland with great difficulty and some loss as they ploughed their way more than knee-deep in salt water across the flats with flashes of lightning their only illumination. In the confusion which ensued among the attacked at this unexpected invasion, the Netherlanders lost their heads and were easily overcome. The Admiral's brother was slain by his own men in the darkness and surrender of the fort was unavoidable.

The Spanish secured their prize and then braved the rising tide and waded on across the second and narrower strait to Schouwen, where they quickly reduced Brouwershaven on the North Sea and invested Bommenede and Zierikzee. Both towns resisted bravely, the former until October 26th, while the latter held out until June, 1576. Its final capitulation proved one factor in the progress of events that had already been set in motion by a series of occurrences that had preceded it, the most important of which was the sudden death of the Grand Commander after a five days' illness (March 4, 1576). Anticipating his death, Requesens attempted to appoint a temporary successor; but his unsigned memorandum was entirely disregarded and the Council of State at Brussels assumed the sole executive authority, pending the arrival of Philip's orders from Spain. That distant ruler did not, however, act with the promptitude demanded by the occasion, while the Prince of Orange did. At the latter's instance, a joint assembly of the

THE PACIFICATION OF GHENT, 1577. (Redrawn from a contemporaneous print.)
The provinces are shown safe within an enclosure symbolising the Pacification. The Belgian lion guards the entrance.

Estates of Holland and Zealand had been convened in March. The result of their deliberations was the adoption of a new Act of Union between the two bodies politic, which replaced the earlier, inefficient alliance.[1]

By its articles Orange was clothed with sovereign powers over the united lands during the continuance of the war. Moreover, he succeeded in making good his theory of extending the zone of responsibility—a theory which was a deep-seated principle. "His Excellency deems it advisable that all regulations, civil and military, should be ratified ... also by the communities ... so that the people should have no ground for complaint that ordinances were made without their knowledge."[2]

Another motion was definitely broached in this Delft assembly, assuredly of a revolutionary character,—the idea of inviting some foreign prince to assume a protectorate. The Prince's phrase, used to Requesens, that the provinces were a fair maid who did not lack wooers, implies an openness in these proceedings. William of Hesse evidently has this plan in mind when he interjects into his letter about the Prince's marriage, his warning that Holland and Zealand may find themselves in subjection while seeking

---

[1] Hierges was stadtholder (Royal) for Utrecht and Guelderland and temporarily for Holland and Zealand at this time, 1575, but he was powerless to prevent these measures.

[2] Muller, *De Staat*, etc., p. 121, Res. of Hol., 1575-76.

protection.[1] Thus it was certainly no secret
even at the early stages, and from the first it was
the Prince's wish. The absolute need of a foreign
potentate at the head of a kind of home rule, constitutional, federal government was an *idée fixe*
with him to the end of his life and one that
brought strange contradictions into his policy,
or rather turned his policy into politics. Surely
it would have been the part of greater wisdom
had Orange been more audacious, more ambitious,
and assumed in his own name an elective monarchical power which would have been free from
the complications accompanying the "protection"
sought here and there by the revolting provinces,
who appealed now to England, now to France,
deliberately blinding their eyes to the fact that
neither the non-commercial Catholic, nor the
commercial Protestant neighbour would do anything for the commercial petitioners, not even
united in their heterodoxy, that might seriously
jeopardise any of their own interests.

There was long uncertainty as to what would
be Philip's move after Requesens's death.

Marvellous it is [writes Morillon, May 28th] that
so little news comes from Spain. It is rumoured
that Don John will have the government, others
in his Majesty's chamber declare that nothing is
determined and that he is probably waiting for
answers from those he has written to. There is talk

[1] Groen, v., p. 228.

of Mme. de Parma and her son. God grant it may be some one who understands the country.[1]

In Madrid every eligible person was discussed in detail but the appointee proved to be one who neither understood nor cared for the "country," except as a convenient stepping-stone in crossing the adjacent channel, for the King's choice did finally fall on his half-brother, Don John of Austria, as rumoured.[2] He was the son of one Barbara Blomberg and Charles V., provided for in his father's will and acknowledged by Philip, who had him educated, let him associate with Don Carlos, and conferred upon him highly responsible appointments at an early age. It was Don John's extraordinary good fortune to be in command of the allied fleet at Lepanto (1571) when the threatened advance of the Turks into western Europe was repulsed, and the admiration showered upon him for the marvellous achievement was sufficient to bewilder a wiser and an older head. Pope Gregory XIII. himself said:

That young chief has proved himself a Scipio in valour, a Pompey in heroic grace, an Augustus in good fortune, a new Moses, a new Gideon, a new Samson, a new Saul, a new David, without any of the faults of these famous men, and I hope in God to live long enough to reward him with a royal crown.[3]

[1] *Cor. de Granvelle*, vi., p. 88.
[2] *Don John of Austria*, Stirling-Maxwell, 2 vols.
[3] Stirling-Maxwell, i., 429.

Others too had suggested that his illegitimate birth need not be a bar to his royalty in any land but Spain. The appointment to the lieutenancy of the insurgent provinces was especially acceptable, because Don John regarded his new office as the opening to a more ambitious career. His brother bade him be very conciliatory to the Netherlanders and to make peace at any price short of licensing heresy. Even with the obstinate Protestants he was to use no more of the harsh methods of his predecessors. Every one who wished to stay at home must, naturally, return to the Church, but non-conformists were to have plenty of time to arrange their affairs before emigrating and to find Catholic friends to look after their property. With various gracious offers at his disposition Don John had no doubt of his speedy success. As soon as the assigned task was accomplished, he meant to take the troops, whose disbandment was clamoured for, and, with their aid, rescue the imprisoned Mary Stuart, whose royal hand would be, he dreamed, a suitable reward for his services. Eventually, might he not be prince-consort to the Queen of Great Britain? It was a pleasant picture that danced before his eyes as he rode, hot haste, to the north. As soon as his dilatory brother had decided on him as Requesens's successor, Don John set off on his journey across France, more like a fortune-seeking adventurer than a staid deputy-lieutenant of a monarch. Disguised as a Moor (so runs the story), accompanied by a small escort, he travelled hastily across France, pausing a single night in Paris, where, according to Brantôme, he went to a court ball and looked on the royal family, without revealing his own identity. He was a handsome, spirited person, even if he fell somewhat short of the Pope's summary of his characteristics, and he was still a youth in spirit, in spite of his thirty years.

When he crossed the frontier into Luxemburg and received the first direct report from his government, the news was startling indeed.

> At last, thank God [he writes, November 5th, to Don Rodrigo de Mendoza], I reached this place the 3d of this month and found the worst possible tidings of these provinces, for only this in which I am [Luxemburg] and Friesland . . . have withstood revolt. The rest are leagued together, calling out troops and foreign aid against the Spaniards, making and repealing laws in their own fashion, under the name of the King, whose name is also used while they are actually fitting up a house for Orange in Brussels and taking steps to admit him in the city.[1]

[1] Stirling-Maxwell, ii. (Appendix), p. 357.
Another letter of his, May 24th, is worth noting as showing the degree of persecution that still existed. "Two heretics belonging to the district of Namur are to be punished as examples. One, who refused to acknowledge himself as a heretic, was found to be in the possession of many bad books of Calvin and other heresiarchs. And the other, ready to repent, confessed his errors and that for nine years he had not been to confessional or received his Creator. Without the books of the one and the confession of the other, we should have been in difficulty. Certain

To return to the early summer of 1576. The Council of State at Brussels administered affairs as well as they could until the capitulation of Zierikzee. "We do here what we can, but everything is slow, for [writes Morillon to Granvelle, from Brussels, May 21st] there are seven governors where there should be but one. *Multitudo imperatorii curiam perdidit.*"[1]

The financial difficulties were a formidable burden to the feeble executive body in the capital. The deficit in the treasury was enormous and the arrears of pay owing to the soldiers amounted to a sum total which it was impossible to collect. The demands of the captains were put off with vague promises. Probably the men were soothed by intimations that they should have a fine share in the booty of Zierikzee, whose fall seemed certain. When that happened, however, the timid Council of State thought it would be politic to deal gently with the city. Excellent terms were granted to the burghers and the soldiers who had stood so patiently at the closed gates, expecting the delight of sacking when admitted, found themselves debarred from their precious privilege. There was a brief moment of sullen resentment at being

---

citizens made capital out of the fact that the above had been questioned out of their house against the privileges and they stirred up other riffraff, whose mouths were stopped when they saw the books burned and the *amende honorable*, and I shall warn the magistrate to be more careful about admitting strangers in future."

[1] *Cor. de Granvelle*, vi., p. 81.

left without either wages or freedom to help themselves; then mutiny broke out in the ranks and the troops became a terror to friend and foe alike. After some wild raiding, the city of Alost was seized as headquarters for the mutineers,—organised under a system of their own, —and the land was kept in a state of abject terror as to the next outbreak of their organised lawlessness.

It was a period of almost superhuman exertion on the Prince's part. No stone was left unturned. Many of his efforts are known.[1] Doubtless there were others whose details have never been revealed. It was all the systematic procedure of a declared revolutionary leader, a procedure honeycombed with the faults inherent in such action. He was fully resolved to leave Philip out of the question henceforth and he used every weapon at hand to undermine royal authority and to ruin the nominal administration. It was the seventeen provinces that he wanted to see united. Holland and Zealand had been under his jurisdiction but neither had ever bounded his interests. His estates were in Brabant, his official life had been passed in Brussels. The confederation he dreamed of was to be as comprehensive as the Netherland circle of the empire erected in 1548, and at this moment of 1576 there is little doubt that he thought the dream was to be realised.

[1] Groen, *Archives*, v., pp. 327-584; Gachard, *Analectes Belges, et passim.*

In the act of union between Holland and Zealand Orange had exerted himself to keep any derogatory mention of the "Catholic" religion out of the articles, and had had introduced the ambiguous phrase that the exercise of *all religion at variance with the gospel should cease* and in so doing had been actuated not only by a desire to see tolerance within the little confederation, but to leave a loophole open for the hoped-for friendship with the great body of loyal Catholics in the other provinces. During the summer of 1576, numerous letters—not copies of one draft but each one written afresh—were showered not only on provincial estates but on municipalities, officials, and private persons, urging corporations and individuals alike to be slaves no longer. He reminded each one of his own grievances and pointed out the necessity of concerted efforts, pledging himself to act slowly and always in accordance with the wishes of the States. How much had Orange to do with the revolutionary occurrences that took place at Brussels? Undoubtedly it was his hand that pulled the wire when a certain Seignior de Hèze suddenly came to the fore. He was a young man with the qualities of a demagogue, full of audacity and energy, and in command of some municipal troops. From the beginning of the mutiny he had inflamed popular indignation against everything Spanish. From August on, he was in close correspondence with Orange, who was probably fully informed of a bold *coup d'état* which de Hèze put into execution.[1]

Suddenly appearing before the Council of State with five hundred men-at-arms, de Hèze arrested the assembled councillors in the name of the Estates of Brabant and assumed the reins of government.

Things went so far that the Brussels folk, determined to be free, apprehended and imprisoned . . . Count Mansfeld, M. de Berlaymont, Viglius, Assonleville, and some others of the Council of State. Several cities seem ready to rise and it is to be hoped that God is going to take pity on these poor lands [wrote Orange to his brother on September 9th].[2]

The actual detention of the councillors,—two in the Broodhuis, the others in their own residences, was not of long duration, but their authority was effectually annihilated. Popular risings followed in other towns and at the same time the mutiny of the Spanish grew more serious. Fear of this unrestrained terrible force in their midst, combined with the Prince's well-directed efforts, finally had an effect. The Estates of Brabant assumed the initiative and invited a convention of deputies from the sister provinces. The resulting assembly called itself the States-

[1] The Spaniard Del Rio was eye-witness to these events and according to him all was in train for accommodation when the habitual artifices of the Prince of Orange overthrew everything. *Mémoires*, i., p. 69, etc.

[2] Groen, v., p. 409.

General, but as all the Estates were not represented, it was, perhaps, rather more like a self-appointed committee of national safety. While this conclave was in session, Orange addressed the following letter to its members—recapitulating in substance what he had said to each province separately.[1]

Understand your own position. Steer yourselves free from this dire confusion, which is the true foundation of tyranny and has been the source of ruin to republics from time immemorial. To do this, union among yourselves is important above all. If you will examine both the famous disasters of ancient history and the calamities of modern times, you will see that in France, Italy, and Germany, as well as in Hungary, Africa, and Barbary, where the Turks ravage at will, internal dissensions in a nation have been the root of all ill. My advice, subject to your correction, is, write to the King that you resolutely refuse to endure longer the incubus of his foreign troops, or to submit to the annihilation of all your rights. Express yourselves clearly, without ambiguous statements. Let no phrase creep in which could be to your future prejudice. Let this letter be signed by all the provincial Estates, and even by the chief monastic orders, and by all individuals of dignity in the land, or in credit with the King, or who ought to look to public weal. This action would act like a spur to your deliberations. Your position would be defined. You would no

[1] Gachard found this undated letter in Paris. It must have been written in October.—*Cor.*, iii., p. 140.

longer be swimming between two waters. You would then be in a position to act together and to feel mutual obligation to defend your action. Weighty deeds must bear the seal of their own importance. The ancients understood this. They used to inaugurate their societies and brotherhoods with elaborate ceremonials, so that each individual felt the sanctity of the common bond. . . . Defensive confederations are no new thing in this land. In the year 1261, Louvain, Brussels, and other Brabantine cities formed an alliance, and there were other similar leagues in 1339, 1368, 1371, 1372, and at many other times. *It was by this persistent course of united effort among weak parties, each defenceless alone, that our vaunted privileges, rights, and customs have been so long maintained.*

The King thinks that the only malcontents here are a band of mutinous, so-called heretical Lutherans, while the country in general would be peaceable and content if there were not one or two leaders who stirred up revolt. In the year 1559, when there was question of the departure of the Spanish soldiers, the King himself said to me, "*Si los estados no tuviessen pilares, no hablarian tan alto.*" Let him see that it is the general voice of the people which speaks, that the Estates are supported in their protest by great and small, by prelates, abbots, monks, and ecclesiastics, as well as by lords, gentlemen, citizens, and peasants. In short, show him that there is no age, sex, condition, or quality of persons which does not participate in the clamour, which does not lend its voice to one will. Then, if he disregard your cry, all the world will declare him wrong, and support your right to oppose such iniquitous tyranny by every means in your power.

Finally, let him see that you are united to us, and that, moreover, you intend to throw yourselves into the arms of the ancient enemy of the House of Austria rather than to endure further insults.

Then what can he do? Separate twigs can be snapped in two easily, but no one is strong enough to break a faggot. Even so, if you are firmly united, Spain and Italy together will not be sufficient to work you ill. See what Holland and Zealand have done in five years, and the burghers who have held aloof, as Amsterdam and Utrecht, have wrought us more injury than our foreign foe. What is our handful of cities to all the Netherlands? . . . Everything is ready. A touchstone alone is needed, and such a touchstone would be a plain declaration of your rights duly signed. With the publication of such a declaration, friends would declare for you on every side. Now, the princes of Germany, the gentlemen of France, the Queen of England, and all other Christian potentates think you do not wish help, because you do not help yourselves. Act with decision, and the people will be a shield and buckler of their rights and will no longer ebb and flow like waves of the sea. Act, and there will be no one who will not haste to your assistance and be faithful to the last drop of blood. Do this, and you will be an example to all free peoples and to all unjust oppressors of republics.

The Prince's arguments prevailed so far that delegates were appointed by the separate provinces to meet persons deputed by himself and the allied provinces in revolt to confer on joint measures at Ghent, the city of his choice.

The Pacification of Ghent

There was a special reason for this selection, as Ghent had shown her temper by asking for a guard of the Prince's own troops to protect her from the mutineers. On October 19th, the deliberations began, and on November 8th signatures were put to the Pacification of Ghent, a compact that bound the southern Netherlands into a defensive league with Holland and Zealand. Very possibly the twenty-five Articles of Confederation would never have been signed had not the mutineers suddenly seized on Antwerp and treated the city with a savage brutality, known as the Spanish Fury.

It is notorious that Antwerp was but yesterday one of the chief ornaments of Europe, the harbourage of all the nations of the world, the nurse of art and industry. . . . The protector of the Roman Catholic Religion, she was ever faithful and obedient to her sovereign prince. Now the city is changed to a gloomy cavern, filled with robbers and murderers, enemies to God, the King, and to loyal subjects.[1]

Such was the message sent by the Estates of Brabant to the Assembly at Ghent, after November 4th, and the words doubtless contributed towards the conclusion reached some days later.

Orange did not appear in person at Ghent, but he was adequately represented by Ste. Aldegonde and Paul Buys. Morillon tells Granvelle (November 5th) how Ste. Aldegonde had the

[1] Bor, i., 733.

sympathy of the meeting so completely that, when he asked for the restitution of the Prince's property, the request was not only granted, but there was a further suggestion that a gratuity would be only proper. Marnix declared that his chief was too generous to think of any personal recompense and that what he had asked for was at his own initiative and not at that of the Prince. Then the deputies were rejoiced that they had not been taken at their word, for they had spoken liberally, without authorisation, and they might not have received the endorsement of their constituents upon their spontaneous generosity.

Several times the rupture of the negotiations seemed imminent because of the religious difficulties; and then it was that the Prince urged nationalism, with adequate protection for the ancient faith, on such men as the Abbé of Ste. Gertrude, who had no intention of deserting the Church of Rome. It was entirely due to Orange personally, to his consistent conciliatory efforts, that any compromise was effected between the ultra partisans of both communions. Very probably a more widely spread agreement could have been reached in 1566 than in 1576. The repressive measures carried on for ten years had effectually checked Protestantism in the quarters where it had originally been the strongest, and zeal for the reformed faith undoubtedly had flagged in the major part of the Flemish Walloon territory, though in certain cities interest was

THE ENTRY OF THE
(Based

ANGE INTO BRUSSELS.
(raving.)

simply latent and flashed out as soon as it was possible.

The Prince had his reasons for hastening a decision. He was fully aware that affairs would take on a different colour once Philip's lieutenant was in the field, and he wished to confront the traveller with an accomplished fact. He was successful. The day of Don John's arrival at Luxemburg, November 3rd, was the very day before the outbreak at Antwerp. Frightened by that, the congress at Ghent ended their hesitation, so that when their deputies went forth to bid a formal welcome to the new governor, they carried the accepted Articles of Confederation for his ratification, before, in their turn, they accepted him. And pending the interchange of pledges, there were stormy scenes.

Don John had been ordered to make peace at any price except allowing heresy. That one exception proved paralysing. The Pacification did not "allow" heresy, but it left religious matters *in statu quo* for further decision. Then Don John could not mention what lay nearest his heart—his design to rescue Mary Stuart. He was quite ready to meet the Netherlanders' wish about the dismissal of the Spanish troops, but as he intended using those same troops in England, to achieve his other purpose, it was necessary that they should depart by sea, and very reluctantly did he concede the point that they should march away on land. The deputies were firm

to a degree that exasperated Don John intensely.
In the midst of one discussion, he actually seized
a candlestick to throw at a delegate's head, as a
more telling argument than any other he could
produce.

The delegates took pains to inform Orange of
every step of their negotiation and to impress
upon him their consideration for his interests.
Final signature to the so-called Perpetual Edict,
signed at Marché-en-Famine, February 17th,
was actually held over, pending the receipt of
the Prince's letter, which never came. He preferred that they should act without him in an
accord that he knew would lead to nothing.
Yet the articles did, indeed, yield many points.
The Pacification of Ghent was endorsed, the Council of Troubles was abolished, Don John was to be
accepted, the soldiers sent away by land, the
ancient charters to be maintained, and the States-
General convened. In return, the States gave
one substantial promise. They consented to pay
off the soldiers.

When the facts are reported to Orange, he
is by no means enthusiastic. The States mean
well, but their zeal is misplaced, etc. He has
no faith at all in Don John, less than he deserved.
"Alva, Requesens, and Don John all had the same
intentions, in spite of their different phrases,"
he said later.

On his part, Don John was constantly exasperated at feeling the touch of the Prince in

The Pacification of Ghent

every detail. He credited him, indeed, with far more influence than he really possessed, for the stranger could not see the difficulties that beset the leader of the opposition. "He is the pilot who is guiding this bark and he alone can wreck it or save it. The greatest obstacle would be abolished if we could gain him over." So wrote Don John to the King, March 16th. After assuring his brother that his name was as hated as that of Orange is loved, the writer adds:

I am negotiating with the Prince about desired assurances, for I see that the establishment of peace, as well as the maintenance of the Catholic religion and the obedience due your Majesty in these provinces, depends solely upon him, and that things are gone so far that a virtue must be made of necessity. If he lends ear to my propositions, it will only be because the conditions are very favourable to him, but we needs must do this rather than lose everything.[1]

---

[1] This letter is partially given by Gachard, iii., p. liii.

On Dec. 3rd, the English Thomas Wilson writes to Lord Burghley that the trial was to be "betwixte Don Jhon and the Prynce for the best game, without hopes of peace or any accorde at all. And suerlie if the Prynce with the States had monie, it is like that some greate exploite would sodeinlie bee done. And no dowte the Prynce is a rare man of greate authoritie universallie beloved, verie wyse resolute in al thynges and void of covetousness and that whiche is worthie of especial prayse in hym he is not dismayed with any losse or adversity, his state being better now than ever it was. God graunte that right maie take place & justice bee doune upon yearthe."

Rel. pol. des Pays-bas et d'Angleterre, ix., p. 68.

This letter seems to prove that Don John was really sincere in his propositions, but Orange persistently refused him credit for any truth at all. To the Prince's mind all Don John's offers were pure sham, and his advice to the States-General was in accordance with that belief. Certainly he was consulted at every step. After a time, Don John, discouraged and embittered by the constant annoyance of this unseen authority ever counter to his interests, began to write to his brother, begging for permission to take up arms again, so that he might beat a sense of their duty into "these drunken Flemish wineskins." He was a soldier and not fitted for the task given him. The more he gave way the more insolent they became. A child or a woman could do the work required of him better than he. But Philip gave him no comfort. On his part, the King was led to believe that his young brother was tricking him and cherishing secret designs inimical to him. Don John was left in a wretched position, trusted by none.

More and more did the Prince of Orange become the personification of the party of the opposition, even though he was not liked by all members of that opposition, and while his theological affiliations were feared and distrusted. A proof of this was the formation of a new alliance in January, 1577, called the *Union of Brussels*, whose adherents reaffirmed their orthodoxy, while asserting their anti-Spanish nationalism. Certain articles were circulated like the Compromise of 1565 and found many signatories, even in the North, though, contemporaneously, there were changes there to the distinct advantage of the Prince. In North Holland, Friesland, Groningen, and other places, Philip's officers were ejected and nominees of the States-General were accepted. In many instances, however, the movement was only partially Protestant. When Haarlem, Amsterdam, and other cities threw off the Spanish garrison and accepted the Prince's, the persistence of the fidelity of Catholics to the Church was quite as firm as had been the tenacity of the Protestants. This was especially true of the citizens of Amsterdam. The city was very reluctant to throw in her fortunes with Orange, and many of the Catholics preferred emigration to accepting the articles offered them. Others resorted to casuistry in order to keep their property and their places. They reasoned that the oaths were demanded illegally and therefore might be taken with mental reservations, that the subscribers did not mean what they swore to "although their words might seem so."

In the spring of 1577, the chief provisions of the Perpetual Edict were fulfilled and Philip's ratification of it was in Don John's hands when he made his long-delayed entry into Brussels on May 1st. In delivering the ratification to the Estates, the new Governor expatiated to the people on Philip's wonderful love for the

Netherlands, but Don John's aspect rather belied
his words, for his mood did not correspond to the
splendour of the official entry into the capital
with all the fantastic forms beloved of the Netherlands. The disappointed young man was firmly
convinced that there was no scope for his genius
within the government, no prospect for his
energies beyond it, and he was thoroughly unhappy. He trusted none of the nobles who
surrounded him, not the weak Aerschot, "the
lamp lighted by Champagny after dinner,"[1] nor
his insignificant brother, Havré, nor the untrustworthy Champagny himself. He knew that they
were jealous of Orange and yet, regarding him
as an aid against Spain, were unwilling to shove
him wholly aside.

Bad and good, all alike want liberty of conscience
and they will never be diverted from this idea by
kindness,—only by energetic measures[2] [writes Don
John to Philip, May 31st]. The people here are
simply bewitched by him [Orange]. They love him,
they fear him, and want him as over-lord. They
tell him everything and do nothing without consulting him (*Ellos le aivisan de todo, y sin èl no resuelven
cosa*).

Three days earlier, Don John reported that
Orange had urged Aerschot not to trust the King
at the risk of his head, saying that Philip had never
yet learned to keep faith with heretics. The Prince

---

[1] Blok, iii., 115.   [2] *Cor. de Ph.*, v., p. 383.

had further said that he was bald and a Calvinist
and as such he would die (*que es ya calbo y cal-
banisto*). The Spanish pun is lost in English.[1]

With complete distrust in everybody, Brussels
did not seem safe to Don John. In mid-June he
retreated to Mechlin, sulked awhile, and then it
chanced that Margaret of Valois passed down the
Meuse to Spa to take the waters at the springs
and to discover if there were any prospect for
an honourable post for her brother, the Duke of
Anjou, in the Netherlands.

Don John went to Namur to give the traveller
hospitable greeting on her way. After seeing her
off, he started to go hunting, but suddenly he
seized upon the citadel of Namur and entrenched
himself within, behind Spanish lances, in a distinctly hostile attitude towards the Netherlanders,
who had so recently feasted him in "his" capital
of Brabant.

The news of this exploit was not well received
at Madrid.

> I regret more than I can express [writes Philip
> to Granvelle, October 17th] these last troubles, and I
> should be very sorry if they should progress so far
> that it would be necessary to adopt a different policy
> than the present. I desire nothing so much in my
> life as to see peace and tranquillity reign in these
> lands,—so as to avoid the need of force and the damage

---

[1] Gachard, *Cor.*, iii., p. lxiv. Don John added that Orange
hated Philip more than anything in the world and would like to
drink the king's blood.

that results therefrom. For this motive and because
my brother's co-operation can not procure us the
desirable boon, as he has, I learn, antagonised the
States by this last revolution of Namur, it seems to
me that it would be well for you and my sister Mme.
de Parma to go to Flanders. . . . Don John will
show you the letters I have written to my brother
so that you may be informed of my plans and
intentions.[1]

It was true that the Estates gradually lost all
confidence in Don John and Orange hastened to
make capital out of their distrust. Skilful arguments were brought to bear. On September 6th,
it was resolved to invite the Prince to come to
Brussels. The arguments used to bring the
majority to this point were not wholly pacific,
and it is more than probable that Orange knew
of the manipulations without wishing to take
cognisance of their details. The disturbance did
not take on a religious character, being indeed
rather more Orangist than Calvinist. Sufficient
ascendancy was gained in the city councils by
the Prince's sympathisers to ensure a warm
reception for him when, on September 23rd, he
made, in his turn, formal entry with public honours
into the city which he had left informally under
a cloud ten years previously. His reception was
graced by as splendid performances as those in
Don John's honour, and there was every appear-

[1] *Cor. de Granvelle*, vi., p. 274.

ance of universal enthusiasm. Orange was at the very zenith of his popularity.

On the other hand, the Spanish troops, whose departure had been so long in dispute, were turned about-face when they reached Genoa and hurried back to the Netherlands under Alexander Farnese, Prince of Parma, son of the former Regent, Margaret. He joined his young uncle at Namur and the era of apparent good feeling was at an end. There was no possibility of a perfect understanding of the situation on Philip's part and without comprehension of the force of Protestant individualism, adjustment was impracticable. *Cretisandum semper cum cretense* was repeatedly urged as an excuse for the use of "political methods" on the part of Orange, and all the negotiations of the patriots will not bear the closest scrutiny.

UNION MEDAL AFTER
RUPTURE OF PEACE NEGOTIATIONS

CHAPTER XVI

SOME FAMILY LETTERS

1576-1578

AS a background to all this excessively complicated play of public events, Orange had now a household of his own for an occasional refuge, a household not, indeed, settled, being now in one town and now in another, but always centred around a devoted wife, ready to aid in public enterprises when a woman's word was possible, and to give the warmest sympathy to her husband at all times. Convent training certainly did not unfit Charlotte of Bourbon for the duties of wife, mother, and intelligent helpmate. She fulfilled them with conscientious pleasure.

The marriage that had seemed almost insensate to the Prince's friends, really gave him a comrade deserving of his confidence and a consort capable of representing him fitly in his absence. The establishment directed by this Princess of Orange was conducted on a very different scale from that Brussels residence to which people had flocked for the sake of the good things standing night and day on the buffet. Often the family were in modest lodgings in some town where circumstances demanded an official sojourn. Instead of there being space and to spare for any visitor with little or no claims upon his host, rooms had to be hired in the neighbourhood to accommodate the Prince's nearest relatives.

In the summer of 1576, when Orange was making great strides towards popularity throughout the provinces, exerting himself so strenuously that he hardly had time to "breathe from morning to night," Charlotte was at Delft, with her small daughter, Louise Juliana,[1] born March 31st. In a postscript to his letter to John (April 4th), announcing the event, the Prince adds:

M. my brother, since writing, yours of the 17th ultimo has arrived, in which you mention that there is prospect that the Duke of Saxony and the Landgrave may try to make trouble about the obligations assumed by you and my other brothers in regard to "her of Saxony." I am not afraid of this, because they really have no foundation for their accusations, and I cannot believe they will take any steps. In regard to my son Maurice, I would be quite willing for them to take him and bring him up, but should be sorry that he should have training like that of Duke Francis van der Lauenburg. So if they come after Maurice, you may answer that you must consult me first, and then we can act as may seem advisable at the moment. At the same time, I could get

[1] Married, 1593, to the Elector Palatine. Her birth made it important to settle the legality of the separation from Anne.

your opinion and that of our relations and good friends.[1]

This somewhat time-serving statement is typical of many of the Prince's political utterances that summer. It is the period of the highest hopes and it is also the period of the leader's most marked opportunism. He is ready to seize every passing advantage and use it as best he can. Never does he let himself be hampered by an inconvenient theory. But the stable element in his life is Charlotte.

Monseigneur: It is indeed to my deep regret [Charlotte writes] that all the labour and pains you have undergone down there have not succeeded according to our hopes. I am especially troubled to hear of the accident to the big ship, and of the loss you have suffered in the Admiral's death, for I do not doubt you will be in much perplexity as to whom to put in his place. The Sire de Viry told me that Count Hohenlohe had brought you some assistance, which I was glad to hear, as I am also to know that you wish me to join you; but as I am still very weak I have not dared to ask your counsel since this first report from Zierikzee, lest I might have new cause for new fear. I will wait here seven or eight days, during which I will, please God, take the air as far as The Hague, to see how I feel. As to your daughter, she is very well. I have asked whether it would be dangerous to take her on the sea. Many say no. Nevertheless I beg you to tell me what to do. I have not failed to show

[1] Groen, v., p. 335.

your letters, as you commanded me, to the Estates. I hope the news from France will be to your satisfaction, and then it will be to mine. I am content if you are, and if I can be assured of your good health, to which I beg you to pay attention.

Your very humble and obedient wife as long as she may live,

C. DE BOURBON.

At Delft, June 2d, 7 in the evening.[1]

It is especially strange that the Prince should have thought, even for a moment, of entrusting his second son to alien guardians, when his eldest son was being so diligently educated directly counter to his wishes. Yet Philip William of Nassau in the University of Alcala seems not to have been alienated from his own kinsmen. In this same summer he writes the following note to Count John. Possibly permission to do this was part of the King's conciliatory policy.

Monsieur: I do not doubt that you will think it strange to have received no news from me in this long time, considering the great obligation I feel myself under to you and to all my relations and friends over there, both from the natural bond of affinity between us, as from the continual assistance you have so loyally shown my father during his adversities. But, knowing the little convenience and dangers of the time and place where I am, I hope that my failure to write will be attributed to them, rather than to default of my duty or negligence. The bearer

[1] Groen, v., p. 366.

of this will give you fuller information, and I beg you to give entire credence to him. May the all powerful God send me the means of deserving all His mercies, and give you, monseigneur my uncle, good health and long life and the sum of your desires.

In recommending myself to your good graces, entirely your very affectionate nephew ready to serve and obey you,

P. WILLIAM OF NASSAU.

To Count JOHN OF NASSAU.

From Alcala, June 30, 1576.[1]

Is it design or accident that the exiled student reduces his first name to an initial and writes out his second in full?

Philip William's own sister, Marie, had been almost as much separated from their father as the Count of Buren, but her lot had been singularly happy in the midst of the Dillenburg household, where she was a devoted granddaughter to Juliana of Stolberg and on terms of filial intimacy with her uncle. There is nothing formal or perfunctory about her letters. They have a tendency to be almost as voluminous as the Prince's, although her pen runs on less easily to the unfamiliar father than to the uncle,—less easily too in French, in which language she writes with pleasant sympathy in her father's affairs, domestic and public.

---

[1] Groen, i., p. 369. MS. in Orange-Nassau family archives. The writing is very clear.

I cannot tell you how pleased I am to hear that Madame has a little daughter and that she and my little sister are doing fairly well. It is a matter for great satisfaction as you wrote me that Madame being *enceinte* suffered acutely from hostile aspersions. Now that Monsieur has won three forts I hope the enemy will not annoy him so closely. As to Zierikzee I trust our Seignior will graciously permit it to be revictualled, etc.

Again, later in the summer, she writes:

Monsieur, my well-beloved father: On the 12th instant I received your letter [and am delighted to hear, etc.] . . . As to my uncle and Madame I know nothing more to tell you than that they are well and we are all here at Count Albert's on a hunt and have taken many stags. I would that Monsieur were here so that you might have a little pastime, for I am very sure you have not any now but much business and worry which troubles me greatly whenever I think of it, but I hope by God's grace that He will soon free you. I am delighted to hear by your last letter that your affairs in Brabant go so well . . . and that the result will be good firm peace, which I desire from the bottom of my heart so that one day I may see Monsieur and Madame in tranquillity.

Further, as to what Monsieur has written me regarding the chamberlain and others in charge of my brother Maurice, that I should give them what seems reasonable, I do not know just what to do. I am afraid of giving too much or too little. I wish you had said how much, but since that cannot be, I will ask my uncle what he thinks I could give and will go by his advice, for certainly the chamberlain has taken great pains and, as I hear, Maurice behaves pretty well. I hope that will continue. . . . From Otweiller in Wetterich, October 15, 1576.

> Your very humble and obedient-to-death daughter,
> MARIE DE NASSAU.

My sister Anne begs me to give you her compliments. She would have liked to write, but it was not possible because she has a bad headache.[1]

Juliana of Stolberg, too, keeps an active interest in her son's projects. She is very solicitous about the articles in the peace that relate to religion.

High-born prince, heart-dear lord and son [she writes]: From the bottom of my heart am I longing for news as to how it goes with my lord in these troublesome affairs. If common rumour be true the imminent peace will impose conditions very irksome to soul and to conscience and Satan will be at hand in sheep's clothing and many pious will suffer. . . . Jesus Christ alone . . . can help in such peril. I implore my heart dear lord . . . to undertake or approve nothing contrary to God and to the welfare of my lord's soul. It is better to lose temporal weal rather than eternal. . . . I implore my lord not to allow himself to be persuaded to go to dangerous places for the world is full of craft. . . .

SIEGEN, April 4, 1577.[2]

Charlotte, too, felt that the "world was full of craft." In a postscript to a letter of May 22nd,

[1] Groen v. p. 428. [2] Jacobs, p. 276.

JULIANA OF STOLBERG
COUNTESS OF NASSAU

she writes to Orange: "Monseigneur: they have made me a present of some Brussels' sausages which I forward to you with the petition that you eat very sparingly of them and that you let the others do all the drinking. I am pretty well and your daughter even better."

The Prince begins to make plans for his other daughters who have grown almost out of his knowledge.

Your Grace's daughter, Fräulein Marie [writes Count John, May 26th], has shown me your letter desiring her to come to Holland. If your Grace wishes this for his own reasons, I will gladly further the plan to the best of my ability. But if my gracious lord is under the impression that she is any burden to me, I should be sorry, and would beg your Grace to banish such a thought and leave her with my housewife and me as long as possible, especially for the sake of my mother. She begins to fail perceptibly and if left too much alone gets melancholy and depressed. She counts much on your Grace's daughter who is very devoted to her grandmother and makes herself very useful with reading, writing, and giving out medicine and confitures and things of that kind. Her Excellency will be very sorry to lose this grandchild and thus have to sit alone. . . . My housewife has so much to do with the children and her housekeeping that she has little time to spare for her Excellency.[1]

The wish to retain her granddaughter seemed

[1] Groen, vi., p. 89.

an eminently reasonable demand in behalf of the old Countess, but her eldest son feels that his own plans for his children are more important, now that he has a suitable chaperon for them and he insists on having Marie and Anne and the ten-year-old Maurice,—the last-named withdrawn from Heidelberg,—sent to the Netherlands. When the Prince makes his entry into Brussels, the Princess thus has his eldest daughters with whom to share her hopes and fears about the precarious honours in the midst of dreaded latent enemies

Monseigneur: I am longing to hear [she writes] that you are back in Antwerp and shall not be easy until I am assured of that and whether Don John has received aid from Mons. de Guise. . . . Our girls, big and little, are well and so am I.[1]

Monseigneur: I arrived in this city [Dordrecht] at one o'clock and came with the boat to the lodgings where I found our little maidens in safety. The elder girls, hoping for your speedy return, would not stay longer in your rooms. They have found a good lodging, but it is farther away than I like, about fifteen houses intervening between our two.

To-morrow your surgeon will commence to treat M. the Count Maurice. . . . We are well and longing for your return. People here tell me that the Estates of these lands have asked you to return and are waiting for your opinion and you can give it better if you are here and if peace is made with Don John. I am sorry too, that M. your brother is away from you.

[1] Groen, vi., p. 172. Elizabeth was born May 3, 1577.

We wish he were here. Please write and ask him to
let you keep the tutor now with Maurice. That
gentleman is anxious at being uncertain about his
engagement and will be disappointed not to be employed permanently, now that he has stayed so long.
Also he ought to know what salary he will have. I
make you rack your brains with my questions, but I
needs must know your wishes. I also venture to
remind you that you ought to thank the Queen of
England for her kindness through her ambassador at
Brussels.[1]

Two days later, October 4th, she writes that
Breda has been delivered up by the Spaniards.
On its return to the Prince's authority many
points for decision are referred to her and she is
most anxious to give wise directions about the
garrison, etc.[2]

A letter of October 7th is happier in tone[3]:

Count John arrived in Dordrecht at one o'clock,
to the great satisfaction of burgomaster and people.
We, the girls and I, are happier than all the rest. We
have all just dined together and drank your health,
Monseigneur, longing for your presence. I will do
my very best to do what you direct, but the citizens
of this city are determined to put their gift in the
shape of a cup, the vase of which is *licorne* set in
silver. It is worth about a hundred pounds. If the
others do the same thing, it will be certainly a proof
of their good will, but I would like it better if all the

---
[1] Groen, vi., p. 173.   [2] *Ibid.*, p. 174.
[3] *Ibid.*, p. 180.

states together would make a present of something
serviceable. [Such a human wish on the part of a wife
who is trying to be economical on uncertain revenues!]
However, Monseigneur, I did not dare check this,
while it is to be hoped that the generality will supplement the shortcomings of the communities. . . . As
to the 1000 florins, I have asked Jen Back to see if
they can be furnished and where I can raise a part,
if he cannot raise it all. We, our girls and I, shall
miss your brother when he goes. While he is here it
does not seem as though you were entirely absent.
. . . We, the girls and I, are very fond of each other
and live very intimately and they take great care of
the little ones. . . .

I have received [October 8th] the present you sent
me from the Queen and I find it very pretty and well
made.[1] As to the signification of the lizard, it is said
that its characteristic is that if a snake attacks a
sleeping person, the lizard will arouse him. I think
it is you, Monseigneur, who have this attribute,—
you who watch over the Estates, fearing that they
may be bitten. . . .

Monsieur, I have just thought that we ought to
give something to the gentlemen who are with M.
your brother. If you approve, I will have your
portrait and mine made in one medallion or apart with
the device that you sent me. If there should be a
little chain to hang them on, tell me what value it
should be.

I hear [writes Orange to Count John, from Brussels,
October 9th] from the governor of Walcheren that
you are in Zealand. I am glad to know that you

[1] Groen, vi., p. 10.

Monseigneur jay resceu
part de la roine que jay
a la sinificacion de la cesar
est quant vngne perso
la cesar de se reueille ze
est atribue guy et veilles
dieu veille par sa grace
nons avons ven ce matin
la marquise de bergue qu
guy est de dixsept ans
quant ze vons voire

Monsieur ze viens
sont pres de monsieur
donner quelq chose s
vre pourtraict et le
a jour avec les devis
fauldroit quelq pet

FACSIMILE OF LET

it qu'il vous a plu mentioier de la
foit bien et iolimet faict quant
nt que lon escript que sa propriete
et quin serpent le veulx mordre
test a vous monseigneur a quy celle
s craingnent quy ne soits mordus
puissyes bien garder du serpan
t madame de merande et sa fille
belle et fort grande pour son age
bien regardee pour vous en dire
n senble ce 8 octobre sur les onse
          devent dine   henres. +

pour les gentilhomes quy
my mesanble leur fauldroit
t que ie face faire en or
en vngne medalle ou
le mendeues et st
our les pandre de quelle

have been well received. . . . Everything here is still ambiguous, as they will not come to a firm resolution, in spite of all my representations. Meanwhile, Don John goes on levying troops and fortifying himself, and his designs will soon be plain. I hope soon to go to Breda, where I shall have my wife come and I hope you can join us. . . .

Since writing the above, news has come that the Archduke Matthias, son of the late emperor, is on his way to the Netherlands, in lieu of Don John.[1]

The item in the postscript was true and significant. A new governor was indeed on his way to the Netherlands not, however, appointed by Philip but invited thither by the nationalist Catholics, to offset the Prince's influence, so steadily on the increase. A small group of nobles took fright at the situation, and the result of their intrigues was the sudden arrival of the Emperor's brother the Archduke Matthias on the scene. A mere puppet, he was simply put forward to give a show of royalty to the government of protest and to overshadow Orange. And how clever the Prince proved himself at this crisis! Instead of showing displeasure at the underhand proceedings of his alleged allies, he accepted their choice—propped up Matthias and ruled over his shoulder. He himself was made Ruward of Brabant, — that ancient title for a temporary governor being revived and bestowed upon him. When Orange took his oath on December 17th, the

[1] Groen, vi., p. 195.

States-General had already declared Don John a public foe. Revenues were henceforth to be at their disposal alone. The Pacification was confirmed in a new instrument; and Holland and Zealand agreed to allow the exercise of the Catholic rites. For the moment, union, moderation and toleration were in the ascendant.

All these events delayed the Prince's return to his family, whose plans were contingent upon his arrival. Charlotte is obliged to go alone to Breda, when that town is at last delivered to its hereditary seignior. "I do not think it can be before Monday or Tuesday [she writes in response to her husband's request that she shall take this duty on herself] because this city wishes to give your brother a banquet on Sunday.

"After closing my letter [she adds] I remember that I forgot to ask your wishes about the exercise of religion at Breda. Must it be secretly, or can I do as I do here?" [1]

Monseigneur: Since the despatches [she writes Oct. 11th] I sent you yesterday,[2] I have been troubled lest you may think that I am inconsiderate with my questions in the face of the difficulties which overwhelm you at present. I assure you that there is nothing I am more anxious to avoid, but the proper observation of the Pacification gives me much anxiety. However, I hope when you come you will be able to provide for it. Until you come I can think of nothing else.

[1] Groen, vi., p. 198.   [2] *Ibid.*, p. 199.

M. Taffin has withdrawn to Dordrecht until I tell him your decision.

Breda proved to be in better condition than was expected, and Charlotte finds her housecleaning a fairly easy task, but she has not the anticipated pleasure of staying there with the Prince. Antwerp seems a more fitting residence for her, and the united family are established in the castle there when the defeat of Gembloux brings consternation to all.

Wellborn, friendly, heart-dear father: I must let you know [writes Marie to Count John], that I have now received about six letters from you, and rejoice indeed at the proof of your goodness to me, and that you have not forgotten poor little Maiken. Indeed, I can not thank you enough. I would have liked to answer at once, but could not as I knew of no messenger to your Excellency, and I did not dare write on an uncertainty. Pray forgive me, and I will do better, with God's help. Pray forgive me, too, that I was so silly at parting from you, and never thanked you for all your goodness to me. I would have liked to do so, but was too sad for words. Your Excellency must take the will for the deed, and rest assured that if my father and all of us can ever serve you, we will not neglect the opportunity, and I hope to remain your true, filial, obedient daughter as long as I live. It was harder to part from you than I dreamed it would be, but as it cannot be otherwise I must perforce be content.

Your Excellency will probably have heard of the

changes which have taken place here since your departure—how our people have suffered defeat, and how the enemy have gained Gembloux and Louvain. I hope to God, things will come out right. The archduke, the Dukes of Aerschot, Havré, and other Brussels nobles are all here, with their wives. . . . I heard that your Excellency arrived safely at Nymegen, and rejoice especially to know that the Guelder folk are glad to have you, but it will be no little burden for you to stay away from home so long, and besides, you will find it very expensive. I only hope that they will deserve all your trouble, and will give you an opportunity of going home. I know how the mother and wife must be longing for you as it is a wearisome time since they have seen you.

Dear father, I must tell you that we are now lodged in the castle, and you can not believe how grievously cold it is. I am afraid if I stay here long, I shall be frozen stiff. Would it not be a joy to wake up and find myself in my beloved little room in Dillenburg—Well-a-day! I hope that may come in time. I must tell you, that your son Philip arrived four or five days ago. I cannot see that he is as pious as your Excellency says he has become, for it seems to me he is roguish and spoiled. I hope, though, that he will, come to his senses and grow rational.[1]

ANTWERP—in haste—Feb. 10th.

It can never go so well with your Excellency, that I would not wish it a thousand times better. How things are here, your Excellency has doubtless heard. The enemy have gained Aerschot, Sichem, and Dietz, where, as I hear, they exercise great tyranny, so that

[1] Groen, vi., p. 297.

the poor people are to be pitied indeed. There is a rumour that the enemy mean to advance to Maestricht and even to Mechlin. All is in God's hands. Further, heart-dear father, I must tell you that the Marquis of Havré is going to England to-morrow or next day, and wants to take my cousin, Count William, with him. As my father perceived that my cousin greatly desired to visit England, to see and learn something of the world, he thought this a good opportunity for him to make the journey in suitable company; he gave his permission and intrusted him to Lier, for which I was very glad, as you well know that he is a God-fearing noble. If my cousin William take him as a model, as I do not doubt he will do, he can learn no evil. Your Excellency would hardly believe how fine my cousin is now. He has grown much more lively than when he left you; I am sure you will be pleased when you see him. You may trust me, if it were not true I would not write it to you. The margrave only proposes to be absent a fortnight. I helped my cousin out with money as well as I could. I hope you will not be displeased at the project.

Your true daughter,
M. F. v. N. and O.

ANTWERP, March 8th, in great haste.

Then she writes again, March 15th, to tell Count John about the travellers in England. There was no need to worry about William. Lier would take good care of him. In dating her letter, she writes first "Dillenburg, in great haste," and adds: "Your Excellency can see where my heart is. As I was about to write 'Antwerp' out popped 'Dillenburg.' "

And again March 19th:

I am sorry to hear that the grandmother is so poorly, but after this long life of toil and trouble, we cannot hope for much else. Further, beloved father, as your Excellency writes that he has heard that I am betrothed to your eldest son, I must assure you that I can not wonder enough how people got hold of such an idea, *in which there is not a word of truth*. It is hardly a fitting time for such matters, and I think too, he cares nothing for me. If there were such a prospect be sure I would tell you at once. My father is thinking of taking Maurice from Breda and sending him to Leiden.[1]

Count John was at this time in Dillenburg, trying to arrange his private affairs, so as to assume the government of Guelderland, to which he had been appointed. The Prince had urgent need of his brother, whose faithful, honest disposition inspired confidence. His was a simple, direct nature, ponderous perhaps and sententious, but eminently reliable. And it was certainly a moment when Orange needed a friend at hand, in whom he could repose implicit faith. There were so many diverse interests to conciliate! The Catholic nobles, the Protestant Hollanders, whose sentiments were known; Elizabeth of England, in one mind one day and another the next; the

[1] Groen, vi., p. 301.

French Huguenots, who yet had to be so treated that the Catholic court would not refuse aid; the German mercenaries under John Casimir of the Palatinate; and Matthias and his backers. The latter were baffled first by the Prince's acceptance of their puppet and then by the complete inefficiency of that puppet.

At one epoch there were actually five different bodies of soldiers on the field,—the Malcontents as the Prince's Catholic critics were called, in Flanders, and the French on the borders, in addition to the Spaniards, the States' own troops, and the Germans come to help them.

The mission of the expedition to England which Count John's son was allowed to accompany, in order to see a little of the world, was to make it plain to Elizabeth that if she were not ready to give aid, the provinces were ready to admit the French troops hovering at the frontier and to accept Anjou's protection, whether she liked it or no. Nothing certain was obtained from her, however, the negotiations with France went on, and there was no dearth of opinions about it.

As to Count John [reports a certain news-gathering secretary of William of Hesse, July 15, 1578], I hear that the Estates of Holland and Zealand wish him as governor in the absence of the Prince of Orange. They offered him 18,000 florins salary. He declined. Now they have sent a special messenger to urge his acceptance, and I think he will let himself be persuaded, urged as he is by the Prince, notwithstanding that the condition of local affairs and the Spanish majority in many cities make him fear an uprising. Don John is turning his army in that direction. . . . The Duke of Alençon (Anjou) has declared roundly that he will have nothing to do with the archduke, but must treat directly with the States. When the archduke heard this, he burst into tears and asked the bystanders if aid could not be brought from Germany to resist the Spaniards without applying to France.[1]

It was indeed a *confusum chaos* where intrigue rather than statecraft was dominant. One anonymous pamphleteer acknowledges that his contemporaries can hardly hope to understand the truth under all the various negotiations and he begs his gentle reader to make a point of contradicting any false statements discovered in the letter he publishes, so that posterity may at last arrive at the truth. He adds that if any man's actions meet general approval something is sure to be wrong, for the public are fools.[2]

One more letter from the Prince to his wife may be given here, as an added picture of his confidence in her:

My wife, *ma mie* : Lauda arrived this morning at about nine o'clock bringing me your letters and those

[1] Groen, vi., p. 416.
[2] Hague pamphlets, 360. Letter dated Rouen, May 25, 1578.

of my brother and of M. de Sainte Aldegonde. As those of M. de Sainte Aldegonde were important I answered them immediately and begged him to give my excuses to you and my brother that I did not answer yours. Since then Count Hohenlohe arrived with your last. Now to answer both at once, I don't know what to say beyond my regret that in this state of affairs we cannot hope to see each other soon. Since I see by your last that some satisfaction can be given to the *commune* I cannot do better than take the advice of the Count of Schwarzburg, Sainte Aldegonde, and you. I am afraid it will be at least a fortnight before I can leave here. For the people are so divided in opinion that it takes time to make them all hear reason. . . . It may be, if affairs end as they now promise to, that I shall render a signal service to the whole country and even to those who do nothing but criticise me. But thank God, I am so accustomed to continual criticism that it does not trouble me, since I have the consciousness of proceeding openly in this matter without heeding anything but the weal and tranquillity of our *patrie*. . . . I hate to see all the dissensions but certainly much prefer to have them speak out openly. . . .

I write all this to you because M. de Sainte Aldegonde tells me that many are interpreting the work I am doing as if another intention were at the root of it, and as if I only wished to aggrandise myself. . . . If it would not put us to shame I would wish that every one knew my condition and in what extremity our affairs are. I am sure they would have more pity for, than envy of us. But one cannot give up. . . . M. de Boussu's illness saddens me greatly, especially as Lauda tells me that the doctors have

378   *William the Silent*   [1576-1578]

little or no hope. Please give me frequent bulletins. ... with affectionate recommendation, my wife, *ma mie*, etc. From Ghent, December 18, *anno* 1578.

Your very good husband for ever,

WILLIAM OF NASSAU.[1]

[1] Archives of the Duc de la Trémoille, Delaborde, p. 179.

ROYAL PEACE MEDAL
1577

CHAPTER XVII

THE UNION, THE BAN, AND THE ABJURATION
1578–1581

IN the summer of 1578, a convention called the *Religious Peace* was adopted by the States-General (July 22d) which embodied the Prince's ideas of a just and equitable *modus vivendi* for fellow-countrymen of different creeds.

The two main points were the absence of religious tests for office and the provision that in any locality one hundred householders of one communion were to be free to celebrate their own rites. The articles were not universally accepted by the constituents of the deputies, Guelderland objecting for Protestant, Hainault for Catholic reasons, and there were all shades of dissension in between. And even when accepted they were not put in force except imperfectly at Antwerp, where the measure met with the greatest degree of practical success. The Reformers came rapidly to the fore as soon as leniency was evinced toward them. Exiles returned from England and very shortly there were enough to fill twelve or thirteen churches. Probably, too, the Prince's residence in the city gave the sectarians a greater confidence, while it also ensured fair play for the Catholics. At the same time, his uniform and consistent refusal to ignore Catholic rights alienated many of his devoted evangelical adherents, whose eyes could see nothing but culpable indifference to truth in his course. The criticism was not only bitter but so indiscriminating as to attack Count John too, although, in point of fact, he had scant sympathy with his brother's liberal views and was far more interested in bringing those of the "faith" together than in any abstract question of toleration for all opinions.

To the Count's strenuous exertions was chiefly due the extension to a wider circle of the alliance between Holland and Zealand, an extension agreed upon in the important instrument known as "The Union of Utrecht," which became in course of time, though somewhat fortuitously, the basis of the constitution of the United Netherlands. It is one of the odd contradictions of the many in the story of the Prince's career and of his apotheosis as Founder of the Republic, that, probably, he had little part in casting this "Constitution," even as the mere confederation that it was, and accepted it with reluctance, many of its tendencies running diametrically counter to his most cherished convictions of the country's best interests.[1]

---

[1] There are divers opinions about the Prince's participation in this document and it must be acknow'edged that credit for it is

The Union of Utrecht is spoken of as an inner bulwark erected by the prevision of the prudent Prince within the outer walls of the Pacification whose crumbling he foresaw. The articles and the many contemporaneous explanations and commentaries show, however, that it was simply a defensive league between those of evangelical sentiments, and of Germanic speech, for the linguistic element was also a feature although one that is frequently ignored.

The fact that the contemporaneous Union of Arras, finally concluded in January, 1579, knit together the provinces predominantly Walloon and Catholic, shows how a tendency towards association of kind lay at the root of both "Unions," which proved to be the germ of final *dis*union in spite of the express assertion, contained in each document, that the signatories meant to adhere to the Pacification of Ghent and to strengthen that larger bond by their smaller inner fortified circles.

The Union of Utrecht became indeed the formal nucleus, as events turned out, of the later state; but the confederation of the seven component parts of that state did not by any means spring into being when the Union was signed, nor were

---

claimed in the *Apology*—yet the circumstances seem to justify the conclusion that he stood aloof and took the best that could be attained, disappointed the while at the result. Fruin, *The Union of Utrecht*, i., p. 38 *et passim*—Muller, p. 192; Blok, iii., p. 137.

all the first signatories comprised in the later republic. The articles discussed in the summer and framed in the autumn of 1578 received the first subscription on January 23, 1579, when Count John set his seal thereto in behalf of Zutphen and of Guelderland. The representatives of Holland, Zealand, Utrecht, and Groningen also signed on that day. On February 4th, Ghent followed suit, on March 23d, several cities of Friesland; July 24th, Antwerp; September 13th, Breda; February 1st, 1580, Bruges and the Free District; February 16th, Liège; and April 11th, Drente.

In a large measure, the "Union" undid and destroyed the work of unification that had been in slow progress since Philip the Good of Burgundy began to build up a realm out of a congeries of tiny states. The individuality of each political entity was reasserted in their articles of mutual alliance, and, in the tenacity with which that individuality was cherished henceforth, seed was sown for much of the dissension that blossomed rankly in the palmy days of the republic. This, in spite of the statement that all the subscribers were welded together as though they were but one province, "*alsof zij maar een provincie waren*. That phrase may be considered the Prince's sentiment, but it remained a phrase only and was never realised in fact.

Just as Orange had been wise in espousing the cause of Matthias, called in by the nobles to

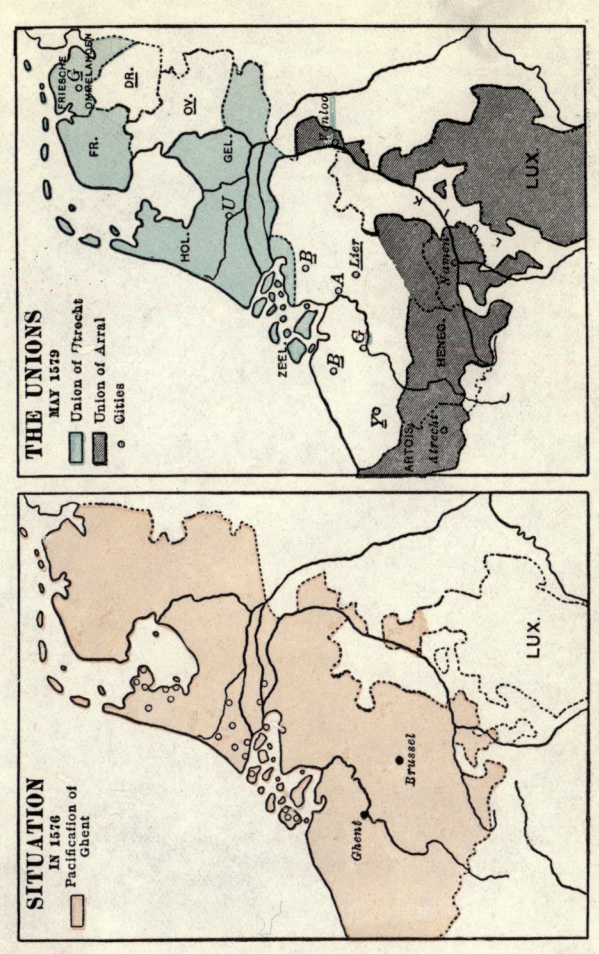

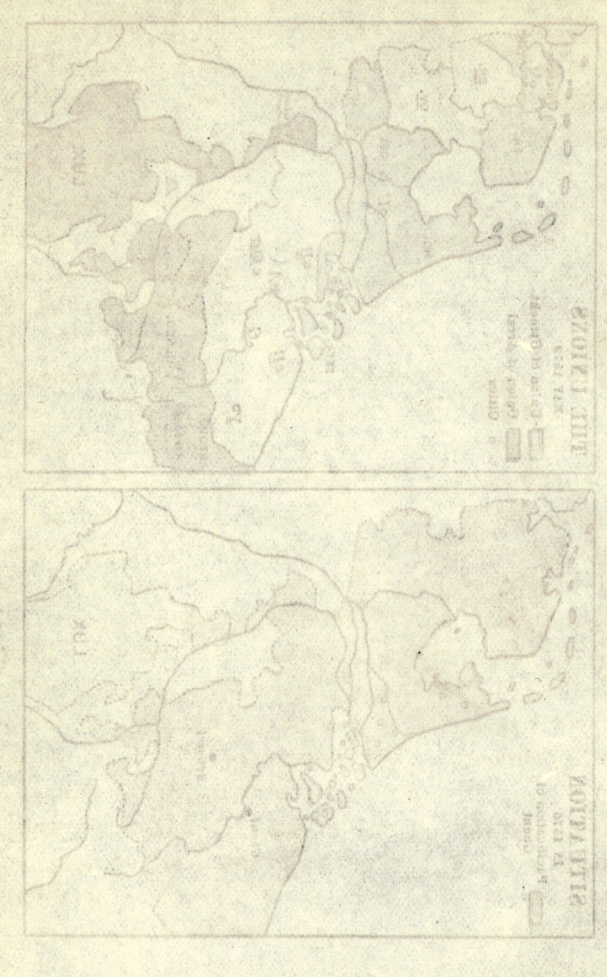

The Union, Ban, and Abjuration

weaken the Prince's credit and check his ascendancy, so he was equally astute in identifying himself with this Union to which he subscribed in May. He had waited thus long "because he cherished the hope of bringing all the provinces into the confederation." There was evident reluctance on his part to realise the truth that the breach between the two sections was to be irreparable—but accept it he did in his wisdom. By that time there was a new Spanish leader to reckon with.

The victory won by Don John at the battle of Gembloux had convinced him that he was on the road to success by arms after his failure in conciliatory diplomacy. He had Alexander Farnese with him, too, to share the responsibility. But there proved to be more disappointments to share than action. The two together could do little, so hampered were they by absence of funds and by presence of sickness in their camps. Don John, too, had changed sadly. When Farnese met his uncle on his arrival he was greatly shocked by his appearance. The emaciated, depressed, careworn man was a very different person from the eager, alert cavalier who had started off gaily from Spain in 1576. When a fever attacked him in August, Don John showed no power of resistance. After a time he was carried to the heights above Namur to try the effects of purer air than that of the camp reeking with pestilence. It was a miserable shelter in which the petted hero of Lepanto spent his last days, an old pigeon house having been hastily cleaned out for his use.

On September 20th the invalid wrote his last letter to his royal brother, who had paid no heed to him for months. "I assure your Majesty that the work here is enough to destroy any constitution and any life," is the phrase with which he ends his summary of difficulties with which he is beset. One sentence begging for specific orders was underscored, thus: "*La orden de como tengo de gobernare.*" When Philip had read this appeal, he wrote on the margin of the letter, "I will not answer the italicised words" "*Lo rayado no yo le dire*". As far as the writer was concerned an answer was needless. Don John was dead when his letter reached Spain.[1]

Before he expired (Oct. 1, 1578) he appointed his nephew his successor until Philip decided otherwise. The appointment was made permanent by the King and thus a new régime began for what remained of the loyal Netherlands.

Alexander Farnese, Prince of Parma, took up the office vacated by Don John and speedily showed himself far better fitted for the work in hand. The two were nearly of an age, Parma being about thirty-three when he entered on his career in the Netherlands. But the better success he met with was not wholly due to his greater skill either in diplomacy or in military affairs. Among the Catholics in the Walloon country there had

[1] Stirling-Maxwell, ii., p. 286.

been a marked revulsion of feeling. They took
fright lest Protestantism might be actually forced
upon them. They wanted nationalism but they
dreaded lest injury to the ancient Church should
follow in its wake. Orange found himself unable
to hold back even those who hated Spain and one
town after another embraced the reconciliation
offered by Parma in the King's name. The situation was far more favourable for such efforts than
it had been in 1576. Then the confederation
had seemed more attractive than loyalty. In
1578 its weakness had become apparent. As the
breach grew wider each party declared that the
other was the culprit in breaking the pledges of
the Ghent Pacification.

There was a curiously quick contemporaneous
comprehension of both facts and the humour of
the situation, if one may judge by a pantomime
exhibited in one of the Paris theatres, representing
this "reconciliation" of the repentant provinces.
Philip is introduced leading a nice gentle cow,
who suddenly becomes restive, kicks up her heels,
breaks loose, and starts to run away. Up rushes
the Prince of Parma and tries to mend the broken
rope while the States-General, too, make their
appearance *en masse*. Some members seize the
cow by the horns; others try to mount on her
back, while others simply stand aside and call for
help. As spectators there are the Emperor, the
French King, and the English Queen,—the latter
sympathising now with the cow and now with

her pursuers. Then Anjou appears and seizes the cow's tail, while Orange and Duke Casimir of the Palatine follow with milk pails and vainly try to milk the animal, until Parma stops their proceedings by getting firm hold of the broken halter and leading the beast triumphantly to Philip, Orange and Casimir being kicked over in transit. The comical side of the passing show was evidently not lost at short range.[1]

Ghent had entered the Union of Utrecht, but the seething unrest in which the city had been ever since October, 1577, showed no sign of abatement. In the spring, Orange sent appeal after appeal thither imploring the citizens to keep within bounds. "You are acting like a wounded man who tears off his bandage, like a lunatic who plunges a dagger into his own heart." His arguments only served to make the rabid reformers distrust his own sincerity. One of the ringleaders, Imbize, declared that Orange was nothing more than a papist in disguise, that he was parleying with France for his own benefit, etc. And the preachers went further. Pierre Dathenus, once a monk, declaimed openly against the Protestant leader. The Prince was an atheist, he could change his creed as readily as his coat, he cared nothing for God or religion, but made an idol of the state and of expediency, he would discard his shirt if it smacked of religion, etc., etc.

For a time, Orange took no notice of these

[1] Strada, ii., p. 42.

calumnies, but finally he adds a postscript in a letter to the Ghent burghers:

> I am informed that Master Dathenus has been stigmatising me as a man without religion or fidelity, as one consumed by ambition, etc. I do not think it needful to reply to his aspersions. I will only say that I am willing to submit to the judgment of all that know me.[1]

The Prince could afford to trust to those who knew him, but, naturally, among his adherents there were many who never came in actual touch and they began to grow cold, and to fall off from his ranks. Probably, however, this chilling of the former fervid enthusiasm for "Father William" was not immediately perceived in the hostile camp. In the summer of 1579 intimations found their way to the Prince's ear that Philip would be glad to make his submission well worth his while. Orange repudiated the suggestion and refused to have his interests separated in any particular from the States.[2] The tentative offer was made in the preliminary stage of an international congress at Cologne, assembled for the purpose of arranging an accommodation between Philip and his subjects. Philip showed his own zeal towards

---

[1] Groen, vi., p. 586; vii., p. 33.
[2] See *Apology*. But there is other testimony. Philip's envoy to the Cologne negotiation of that summer wrote in full to the King. See also Gachard, *Cor.*, iv., p. c. *et seq*. This was but one instance of the frequent efforts at international arbitration of the time.

that end by sending five august councillors with
the Duke of Terranova at the head to represent
him. All the powers of Europe were there by
proxy and they did not fail to bring skilled chefs
to help out their diplomacy with fine banquets.
But diplomacy, dainties, and wines alike were
incapable of reconciling the irreconcilable. No
peace at large was effected, while the gradual and
increasing defection of many from the party of the
rebels became known and soon convinced Philip
and his advisers that the tide was turning in the
King's favour, and if the Prince were only not
there to hold any back by the direct exercise of
his personal influence, the force of the rebellion
would be broken completely.

The clemency of your Majesty could lead them
[the Netherlanders] to repent [wrote Granvelle to
Philip, November 13, 1579] and refuse to expose their
life and their property any longer for the Prince of
Orange. As regards the Prince, it might be well to
follow the example of all the potentates of Italy and
offer a reward of 30 or 40,000 crowns to any one who
would kill him or deliver him up alive. As he is
pusillanimous, the very terror that such an offer
would inspire in him would be of a nature to cause his
death; or some desperate fellow, having seen the edict,
published in Italy and France, will be seduced by the
hope of gain and ready to strike the blow.[1]

This advice was followed. The King let loose

[1] *Cor. de Granvelle*, vii., p. 496.

over Europe a formal Ban, declaring that William of Nassau, Prince of Orange was an outlaw and that his death would be a public benefit. In the document, Philip rehearsed the story of his grievances, how Alva had gone beyond his instructions and imposed an unadvisable tax upon the provinces, how Orange had made capital out of that political mistake and had hastened back to the Netherlands from Germany to excite the King's subjects to rebellion. He had promised to be loyal to the King and to maintain the Catholic religion,—promises ruthlessly broken to God and man alike. He had married an abbess during the lifetime of his legal wife. The King had patiently tried to pacify this restless and contumacious malcontent, the one hostile element among his loving subjects. His late beloved brother had also vainly endeavoured to bring this obdurate rebel to terms. Orange did not desire peace. He had gone steadily onwards in rank rebellion, finally having himself elected Ruward of Brabant by a tumultuous and unruly assembly.[1]

Therefore, for all these just reasons, for his evil doings as chief disturber of the public peace and as a public pest . . . we banish him forever and forbid all our subjects to visit or communicate with him in public or in secret. . . . We declare him an enemy of the human race . . . and in order the sooner to remove our people from his tyranny and oppression,

[1] Dumont, *Corps diplomatique*, v., p. 365.

we promise, on the word of a king and as God's servant, that if one of our subjects be found so generous of heart and so desirous of doing service to us and good to the public, who has any means of executing this ordinance and ridding us of this said pest, either by delivering him to us quick or dead, or by depriving him at once of life, *in any way*, we will give the said person or his heirs, landed estates or cash at his desire, to the amount of 20,000 golden crowns. If he has committed any crime—of any kind whatever—we will pardon him; if he be not noble, we will ennoble him for his valour, and if the principal takes other persons for his assistance in his enterprise, we will reward them according to the service rendered, pardon their crimes, and ennoble them too.

This proclamation was sent to the Netherlands with orders that it should be published by the governors, "so that none can claim ignorance." The Prince of Parma was very loath to do his uncle's bidding in regard to this Ban. He thought it was possible that Orange might win more sympathy than obloquy if he were so publicly offered as a mark for the dagger of any assassin. He had proposed to take advice of the reconciled provinces on the subject. Philip set aside this suggestion, but Parma did not hasten to execute the final commands. The Ban was not printed until July 2nd, and not really published by the councils until late in August, 1580.

The Prince's answer to this proscription is a

long document, already referred to as the *Apology*.[1] It is addressed to the States-General and has nothing apologetic in its tone. Though written in the first person and purporting to come from the Prince, its composition has been attributed to Pierre Villiers, a reformed minister, and again to Hubert Languet. In the writings of the latter there are, indeed, many phrases like those in the *Apology*. Still it cannot be denied that the mark of the Prince's mind is evident throughout every paragraph to anyone familiar with his letters, formal and informal. It certainly is not a work of literary art. It falls far short of Languet's style in his letters to Philip Sidney. It is too long, too verbose, and loosely put together.

If the King were scathing in his denunciations of the rebel leader, it must be conceded that the latter (assuming that Orange endorsed if he did not frame the sentences) repaid him in kind and showed an equal hospitality towards all damaging rumours about the King's deeds without discrimination between the proved and the unproved. Philip's character is painted in the darkest colours and every idle imputation is referred to as a fact.

The whole story of the Prince's life, his relations with the late Emperor and the present King are reviewed. The writer defends his every loyal action up to the time of Alva's coming, and justifies himself in his disloyal course since that date,

[1] Dumont, v., p. 384. *Apologie de Guillaume de Nassau.* Editor A. Lacroix.

as he claims that Philip had forfeited all his hereditary rights to the individual provinces by his violations of the time-honoured charters of the land. He quotes Demosthenes in saying that distrust was the bulwark of a nation against tyranny. Philip himself had planted distrust deep in the hearts of his would-be obedient subjects, and a free people had revolted, as had happened before in similar but far less aggravated circumstances. He reminds Philip that "I was born a free lord and have the honour of bearing the name of an absolute prince, although my principality is not of great extent." He points out that the imposition of the taxes had been unfair, unjust, and entirely illegal, but that the people had protested, not only against them but also against the suppression of liberty of conscience. He defends bitterly his personal reputation.

It suffices for me to say in one word to you, gentlemen, and to all Europe, that every Spaniard or Spanishised person, no matter of what rank he may be, who says, or who will say, as this infamous proscription asserts, that I am a traitor and a miscreant, that same person has spoken falsely and against the truth. . . . If you, gentlemen, judge that either my absence or my death can serve you, I am ready to submit to your judgment. Here is my head, over which no prince nor monarch but you has control. Dispose of it for your welfare, for the preservation of your republic. But if you judge that the mediocre experience and industry which I have acquired by patient toil, if you judge that the remnant of my property and my life can serve you, take them and let us work together for the defence of this good people. If you will continue the favour you have hitherto shown me, make your resolution for the preservation of this land and *"je le maintiendrai."*

On December 13th the Prince appeared before the States-General, sitting at Delft and was present at the reading of his letter, accompanying his *Apology*.

Messieurs: You have seen a certain sentence in the form of a proscription sent hither by the King of Spain and published by the Prince of Parma. . . . I have taken the advice of many notable persons . . . and am counselled to do nothing to satisfy my honour but to publish a statement showing how unjustly I am accused. Recognising you gentlemen, alone, as my superiors, I present to you my *Apology*, in which I not only unmask the impostures of the foe, but justify my every action as legal.

He ends by saying that he had tendered his resignation again and again to the States, but he was still ready for the future as he had been in the past to lay down his life for his country's good. He expressed a hope that his paper would be printed, so that "the whole world may judge my case."[1]

Four sessions (December 13th to 17th) were consumed in hearing and discussing the *Apology*.

[1] *Res. des états-gen.*, Dec. 13, 14, 17, 19. Gachard, *Cor.*, vi., 41.

It was finally resolved that the Ban was as insulting to the Estates as to the Prince; and a vote of entire confidence in the latter was passed. His answer contained nothing but the truth, etc. He had accepted office only in response to earnest entreaty and they refused to consider his resignation. Thus he was completely supported by his official chiefs.

The Ban declared the Prince without the pale of the law and it was natural that his answer should give the best view of himself as not only within it but standing on the loftiest pinnacle of right action. There is an instinctive aversion to hearing self-praise,—therefore there are parts of the *Apology* which leave the reader cold. Again, there are many inaccuracies of statement, when checked by other evidence. Part of the apparent self-appreciation, as part of the inaccuracy, may be due to the secretary, whether he were a scholar like Languet or a mere scribe, part to forgetfulness of items when events have crowded so close upon each other. If Orange were the author the *Apology* does not show him at his very best. But allowance must be made. He was sorely tried. One noble after another had passed from his camp to Parma's as though leaving a sinking ship and he had to bear other attacks on his honour from behind his back in addition to the Ban.

Since my *Apology* was written a false letter forged by my enemies has fallen into my hands, purporting to have been sent by me to the Duke of Anjou, or as they say, Alençon, and intercepted by them. Copies have been distributed over Christendom. This letter is so uncouth in style and in matter that anyone might by casual reading discover that it is but an impudent invention, unworthy of answer.[1]

In the forged letter occur the following passages:

As to religion, that is plain and clear. No sovereign ought to be hampered by consideration of it. By means of the fortresses and garrisons your Highness will easily master the chief Flemish and Brabant cities, even in face of opposition. *Afterward you can compel them without difficulty to any religion which may seem* conducive to the interests of your Highness.

Such words were well calculated to cause distrust in the minds of those already weakened in their allegiance to Orange by zealots like Dathenus. Defection had begun to be very serious even before the publication of the Ban.

"It is rumoured [writes Count John to his brother] that the eldest son of my brother-in-law de Berghes has taken a regiment over to the Prince of Parma. I still hope for the best and shall hear within two days."[2] The rumours proved true, and this defection of one of the Nassau family was a heavy blow.

[1] To the States-General. Groen, vii., p. 380. In the collection of pamphlets at The Hague, there is abundant evidence of the wavering public opinion at this epoch. *Apologie*, p. 37.

[2] Groen, vi., 642.

"I could not leave the Prince just now [writes Count John, July, 1579], as he is deserted by nearly everyone except the Governor of Friesland and myself."[1] Even this modest numbering of the Prince's friends proved an over-estimate. The said governor was George de Lalaing, Count of Rennenberg. In March, 1580, he too deserted and received "as the price of his virtuous resolution to return to his sovereign, 10,000 crowns down, 10,000 in three months, and a pension."

Even though realising his brother's lonely position, Count John became more and more desirous of resigning his own office in Guelderland. His position there was painful in the extreme. No salary for his services was forthcoming. Often he had no cash for baker or butcher and his house was out of repair. Not only did he think the political future dark but he was anxious to give his entire attention to his private affairs. His wife had died. His motherless children, whom he was trying to educate at the least possible expense needed his care. Moreover he felt that it was incumbent on him to take a new wife. Indeed his first thought in that direction came very promptly after his loss, as is evident from this letter to his confidential friend:

Dear Doctor Schwartz: In order to have your advice freely on a certain matter, I will not conceal from

[1] Groen, vii., 35.

you a vision I had about it. On the 21st of last July,
I was very anxious at having had no news from my
sainted spouse. Just as I was going to bed, I called
my servants in to know what they had heard from
her Excellency, and felt, although they would answer
nothing, that all was not well with her. Then I went
to sleep, very heavy hearted, and that same night
I thought I was married again to the Fräulein we
were speaking of, and I dreamed it so often that I was
annoyed. On the following morning when the sad
tidings were announced to me by my servants and
the Prince's messenger, sorrow made me forget my
dream; but after the lapse of several months, when
the dowager electress was suggested to me among
others, not only did that dream occur to me, but also
something else. As far as I know I have never spoken
a word to the maiden all the days of my life, but I
remember hearing both from my sainted spouse and
from the Prince's daughter, that she had quite an
inclination for me. Once she sent me a message
through my late wife and my niece that I might always trust her. Of course, my marriage with the old
electress would be pious, virtuous, and on many
accounts advisable for me; moreover she has borne
her cross, knows how to treat gentlemen, and when
she should be patient, but as she has already had
two husbands and is rather older and taller than I am,
I do not feel altogether drawn towards her.

The Prince rather favours the old one, while the
Princess and the Prince's daughters prefer the young
lady. So I have come to the conclusion you will see
in the enclosed instructions. Will you, in as quiet a
manner as possible, make inquiries about this person,
what kind of a mind, head, and character she has,

and then talk to my mother about it at the first opportunity? If there be no reason why such a marriage should not take place with conscience and honour, just begin the negotiations. Do not allow any needless gossip [*allerhand unnütz Geschwetz*].[1]

On April 9, 1580, John sends Count Ernest of Schauenburg a long epistle. After descanting on affairs in general he says:

The States-General will meet in eight or ten days to discuss three points: item,—government for the whole Netherlands; item,—the better maintenance of military affairs; item,—how to come to an understanding with Alençon. The land is loath to take this step, but there is no other alternative, etc., etc. The Prince, thank God, is pretty well, and so are his wife and children. He is in fairly good spirits in spite of incredible labours, dangers, and fatigues. You could not believe that any man could endure so much, and you would rejoice if you could see him. His two eldest daughters are not yet married; perhaps something will be done about it soon. Count Gunther and his wife are fairly well, as times go. His Honour manages to have plenty to eat and drink, and to gather a pleasant company around him. Nothing is lacking to him except that he is not sufficiently paid, and he is often tormented with the gout, and my sister with the toothache. If his debts were only settled they would certainly lead a stately existence. Until that happens, his Honour, as well as I, is driven to borrow money from time to time, and

[1] Groen, vii., p. 323.

he is often forced to send both his plate and my sister's jewels on a little pleasure trip. As for myself, I keep fresh and sound, but am very poor, and tired out with so much work. If I wanted titles, or were willing to enrich myself without remorse or consideration for the nation's stress, I have had opportunities enough to do so, etc.[1]

There was soon greater reason for a new mistress at Dillenburg, for when Count John finally took a leave of absence and returned home, he was too late to say farewell to the mother about whom his own family life had centred for so many years. To the very last, Juliana of Stolberg kept in close touch with her distant children. In the midst of a fever which attacked Orange in June, he writes to her apologising for being so bad a correspondent. She would understand if she could see his pressure of business. He promises that Marie shall write, and Charlotte does so by the same courier, speaking of her husband's overweight of work, of his fever and recovery, adding modestly as a loyal daughter-in-law, who feels that she is of less importance to the Countess than her son and grandchildren:

As to myself, I am as usual and very happy with our big and little children and only wish I might have the honour of seeing you once more in this life. My eldest, Louise Juliana, says you would love her the best because she has your name. She begins to speak German and is tall for her age.[2]

[1] Groen, vii., p. 327. [2] *Ibid.*, p. 367.

These letters were the last ever written to the old dowager, who had given so many offspring to the world and yet passed out of it without either son or daughter by her side. Juliana's married daughters were all scattered far and wide. One granddaughter there was in Dillenburg, the eleven-year-old Emilie, the Prince's child, whom he had scarcely seen since her unfortunate mother gave birth to her. John's little boys had been sent away with due consideration to that ever-needful economy in the plans made for them; and Fräulein Juliana had been placed under the charge of the Landgravine "without costing us a penny," as the sympathetic and economical Dr. Schwartz informs the Count.

Thus it chanced to be a favourite nephew, Count Ernest of Schauenburg, staying at Dillenburg, who was the sole kinsman to hear Juliana's last good-night and her wish that he should have "what his soul and body needed and a pleasant morrow for the next day." That was on the evening of June 17th. To her own next day there was no full morrow, though she was still able to give a silent blessing to Ernest before death came at eight o'clock. The word of her serious condition reached even her nearest children too late for them to be at her bedside in time.[1] Her daughter Elizabeth and the Count of Solms-Braunfels travelled hastily through the summer night and arrived after her voice was

---

[1] Jacobs, *Juliana v. Stolberg*, p. 276.

WILLIAM OF NASSAU, PRINCE OF ORANGE, 1581

silenced. Only a few of the many children and cousins were present at the funeral, on June 22nd, but their absence was not from lack of respect or affection. Juliana's memory was warmly cherished. Twenty maidens, big and little, were known by their grandmother's name at the time of her death, and it would be difficult to enumerate all her namesakes in the European courts between 1580 and 1909, when the wee Princess Juliana of the Netherlands revived memories of, and tributes to the ancestress, freshly honoured in her baptism.

More than a hundred living descendants survived the Countess of Nassau. In three hundred years the male lines have died out, in spite of the very large families in each generation. But through the daughters there are still many survivors of her blood and some of the soundest and most intelligent men and women of the royal families could trace descent to her.

The loss of his mother hastened both John's departure from Guelderland and his marriage plans. He was glad to get home where he could settle affairs to his liking without being called on to cudgel his brains over insoluble problems or to attempt to satisfy discontented as well as alien people. In regard to a second alliance, he decided that the late Elector Palatine's daughter Cunigunde was a more suitable *partie* than her stepmother.[1]

---

[1] The dowager was Emilia de Nuenar, widow of **Henry Brederode** before her marriage to the Elector-Palatine.

The complaisant Dr. Schwartz admitted the desirability of giving weight to the Count's dream as to his choice, and further offers the opinion that certainly "it would look odd to see the Countess taller than the Count when they were in company or walking on the street together." The wedding was celebrated in September. Charlotte's letter of congratulation, accompanying the Prince's regrets that they could not be present, is very cordial. She had loved the bride as a sister in the Heidelberg days and looks forward to greeting her soon in their new relationship.

To what degree did these family matters really influence the Count's retirement and how large a part did his distrust of his brother's French policy play in his extreme reluctance to take a prominent rôle in Netherland affairs? Probably his anti-French prejudice was a factor. He seems to have felt far more at ease in discussing the complications of Netherland affairs and the dangers of this scheme of protection with the Landgrave, with Lazarus Schwendi, and with other Germans than with Orange. All the above concluded that it was a terrible medley, a *confusum chaos*. There was complete concensus in this opinion, whether expressed to the Prince himself or to others about his affairs. And letters of cautious advice were fairly explicit. "*Do not go too far with* the slippery and treacherous French, under whose sail neither state nor prince has ever entered port." "Do not commit the grave error of driving out the Archduke, whose presence has preserved your authority through confusion." "Believe, when God blinds men, then destruction, is at hand." "There will be a more bitter feeling against the French than the Spanish King, who is lord by nature and can thus justify himself."

One answer to these warnings drafted by Orange was couched in such bitter terms about German lukewarmness that the Prince thought it impolitic to send it. A second is more moderate, but he makes it plain that he cannot accept any advice of the kind offered.

Those who owed us aid are deaf to our prayers. What can we hope from reform within the Church? Germany's experience has proved the futility of such a scheme. Was not the Council of Trent as long as the trunks of ten elephants, only to end in a flat condemnation of Protestants as heretics and excommunicants?[1]

These lands are in more danger than is Germany. If you realise, as you seem to do in your letters, that it is impossible to remedy the troubles without granting free exercise of religion, I fail to see your ray of good hope, as there is the same disposition as ever to root out pure religion. In my simple judgment, your phrase can be turned "when God blinds men, their ruin is at hand." For they [the enemies of religion] will not see the deplorable condition of Christendom, the ruin of flourishing states, and the advance of the Turks, and think only of extirpating

[1] Groen, vii., p. 230.

those whom they ought to protect. So, monsieur, it seems to me that if this land, seeing itself so ill treated, resolves to change its prince,—which I am not yet sure it will do,—the blame should be cast on those who are the cause, and not on the poor sufferers.

And if, in this case, they find themselves obliged to abandon the Archduke—whose humble servant I am, and I would feel more than any living man if harm or indignity came to him—it is not their fault, but the fault of those who from lightness of heart, or from some trivial reason, have withdrawn their hand from him, and abandoned him entirely. Is it not true that his imperial Majesty refused to acknowledge his title of governor, which other strangers accorded him? Also, in this last treaty at Cologne, his Majesty's commissioners were surprised that the States-General of this land demanded him for governor, and rejected that article entirely. Besides, not only by connivance, but also by express testimony, verbally and in writing, they have approved the act of the provinces who separated from the "generality" of the Estates, and allied themselves to Spain, by which his Highness was deprived of his governorship, with the same frivolity with which they summoned him, without even informing their allies of their action.

If the Emperor and Princes made so little of having approved his rejection, what hope could be given to the people, of aid from him, abandoned by every one, even by those who are the nearest, and have the strongest reason to wish him to remain? What fault can be imputed to those if, in their necessity, they turn to another? Everyone knows that I have done my best to honour him, though I was not consulted on his coming. . . . Schwarzburg and M. des

Pruneaux assured me that, if I could hold the treaty with M. Anjou in abeyance for three months, I would do service to the House of Austria.—The negotiation has not only been delayed three months, but nearly two whole years, by which any one can see that we have not thrown ourselves headlong into the arms of the French. His Majesty had plenty of time to come to a decision had he wished. You undoubtedly mean well, but there are pensioners of Spain about the Austrian court who have done their best to do us damage.

As to the slippery and fraudulent nature of the French, pray, what title can be given to the Spaniards and the Spanishised, who have thrown not only their subjects, but their allies into servitude and destitution? The reputation of those who had these provinces under their domination is far worse than the fame of those who united Brittany, Guienne, Burgundy, or Piedmont to France.

The Prince's mind was completely made up and in spite of difficulties and criticism he paved the way for Anjou's coming to the Netherlands as protector. The Treaty of Plessis les Tours, providing for this event, was ratified by the States-General on December 30, 1580, and further confirmed in France by the Treaty of Bordeaux, January 23, 1581.[1] Before the reception of this French quasi-sovereign, a determination had been reached to abjure Philip's sovereignty; to sever definitely a tie which it was claimed depended from God himself.

[1] Lavisse, v., p. 198.

The Flemings [says the royalist Renon de France] violated the faith which Nature herself teaches each nation to cherish for her legitimate sovereign.[1] Many people trembled with apprehension, which was increased by a terrible earthquake felt in Flanders and as far as Paris.[2]

Undoubtedly many did tremble at the audacity of the snapping of feudal claims, but the action proceeded with calm deliberation of legal procedure. The States-General removed their sessions from Delft to Amsterdam, from Amsterdam to The Hague, and there in the great hall of the ancient Count's palace, Philip was declared deposed from his hereditary rights and from the sovereignty into which he had been so solemnly introduced a quarter of a century previously. Representatives from Brabant, Guelderland, Flanders, Holland, Zealand, Friesland, Mechlin, Overyssel, and Utrecht were present. In the articles of the Union of Utrecht it was stipulated that the charter of Brabant, known as the Joyous Entry, should be valid for all provinces. There were special reasons for this, as that charter justified rebellion in case the privileges therein granted were infringed by their Duke. This same charter was now used as a warrant for discarding the sovereign altogether. The article upon which the right rested runs as follows:

In case that we, our heir or successor infringe any

[1] *Hist. des troubles*, etc, iv., p. 564.   [2] Strada, ii., p. 135.

of the aforesaid privileges in all or in part, in any manner whatsoever, we authorise our aforesaid good people that they should offer no further service nor obedience to us, to our heir or to our successor.

Thus the abjuration was distinctly an act of throwing off the feudal bonds between vassals and overlord.[1] It looked backwards to the Middle Ages, not forward to the sentiments rife at the time of the American and French revolutions. It was not a declaration of independence but a simple division between state and a sovereign, division pronounced, indeed, after a new lord had been chosen. Certain phrases in the document of abjuration seem, to be sure, strangely suggestive of the American Declaration of Independence, but there is a different light behind them, radiating from Mediæval times and not

[1] The reformed had grave doubts as to whether they might legally abjure the king. Both Roman law and the Bible seemed to be against it (Romans iii., 1 and 2). Calvin's solution was that states were ordered by God. Groen says that at the abjuration republican principles are put to the fore because the Catholics would have been frightened if too much stress were laid on religious reasons. But a deliberate intention like that seems open to doubt. Mediæval rather than modern notions predominated in the Netherlands. The foundation of the relation between prince and people was the oath of homage. If the nation were to break the oath, they would lose their privilege; if the prince broke his, then he lost the sovereignty. A certain number of people never considered themselves freed by the abjuration. It was only after the accession of Philip III. that this school felt free. No oath had ever been taken to him. (*Staatsinstellingen in Nederland*, p. 51. Muller, p. 260.)

from ideas of natural rights and universal liberty.

The state of affairs had been absurdly illogical. The name of King Philip II. had been scrupulously inserted in all declarations of war against him. The fiction that his honoured right hand knew not what evil his left hand, as represented by his Netherland lieutenants, was doing, was zealously maintained. But the conviction that action could only be performed in the name of one supreme ruler was deep seated. The Prince might easily have been that one, but he would not. He wanted prestige and power behind him and was ready to enhance the prestige while holding the power in leash.

As the abjuration introduced no new situation, as it simply phrased and formalised a condition that had existed in Holland and Zealand for nine years, plans were quickly matured for the acceptance of the French prince who had so little to recommend him individually. In the face of all the discouragement of the last few months, Orange yet saw his own views adopted and his dreams of the French protectorate come true. But there was Matthias! He was the shadow of Philip's shadowy authority in the revolted provinces. With the abjuration of his cousin's sovereignty his own office expired *per se*. His resignation was accepted without regret, he set off for Germany in October without taking leave, and it is quite probable that the 50,000 florins pension

CHARLOTTE DE BOURBON, 1581
PRINCESS OF ORANGE

voted to him by the States was a gift as empty as his own authority.

Until the arrival of Anjou, now governor-elect, the Prince was to administer the government. So it was resolved by the "generality," without the assent of Holland and Zealand to the temporal phrase. They put no time limit in their articles accepting Orange. They intended to consider Anjou only as governor of their allies.

Thus the seventeen provinces were to be severed in three portions, one under the Prince of Orange allied to the second under Anjou, and the third under the Prince of Parma, though, of course, Parma claimed to be governor over all. The inhabitants of the first two were asked to take the following oath:

I solemnly swear that henceforward I will neither respect, obey, nor recognise the King of Spain as my prince and master; that I now renounce the King of Spain and consider myself absolved from the allegiance I formerly owed him. At the same time I swear fidelity to the United Netherlands, namely, the provinces of Brabant, Flanders, Guelderland, Holland, Zealand, etc., etc., and also to the national council and superior body established by the Estates of these provinces; and promise my assistance according to the best of my abilities against the King of Spain and his adherents, and all other national enemies. This is done and resolved in the assembly of the States-General of the United Netherlands in The Hague, July 29, 1581.[1]

And for the "generality," connection with Spain was at an end, even though some portions later shifted over to the other side.

[1] Renon de France, iv., p. 565.

STATES-GENERAL MEDAL

UNION OF UTRECHT

CHAPTER XVIII

THE FRENCH PROTECTOR

1581–1582

THE remainder of the Prince's life—life henceforth ever under shadow of the Ban—was consumed in herculean efforts to establish, justify, and support the French puppet set on the stage at last, at the end of the long negotiation between France and Orange. Puppet is not the proper term, perhaps; the Duke of Anjou was by no means the complete nonentity that Matthias had been. He was, however, nothing more than a wretched, degenerate young man, seeking a foreign career as cadet of his House, and decidedly inferior to the monarch deposed to make place for him. The one difference that made him more acceptable for the moment should weigh against this French Duke in judging the sincerity of his motives as compared to the Spanish King's. Posing as a devout son of the Church, Anjou was yet ready to sanction the creeds forbidden by her edicts, as Philip could not bring his mind to do for any political advantage whatsoever. There were plenty of critics in and out of the Netherlands with sufficient clearness of vision

to perceive that it was not to Anjou's good that
he suppressed his own convictions in order to
acquire the government desired by him and still
more by his mother, who wanted to see the four
crowns that had been predicted for her sons
gained without any more deaths among them.
The iron quality of Orange's will was proven
by his persistence in this matter, contrary to the
counsel of every friend. Proverbs, predictions,
and prayers were hurled at his head. And he
met each argument with perfect calmness. To
Count John's lengthy, cautious pleas he replied
that the man fallen among thieves did not refuse
the aid of the Samaritan of different faith, after
the priest and Levite had passed him by.[1] To the
remonstrances of others, it was urged that a
dog whose faults were known could be made a
safe guardian of a flock, if properly muzzled.
"Not what we wish the most, but what we can
attain," he repeated in many different forms to all
who were honestly pained to see him transferring
the struggling provinces from frying pan to fire,
a homely phrase often used in the interminable
discussion and comment of the time.

During the autumn of 1581, Anjou was busy
with another courtship besides that of the "beautiful
maid," in whom Orange had personified the
Netherlands. He was also wooing the Queen of
England.[2] As Elizabeth Tudor was born in 1533

[1] June 20, 1581. Groen, vii., p. 573.
[2] Anjou went to England in the summer of 1581.

and thus was exactly the same age as the "bald and calvinistic" Orange, she counted forty-eight years to her suitor's twenty-eight, but none the less the clever politician was at one and the same time a vain woman, open to flattery and ready to be persuaded by, assuredly to give complaisant ear to, Anjou's hollow assurance that he loved her for herself alone. There was a certain boy, seventeen years old in that year 1581, who could have made an irresistible comedy of the farce enacted at Elizabeth's palace, had he only taken a contemporaneous theme for his wonder-working pen and simply thrown actual phrases used into a dramatic form. Shakespeare would have needed no invention to make the truth funnier than any fiction, had he portrayed Elizabeth playing fast and loose with the offers of her "dear frog," now exchanging rings with him, now calling him her future husband, and now promising to be a sister to him. Perhaps it was his extremely uncouth appearance that finally induced her to reject him as a spouse, but the rejection was not pronounced until the ridiculous courtship, honeycombed with insincere phrases, had gone on for many months between the shrewd spinster and the undersized, puny, ill-shaped dukeling.

François Hercules of Valois certainly was no personality to charm any one. His face was pockmarked, his skin blotchy, his nose almost double. The general impression was that, at the end, Elizabeth found him too hideous to endure. She did not, however hurt his feelings by any such straightforward, bald statement. She did not take back her ring and she did escort him as far as Canterbury on his way to the coast, and commissioned her favourite, Leicester, and a noble train to accompany him over to the Netherlands and to deliver her own letters to the States, desiring that Anjou should be treated as if he were her "second self." Elizabeth and Orange were really two of the cleverest people in Europe at this epoch; both perfectly able to see through motives and the character of the whole tribe of Valois, but in their relations with Anjou, Elizabeth showed herself far wiser than the Prince. She flattered him and dropped him; Orange held fast, convinced, as he stated, that a muzzle and a leash were sufficient guard against any harm that might come from a vicious protector. He banked on two supports, Elizabeth's hand stretched out from England to prop up her betrothed husband, and King Henry's hand from France to hold his brother firmly in the new seat, which he wholly approved, not because he wished him well but because France was thus relieved of Anjou's presence. Orange simply played for high stakes, fully conscious of the risks.

At the very spot where Philip, Duke of Brabant, Count of Flanders, etc., had bade Orange an ungracious farewell when he set sail for Spain in 1559, the Prince welcomed the man whom he meant to clothe with dignity taken from the

King of Spain. Leicester, Philip Sidney, and the other Englishmen witnessed a magnificent, almost regal reception, although the provinces actually involved in the transaction were only a small geographical fragment of a tiny country. And equally magnificent was the progress to the outskirts of Antwerp, where Anjou received homage and gave his own pledge to his self-offered subjects, before being admitted within the city walls. This was strictly in accordance with ancient usage on the reception of a new duke, but it also fitted into the programme of "muzzling" this particular French puppy.

Orange himself placed the ducal mantle on the new incumbent's shoulders.

As he buttoned it [says a contemporary] he used words noted by his suite and all the company: "Monseigneur, this button must be securely fastened, so that no one can snatch the mantle from your Highness." Then as he put on the hat, he added: "Monseigneur, I pray God that you may guard this dress carefully. Now you are indeed Duke of Brabant." Many of the bystanders would willingly have wagered that the button was not firmly buttoned nor the hat securely set and the end justified that prognostication.

In all the ceremonies the most precise pledges were demanded, and apparently the Duke was hedged in by precautions that ensured a strictly constitutional, limited exercise of authority, before the Joyous Entry was made into Antwerp.

The whole performance was marked by a mediæval disregard of international equity. France, Spain, and England were not at war with each other. Yet here was the brother of the French monarch calmly accepting titles and prerogatives belonging by heritage to the Spanish King, possessions and dignities which the heir to the Duke of Burgundy had not the remotest idea of renouncing. Moreover, the incoming "Duke of Brabant" came direct from the English Queen, being generally regarded as her fiancé, and accompanied by her accredited envoys, while she continued to write pleasant notes to her brother of Spain when the spirit moved her.

Surely these events were on the last glimpses of the confused theories of the Middle Ages,—not the initial steps of democratic participation in a federal government.

While Orange was thus setting up a golden image, the golden reward offered in the Ban for his own removal began to stimulate various persons. The liberal offer appealed to bankrupts wanting money, to criminals desirous of rehabilitating themselves, and last, but not least, to fanatics who honestly believed that Orange was a danger to the eternal life of many thousands by encouraging them in religious anarchy. It chanced to be a bankrupt who instigated one assault on the Prince and one that was nearly fatal.

ORANGE MEDAL

ANJOU MEDAL

At Antwerp the many discordant elements latent in the new alliance peeped out immediately between the folds of the magnificent inauguration drapery. The new sovereign was dissatisfied with the private celebration of the mass at the Abbey of St. Michael where he was established. He demanded public rites in accordance with the provisions of the Religious Peace and only obtained some grudging concessions at the Prince's instance. During the first month of the new régime, many weak spots appeared in the compact, and there was instant readiness to suspect bad faith on the part of the French when Orange was suddenly shot down in his own house on March 18th.

It was a Sunday. The Prince had heard a sermon in the chapel of the citadel and afterwards went to midday dinner, accompanied by several guests, the French ambassador, M. de Laval and M. des Pruneaux being of the party. In the evening all were to sup at a great banquet offered by the new Duke of Brabant to the States-General and others in commemoration of his birthday. The repast at the Prince's house was no banquet but a family meal where all the household was present, including the fourteen-year-old Maurice and two of Count John's younger sons. The conversation was lively and the company lingered long over the dessert. Then as the Prince led the way out of the dining-room he paused to comment on the tapestry, in connection with a remark regarding it made by one of the guests. He was just about to pass on through the door, still looking upward, when

suddenly [writes W. Herlle to Lord Burghley] a person of small stature and less representation (of the age of three or twenty-four years, [*sic*] ill clad, and of face pale, drawing to a black melancholick colour, shaven, saving the upper lip, whence a thin black hair began to issue) presented himself as though he had some request to exhibit and once being put back by a halberder, still persisted and suddenly discharged a pistol (that he held unseen) at the Prince, which by reason of overcharging recoiled in his hand and made the piece and bullet to mount upwards from his level, taking the Prince between the ear and the end of the jaw of the right side, passing clean through the left cheek, without offence to the arterye, the jaw, tongue, or tooth (as yet hitherunter is said) saving that it grated upon one tooth, whereat the Prince nether staggering, nor astonyed, beheld the fellow, till he, amazed with his own fact, and bound as it were to the place by a divine power, let his dagger fall to have made away, whereat one Bonnyvet stabbed him in the breast, and then he was presently slain in furie by the company much against the Prince's will, who cried still to save him, but in vain, for he had in less than a moment no less than thirty-three mortal wounds given him.[1]

---

[1] Groen, Supplement, 221. The story is given in a contemporaneous pamphlet entitled: *Bref recueil de l'assassinat commis en la personne du tres illustré prince d' Orange Comte de Nassau* etc., Antwerp, 1582. The Dutch version seems to have contained a few more details.

The Prince was so completely off his guard that the assassin was able to get within very close range so that his victim's hair and beard were actually singed by the bullet.[1] It was all so quick that none knew what had happened, Orange least of all. Indeed, he thought that a fragment had simply fallen from the ceiling. His first breath after the shock was used to say, "Do not kill him. I forgive him my death," and to the Frenchmen, "What a faithful servant his Highness loses in me."

Then, still on his feet, but unable to walk alone, the wounded man was helped to his bedroom amid the frightened cries of his children and the consternation of the other bystanders whose first thought was that another St. Bartholomew was initiated. Maurice showed extraordinary self-possession and stood quietly by the assassin to make sure that no papers were taken away. The first look at the dead man showed that his thumb had been blown off in the discharge of the pistol, so that he—Jaureguy proved to be his name—had been unable to defend himself with the dagger found in his trunk hose. Everything discovered upon the man's person was given to Maurice, who was then persuaded to go to the common room of the house, his find sheltered by the cloak of a faithful

---

[1] Hooft says that the wound was cauterised by the fire and an immediate hemorrhage was thus prevented by the proximity of the weapon.

servant. A cursory examination of the papers
convinced the young Count that everything
written was in Spanish and the servant hastened
back to show the Spanish writing and to exonerate
the French from the first suspicions of rank treachery. It had even been thought that the very
slayer of the assassin was his accomplice. Maurice
soon returned to the hall, bringing a cross, an
Agnus Dei, a green wax candle, and two bits of
toad skin, supposed to be charms, besides the
packet of papers. These last contained, in
addition to prayers, vows, and correspondence,
two letters of credit,—one for 2000 and the other
for 877 crowns,—with memoranda of advice, all in
Spanish and by Spaniards. There were a book
of hours, a Jesuit catechism, and two tablets containing a detailed account of Jaureguy's plan.
Gifts were promised to the Virgin Mary, the
angel Gabriel, and the son of Christ,—*even of
Christus eenen zoon had*, remarks Meteren,—for
intercession with the Almighty in behalf of his
success. He pledged himself to break his fast
with nothing but bread and water for a week if
he escaped alive. Presents to various shrines
were distinctly specified while magic as well as
spiritual aid was invoked by a charm which was
to render the wearer invisible as soon as he had
wrought the will of God. That Jaureguy conscientiously thought that God willed the Prince's
death there can be no doubt. His master, who
instigated the deed was moved by sordid motives.

There was no delay in communicating the main facts to Anjou who showed promptitude in convening the States council and in issuing a proclamation ordering anyone who had any information of any kind to give it up immediately. The whole story was thus speedily unravelled and an attack on the French was warded off when it was proven that the knowledge of this particular attempt on the Prince's life was confined to but few people. The facts were as follows. Caspar d'Anastro was a Spanish merchant living in Antwerp. Just on the verge of bankruptcy he was attracted by the liberal offers in regard to Orange and signed a contract with Philip, pledging himself to work the desired end in consideration of 80,000 ducats and the cross of Santiago. Access to the Prince's presence was very easy, but, naturally, escape with a whole skin after the murder was problematical and the merchant had no desire to sacrifice his own life. He made a confidant of his cashier by the name of Venero, who mingled his tears with his master's over the financial stress and suggested Jean Jaureguy as an excellent tool to obtain the large sum so conveniently offered.

Out of religious zeal or from devotion to his master, Jaureguy consented to run the risk. At least it seems so, for his own share in the spoil was to be only 2877 crowns. A certain Dominican monk, Zimmerman, certainly confessed and possibly absolved him before the deed, which he carried through on the 18th. Anastro wisely went to

Calais before the date set and thus avoided the unpleasant results that befell Venero and Zimmerman upon whom popular indignation fell.

Venero made full confession and there is some doubt whether Zimmerman refused to break the faith of the confessional, but both were promptly executed on March 28th, ten days after the crime, though saved from the horrible tortures to which they might have been subjected by the kindly thought of the wounded victim:

M. DE STE. ALDEGONDE:
I have heard that to-morrow they are to do justice to the two prisoners, accomplices of the person who fired on me. For my part, I would willingly pardon the offence against me, but if they have merited rigorous punishment, I beg you to ask the magistrates not to inflict torture but to be content with a quiet death.
       Your good friend to do you service,
                    WM. OF NASSAU.[1]

The first grief of the Prince's own family at the crime was piteous enough. Charlotte fell into one swoon after another, and the children's cries were heard all over the house, but wife and daughters soon regained the calm that Maurice had never lost and devoted themselves to the Prince's care. The English Herlle says that two points militated against the patient's recovery: that he was given to over-eating and had been imprudent

[1] The original of this does not exist. It is thus given in the *Bref recueil*.

at the dinner table from which he had just risen, and that his brain and mind were never at rest.[1] The last was certainly true. He was forbidden to talk, lest the wound should open, but he used his tablets from the first and wrote message after message, calculated to protect the French and to keep the public affairs in motion while he was invalided.

The news of his death flew over Europe and the belief that Orange had been disposed of for good and all was very hard to dislodge. Granvelle was very loath the accept the truth.

I believe [he writes as late as May 12th] that they tried to hide his death for some days and let it be bruited about that no one was admitted to his presence except his physician. Aldegonde has attached himself to the Duke of Anjou, who finds him very useful. I wish, considering his devotion to the Prince of Orange that he had let himself be buried with him as favourite wives are interred with Indian princes. However it is, Alençon will find it hard work to adapt himself to Hollanders, Zealanders, Friesians, Flemings, and Gelderlanders and others whose language he does not know. With his slipper nose [*nez de pantouffles*] he will have hard work to win the popular favour, possessed by the Prince, who was skilled in acting as a boon companion, talking and drinking with everyone and cajoling them to his will.[2]

---

[1] Groen, viii., p., 98.

[2] In this letter, as in many others, Granvelle dilates on the absurdity of sending Spanish ambassadors around Europe not conversant with the various languages. *Cor.* x,, p. 168.

While the Prince's enemies were rejoicing at the end, that had not come, the patient progressed towards recovery with some drawbacks.

Here we have been in great terror [wrote Marie of Nassau] thinking my lord must surely die. A fortnight after the shooting he had such a bleeding from a vein that was slightly grazed, that we gave up all hope. The hemorrhage lasted several days. He resigned himself to death, and bidding us all good-night, said, "It is over with me."[1]

You cannot believe how troubled we were to see my lord in such pain, without being able to relieve him.

Never shall I forget that day. But he has been saved by a miracle. There has been no hemorrhage now for fourteen days, and the doctors and barbers think he will be completely restored to health. He has to keep perfectly still, and is not allowed to speak more than is necessary. That is the reason why Philip [Engel, the secretary] has not answered your queries. The doctors forbid my lord doing any business at present. I wish it were possible for your Excellency to see how my lord is changed and emaciated. There is really nothing on him but skin and bones. I hope his flesh will soon come back when he begins to eat.

Up to now he has had no meat; nothing but bread, water-soup, and things of that kind, for he cannot yet chew easily, but I believe in a day or two he is to be allowed to begin to eat and try how it agrees with him. In the greatest haste, March 18th.

[1] To Count John, April 18th. Groen, viii., 87.

Your Excellency's wholly devoted and true daughter to the end of my life.

M. F. v. N. v. O.

"March 18th," Marie writes, when the date should have been a month later. It is as if Jaureguy's pistol shot had stopped the dial for the Prince's family. The loss of blood from this hemorrhage was terribly serious. Twelve pounds is mentioned by van Foreest as what the Prince told him. The flow was checked with great difficulty, because a bandage tight enough to be effective would have choked the invalid. Hooft says that a simple and new expedient devised by Anjou's own physician, Leonardo Botelli, proved efficacious. The pressure of a broad firm thumb upon the vein was found sufficient to check the flow of blood, so a succession of attendants relieved each other night and day until the hemorrhage ceased and the wound closed.[1]

Every day now, thank God, finds *me her* better [writes Marie to her uncle]. He has now tried to eat a little and it tasted pretty good. Mastication is still difficult, but I hope that will come right in time. We have reason to be grateful that it has come as far as this. I made your Excellency's excuses to my lady as your Excellency requested. [It is very odd to mark Marie's changes from "Fatherly uncle" to formal titles.] It was not necessary. They never

[1] This story seems so plausible that it is given here, though it does not appear in the best authorities.

doubted your Excellency's good will and we well
know how the calamity would have grieved your
Excellency. I beg your Excellency to forgive my
bold speaking in my last letter. I could not really
help it, for it annoyed me a little that we heard
nothing from your Excellency. As your Excellency
was away from home and had no opportunity, as
your Excellency has written me, it was not your
Excellency's fault, so forgive me that I blamed your
Excellency wrongfully.[1]

It is easy to see that the writer has indeed been
keenly hurt at her uncle's silence over an event
that stopped time for her. It is just possible that
Count John steadfastly refused to believe in the
alleged French innocence of the attempted crime
and felt that his brother was simply paying the
penalty of his headstrong course in a wrong
direction,—so that he was not too ready with his
sympathy. That he was grieved admits of no
doubt. He was not like Anjou, anxious for his
elder brother's shoes. And whatever the Nassau
faults were, lack of family affection was not one
of them.

On the day after the above letter, Orange was
able to sign a long epistle to Count John and from
that date on the proofs of his resumption of
activity are many.

Jaureguy's bullet failed thus in its direct aim,
but it found its victim. Charlotte of Bourbon
was completely exhausted by her terrible anxiety

[1] Groen, viii., 89.

and unceasing devotion to her husband and was thus in too enfeebled a condition to withstand any illness. Just as Orange passed out of danger she was attacked by a fever to which she succumbed on May 5th.

What a diversity there was between Charlotte's two life experiences! Yet the first in the convent to which she was driven, not called, and the executive rôle of lady abbess that she was forced to play, gave her excellent training for the household which she administered and for the education of the six little daughters she brought into the world, with thankfulness for every one. Every word she has left in her clear, forcible handwriting, shows complete identification with her husband's interests, public and private, and reveals the high standard she had set for her wifehood as a profession. If Orange had hoped for any political advancement from his alliance with the refugee abbess, he was doomed to disappointment. The dubious French alliance was made through other channels, while the loss of German friends caused by the Bourbon marriage had certainly been very serious. Prudentially then, the Prince's friends were right in their apprehensions but from a personal point of view Orange had builded better than he knew. The marriage was singularly happy and from the beginning Charlotte was a loving and devoted wife, very moderate in her demands on life and very grateful for all that fell to her lot. With each of the seven years she seems to have assumed a larger part of her husband's burdens and to have acted as his viceroy and agent in a painstaking, intelligent way.

She left six little girls under seven years old. The first had been named Louise Juliana for the Duke of Montpensier and her grandmother; the second for Queen Elizabeth; the third, born in 1578, when it was hoped that a reunion of the seventeen provinces was still not impossible, was called Catherine Belgia, and had the States-General and Catherine Schwarzburg, for whom she was also named, as her sponsors. On September 9th, the States-General decreed that an income of three thousand pounds a year from the estate of Linghen should be paid to their godchild. In 1579, Charlotte Flandrina was born in Antwerp and to her the Estates at Ghent voted an income of two thousand florins.[1]

The father's ruwardship was acknowledged in the name of Charlotte Brabantina, who was followed by the sixth baby (1581), named Emilie Antwerpiana, in honour of her birthplace, Antwerp, which presented its godchild's nurses with three hundred florins.

With the Prince's migration from one city to another, there was little luxury and less comfort for his family as said before. But he was not subjected to complaints from this wife. She made light of the inconvenient barracks and cold lodgings, in which they had to find quarters from

[1] Groen, vii., 333.

time to time, and found real happiness,—the
surprised happiness of one who might have missed
that side of life—in "our big and little girls."
It was all so much richer than the convent or
the dependence of the electoral court! She lived
down the obloquy that had been cast on her for
her change of faith and of profession and the
sterling worth of her character was gradually
but ungrudgingly acknowledged by all the Prince's
friends who had been filled with consternation
at the marriage.

All disparaging rumours about the new companion
of M. the Prince of Orange . . . must be relegated
to the rank of calumnies [writes loyal Count John to
the Landgrave a few months after the marriage so
dreaded by both]. Every day travellers from Holland, especially those who have stayed with the
Prince's noble spouse, bear testimony to her qualities,
testimony which could not be more favourable, in
spite of her detractors. To enable you better to
sound the depths of the odious aspersions I enclose
a note written by her Grace the princess to Mme. my
mother.[1]

Charlotte's father, too, finally abandoned his
wrath and readmitted his daughter into his good
graces[2] before his death. He was quite ready to
be interested in his namesake, Louise, and to
accept childish gifts made to establish relations
between the six-year-old little girl and himself:

[1] Groen, v., p. 312. Nov. 21, 1575.
[2] By a formal act June 25, 1581. Delaborde, p. 259.

My grandchild: You have achieved no slight thing in learning to net at your tender age as I can see by the belt of pretty violet silk bordered with silver lace which you have sent me. This shows me that you are eager to learn and to be a good child since you can do so much already. Nothing could have pleased me more . . . than to have had your first netting work dedicated to me. You could not have given it to any one who would have prized it more or who loves you better than I, both because you are my grandchild and because you are my godchild and bear my name.[1]

These were gracious words to the innocent child after his anger against her mother ten years before. His young wife, too, Catherine of Lorraine, was not backward in claiming the honour of being a grandmother. There is a pretty little letter of hers to this same Louise expressing somewhat pedantic pleasure in the virtues of "my grandchild."

To show you how much I think of you I send you a little gift of a phœnix, begging you to accept it with as warm a heart as I send it, hoping you will take good care of it for love of me.

                Your very affectionate grandmother,
                    CATHERINE DE LORRAINE.
From Champigny, July 15, 1581.

Charlotte's official correspondence with her children's sponsors shows her infinite solicitude

---

[1] Louis de Bourbon to Louise Juliana of Nassau, Jan. 5, 1582. Archives of the Duc de la Trémoille, Delaborde, p. 291.

for their legal interests and her will made in 1581 is an interesting document in its careful distribution of her effects and in its loving memory of every one who had been faithful to her. She begs the Prince to keep for the children Mme. Tontorf, "who has served me for twenty years" and thus must have come from Jouarre with her mistress. François d'Averly, Sr. de Minay, too, receives three hundred livres as pension and other charges during his life "in recognition of the service he rendered me, having accompanied me from France to Germany and stayed by me for three years at Heidelberg to assist me in my affairs." Secretary, tailor, steward, coachman and equerry all are remembered each by name in addition to the higher officials of the household. She was evidently one of those rare women to whom every underling was an individual and it is easy to believe that the mourning for her loss was no perfunctory service.

CHAPTER XIX

ANJOU'S FAILURE

1582–1583

AGAIN it had been due to the one indomitable will alone that the Prince's protégé was carried safely past the dangerous crisis of March 18th for the time being. The suspicion of black treachery towards Orange was not easily allayed. The vision of a repetition of Coligny's fate was vivid and the desire of the Netherland troops to fall upon every Frenchman in the city was only curbed by the assurance of one of their captains, Lion Petit, that he had forced his way into the Prince's room and seen him in life with prospect of recovery. Then Orange, speechless as he was forced to be, made his influence felt through Aldegonde without, as long as he lay helpless within the house. If ever personal suggestion told, it did then, and Anjou was retained in his place, though in an atmosphere that was somewhat chilly. When Orange was on his feet again, the installation of the French Prince as Count of Flanders took place duly at Bruges, with a burst of allegorical joy to assert loudly the perfect satisfaction of the Flemings at their new acquisition. By that time Holland and Zealand had fully resolved that they would not follow suit in this game of conferring titles. There fervent adherents of the Prince were determined that Orange and Orange alone should be Count of Holland.[1]

It is amusing to read references to the title in the correspondence of Granvelle, Parma, and other royalists. It was their opinion that Orange systematically sought it by every political machination, in which he was an adept. As a matter of fact he did not want it, not because he was unambitious, but simply because he deemed the bestowal of the dignity upon him a disadvantage to his larger plans. He was not wholly at one with the ideas of his ancient government. Holland and Zealand were bent upon furthering their own provincial prosperity in commerce and in fishery. Orange wanted prosperity for the Netherlands united in persistent efforts to gain a commonweal.[2] He was perfectly willing to see compromises here and there, if sacrifices were needed to attain that weal, and he was impatient with the reluctance of the provinces to relinquish some private

---

[1] "Although his authority is nowhere so great as with the Hollanders and Zealanders, yet many persons think that he will have greater difficulty in persuading them to submit to Anjou's rule than the rest," was Hubert Languet's prophecy in writing to Philip Sidney, Feb. 27, 1580.

[2] P. L. Muller, *De Staat der vereenigde Nederlander in de aren zijner wording 1572-94*: "What Washington did under somewhat similar circumstances—the establishment of a federal government of semi independent units,—Orange failed in. The times were not ripe " is the author's summary.

gain for the public good. The sovereignty of
Holland and Zealand held temporarily by him in
1581 could have been made permanent then, had
he not tenaciously cherished the hope of seeing
it conferred on Anjou with the rest of the bundle
of Netherland titles. The two provinces had,
however, been equally tenacious in accepting
Anjou only as the sovereign of their allies and
when, after a little experience, he duly proved
even less attractive in that capacity than had
been expected, there was a return to the original
proposition in the councils of Holland and Zealand;
and the decision to confer the title of Count,
considered to be in abeyance, upon Orange and
his heirs, was further discussed and met with the
approval of the majority, though not of all. The
negotiations were of long duration though intermittent and secret. After the Prince's recovery
in 1582, greater pressure was brought to bear
upon such constituents as were reluctant to give,
and upon Orange, still more reluctant to take,
pressure which resulted in his final acceptance
of the proffered countship of Holland and Zealand
on August 14, 1582, a month after Anjou's inauguration as Count of Flanders and after the latter's
acceptance, too, of the additional titles of Duke
of Guelderland and Lord of Friesland. The fact
was not, however, immediately made public.
The offer and its acceptance were mere prelimin-
aries. So-called letters of *Renversal* were to be
drawn up and delivered, a new constitution

agreed to, and the formal inauguration celebrated. All this hung fire during 1583.[1] Possibly Orange was still hoping to divert the title towards Anjou, to prevent the fragmentary character of the political status of the French "protector."

The fashion in which the European world received a great reform movement, of universal interest but bearing the papal seal, in this year of 1582, showed how all events were still shadowed by the theological differences of the time and how slow the shadow was to move on. For a long period the year's seasons had been seriously

[1] In the spring of 1583 there was fresh agitation and resultant action. On March 26th, the formal act of recommendation was passed by the Estates of Holland and on April 5th was entrusted to a committee consisting of Sr. van Boetzelaar van Asperen, the advocate Buys, and Dr. François Maelson to have the seals of the cities set thereon. This act comprises simply the recommendation and the reasons, without stating the conditions stipulated later. It was sealed in the name of three nobles and by the secretaries of twenty-five cities, representing all remaining places in Holland. One copy was given to the Prince, one was preserved in the state archives. Nothing remained but the fulfilment of the conditions and the formal exchange of oaths. The circumstances were quite different from those obtaining in 1576. Before it had been delegated, now it was sovereign, authority offered, limited by the States. His successor was to be chosen from the Prince's legitimate male heirs. This clause was intended to exclude Philip William.

There were numerous hindrances to the completion of the affair. Kluit says the chief were fear of France and of Anjou and the suspicion of the other provinces. Holland was anxious to take no step without Zealand. Middelburg, Gouda, and Amsterdam made difficulties of one kind and another, fearing lest their private privileges, their particular commerce, etc., might be jeopardised. Kluit, i., p. 287; Muller, p. 312.

out of gear. The several minutes of excess of the Julian calendar over the solar year existing from the inauguration of that calendar had amounted to a discrepancy of ten days between the two by the sixteenth century. Pope Gregory XIII., accordingly, finally ordered the enforcement of an edict of the Council of Trent and issued a mandate that ten days should be omitted arbitrarily from 1582, so as to bring the two years into harmony. After October 4th, October 15th was to be written, and Easter and other festivals thereby restored to their wonted seasons. It was further provided that 1700, 1800, 1900 should be leap years, but not 2000, to avoid the recurrence of the error.

Protestant nations were not inclined to obey the mandate, because it emanated from Rome. Holland and Zealand, possibly because they were for the moment in close affiliation with Anjou, agreed to accept the alteration and thus they were grouped with France and other Catholic lands that made the change, instead of with England, which adhered to the old style until the eighteenth century. Flanders, Brabant, Artois, Hainault, Holland, and Zealand celebrated Christmas after December 15th; Guelderland, Zutphen, Utrecht, Overyssel, Friesland, Groningen, and others adhering to the "old style" for another long period, as Russia does to this day.[1]

[1] The acceptance in 1583 by Protestant Holland aroused some indignation among Protestant neighbours. Landgrave William

ANJOU MEDAL

ANJOU'S TREACHERY

In spite of the Prince's personal success in propping up Anjou and in persuading the people to obey him, he did not succeed in making him happy. The young Frenchman strained impatiently at his leash and felt hampered and restricted in his authority. He was thoroughly miserable in the midst of the people who had welcomed him as a saviour. His English fiancée took upon herself to call Orange seriously to task for the shortcomings of the Netherlands. They had no right to invite an honourable lord to their shores and then to leave him ill paid and forced into a secondary part. "Take care that Monsieur is not driven too far," was her concluding warning. There were people at hand in Anjou's suite ready to assure him that his treatment was already far beyond bounds.[1] They harped on the fact that he was unceasingly playing second fiddle in the state orchestra, as ill befitted a son of France.

---

writes a characteristic letter to the electors of Saxony and the Palatinate, protesting about the proposition, most inconvenient to farmers accustomed to plant by the festivals "as they now are" and to pay their rents on the appointed time. He counts the Gregorian ordinance as a piece of "papal politics" that should be completely ignored by all good Christians. It may be noted that owing to Holland's early change in style, New York, as New Netherland, was the first American colony to adopt it. The Dutch style was abandoned when the colony passed to the English in 1664, resumed in 1673, and abandoned again in 1674.

[1] "*Orange gouverne tout, Sainte-Aldegonde conseille tout en attendant que tout soit emporté par le diable*," was the French version of a doggerel sung in the street.

Why go on taking a little meagre authority, meted out by these purse-proud burghers, and sharing, moreover, that modicum with the Prince of Orange? Assert your rights at one bold stroke. Make yourself master of Flanders. France is at your back.

Anjou had neither an inherited nor an acquired distaste for treachery. The arguments fell pleasantly on his ear and he made his arrangements accordingly.

In January, 1583, in the seclusion of his bedchamber, after he had retired for the night, Anjou recounted the tale of his grievances to his confidential friends and declared that only two courses were open to him,—to leave these ungrateful and parsimonious Flemings to their own devices, or to show them once for all that he was a man of mettle. He had decided on the latter. He proposed that Dunkerque, Dixmude, Termonde, Bruges, Ghent, Vilvoorden, Alost, and other important places should be seized simultaneously by his trusty French troops, sent thither to quell tumults that could be purposely excited. He himself would take measures to assure himself of Antwerp. The project was highly approved by those in whom he confided, as he was very careful in his choice, and Frenchmen known to be devoted to Orange had been sent away on various pretexts. Later, some of those present disclaimed knowledge of the plans.

The Marshal de Biron [according to Bentivoglio],

was among the confederates. Bor says that he approved the work in hand but his daughter told me that her father took in no more than a pinch of it and assured the Prince of Orange that Monsieur cooked the project so secretly that no odour was wafted abroad.[1]

When his friends evinced full sympathy with his plan, Anjou leaped from his bed, unclad as he was, and knelt down to implore God's blessing on his enterprise, designed to avenge insults to the Church as well as to himself.

The unsavoury plot was not, however, wholly unsuspected. Distrust and uneasiness tainted the air. The captain of the guard felt their presence sufficiently to warn Orange, who reassured him by his own confidence in the protector's good faith, though he agreed to precautionary measures, usual under fear of an attack. At the same time, the Prince made a display of his own confidence in Anjou by sending the burgomaster to inform him of the accusation, and Anjou promptly despatched a private message on the evening of the 16th, protesting that he would die for Antwerp, but injure it never.

Orange was in the habit of saving his strength by staying in bed late in the mornings, often disposing of certain business before rising. The early hour of seclusion in his room had another advantage, that of affording a time for confidential

[1] Hooft, p. 184.

conversation. He was still in this retirement when Anjou sought him, on the 17th, ready to act out the part of injured innocence. Orange seems to have accepted his assurances, but at the same time he refused to go with the Duke to a review of the troops outside the city walls and strongly advised him not to leave Antwerp that day. An hour or two later, Orange accompanied the city officials to wait upon Anjou in formal ceremony. That interchange of intimate and ceremonious morning visits was the last personal intercourse between the two men. They never looked on each other's face again. Orange returned to his own dwelling on the other side of Antwerp, and Anjou sat down to his noonday dinner. While at the table, a letter was delivered to him which agitated him greatly. He read it, and stuck it in a little muff that he carried on his arm. Then he left the table, ordered horses, mounted, and, after exchanging steeds, as the first brought to him seemed restless, he rode off out of the Kipdorp gate, followed by two hundred men. As he crossed the drawbridge the Duke waved his hand to the troops, saying "There is your city. Go and take possession of it." This was between twelve and one o'clock and the burghers were at dinner when the cries of "*Tue, Tue! Vive le duc d'Anjou! Vive la messe!*" rang through the streets.

The aroused burghers were totally unprepared; but they did not lose their heads, and made a good fight with any and every missile that came to their hands. From the roof tops they hurled tiles, from the windows heavy furniture, etc., to such good purpose that a large number of the foe (exactly 1583 of them according to Hooft) lost their lives. It was a mad turmoil, while the fray lasted. The citizens for once all worked together. "Rich, poor, young, and old displayed an equal zeal. Beggar, Papist, Lutheran, were forgotten names."

"Do not shoot, burghers," cried Orange, when he arrived on the scene of action, somewhat late,— "It is simply a misunderstanding." Perhaps it was as well that victory was practically gained before he came, for the burghers were probably not in the vein to rate this patent assault upon their town, with its evident treacherous intent, as a simple "misunderstanding." The attempt failed of its object. In this so-called French Fury, the burghers, looking to their own defence, fought far more effectively than had the mercenaries in repulsing the Spanish Fury of seven years previously. Moreover, the very self-confidence of the French was their undoing in the face of the unexpected and obstinate resistance they encountered.

Anjou, disappointed and baffled, betook himself to Termonde with his troops, losing a good many on the way from an overflow near Mechlin where a dyke had been cut to impede him. His first letters, dated from Termonde, January 17th, are marvellously audacious. To Orange he stated that the events of the day were caused by the indignities he had suffered and he begs the Prince to see that no harm came to his people. At the same time, he wrote in a high-handed way to the States-General, and sent two gentlemen to the magistrates and colonels to "explain everything." He even requested that his furniture and clothes should be forwarded, prisoners surrendered, and supplies furnished for his men. Further he intimated that, ill-requited as he had been for his loving kindness to the oppressed Flemings, still he *might* forgive and forget![1]

You will have heard the result of Alençon's [Anjou] augustly offered help [wrote the Landgrave, January 21st, o. s.]. The people there had better look sharp and not let their mouths be smeared with honey. It can be seen clearer than the sun [*clarius sole*] from this transaction that, no matter what is said, the intention is to uproot religion. You have often heard me say that I could not wonder enough at the prince's course in entrusting the defence of this same religion to the enemy, in commending the lambs to the wolves. *I* never expected any good result.[2]

In Germany this most natural dictum was echoed from mouth to mouth, while Elizabeth of England and Catherine de' Medici were inclined to opposite views. "I do not know what the immediate cause was [wrote the former], but I do remember

[1] Bor, iii., p. 344, etc.   [2] Groen, viii., p. 141.

that Monsieur has often complained to me about the wrongs and indignities he has suffered." [1]

Catherine assured the Prince that she suspended judgment until she had further details of the occurrence, for she could not believe Orange guilty of the base ingratitude that appeared on the surface. [2]

Orange answered Elizabeth that full reports had already been sent to her. "On which testimony, Madame, I do not doubt that you will be able to judge fairly who deserves blame and who not. . . ." [3] And his conclusion implies that extraction from the confusion in which they are involved is almost beyond human aid, with which words he remains the Queen's humble servant. Catherine's letter was acknowledged in dryer terms with the assurance that the Prince would have believed no testimony but that of his own eyes in regard to the tragic events. [4]

It is evident that Orange understands the character of the Valois perfectly, yet he steadfastly refuses to repudiate the whole clan once for all, with the contempt deserved by Anjou's shameless treachery. When the magistrates and military officers of Antwerp pressed him for a definite recommendation of future policy he answered that he was reluctant to express his opinion, ill equipped for action as he was, and then he proceeded to rehearse the story of Anjou's rela-

[1] Groen viii., 142. [2] *Ibid.*, p. 147.
[3] *Ibid.*, p. 157. [4] *Ibid.*, p. 158.

tion to the States-General, acknowledging that all agreements were virtually annulled by his duplicity.[1] Three courses were open to the Netherlands: (1) reconciliation with Philip; (2) dependence on themselves; (3) reconciliation with Anjou. The first was incompatible with the preservation of the reformed religion. The second seemed to him also impracticable, from their lack of funds, lack of central power, of central interest, of central responsibility. Each province was intent on local self-interest rather than on the common weal. To his mind, therefore, the last course was the sole one to adopt. "With France to back him, Anjou is our best and only hope."[2]

The advice could not be other than unpopular. Every one felt capable of judging for himself. In his first letter, Anjou had at least acknowledged that he had tried a *coup d' état*, but alleged that his action was necessary to save him from being "a Matthias," so unworthy was the treatment accorded him. After a little, however, his tone changed, and became more high-handed and more insolent in the mendacious assertions that the whole disturbance had been accidental and due to the insubordination of his troops.[3]

The Prince's persistent advocacy of reconciliation with this patently unreliable protector

---

[1] Groen, viii., p. 149. *Cor.*, v., p. 95.

[2] *Ibid.*, p. 202. This is not the speech but an outline of the arguments.

[3] Bor., iii., p. 348. Letter to Henry III.

brought down a shower of abuse on himself. One
pamphlet declares him to be corrupt, ambitious,
self-seeking.[1] The old forged letter to Anjou,
long since disproved as emanating from Orange, is
laid to his charge afresh. He was an atheist,
having characterised religion as *een curieuse en
subtyle sake*, etc. His speech to the magistrates
and others was promptly printed with a bitter
commentary added thereto and circulated widely.[2]

No wonder that the negotiations that followed
were spiritless and dreary. The hesitating confidence in the French alliance had, primarily, only
been coaxed into existence by the Prince's efforts.
The second reconciliation was a mere mirage
above a quicksand where no one could step
without being clogged by the mire.

In the hot outburst of indignation, the title
of Duke of Brabant was considered again vacant
and offered to Orange, as that of Count of Holland
had already been. He declined it, bound as he
was to restore Anjou to that dignity.

"Thank God that he inspires you to reconcile
me and the States happily. I trust with His aid
this compact will endure for ever. Certainly
there will be no breach of faith on my part."[2] So
wrote Anjou to Orange in recognition of a new
provisional arrangement, signed between him and
the States-General, March 26th and 28th.

---

[1] Hague Pamphlets, 648. *Claer Bewij's dat de Prins van
Orangien*, etc. Printed at Cologne, Feb., 1583. *Ibid.*, 663.

[2] *Cor.*, v., 123.

Anjou was to deliver up the towns he held, to receive thirty thousand florins for his troops, and to wait at Dunkerque for the "perpetual" treaty to be arranged later. The other articles in the March pact are not worth considering, because they proved empty words. Anjou never again set foot within the Netherlands.

In the midst of this most unsatisfactory state of affairs, Orange entered upon his fourth matrimonial venture. That his bride was French was a fact that militated against him in popular estimation. But in other respects she was an eminently suitable *partie* for the leader of a Protestant revolt, a far more suitable friend than any Bourbon or Valois. It was Louise de Coligny, daughter of the late admiral and widow of young Charles de Teligny,[1] who had fallen a victim on the same St. Bartholomew night which had seen Coligny's death. At seventeen the young Huguenot girl had been thus bereft of husband and father in a single night.

The incidents of her own escape from destruction are unknown, but it was effected as well as that of her young step-mother Jacqueline de Montbel, who had been married to Admiral Coligny on the same day that Louise became Teligny's wife. The two fled to Switzerland, where the admiral's posthumous child, Beatrice, was born in December. Then came years of

---

[1] At an earlier date this same Teligny had acted as messenger to Charlotte de Bourbon at Jouarre from Jeanne d'Albret.

LOUISE DE COLIGNY, PRINCESS OF ORANGE.
(Based on an old engraving.)

poverty, for the Coligny property as well as the private estates of the two widows were confiscated. Greater misfortune, too, was in store for Jacqueline. She was accused of sorcery, magic and compacts with the devil and thrown into prison, where she spent many years. In August, 1576, Louise accompanied her brother Andelot back to France and was reinstated in a portion of Teligny's estate, Lierville in Beauce being returned to her. There she established herself and lived quietly with little known record of her adventures for five or six years.

It is strange [says Brantôme] how Mme. de Teligny has taken on grace and agreeable manners in that rude and barbarous land of Switzerland. The world is wondering how countries so hard, so rural, and so rough could have turned out ladies as accomplished and cultivated as in other lands, so sweet, courteous, and good. But it must be remembered that the foundation of Louise's education was in France and first impressions are the important ones.

In her youthful days when hope ran high in the Huguenot camps Louise had known Louis of Nassau. He had been one of the intimates of the family circle and had witnessed the two marriages of 1571. Whether the young girl had ever seen Orange is uncertain. If a meeting took place it must have been between 1568 and 1572, during the four years preceding the massacre, when Louise was a mere child. In 1583, she was a fine young woman whose twenty-nine years with their discipline of misfortune were sufficiently suited to the Prince's fifty, and whose sympathies, hereditary and individual, were naturally in close touch with the religious side of the cause Orange was espousing, though probably she was more fervent in her point of view than he. The negotiations for the alliance were made, as mentioned in the announcement to the Estates of Holland, before the January deed had thrown fresh suspicion upon everything French. Orange was not the man, however, to be turned from a purpose by a wave of feeling that might have swept subsidiary events into the same category as the main issue. He proceeded calmly with his private alliance, as already arranged. On April 7th, Louise de Coligny arrived in Zealand, on the 11th at Antwerp, where she was quietly married to the Prince on the following day and the event was publicly honoured by salutes of cannon and ringing of bells.

"You will have heard, Monsieur, how his Highness made an accord with the States and how my father married Madame de Teligny on the 12th instant."[1] Such were the laconic words with which Maurice mentions the family event to his Uncle John, to whom later the bride sends the following note by his secretary, Philip Engel:

I hasten to assure you how honoured I feel that God put it into the heart of Monseigneur the Prince

[1] Groen, viii., p. 189.

to take me for his companion; I recognise, too, his
further favour in giving me as kin so many noble
lords who cherish the fear of God, among whom you,
monsieur, hold the first rank.[1]

Antwerp had offered public honours on the
marriage but the Prince was no longer popular
in the city. The people could not understand
his motives in endeavouring to reinstate Anjou
in the authority he had misused to their personal
injury. They counted all the French promises
as too fragile for handling. In July a disturbance
took place on some side issue, just as Orange
was leaving Antwerp. An angry crowd with its
suspicions easily excited rushed to the gate and
forced him back with the cry, "Traitor, he is
bound to deliver Antwerp to the French." A few
days later there was a report that he was about
to fortify himself within the citadel. The mob
threatened to attack his person and were only
calmed with difficulty. The timid magistrates
were afraid to punish the offenders, easily identified though they were, and this official failure to
count his interests and his integrity one with those
of the government wounded Orange deeply.

He was just then preparing to go to Middelburg
to meet the States-General in session. After the
disturbance he hastened his departure and left
Antwerp on July 22d, not to return there again
for residence. He felt Holland to be more friendly

[1] Groen, viii., p. 228.

than Brabant and he established his family at Delft in the old convent of Ste. Agathe, whose name is lost in that of the Prinsenhof. Louise Coligny found her first land journey in her adopted country a trying experience.

> She told my father [says Aubéry du Maurier] that she was greatly surprised at the difference between French and Holland customs. She was placed in an open waggon instead of a carriage, with no seat but a board, and in the short distance between Rotterdam and Delft she was almost shaken to pieces.[1]

Just one year was left to the Prince to rest at this stage of his life journey, a year important for his descendants, however, for there in Delft, at the Prinsenhof, was born his twelfth child and third boy, Frederick Henry, who alone of his three sons left heirs to the Nassau name. The Protestant kings of Denmark and Navarre were sponsors for the child, together with the Estates of Holland, Zealand, and Utrecht. Representatives of the Queen of England were there, and the baptism was a notable international Protestant event. Indeed there seems to have been a return to the Prince's ancient lavishness in the arrangements, for one minister at Leiden felt called upon to rebuke from his pulpit the extravagance of the banquet. The occasion was, moreover, utilised for political discussion. "Under shadow of taking

---

[1] *Mémoires*, p. 286.

part in his son's baptism, he summoned me from Antwerp [says Ste. Aldegonde, then burgomaster of that city] and opened his heart confidentially." [1]

After this conference, Aldegonde was left convinced that Orange was indeed working steadfastly for what he believed to be the best interest of the Reformed Church and he took to heart his warning that Antwerp was in imminent danger from Parma's advances. Another year and the fall of the Brabant seaport showed the clearness of the Prince's prevision. But he was no longer living to see his prediction verified.

His patient, unaided efforts, unsympathised with by friend and foe alike, to hold fast to the French alliance were finally ended by the death of Anjou on June 10th. During the last four months of his life the Duke proved his unworthiness still further by entering into negotiations with Parma, as revealed later. Anjou had not the slightest conception of integrity, truth, or justice, and his mind, like his person, was corrupt and contaminated. In his case the suspicions of poison, usual in regard to every death, were natural enough, so wretchedly diseased was his body, sweating blood at every pore, but the suspicion does not seem to have been substantiated. Valois life was corrupted from its birth.

The event was decisive, but before its actual occurrence Orange had so far accepted the situation that he began to press for the completion

[1] Groen, viii., p. 405.

of the bestowal of the Countship of Holland upon himself. He thought it due to his own dignity that his acceptance of the title which the Estates had urged upon him at their own initiative should be sealed legally.

Early in July he presented the following memoir[1] to the States of Holland:

Gentlemen: We must remind you, that you, together with the people of Zealand, voluntarily gave us certain acts declaring that you took us for your count and lord, and upon such terms as might be arranged . . . the same act being dated March 29, 1580. Some time afterwards, in the month of August, 1582, you were pleased to send certain deputies to us at Bruges, expressly to urge us to make an end of the affair, and asking us to state the conditions upon which we would accept the dignity. After you had seen the said conditions stated in articles, you wrote to us the —— of ——, '83 [sic] that you approved them. Since then you have written to all the provinces which remain united, advising them of your resolution to make us your count and lord. In last December, you, before an assembly of all the States, presented to us the letters of acceptance that you had received from our person, duly sealed with the city's seals, together with the articles you had agreed upon, which had been signed by all the cities except Amsterdam and Ter-Goes.

[1] Groen, *Archives*, viii., 428. On the margin is written: "Presented by his Excellency to the States of Holland, in the beginning of July, 1584." Groen says this document is not in the Holland register.

This matter has been discussed so often in the States of Holland and also in the private assemblies of the cities, and imparted to the other provinces, that it cannot remain hidden or secret.[1] It is not only public property in these lands, but there is no kingdom or country in Christendom where it has not been discussed. As it is patent how long the affair drags on, every one has the right to draw his own conclusion, as each will do, according to his sympathies. And as it behooves you and us to heed the common weal above all, public honour ought to be cherished. Nevertheless, you cannot be ignorant of the fact that opportunity is given to people to gossip about it.

If the affairs of the land were well conducted meanwhile, this inconvenience might be borne, but you know that the contrary is the case and that uncertainty in all quarters of this republic causes a confusion, or great imperfection in many things, as reformation in all directions is postponed until affairs are on a fixed basis. People talk and act without restraint, with no fear of punishment, and if we, having as little authority as we have, should arrest any one in the course of justice, we should be criticised at once, as though we were acting privately and not in behalf of the whole land and republic.

All these considerations move us, gentlemen, to beg you in a friendly manner, to terminate this business and help us to uphold our honour and reputation, as well as to help you to establish all affairs in such a state and order that the land and republic may be thereby benefited. While you delay your

---

[1] The first offer *was* secret.

resolution about the formal inauguration, see to it, above all, that some temporary steps are taken, so that these annoyances may be obviated. . . .

Meanwhile, awaiting the solemnisation of the affair and the decision of Zealand, may it please you to determine what title we shall use in letters and ordinances, and also what seal in despatches, so that all the business of the land may be expedited.

In spite of the fact that matters had been pushed so far and that the publicity justified the Prince's remonstrance at the delay in completing the gift, objections continued to be put forward. The most vehement protest was made as late as June, 1584, before the council of Amstersterdam, by C. P. Hooft, the father of the historian. He argued that no advantage was to be gained from the action and that this individual action of Holland was an infringement of the "Union of Utrecht." His opposition was, however, not well received by his fellow councillors and there is little doubt that the Prince's remonstrances would have borne fruit had there only been time. Coins were actually prepared (at least so says Strada) with the inscription *Nova moneta comitis Hollandiæ ac Zelandiæ*. But the day of inauguration never dawned.

CHAPTER XX

THE ASSASSINATION

1584

WHILE the title of Count of Holland hung in the air over the Prince's head a motley crew of zealots and outlaws followed in Jean Jauregy's wake, with more or less uncertain step. The summary justice dealt out to the unsuccessful assassin was sufficient to divert the second class from their purpose when they came in close range of the dangers which would inevitably threaten their own life and limb and in all probability leave them no time to enjoy the reward even if they won it.[1] Parma was beset

[1] In the midst of the inauguration of Anjou as Count of Flanders at Bruges, one plot had been unmasked, directed against that "protector" as well as the Prince of Orange, in which young Lamoral d'Egmont was shamefully implicated. Orange had been very kind to him, not needing the mother's dying injunction to take an interest in the son of his unfortunate friend, and his kindness was ill requited, if the accusation were true that Egmont had meant to poison him at his own table. The young man was allowed to escape to France. His elder brother had gone over to Parma in 1580. *Wreede Turkshe wonderlycke verhaalinge van dit letste verraet tegen Ducks Dangu en tegen den edelen P. v. Orangtien.* Leiden, 1582. The brochure contains two letters, July 25th and 27th.

by many candidates for blood money and he did not always find it an easy task to distinguish the real rogue from the false. For instance in April, 1584, a certain Frenchman, Get or Gott, was taken prisoner by one of the Duke's captains, Roubaix. Though Get offered to pay high in service for his freedom, the various pieces of treachery suggested as the price to him did not seem feasible. Then Roubaix asked whether he could not make way with the Prince of Orange. Yes, indeed. That was perhaps within his power. He had peculiar facilities for the task, being intimate with one of his stewards and having free access to the kitchen; he might try his hand at poisoning the Prince's food. Roubaix was rather incredulous as to whether either intimacy or presence in the kitchen were sufficient to ensure the right cup reaching the right lips. Then Get explained to him how a certain little pot often stood on the fire, filled with eel soup for the Prince's own consumption. The cover was perforated to allow the emission of steam. The inference was clear and Roubaix took the bait. But first, he asked the man's motives. Get's answer was that the French were so out of favour in Flanders that it was almost impossible for one of his nationality to pick up a living. He was poor and Philip's high reward would suit his circumstances excellently.[1]

---

[1] *Cor.*, vi., p. 121, etc. *Lettre du marquis de Roubaix au prince de Parme.* Much of the story of the murder is contained in this volume vi.

The story as reported did not carry conviction to the Duke of Parma, but he bade Roubaix release his prisoner, if he thought best, and take the chances that good might be done. Get hastened straightway to Orange and boasted that he had refused to play him false. And thus lies passed back and forth.

At last a true zealot came on the scene, impelled to action by other motives than the hope of the reward and not easily paralysed by fear for his own safety. He was a man of twenty-eight, and possessed of some education, but a poor, wretched looking piece of humanity to cherish the purpose of ridding earth of the Prince of Orange by his own hand. Occasionally an inordinate vanity is allied to an insignificant personality and so it was in the case of this Balthasar Gérard. As he crept about, unheeded wherever he was, he loved to think that he was going to prove himself a giant of action to the big self-sufficient brutes who paid him no more attention than is given to a small garter snake, deemed innocuous, as it crosses a path.

Delft was not indeed an Eden in the early summer of 1584, when this creature wormed his way into the Prince's little court, established there in the roomy old convent on the canal; but the domain was a pleasant, quiet spot, peacefully removed by water and a street from the bustle of the great market place. Under the roof, were gathered almost enough women to people the ancient cloister. There were the Prince's sister, the Countess of Schwarzburg, Marie and Anne of Nassau, his elder, and the five small girls, his younger daughters, in addition to Louise de Coligny and her baby. Four other children were in as many different places. The elder sons were university students, one in Spain and one at Leiden, the thirteen-year-old Emilie had never left the friendly shelter of Dillenburg, and one of Charlotte's daughters was under the charge of her grandfather, the Duke of Montpensier.

The early summer weeks of 1584 seem to have been a time when Orange was simply pausing until the countship was settled. As he waited, there were anxieties enough to occupy his thoughts. They were plain to view. That he foresaw Antwerp's capture showed no miraculous second sight. Even the jokers of the day were already predicting it. "Antwerp is to let from the Michaelmas term," was a sign posted up at Lierre. In regard to that city, the trouble was from without. At Ghent it was the internal seething of the burghers that threatened to boil over.

. . . We have had reliable information that certain Ghenters are in treaty with the Prince of Parma. I only wish that your theologians would explain the conscience of people ready to abandon their brethren. . . . I hear that Dathenus is one of the councillors in this most honourable capitulation.

A touch of bitterness is evident in these words

written by Orange to his brother in March.[1] The main part of his letter is devoted to a discussion of a pamphlet intended to affect public opinion and prevent any further appeal to France.

The author spends much time in contrasting the ample resources of the King of Spain with my scanty power and in describing the doubtful outcome of the war, the uncertainty of the popular will, etc. Then he proceeds to touch on the ill opinion that some of the reformed have conceived of me, because of the treaty with the French, and of the slight confidence there is in any friendship with them, their past faults, the meagre resources of the Duke of Anjou, the improbability of the [French] king letting himself be involved in a war against so grand a monarch. Finally he attacks our House. . . . As to my honour, I may, in speaking to my brother, express myself more strongly than to a stranger. Is there any human being who has . . . worked more, suffered more, lost more than I in trying to plant, advance, and maintain the churches?

Then he recapitulates the old arguments in favour of the alliance with Anjou, an alliance which destiny itself had severed, as already said. And by that time the Prince's own days were numbered.

It was early one July morning, when certain official letters from France, containing despatches relating to Anjou's death, arrived at the gate of the Prinsenhof in Delft and were immediately

[1] Groen, viii., p. 339.

delivered to Orange. He ordered the messenger brought at once to his bedside, that he might gather further details from his lips. Such complete careless trustfulness was wholly unexpected by the man, not a mere messenger, but a fanatic, the above-mentioned Balthasar Gérard, whose life was dedicated to the Prince's death. The man was simply overwhelmed with regret that he had no dagger convenient to his hand at such a wonderfully opportune occasion for the execution of his scheme. Meanwhile, Orange, absorbed in his news, lay there in bed, unprotected and totally unsuspecting that his humble visitor was harbouring murderous thoughts at the very moment when he stood before him, hot from his ride, cringing and respectful in his answers. It was not his first appearance at Delft and Orange was confident that he knew all that was necessary about the man to make him safe to have under his roof. He was a poor, persecuted Calvinist from the Franche-Comté in whom the Prince had been interested a few weeks previously.[1]

At the beginning of May the Prince's confidential secretary Villiers had counselled him to receive a letter from this stranger, in which he humbly offered his service to the Prince, so that he "might remain where he could worship God without

[1] The details of the story are taken from Gérard's confession, his answers under torture, the *Relation officielle*, letter of the Burgomaster Aerssens and other letters. See *Cor.*, vi., and *De Moord van 1584*. The Hague, 1884.

fear of death" and begged that some one be deputed to hear his story. Orange delayed giving further attention to the request for a time, but at last, wearied by the petitioner's importunity, he bade Villiers examine him. Gérard was ready with his tale, carefully fabricated with extraordinary dramatic ability and careful attention to local colour. It was as follows: He was one François Guion, native of Besançon. His parents had been driven into exile from their little home on the bridge, because they were Huguenots, and when they had ventured to return to Besançon on the rumour of better times, they had met their death in company with brethren of the Faith in June, 1575. He, François, had continued to cherish the true religion, but insults from the papists induced him to seek a refuge where he could be free to follow the dictates of his conscience. In 1582 he had arrived in Luxemburg on his way to the Prince of Orange, but could not proceed further on account of poverty and ill health. Then he took service with one Dupré, his cousin, secretary to the Count Mansfeld, royalist Governor of Luxemburg. "But as it was very difficult to please the Lord with secret service, I feared I would fall under divine wrath. Therefore I left my master, after having taken copies of the said Count's seals in red wax."

A certain priest had suspected him of laxity in the observance of Catholic rites. To escape him he had tried to go to Trèves under pretence of taking communion at Easter. The priest followed him and in self-defence Gérard had slain him and then fled to Holland for safety. He was in a position to render valuable service to Orange, by means of the stolen seals which he displayed.

Gérard had outlined this story previously to one of Parma's councillors with the words, "This and other rubbish I intend to relate to the said Nassau, so as to gain access to his presence as preliminary to the execution."

The tale was indeed a skilful fabrication, propped up on a few truths, among which were the stolen seals. The man was not "François Guion," an orphaned Huguenot, but Balthasar Gérard, a devout son of the ancient Church, who believed from the bottom of his heart that Orange was a public pest. In 1577 he had been reproved for his expressed wish to kill Orange and reminded that Philip was probably desirous of preserving a valuable captain to his service, thinking he would at last be reconciled with his lawful sovereign.

Giving ear to this remonstrance [says Gérard in his confession] I left all to God and his Majesty. But when I heard, about three years ago, that his Majesty had issued a sentence of death against the said Nassau in the form of a proscription, and as the execution of justice and the King's will seemed long delayed, I put my private affairs in order, left Burgundy, and came hither on purpose to carry out the said sentence. This was in February, 1582.

The report of the Prince's death in March of the same year seemed to relieve Gérard of a charge. Then it was that he entered the service of his cousin Dupré in Luxemburg and possessed himself of Mansfeld's seals. Various events conspired to detain him in Luxemburg after he had assumed the burden of his task again, and it was not until March, 1584, that he made any advances towards fulfilling his vow. A Jesuit at Trèves tried to dissuade him from his dangerous business, being, indeed, chiefly concerned about a possible misuse of the stolen seals.

It was upon this priest's advice that Gérard went to Tournay for the express purpose of getting Parma's sanction upon his enterprise, so as to dignify the proposed crime into an authorised execution of justice. On March 21st, Parma gave him an audience, but was not very favourably impressed by his visitor and refused to advance any money. Vague promises from Councillor d'Assonleville that the King would fulfil his promise and that the doer would be immortalised if the deed were done, were all that Gérard attained. At the same time he was warned of his personal danger and of the necessity of not compromising Parma. With this meagre encouragement, the assassin was obliged to content himself. He confessed himself again, left two more written statements and went on his way, with the result, as related before, that he was accepted in Delft at his word and was allowed to linger around the

Prinsenhof, without being questioned further. Thus he had an opportunity to study the ins and outs of the Prinsenhof and to make careful plans for his own escape in case of need.

His course of action was interrupted by the unsuspecting Prince, who asked Noël Caron, Lord of Schoonval, to take "Guion" with him from Holland to France, so that he might deliver his seals (they were *cachets volants*, easy to attach) to Marshal de Biron, at Cambray, thus stationed close enough to Luxemburg to be able, possibly, to utilise them.[1] "Guion" was not pleased at the offer, which removed him from Delft and the vicinity of his game, but he did not dare refuse his patron. He was uneasy, however, until Schoonval entrusted him with return despatches to Orange, so that he had an excuse for going to Delft. That was how he came to be standing there in the seclusion of the Prince's bedroom on that July morning, longing for a dagger to his hand, that he might use it pat. When dismissed from the Prince's room, no one bade him be off from the premises and he waited patiently for his second chance. He acted out his rôle of Calvinist refugee with remarkable skill. He was diligent at sermons (this was the item of his part that he deemed most perilous to his soul!) and was never seen without a psalm-book or some other Protestant

---

[1] In the meantime Mansfeld had substituted seals of a different pattern so that no advantage could have been gained by the foe through the stolen *cachets volants*.

volume in his hand. He even made friends with
the porter by borrowing a Bible and insinuated
himself into the fellowship of various other
members of the household on the score of his
theological brotherhood. He willingly consented
to carry despatches back to France, saying that
there was nothing now to keep him in Holland,
except his want of money, confirming the statement by displaying the holes in his shoes. When
this extreme poverty was reported to Orange, he
ordered twelve crowns to be given to the man.
This was done on Sunday, July 8th. Thus supplied
with funds by his intended victim, Gérard bought
a little second-hand pistol from René, one of the
Prince's guard. It was out of order, so he bought
two more from Sergeant de Forest, serving in
the company of Captain Caulier. These stood
his test, but he had not the balls he wanted, and
it was too late to make his plans and finish his
business on Monday.

On Tuesday, July 10th, the Prince and his
family came down-stairs to their midday dinner.
Gérard pressed up to the stairway and drew close
enough to Orange to ask for his passport. Louise
de Coligny noticed the trembling voice and asked
her husband who the wretched looking person
was. He replied that he was a man who wanted to
carry a message and they went in to dinner
without further thought. Gérard took the time
to get his pistols ready, loading one with three
and one with two balls. He was seen near the

stable and soon afterwards leaning against a pillar at the door of the dining-room. Within, the dinner was in progress. Rombert Uylenburgh, a Frisian, was the sole outsider. The Prince's three daughters, wife, and sister made up the rest of the party. Accustomed to use meal-time for certain kinds of business, Orange kept the conversation upon affairs in Friesland throughout the repast. As the party left the table about an hour after noon, Colonel Morgan, an Englishman, and several other people came into the hall. Orange exchanged some further words with Uylenburgh and then with Morgan. As he passed through the door and turned towards the stairs, Gérard came very close to his person, asking for the passport, and discharged the three balls into the Prince's body.

The stricken man gasped, "My God, take pity on my soul; my God, take pity on this poor people!" and then tottered. His equerry supported him to the stairs, upon which he sank, unable to utter another word, except a feeble "yes," in answer to a question in German from his sister, the Countess of Schwarzburg, whether he commended his soul to Jesus Christ. Then his voice was silenced, while his eyes still expressed sorrow as they looked on his sister. A little later, he was lifted from the stairs to a bed and carried into the dining-room, where he soon breathed his last.

Such is the official account and none of the Prince's own people denied the utterance of the

WILLIAM OF NASSAU, PRINCE OF ORANGE, C. 1583

last words accredited to him, words that have been treasured as a sacred legacy, as a signal proof of his devotion to the people. Their authenticity has not passed unchallenged by his enemies and by historical critics, but the burden of proof seems to be in favour of their truth.[1]

In the first confusion the murderer almost succeeded in effecting his escape. He had prepared two bladders and a little tube for inflating them to aid him in swimming the moat behind the convent, so that he could reach the horse standing saddled and bridled for his use without the town. Balthasar did, indeed, manage to reach the rampart and was about to spring into the moat, when a lackey and a halberdier seized him. "You villain," said one. "No villain I," he replied. "I have only fulfilled the King's behest." "What King?" "The King of Spain, my master." When they took him back into the Prinsenhof, he cried, "Ah! door, door, thou hast deceived me, I see I am a dead man." He was taken into the janitor's room, where he wrote his confession.

The hand that had once protected Jaureguy's

[1] Two reasons are urged to prove that the phrase was fabricated. The first is that given by Morillon (*Cor. de Granvelle*, xi., p. 81), that it was impossible that the *Orangier* could have said so much immediately after dinner, when he was always speechless from his libations. The second was that given by Bentivoglio that the nature of the wound rendered any utterance impossible.

Fruin's answer to the first is that had the Prince been incapacitated for speech or work from noon on, he would never have given Philip so much trouble; to the second, that the heart was not hit directly by the bullet. *Verspreide Geschriften*, iii., 65.

accomplices from torture was powerless now to aid this man, and the worst suffering that human ingenuity could invent was inflicted upon him in order to wrest complete information from the lips of the culprit. He evinced wonderful courage and steadfastness. In his first confession he told the truth about himself, but determinedly refused to incriminate any one and did not mention that the Jesuit at Trèves, a Grey Friar at Tournay, the Councillor d'Assonleville, and the Duke of Parma were all accessory before the fact. There was not the faintest show of repentance. He declared unflinchingly that were he one thousand leagues from Delft he would return to slay the archheretic who had ruined the land. During four successive days torture was applied to elicit further details and a little more information was gained, but no repentance. Gérard steadfastly maintained that his act was righteous and enjoined of God.

On Saturday, July 14th, the assassin was executed in a horrible manner, but never once during his agony, according to the testimony of Aerssens[1] the "heretical pensionary" of Brussels, did he say "*Ay my.*" After his right hand was burned off, filling the market-place with smoke and ill-odour, he made a cross with the maimed stump of his arm. His executioners declared that witchcraft alone could have enabled the condemned to show such Spartan endurance, while the

[1] *Cor.*, vi., p. 195.

Catholics held that only the blessedness of his deed could have fitted the holy sufferer to bear his martyrdom as became a saint.

Popular indignation probably found some relief in the hideously vindictive character of the execution, and the wrath of the people was kept alive by freedom to look upon the murdered man for many days, as he lay in state while the crowd streamed by. Criticism and distrust in his regard were forgotten and the construction of a shrine for hero-worship began in public memory at once, on the corner-stone of regret for the shortened life. It was, indeed, far too brief for its capabilities.

At the time of his death William of Nassau was fifty-one years, two months, and sixteen days old. In person, he was of about average height, his figure was rather spare, but well built. His head was excellently proportioned, his face rather thin, his complexion brunette, his eyes brown, with a pleasant expression. He wore his auburn beard slightly pointed. As a young man his hair, of the same colour as his beard, was thick and luxuriant. In later life this grew thin and he is represented with a little cap. It will be remembered that he called himself a bald Calvinist, with a play of words that cannot be rendered in English.

His old physician, Petrus van Foreest, present to pay him the last honours of the science that had once brought him back to life, declared that he was remarkably sound of heart and limb and destined by nature for many more years of activity.¹

During the weeks that intervened before the funeral, one artist, Christian Jansz. van Bieselingen, managed to defy the express prohibition of the States-General against any portrait of the dead Prince and succeeded in sketching him on his bier. The States had issued their order in fear "lest the enemy obtaining possession of such a picture, might ridicule it."²

On August 3d, a great public funeral took place. Official and private mourners in stately procession escorted the body to the "New Church," across the market-place, and saw it laid under the pavement, now covered by an elaborate monument. The two nearest kinsmen, Count John and Philip William, were missing, but Maurice and his cousins were there to listen to the "brief and consoling sermon" from the text, "Blessed are the dead that die in the Lord . . . and their works live after them." And in regard to both life and works there were many opinions outside the church.

The announcements of the murder promptly sent off by the Estates and the States-General were not the only official notifications despatched

---

[1] Dr. Van Foreest has left a detailed account of the process of embalming. See Fruin, iii., p. 40.

[2] See *Oud-Holland*, 1889, p. 281. A sketch of the Prince's head after death is in the Prinsenhof, but it is not certain whether this is the sketch referred to.

from the Netherlands. The Duke of Parma sent
Philip his warmest personal congratulations that
fitting punishment had at last been meted out as
penalty for crimes against God, Christianity, and
the King. Further, he declared that the relatives
of the assassin "now in glory" should at least
reap the fruits of his noble sacrifice. Gérard's
family were fully in sympathy with this idea and
hastened to make themselves known. Twenty-five
thousand crowns were not easy for Parma to raise
at the moment, but he drew up five reasons why
the claim ought not to be ignored and suggested
that some of the victim's confiscated estates in
the Franche-Comté might be used to liquidate
the debt of honour. Liévremont, Hostal, and
Dammartin were accordingly bestowed upon
Gérard's four brothers and three sisters, together with a patent of nobility, this last given,
indeed, only after ripe deliberation, as it was
dated March 4, 1589.

Cardinal Granvelle, too, was profuse in his
expression of satisfaction at the final success of
the Ban, and wrote:

Alençon died on the tenth of June, Orange on
the tenth of July, and it would be little loss if the
queen mother were to die on the tenth of August.
Alençon and Orange are in the right place and the
martyrdom suffered by our good Burgundian in
executing so heroic an act ought to have fitting
recompense.[1]

[1] *Cor.*, vi., cxxvi.

Such are sentences from different letters. The violent and treacherous death was thus accepted as being a mere act of justice somewhat irregularly performed, owing to the exigencies of the situation. Contemporaneous criticism of Philip for setting a price upon his antagonist is not harsh. It was not until one hundred and sixty-four years later that the Ban was cited as an instance of a "law contrary to nature and the ennobling of the assassin subversive of the ideas of honour, morality, religion." But in this generalisation Montesquieu was moved by modern, not by past theories.[1] In the sixteenth century there was no horror of arbitrary acts affecting life and death.

It is said that Calvin wrote to the King of Navarre (September 30, 1561):

Honour, glory, and riches shall be the reward of your praise, but above all do not fail to rid the country of those zealous scoundrels who stir up people to revolt against us. Such monsters should be exterminated as I have exterminated Michael Servetus, the Spaniard.[2]

Philip of Spain had no greater conscientious scruples about removing William of Orange than the Genevan reformer had in disposing of the heretical Spaniard. The "you, you, you," with which Du Maurier makes him characterise Orange as the root of all evil in 1559 had remained in his mind ever since, as the simple embodiment

[1] *L'esprit des loix*, xxix., ch. 16.   [2] Quoted. Original not found.

of the twenty-five years' trouble in the Netherlands. From his point of view, William of Nassau, a German nobleman, with every reason for unquestioning loyalty to the King's family, had forfeited the right to exist within, while he would not go without, Philip's hereditary domains. Glance at the formal arraignment in the Ban. Many of the articles in the brief were literally true. The Prince of Orange had been a favourite of the late Emperor and had been distinguished by highly honourable appointments at an early age. Even at this epoch, gratitude and party loyalty are not considered out of place in recognition of official gifts, so that Philip's grieved surprise at the Prince's failure to be bound to his side by past favours is comprehensible. From the moment when the monarch's presence was removed from the Low Countries, Orange certainly threw his full weight into the balance of opposition to his dearest wishes. While still in the Council of State, still a high official, a confidential lieutenant of the absent King, he had countenanced rebellious proceedings. Though his formal resignation was an honourable termination to what might be termed overt acts, his resumption of the vacated offices at the point of the sword was flat rebellion. His persistent reiteration that he was simply opposing an unworthy servant in behalf of king, of law, and of people, was surely specious logic, even though it seemed perfectly to endorse the King's own assertion that all the trouble sprang from Alva's imposition of an unpopular tax "as we had never ordered him to do," and that Orange made capital out of the error by "stoking" the fires of discontent while he himself was hastening to change his Netherland policy as soon as he saw the conflagration. Again, it is not surprising that the most Catholic King should characterise the liberty of conscience in the Netherlands as simple dire confusion of religion (*liberté de conscience ou à vray dire, confusion de religion*), considering how little unanimity there was among the reformers of different creeds.

Moreover, it was perfectly true that the Nassau brothers and other Germans were placed in responsible positions in the face of the principle phrased in an early stage of the revolt that Netherland offices should be barred to all foreigners (*uitlanders*) without property interest at stake.

Again in 1577–78, when Don John was honestly trying to carry out a conciliatory policy, Orange did undoubtedly exert every nerve to discredit him, and when a mighty effort was made to arbitrate the differences at Cologne, Orange imposed impossible stipulations before he would consent to participation. He was right. The conflict was irrepressible and had to be fought out. This was plain to such contemporaneous observers as Sir Francis Walsingham, who states his own opinion to Lord Burleigh (report of a con-

[1584] *The Assassination* 475

versation with Catherine de' Medici, August 3, 1581)[1]:

But for the present, whoever doth consider to what extreme degree of alienation from the King the said subjects of the Low Countries are grown unto having beaten down his Arms and renounced his Government, how impossible it is to draw the Prince of Orange any ways to trust the King or the King to be reconciled unto him in respect of a book written by the said Prince wherein the King's honour is greatly touched, shall see no reason to hope for any reconciliation and that the Authors of that device do propound the same but for a delay to serve the King of Spain's turn.

Thus the two men had confronted each other, the one consistent of purpose and supported by certain inherited principles regarding just monarchical power and divine authority;—the other often inconsistent because he was, perforce, feeling his way among new conditions which had to be adjusted. Which of the two failed? Was it the King, convinced that safety to soul and to human society was only obtainable by the maintenance of the ancient Church as supreme caretaker of all? Or was it William of Nassau, with his opportunist endeavours to minimise all theological shades of difference and to establish one code of ethics and religion as a working basis for a harmonious *modus vivendi?* Which of the two was the victor?

[1] Digges, *Compleat Ambassador*, p. 432.

In 1584, Philip's policy looked almost completely triumphant in the realms where the sun never set. As far as the Netherlands was concerned, Protestantism was pretty thoroughly exterminated in the Walloon regions, where it had first been militant. Out across the ocean in the lands under Spanish rule, obedience to Rome was being consistently enforced. In the very years when the outbreak in the Netherlands was coming to a head, 1562–67, Philip's servants were busied in giving "Christian souls" to the Seminole Indians of Florida—lately named for the Eastertide,—and to the natives of his own namesake islands. In the Philippines, there was no pitting of strength with the Reformers. The devoted missionaries that went thither with Legaspi in 1565 were followed by an unbroken line of successors who succeeded gradually in converting all the Filipinos to some semblance of the Roman Catholic Faith.

In America, it was different. The message of peace was carried in one hand, while a sword was waved menacingly in the other, and for a time the sword gained its end. Spanish emigration laws were drawn up with much concern for the salvation of the aboriginal population. People of bad morals and questionable doctrine were to be excluded from the fair new world so that the virgin soil should not be contaminated. Theoretically at least, the western hemisphere was not regarded by Spain as a refuge for undesirables. Evil-doers and those tainted with

pernicious heresy were to have no foothold on
the earth, if Pope and potentate could keep them
away. The conversion of the savage had been
the primary reason for the papal approval of the
"division of the world like an orange" between
Christian princes in 1494, and to that ideal Philip
was true, with a certain temporary success, not
only in conversion to the Church, but in checking
the spread of Protestantism.

Glance at one episode in America. The French
forestalled the English in the idea of colony-
building in America by non-conformists. During
the years 1562–67, when Orange was still cherishing hopes of seeing the Netherland provinces
administered by home rule while faithful to their
hereditary absentee prince, Gaspard de Coligny
was trying to found a little Protestant state on
American soil. One effort was abortive,[1] but
finally a body of Huguenots under one Jean
Ribault were despatched to Florida. Wise ideas
of colonisation were wanting in their methods
of action, in their plans of settlement,—but that is
neither here nor there. The emigrants were established at the mouth of the St. John's River and
might eventually have learned how to develop
a new country to the best advantage, had not

[1] This stanza was attributed to some of the first party who did not find Florida to their taste:
> Qui veut aller à la Floride
> Qu'il y aille, j'y ay esté
> Et revenu sec et aride
> Et abbatu de povreté.

Philip II. sent Pedro Menendez to expel the trespassers from his domain. Menendez gives his own account of how he fulfilled his commission.[1] It is a perfectly simple and direct statement that he took the fort and killed two hundred and thirty heretics. Another band was met at a distance from the fort.

We told them how we had taken their Fort and hanged all within, because they had built it without your Majesty's permission and *because they were scattering their odious Lutheran doctrines in these provinces*. . . . After much talk they offered to surrender if I would grant their lives.

The spokesman was assured that Menendez would act as God had ordered.

Then he returned and they came to deliver up their arms. I had their hands tied behind them and had them stabbed to death . . . deeming that to punish them in this manner would be serving God, our Lord, and your Majesty. Hereafter they will leave us free to plant the Gospel and enlighten the natives. . . .

It was a clear massacre in cold blood. Sixteen artisans alone were preserved for their craft. There were also about fifty women and children under fifteen not slain at the first. These last caused Menendez embarrassment. He did not exactly want to butcher them, but it "causes me deep sorrow to see them among my people on

[1] Letter to Philip, *Unwritten History of St. Augustine*, 1909.

account of their horrid religion." He felt it important to keep the air pure from taint because "in a few years this land will be a suburb of Spain, reached in forty days."

Thus was doctrine exalted above human life, even out in the wilderness, and for human sufferings there was not the slightest pity. The world has grown softer hearted since those times. In a New England State lately, a just capital punishment was long delayed, because no executioner could be found to fulfil the law's decree of taking life for a life.

At the end, however, the severity counted for nothing. Philip failed. The Church he loved could not check the growth of the Protestant faith, and the omnipotence of Spain proved to be a chimera, like his paramount authority in the Netherlands. When he met his own death his policy had met defeat everywhere. By that time, Henry IV. had beaten him in France, the Nassaus ultimately defeated him in Holland, and the English conquered him on the sea. He was bankrupt, his country ruined, his dream of the universal predominance of Catholicism at an end. He alone still believed in his dominance—but his failure was certain. The time-spirit of the sixteenth century was an opponent he could not down. In his day Spain was the richest nation of Europe,—to-day the national wealth is rated at $6,000,000,000, $1,000,000,000 less than that of little Belgium. Its population is about 19,000,000, yet its total exports and imports are about $338,000,000, compared with $1,900,000,000 for the Netherlands, with 6,000,000 of population. Spain's indebtedness is the largest per capita indebtedness in Europe. The individual demands for the advantages of civilisation are meagre—4700 is, for instance, the sum-total of her post-offices; Canada, with half Spain's population, has 10,800.[1] Spain is indeed Europe's last stronghold of mediævalism, and Philip it was who set the standard for her methods.

Turning from the triumphant survivor who failed to the fallen opponent, there is greater difficulty in judging of the ultimate effect of his life and of his real character. William of Nassau was by no means a simple personality. Nor can he, like Philip, be framed in his past and judged through the medium of the atmosphere in which he lived. In so many respects he was not of his epoch. He could have held his own in the nineteenth far better than in the sixteenth century. In regard to his effect, compare him with Gaspard de Coligny. The latter was the leader of men whose own enthusiasm spurred them on, who turned to him for sympathy and advice because he drew his religious inspiration from the same source that they did. He was only eminent among others of his kind. Orange, on the other hand, forced an action,—that of political revolt, and put himself at the head of the actors. He was the

[1] Summaries of December, 1909.

soul and mainspring of all,—even while his opinions were strangely at variance with his followers. Yet with his fall, his cause did not perish, while Coligny's death meant the death-blow to the political recognition of the Huguenots for which he was striving. The stream of the movement was drained of its vigour, though it continued to exist until the revocation of the Edict of Nantes, when it dwindled into a tiny stream like the brook at the base of a ravine.

On the other hand, after the Prince's death, before the sun set on that July 10th, a definite resolution had been adopted by the States-General that they should "look to the safety of the land, cities, places, and soldiery, both in the camp and elsewhere under our authority, to the end that no chance be given to the foe to bring our affairs into confusion."

Two bodies were in session at Delft,—the Estates of Holland and the States-General of the provinces in revolt. They it was who acted as executive and sent out formal announcements of the loss they had suffered. New responsibility was shouldered by them and the fight went on. What had been initiated under Orange had gained too much momentum to stop.[1]

---

[1] *De vergadering der Staten-Generaal op 10 July na den noen.* J. Huizinga in "Bijdragen voor Vaderlandsche Geschiedenis" 4de reeks, 1907, p. 361. The writer has proved that credit is due to the united deputies, not alone to Holland, as has been believed. Nor was there a hurry call for convention. The deputies were on the spot, transacting regular business.

Orange has been compared to Cromwell, to Washington, and to Lincoln, as well as to Coligny. With the first there seems comparatively little in common. In regard to the other three, it may be conceded that Orange fell below their standards in certain elements of moral fibre. The fact that there were different ethical principles in his epoch is not full explanation of the differences. The words and phrases used by him and his contemporaries are perfectly explicit in theories of veracity and of justice that were never lived up to.

Possibly Orange resembles Lincoln more closely than he does any other leader, in spite of the fact that the one was the flower of an hereditary aristocracy, and the other of a pioneer democracy. The similarity consists in the possession of distinct political ambition because each felt that he could achieve the end desired, and in devotion to an ideal state, a state sprung from or consisting of a union of political entities, a state with a nice balance of power, the whole state being the first consideration to each man in contradistinction to the sectional, religious, or personal aims which were engrossing many of their fellow workers. In the identification of Lincoln's name with the abolition of slavery as an institution, it is now forgotten how bitterly fervid abolitionists criticised him for his dilatory steps towards freedom for all, for his persistent attention to the preservation of the Union as the first thing needful, prior to his assumption of authority in the burning question that was consuming them.

Wrong as we think slavery is, we can yet afford to let it alone where it is because that much is due to the necessity arising from its actual presence in the nation, but can we, while our votes will prevent it, allow it to spread into the national territories and to overrun us here in these free States.

This ante-bellum utterance of Abraham Lincoln at a moment when compromise and averted war still seemed possible, may be counted as indicative of the same mental conception of responsibility as that of Orange which called down the virulent attacks of Dathenus and his friends when they murmured that the Prince was jockeying with the truth. "I am approached with the most opposite opinions expressed on the part of religious men, each of whom is equally certain that he represents the Divine will," said Lincoln (September, 1862), and the epithets that were applied to Father Abraham in the press and pulpit of the time were not wholly different from those hurled at "Father William." At the same time, slavery was as repugnant to Lincoln as inquisition into, and persecution for, private beliefs were to Orange, while the one recognised political expediency and even property rights, the other religious rights, in those of different views. A certain trip down the Mississippi River taken by Abraham Lincoln as a boy when the aspects and conditions of a slave market impressed him indelibly with the iniquity of the "institution," may be compared to the impression, —traditional though it may be,—with the shock felt by the Prince in 1559, when Henry II. confided to him the plans for enforcing the Inquisition as they rode through the forest of Vincennes. Nevertheless, while abominating the tyranny of the institution and stemming the way to its entry into virgin territory, Lincoln still was unwilling to hasten to sweep away legal rights, just as Orange was unwilling to ignore the rights of Nationalist Catholics. Both men worked very gradually through a long political experience, when compromise still seemed feasible between conflicting interests, and when certain issues were subordinated to what each leader considered *national* necessities. Orange went further in this spirit than did the American. In phrase more vigorous than elegant, Lincoln declared that he never attempted to stroke "the back of a political porcupine," a task that Orange may be charged with undertaking in his negotiation with Anjou, in his persistent choice of France as an ally.

Again, in their relation with the public, there is a marked similarity between the Prince and the President. Lincoln pursued a consistent policy of taking the people into his confidence. Orange never lost an opportunity in the successive readjustment of political conditions in Holland, in her successive unions with Zealand and the

extension of those unions to her sister provinces
of bringing the smaller towns to the fore, of extending the responsibility for concerted action.
Yet he was never aided by whole-souled enthusiasm for a United Netherland free from Spaniards
—such enthusiasm as Garibaldi and Cavour found
in fighting for a United Italy free from Austrians.

Such likeness as exists between Orange and
George Washington lies rather in the facts of provincial rebellion against distant sovereigns than
in traits of character common to the two men.
George Washington was built on fairly simple
lines and one portion of his life, one phase of his
career was consistent with another. William of
Nassau was a complex and intricate personality.
Had he been born at an earlier date in the century,
he would probably have been, like his uncle, a
loyal courtier to the end of his life. He was a
worldling, wanting wealth, power, and position
for himself and his kinsfolk, ready to accept political methods, long content to count a State Church
as part of useful state machinery, with little real
feeling for religion. This has been said again
and again throughout this story and it is hardly
necessary to repeat it. Yet the thought of that
early attitude comes back as the conviction is
forced upon one that from it the man grew to
accept a real religious belief which completely
differentiates him from Elizabeth of England and
Henry of Navarre. His toleration was not the
political and ecclesiastical compromising of the

one, nor the cynicism of the other. It is curious how little he was really aided in his plans by his peculiar attitude towards theological controversy. Those words referred to, "*Het geschil is te kleen om gesplijt te blijven*," "The difference is too petty to justify your divisions," as an utterance made by him in 1567 when urging Lutherans, Calvinists, and Anabaptists to come to some agreement of faith, never helped his cause. All three sects alike simply distrusted him because he found "petty" what they exalted into essential truth. Coligny with his single-mindedness might have gathered more uncompromising and more closely serried ranks under his standard. And, if guessing be justifiable on hypothetical historical premises, the conjecture might be hazarded that had Orange been alive from 1815 to 1830, a united Netherland realm would still exist. His cast of mind was three centuries out of place. Strange, though, that his theories of toleration finally enhanced the reputation of Holland in that regard beyond her deserts! It was not until long after his death that many narrow barriers to personal liberty were removed. The progress towards political eligibility, irrespective of creed, was very slow in the Netherlands. Even in New Netherland the spirit of intoleration was rampant. Lutherans and Quakers found no welcome, but inconvenient restrictions at the infant port of New York in the middle of the seventeenth century,—and the restrictions were not dead letters.

One of Brandt's stories is delightfully typical of the Prince's own propensity to ignore theological disputes. During a passing visit at Utrecht he chanced to select the church for his Sunday devotions where the pastor, Hubert Duifhuis, was suspected of dangerous liberalism. A deputation of burghers waited on their visitor at once to remonstrate against his showing sympathy with the criticised dominie.

"Oh, I simply said I would go where there was the best preaching," he answered, "and they carried my cushions thither. I knew nothing of the controversy. The sermon was excellent. Next time I will hear the other minister."

Probably neither faction was pleased and both were puzzled by the indifference. Another instance of his attitude of mind is the course he pursued in Antwerp in 1578 when he refrained from going to church because the political situation was so delicate. This fact appears in a certain letter written by a deputy to the States-General, sitting at Antwerp, to his constituents at Tournay. Barthélemy Liebart was evidently in the habit of keeping his friends informed. Regarding the transactions of September 10th he wrote [1]:

When the Prince of Orange had announced that God had given him a daughter whom he wished to have baptised, he said *that he had abstained from the*

[1] *Cor.*, vi., p. 311.

exercise of his religion for more that a year, but now, considering that it was freely exercised publicly in this city (as in the house of the Jesuits, in the castle chapel, and in two other places in the said city) he was determined, henceforth, to suit his own convenience in public, but desired to inform the Estates first of his intention so that they would not take it ill. Whereupon *no answer was given*, either because they wished to pass by the point in silence or because they wished to leave it to his discretion.

Here, too, it is probable that the middle course persistently pursued by Orange had excited much adverse criticism from friend and foe.

The Prince shows at his best in his relations with his own family. In following the mass of Nassau correspondence, intimate and semi-official, the reader is inspired with a sense of fundamental trust in the man, sufficient to overbalance the criticism evoked by the blots—and not all were trivial—that mar his great qualities. Not only trust but profound sympathy. For the leader's loneliness often comes into sharp relief. He was self-reliant but by no means self-sufficient. Indeed during certain periods of his career, the solitary character of his mind, as well as of his political position, is pathetic. The desire that he had to be justified of men is very dominant. It was an appeal for sympathy from somewhere.

Between the contradictory adjectives applied to him, it is difficult indeed to select one that is perfectly apt, though it is comparatively easy

THE STAIRCASE IN THE PRINZENHOF.
(From an etching in *De Moord van 1584*.)

to discard the one most closely identified with him. The term *silent* or taciturn is so singularly inept that it is hard to see how it ever became attached to the genial, social Prince, clever in turning his memory for names and faces to good account, with a warm word for high and low; one who made a friend every time he took off his hat; one who actually excited criticism because he relieved the strain under which he lived by his evident enjoyment of general unrestrained table talk, interspersed with jesting stories. "Some wiseacres," says Hooft, "were annoyed at this, not realising that deep anxiety underlay the merriment." Here again is a passing resemblance to Abraham Lincoln. Silent Orange never was, though always astute. Very probably it was a misquotation that turned a term *sly*, often applied to him, into the *taciturn*, used first by inimical and gradually adopted by friendly Belgian writers, even such as Gachard.[1]

[1] Fruin has discussed this question (vii., 404). In a pamphlet of 1574, *Ontleiding van Pandora*, occurs this sentence: "When Titelman, the furious inquisitor of Flanders, heard that Egmont and Hoorn were arrested, he said, 'If sly William has escaped, the joy will be of short duration'" (*Als sluwe Willem het ontkomen is zal de vreugde toch van korten duur zijn*). This phrase with Granvelle substituted for Titelman is to be found in the third edition (1608) of Van Meteren. Strada copies the story and *taciturnus* in Latin, *zwiiger* in Dutch, then took root in story. Fruin shows that in Granvelle's known letters prior to 1568, his usual characterisation of the Prince is as a young and thoughtless person. One single contemporaneous use of the adjective occurs in the diary of a Groningen peasant, Abel Eppens, but that seems to be the sole instance of it. Fruin protests against the adoption of the epithet, as does Blok. See *Bijdragen*, v. viii.

Nothing is more typical of the Prince's dominant characteristic—his inclination to seize on passing opportunities—than the names selected for his children. They reflect the colour of successive phases of his career. In 1554, when the eldest boy was baptised, the Nassau *William* yielded first place to Spanish *Philip*. Naturally, too, *Marie* was named for the Queen, under whose regency her father was loyal lieutenant to the Emperor. It was also natural that he should permit the great Elector's daughter to remember her father in *Maurice* and herself in *Anne*. Then come Charlotte's six daughters. It was hoped that *Louise* would please the Duke of Montpensier, but *Juliana* was not chosen for political reasons. That was given in natural respect and real affection for Juliana of Stolberg. During the years when the others were born, one after the other, new friends were to be won to the cause. The second girl, *Elizabeth*, was godchild to the English Queen, who, it was hoped, would prove a fairy godmother in her gifts to the Netherlands. Then *Catherine Belgia* symbolised the brief union of all the seventeen provinces and the States-General were her sponsors. *Flandrina*, *Brabantina*, and *Antwerpiana* were all three named in the hopes of exciting especial feelings of loyalty from provinces and cities for the father's plans, and the godfathers were numerous in their official capacity. Last came *Frederick Henry*, whose godfathers, the kings of Denmark and Navarre, were chosen, perhaps, with the intention of showing that the alliance with the French Catholics was to be definitely abandoned.

Even if William of Nassau were not the personification of certain qualities that go to make the popular hero, nevertheless he fully deserves to be ranked among the marked men of the world. He is eminently conspicuous. He towers far above the crowd. He was not like any one else, yet he was so intensely human in both his virtues and his failings, that he is perfectly comprehensible to a later age.

Instead of climbing up to luxury from humble beginnings, as political leaders often do, his career was marked by a change from luxury to poverty. The years of wandering and deprivation were great contrasts to the time when he gave expensive and fantastic banquets on table-cloths made of sugar. That he was ambitious may be granted, but, as said before, it was an ambition for a purpose to which his own status was repeatedly subordinated, an ambition that gave him courage to endure hardship and sacrifice. From having an extravagant and costly wardrobe, the time came when he knew which suit had been sent to the tailor's for repairs, when the once lavish host could make the closest calculations how he could manage to afford a little gift and what table utensil could be spared.

One charge repeatedly made against him is that of cowardice. That his bent was towards peace rather than war is certain, but assuredly, he never allowed considerations for his personal safety to interfere with his plans. His early experiences on the French frontier accustomed him to danger, and though it chanced that he did not take an active part in the pitched battles of his Huguenot allies nor of his own cause, it could not have been cowardice that drove him from the field. He was always exposed to personal peril and always conscious in taking the risks. Warnings were entirely disregarded. He visited Leiden, reeking as the city was from pestilence; he was so little watchful in Brussels that his wife begged him at least to sup within his own walls, and he took scant precautions for his protection even after he was declared a free target for any aim.

In stamping him as statesman rather than general, it must still be acknowledged that in spite of the rebuffs he met, nevertheless Alva was baffled, Requesens discouraged, and Parma kept at bay; and during all the fourteen years when these experienced generals were at work, it was *de facto* the Prince of Orange who was responsible for their discomfiture. In certain enterprises, as in the relief of Leiden, he showed, or at least encouraged, a disregard of stereotyped methods that was extremely effective. War was not the science it became later, and undoubtedly the Prince's military technique was far inferior to that of his son, Maurice. But he himself was potent in what he did. The failures that overwhelmed him were inevitable from the nature of things, but the seeds of success which were planted in the sturdy little nation fell from his hand to blossom later. Holland is right in calling him *Pater patriæ*.

STATES-GENERAL MEDAL

ORANGE MEDAL

THE WILHELMUSLIED

Written and adopted in 1572, the authorship of the verses has never been decided. It has been attributed to Philip Marnix, to Coornhert, and to an unknown follower of Orange. A late investigator decides that there is no proof of Marnix's authorship, and thinks that one J. P. Howaert (1533–1599), a professional *rederyker* or rhetorician, was the author, while Prof. Blok suggests Adrian Saravia. See Fl. van Duyse, *Het Oude Nederlandsche Lied*, den Haag, 1905, and Blok's *Bijdragen* Nʳ 4, 1910. The three stanzas are fair examples of the fifteen composing the song. The air was an old one.

I

Wilhelmus of Nassau,
  I am of German line,
And faithful to the Fatherland
  Bide I, till death be mine.
As sov'reign Prince of Orange
  I am undaunted, free;
His Majesty of Spain
  I've honoured loyally.

I

Wilhelmus van Nassouwe
  ben ick van deutschen bloet;
den Vaderlant ghetrouwe
  blijf ick tot in den doet,
Een prince van Oraengien
  ben ick vrij, onverveert,
den coninc van Hispaengien
  heb ick altijt gheërt.

4

My life and all that is my own
　I to your cause confide;
My brothers, loyal gentlemen,
　Stand faithful at my side.
Count Adolf we left lying there
　In Friesland's woful fray,
His soul in the eternal life
　Awaits the Judgment Day.

15

Before my God I dare assert,
　Before His Sovereign might,
That at my hand the King of Spain
　No slur has met nor slight.
But that to God, the Over-Lord,
　The Majesty supreme,
In Justice I submit myself
　To honour and obey.

4

Lijf ende goed te samen
　heb ick u nict gheschoont.
mijn broeders, hooch von namen,
　hebben 't u ooc vertoont.
Graaf Adolf is ghebleven
　in Vrieslant in den slach,
sijn siel in eeuwich leven
　verwacht den jongsten dach.

15

Voor God uil ick belijden
　en Sijner groter macht,
dat ick tot ghenen tijden
　den coninc heb veracht,
dan dat ick God den Heere
　der hoochster majesteit
heb moeten obedieren
　in der gherechticheit.

BIBLIOGRAPHY

An excellent and discriminating résumé of the sources for this period (1533–1584) is given in Blok's *History of the Dutch People* (English version, New York, 1900), vol. iii., p. 500.

See also Pirenne, *Bibliographie de l'histoire de Belgique* (Bruxelles, 1902) and the bibliographies in *Cambridge Modern History*, vol. iii., p. 98, and in *Histoire générale du ive siècle à nos jours* (Lavisse and Rambaud, Paris, 1895), vol. v., p. 203.

The following list comprises simply the printed volumes referred to directly and indirectly in the text. In many cases others might have been used. Practical use of the list leads insensibly to the general and collateral literature of the XVI. century, which of course, is not specified here. The dates and theological bias of the important contemporary writers are mentioned.

Archivalia:

The Hague.—The most important correspondence of William of Orange has long been accessible in the *Archives ou correspondance inédite de la maison d'Orange Naussau* edited by M. Groen von Prinsterer in eight volumes (Leiden, 1835–1847). The papers selected from those at The Hague are supplemented by the results of Groen's investigations at Besançon, Paris, Brussels, Cassel, and Wiesbaden. Comparison of the printed matter with such originals as exist in the *Koninklijke Huisarchief* proves that the scholar, learned and conscientious though he was, did not always use the most approved methods of editing. His own political and theological bias is constantly betrayed or rather conscientiously indicated in the turn given by his selections, notes, and omissions.

Brussels.—M. Gachard, archivist of Belgium, furnished a complement to the above series in his *Correspondance de Guillaume le taciturne* (6 vols., Bruxelles, 1847–1866). The bulk of these papers are in the archives at Brussels, but many more were collected from Paris, London, Madrid, and Simancas. Only those originals to be found at Brussels have been compared with the printed matter. A greater degree of accuracy is evident in this work than in that of M. Groen. At the same time the material, mainly official, is far more colourless and thus less useful for biography, pure and simple. There are nearly 2000 documents in these two series and their supplements, about 1000 of which emanate from William of Orange. Many other letters, autograph signed or in contemporaneous copies, are scattered through the publications mentioned in the lists. Sometime these last will be more available when the suggestion of the Commission of Advice for *s'Rijks Geschiedkundige Publicatiën* takes effect and a complete collection of the Prince's letters as a supplement to the work of Groen and Gachard is issued.

It is a matter of regret that many an interesting letter, never published, had to be discarded for one already printed because the latter did better service in telling the story.

Bibliography

Acts of the Privy Council of England. New series, v. viii., A.D. 1571–1575. Ed. JOHN ROCHE DASENT. 1 v., 8vo. London, 1894.

ADY, MRS. (JULIA CARTWRIGHT), *Isabella d'Este (1474–1539).* 2 v. London, 1903.

Apologie de Guillaume de Nassau, Justification, etc., Ed. A. LACROIX. 1 v., 12mo. Bruxelles, 1858.

ARNOLDI, JOHANNES VON, *Historische Denkwürdigkeiten.* 1 v., 8vo. Leipzig, 1817.

——*Geschichte der Oranien-Nassauischen Länder und ihrer Regenten.* 3 v. in 4, 8vo. Hadamar, 1799–1816.

AUBÉRY, LOUIS, Seignior du Maurier (d. 1687), *Histoire de Guillaume de Nassau avec des notes politiques, historiques, et critiques par M. Amelot de la Houssaye.* (Work was formerly known as *Mémoires*—author was Protestant, son to French ambassador in Holland.) Londres, 1754.

BAKHUIZEN VAN DEN BRINK, R. C., *Het Huwelijk van Willem van Oranje met Anna van Saxen.* 1 v. Amsterdam, 1853.

——*Studien en schetzen.* 4 v. s'Gravenhage, 1877.

——*La première assemblée des états de Hollande en 1572,* in "Les archives du Royaume des Pays-Bas." Recueil de documents inédits. 1 v., 8vo. La Haye, 1857.

BEAUFORT, L. F. DE, *Het leven van Willem I, prins van Oranje.* 3 vols. Leiden, 1732 (published anonymously).

BENTIVOGLIO, GUIDO (Cardinal, b. 1577, d. 1644, Catholic and royalist). *Della guerra di Fiandra.* 3 v. Milano, 1806.

BIZOT, PIERRE, *Histoire métallique de la république de Hollande.* Vol. i. Paris, 1688.

BLOK, PETRUS JOHANNES (Professor at Leiden, since 1894), *Eene Hollandsche stad in de middeleeuwen.* 1 v.

——*Eene Hollandsche stad onder de Bourgondisch-Oosterijksche heerschappij.* 1 v. s'Gravenhage, 1883–1884.

——*Correspondentie van en treffende Lodewijk de Nassau.* 1 v. Utrecht, 1887.

——*Lodewijk van Nassau (1538–1574).* 1 v. s'Gravenhage, 1889.

——*De slag op de Mookerheide, 1574.* Groningen, 1891.

——*De watergeusen in Engeland, 1568–1572.* 1 v. s'Gravenhage, 1896.

——*Geschiedenis van het Nederlandsche volk.* Vol. iii. Groningen, 1896. English translation by Ruth Putnam, New York, 1900.

―――― *Archivalia belangrijk voor de geschied enis van Nederland. Verslag aangaande een onderzoek in Duitschland. Verslag aangaande een onderzoek in Oostenrijk. Verslag aangaande een onderzoek in Engeland. Verslag aangaande een onderzoek in Parijs.* s'Gravenhage, 1888–89. '91 and '97.

BOR, PIETER CHRISTIANZ (b. Utrecht 1559, d. 1635, Hollander and Protestant), *Oorspronck, begin ende aenvang der Nederlandscher oorlogen.* 6 vols. Amsterdam and Leiden, 1621.

BÖTTIGER, KARL WILHELM, *Wilhelm's von Oranien Ehe mit Anna von Sachsen*, in Raumer's "Historisches Taschenbuch." V. vii., p. 81. Leipzig, 1836.

BRANDT, G. (b. Amsterdam 1626, d. 1685, Hollander and Protestant), *Historie der reformatie en andere kerkelijke geschiedenissen in en omntrent de Nederlanden tot 1600.* 4 vols. Amsterdam, 1677–1704.

BURGON, JOHN W., *The Life and Times of Sir Thomas Gresham* (b. London 1519, d. 1579, Protestant). 2 v., 8vo. London, 1839.

BUSSEMAKER, DR. TH., *De afscheiding der Waalsche Gemeente van de generale unie.* 2 v., 8vo. Haarlem, 1895.

―――― *Opgave vom hetgeen de "Coleccion de documentos ineditos para la historia de España" betreffende onze Vaderlandsche Geschiedenis bevat.* Bijdragen, 1896. 3d series, vol. ix., pp. 352–458. Bussemaker's article is a useful guide to the *Coleccion* (3 vols. Madrid, 1842–95).

Calendar of State Papers. (Spanish, 1568–1579.) Preserved principally in the archives of Simancas. Ed. MARTIN A. S. HUME. London, 1894.

―――― (1572–74) Preserved in State Paper Department. Ed. ALLEN JAMES CROSBY. London, 1876.

Calendar of the Manuscripts of the Marquis of Salisbury (Cecil Papers). Hist. Manuscripts Commission. v. ii. London, 1888.

CARNERO, A., *Historia de las guerras civiles que ha avido en los estados de Flandres des del anno 1559 hasta el de 1609.* (Spaniard, served as soldier in Flanders, 1585). (folio.) Brussels, 1625.

DASENT, JOHN ROCHE (editor), *Acts of Privy Council of*

England. New series, v. viii.–xiii. (1571–1582). 8vo. London, 1894–1898.

DELABORDE, COUNT JULES, *Charlotte de Bourbon.* 8vo, 1 v. Paris, 1888.

——*Louise de Coligny.* 2 v., 8vo. Paris, 1890.

DIGGES, SIR DUDLEY (b. 1583, d. 1639), *The Compleat Ambassador.* 1 v., folio. London, 1655.

Documents concernant les relations entre le duc d'Anjou et les Pays-Bas (1576–1583). 3 v. s'Gravenhage, 1886–91.

Documents hist. inédits concernant l'histoire des Pays-Bas (1577–84). Ed. KERVYN DE VOLKAERSBEKE and A. DIEGERICK. 2 v., 8vo. Gand, 1849.

DUMONT, J. (editor), *Corps universel diplomatique du droit des gens.* Tome v., partie i. London, 1727.

FRUIN, ROBERT (professor at Leiden, d. 1900), *Verspreide Geschriften met anteekeningen, toevoegsels en verbeteringen uit des schrijvers nalatenschap.* Editors, P. J. Blok, S. L. Muller, S. Muller. 10 v., 8vo. s'Gravenhage, 1900–1905.

During a long lifetime Fruin wrote upon the important episodes of the Eighty Years' War as occasion arose. It was only after his death that the scattered articles were collected. Those referred to or followed in this volume are the following:

——Het karakter van het Nederlandsche volk, i., 1.

——De drie tijdvakken der Nederlandsche geschiedenis, i., 22.

——Een Hollandsche stad in de middeneuwen, i., 49.

——De Nederlandsche beroerten in de 16ᵉ eeuw uit een katholick oogpunt beschouwd, ii., 1.

——De overwinning bij Heiligerlee, ii., 84.

——Prins Willem I. in het jaar 1570, ii., 111.

——Nederland in 1571 betrokken in de politiek der groote mogendheden, ii., 167.

——De Gorcumsche Martelaren, ii., 277.

——Prins Willem in onderhandeling met den vijand over vrede, 1572–76, ii., 336.

——Het beleg en ontzet der stad Leiden in 1574, ii., 385.

——Over eenige ziekten van prins Willem I., iii., 40.

——De onde verhalen van den moord van prins Willem I., iiI., 65.

——De laatste woorden van prins Willem I., iii., 86.

FRUIN, ROBERT, Het oudste geschrift van Philips van Marnix, vii., 93.
——Een anoniem pamflet van 1567 toegekend aan Marnix, vii., 99.
——De oprichting der nieuwe bisdommen vin Nederlanden, viii., 298.
——Alva's bril, viii., 373.
——Willem de Zwijger, viii., 404.
——De Zeventien provinciën en haar vertegenwording in de Staten-Generaal, ix., 1.
——Belasting bij quoten in 1577, ix., 29.
——De unie van Utrecht, ix., 37.
——Over 't woord haagpreek, viii., 307.
Not included in collected works:
——*Tien jaren uit den tachtigjarigen oorlog 1588–1598*.
——*Geschiedenis der staatsinstellingen in Nederland tot den val den Republick* uitgegeven door Dr. H. T. Colenbrander. 1 v. s'Gravenhage, 1901.
——De Nederlandsche ballingen in Engeland, 1568–1570. *Bidr. v. vaderl. gesch.*, 1892, IIIe R. dl. vi.
In addition to these many of Fruin's reviews on Motley, Groen, Kervyn, etc., are interesting.

GACHARD, LOUIS PROSPER, *Correspondance de Guillaume le taciturne.* 6 vols., 8vo. Bruxelles, 1847–57.
——*Correspondance de Philippe II. sur les affaires des Pays-Bas.* 5 vols., 4to. Bruxelles, 1848–70.
——*Correspondance de Marguerite d'Autriche avec Philippe II.* (1559–68). 3 vols. Bruxelles, 1867.
——*Correspondance d'Alexandre Farnese, Prince de Parme, avec Philippe II., 1578–1579.* Bruxelles.
——*Correspondance du duc d'Albe sur l'invasion du comte Louis de Nassau.* 1850.
——*Actes des États-Généraux des Pays-Bas.* 8vo. Bruxelles, 1861.
——*Documents inédits concernant l'histoire de Belgique.* Vol. i., 8vo. Bruxelles, 1833.
——*Analectes Belgiques; recueil de pièces inédites*, etc. 3 vols., 8vo. Bruxelles, 1830.
——*Relations des ambassadeurs vénitiens sur Charles Quint et Philippe II.* Bruxelles, 1856.

GRANVELLE, CARDINAL DE (Anthony Perrenot, b. Besançon 1517, d. 1586), *Papiers d' état de.* Ed. Ch. Weiss. 9 v. Paris, 1841–52.
——*Correspondance de* (faisant suite aux *Papiers d' état*). Ed. E. Poullet and C. Piot. 12 v. Bruxelles, 1878–97.

GROEN VAN PRINSTERER, GULIELMUS, *Archives ou Correspondance inédite de la maison d' Orange Nassau.* Vols. i.–viii. and supplément. Leiden, 1835–1847.

VAN SOMEREN, J. F., *La correspondance du prince Guillaume d' Orange avec Jacques de Wesenbeke.* Supplément au recueil de M. G. Groen van Prinsterer. 1 v., 8vo. Amsterdam, 1896.

GUICCIARDINI, LUDOVICO (b. Florence 1523, d. 1589, Italian, fairly impartial), *Descrittione di tutti i Paesi Bassi.* 1 v., 4to. In Anversa, 1581.

HARRISON, FREDERIC, *William the Silent.* 1 v., 8vo. London 1897.

Historisch Genootschap te Utrecht. In the works published by this society are numerous valuable articles. The series are: *Kroniek*, 6 series, 30 v., 1846–1875. *Berigten*, 7 vols., 1846–1863. *Codex diplomaticus*, 1st series, 1 v., 1842; 2d series, 6 vols., 1852–1863. *Bijdragen en Mededeelingen*, 24 vols., 1877–1903. *Werken*, 84 vols.

HOOFT, PIETER CORNELISZ. (b. Amsterdam 1581, d. 1647, Hollander and Protestant), *Nederlandsche historien.* 1 v., folio. Amsterdam, 1656.

HUIZINGA, J., *De vergadering der Staten-General op July 10 1584 na den noen.* Bijdragen voor Vaderlandische Geschiedenis. 4de. reeks, vi., 1907.

HUME, MARTIN A. S. (also editor of *Calendar*), *Philip II. of Spain.* 1 v. London, 1902.

JACOBS, DR., Ed., *Juliana von Stolberg, Ahnfrau des Hauses Nassau-Oranien.* 1 v., 8vo. Wernigerode, 1889.

KERVYN DE LETTENHOVE, Baron J. M. B. C. *Documents inédits relatifs à l' histoire du XVIe siècle.* 1 v., 8vo. Bruxelles, 1858.
——*Les huguenots et les gueux* (1560–1585). 6 vols., 8vo. Bruges, 1883–1885.
——*Relations politiques des Pays-Bas et de l'Angleterre sous le règne de Philippe II.* 11 vols., 4to. 1892–1900.

KLUIT, A., *Historie der Hollandsche staatsregering tot het jaar 1795.* 5 v., 8vo. Amsterdam, 1805.

KNUTTEL, Dr. W. P. C., *Catalogus van de pamfletten verzameling berustende in de koninklijke Bibliothek.* Eerste deel-Eerste stuk 1486–1620. 1 v. s'Gravenhage, 1889.

——*Lijst van Engelsche vlugschriften betrekking hebbende op de Nederlandsche geschiedenis tot 1640.* s'Gravenhage, 1886.

LACROIX, ALBERT (editor), *Apologie de Guillaume de Nassau, Justification,* etc. 1 v., 12mo. Bruxelles, 1858.

LA PISE, JOSEPH DE (b. Orange 1589, d. 1648), *Tableau de l'histoire des princes et de la principaute d'Orange.* 1 v., folio. La Haye, 1639.

LENZ, MAX, *Briefwechsel Landgraf Philipp's des Grossmütigen mit Bucer.* 2 vols., 8vo. 1887.

MARNIX, PHILIPPE, Seigneur de Sainte-Aldegonde (b. Brussels 1538, d. Leiden 1598, Ultra-Protestant and Nationalist), *Œuvres de* [Lacroix ed.]. 2 v., 8vo. Paris, 1860.

MÉMOIRES

Mémoires et Correspondance de Duplessis-Mornay (Philippe, Seigneur du Plessis-Marly, b. 1549, d. 1623. French Protestant, resident in Netherlands 1581–1582). Edition complete, 12 v., 8vo. Paris, 1824.

Mémoires de Claude Haton, curé du Mériot 1553–1582 (b. 1534, d. after 1605. French priest, soldier, and writer). Ed. Felix Bourquelot. 1 v., Paris, 1857.

Mémoires de Michel de la Huguerye (b. 1545, Protestant and devoted to Louis of Nassau). 3 v., 8vo. Paris, 1877.

Mémoires de Marguerite de Valois (b. 1553, d. 1615) [ed. Ludovic Lalann]. 1 v., 24mo. Paris, 1858.

Mémoires de la vie de François Scépeaux, sire de Vieilleville (b. 1510, d. 1571, French), *composés par Vincent Carloix son Secrétaire.* 5 v., 12mo. Paris, 1757.

Mémoires de Pasquier de la barre, 1565–1567 (official at Tournay. Protestant, executed Dec. 1568). 2 v., 8vo. Bruxelles, 1859.

Mémoires de Pontus Payeu (ennobled 1582, Catholic Royalist). Ed. A. Henne. 2 v., 8vo. Bruxelles, 1851.

Mémoires sur les troubles des Pays-Bas, 1576–1578. Martin Antoine del Rio (b. Antwerp, 1551, d. 1608, Royalist and Catholic). Ed. Delvigne. 3 v., 8vo. Bruxelles, 1869.

Bibliography

Mémoires de Viglius et d'Hopperus (Wigle van Aytta, b. 1507, d. 1577, Netherlander and nationalist while faithful to Philip, Catholic) (Joachim Hopperus, b. 1523, d. 1576, Royalist and Catholic, Netherlander). Ed. Alph Wauters. 1 v. Bruxelles, 1858.

MENDOÇA, B. (d. after 1600, Spanish and Catholic), *Commentaires mémorables des guerres de Flandres et Pays-Bas, 1567–1577.* Avec une sommaire description des Pays-Bas. Paris, 1591.

METEREN, EMANUEL VAN (b. 1535, d. 1612, Protestant and Netherlander), *Belgische ofte Nederlandsche historien van onzen tijden tot 1598.* 1 v., folio. Delft, 1605.

MOTLEY, JOHN LOTHROP, *The Rise of the Dutch Republic.* 4 v. Philadelphia, 1898.

MULLER, P. L. (also editor), *De staat der Vereenigde Nederlanden in de jaren zijner wording 1572–1594.* 1 v., 8vo. Haarlem, 1878.

Nederlandsche Liederboek. 2 v., 12mo. Ghent, 1892.

NIJHOFF, Dr. D. C., *Staatkundige geschiedenis van Nederland.* 2 v., 8vo. Zutphen, 1893.

——Notes to Dutch translation of Putnam's *William the Silent* (*Willem de Zwijger*. 2 v. s'Gravenhage, 1897).

Orange, principality of, and its Protestant exiles. Pamphlet. British Museum.

ORLERS, JAN VAN (b. c. 1580, d. 1618, Protestant), *Généalogie des comtes de Nassau.* 1 v., folio. Leiden, 1630.

PHILADELPHE, EUSÈBE (pseudonym), *La réveille—matin des Français et de leur voisins.* 1 v., 8vo. Edinbourg, 1574. (Protestant pamphlet.)

PIRENNE, HENRI (Professor at Ghent), *Histoire de Belgique.* Vol. iii., 8vo. Bruxelles, 1907.

RAUMER. F. L. G. VON, *Geschichte Europas seit dem Ende des 15 Jahrhunderts.* 8 v., 8vo. Leipzig, 1830–1850.

——*Historisches Taschenbuch* (editor). Vol. vii. Leipzig, 1836.

REIFFENBERG, LE BARON DE (editor), *Correspondance de Marguerite d'Autriche, duchesse de Parme, avec Philippe II.* 1 v., 8vo. Bruxelles, 1842.

RENON DE FRANCE, RANULPHE (b. Douay 1556, d. 1623, Catholic nationalist), *Histoire des troubles des Pays-Bas.* Ed. G. J. C. Piot. 3 v., 4to. Bruxelles, 1886–1891.

SCHLIEPHAKE, F. W. TH., *Geschichte von Nassau.* 6 v. Wiesbaden, 1867.

STIRLING-MAXWELL, Sir W., *Don John of Austria, 1547–1578.*
2 v., folio. London, 1883.

STRADA, FAMIANUS (b. Rome 1572, d. 1649, Jesuit), *De Bello Belgico.* 2 v., folio. Roma, 1640.

THOU, JACQUES-AUGUSTE DE (b. Paris 1553, d. 1617, Catholic but opposed to Council of Trent), *Histoire universelle, 1543–1607.* 16 v., sq. 4to. Londres, 1734.

VAN LOON, GERARD, *Histoire métallique des xvii provinces des Pays-Bas.* Vol. i., folio. La Haye, 1732.

WOODS, FREDERICK ADAMS, *Mental and Moral Heredity in Royalty.* 1 v. New York, 1906. (Interesting as showing Nassau blood in reigning families. Conclusions not sure.)

INDEX

(CONTENTS OF LETTERS NOT INCLUDED)

A

Abjuration of Philip II., 405 *et seq.*
Aerschot, Duchess of, 54, 88
Aerschot, Duke of, 157, 169, 354 *et passim*
Aerssens, pensionary of Brussels, 468
Albornoz, Juan de, 247
Albret, Jeanne d', 300; letters to Charlotte, 303, 312, 313; her death, 313
Alcabala, the, 230
Alcala, University of, 361
Alkmaar, siege of, 243 *et passim*
Alost seized by Spanish mutineers, 341
Alva, Duke of, 68, 70, 71, 189, 200, 204; letter to Philip II., 206; and the tenth penny, 229 *et seq.*; opinion about the Brill, 231; and Estates, 248; retires, 249, 250; mentioned, 350, 492 *et passim*
Amsterdam, troubles in, 178, etc.; 353 *et passim*
Anastro, Caspar d', 421
Anjou, Duke of (François Hercules of Valois, Duke of Alençon), 355, 365, 375, 409, 411 *et seq.*, 413, 437, 441, 444; death of, 451
Anne of Lorraine, 15, etc.
Antwerp, population of, 170; Cathedral restored, 176; French Fury in, 440; offers public honours to Orange, 449; 458 *et passim*
Aremberg, Duke of, 135, 169, 198 *et passim*
Assonleville, Councillor d', 468
Aubéry, Louis, Sr. du Maurier, 78, 472
Aumont, Sieur d', 312
Austria, Don John of, birth and fortunes, 337; appointed regent of Netherlands, 338; his dream of rescuing Mary Stuart, 338; arrives in Luxemburg, 339; in Netherlands, 350 *et seq.*; his sincerity, 352; falls ill, 383; dies a disappointed man, 384
Austria, Margaret of, regent of the Netherlands, 12
Austria, Margaret of, Duchess of Parma, regent of the Netherlands, 76, 78; letter to Philip II., 140, 153 *et seq.*; receives the petition (1566), 165; anxiety about the preaching, 178; refuses Prince's resignation, 180; tries to stop Alva's coming, 189
Austria, Matthias of, 369, 375 *et passim*
Averly, George d', 305, 310, 431
Averly, François d', Sr. de Minay, 305, 431
Avila, Sancho d', 258

B

Bartholdus Wilhelmi, 244
Bartholomew, St., massacre of, 237, 240 *et passim*, 312
"Beggars of the Sea," 223
Bentivoglio, 438
Berghes, Count de, 395
Bergues, Marquis de, 152
Berlaymont, Count de, 135, 169 *et passim*
Berlepsch, Volmar von, 208 *et seq.*
Bernard, Hans, 58
Biron, Marshal de, 464
Bishops in the Netherlands, 116 *et seq.*
Boisot, Admiral, 254, 268 *et passim*, 276
Bonnard, Claude, 298 *et passim*
Bossu, Count van (Maximilian de Hennin), 233
Botelli, Leonardo, 425
Bourbon, Anthony de, 300
Bourbon, François de, 330
Bourbon, Louis de, Duke of Montpensier, 297; marries a second time, 303; anger at Charlotte's flight, 307; letter to Elector Palatine, 307; 429, 458
Bourbon, Louise de, abbess of Farmoutiers, writes to Orange, 330
Bouton, Claude, 35
Brabant, Estates of, call a convention, 343; Ruward of, 369; title of duke offered to Orange, 445
Brandenburg, Hans of, 109
Brantôme quoted, 339
Breda, 35 *et passim;* peace conference at, 294; evacuated, 367
Brederode, Henry van, 151, 161 *et seq.*
Brett, Marie, 310
Brill, the, captured, 223 *et seq.*
Brunynck, letters to Count John, 279

Brussels, 52 *et passim; coup d'état* at, 342
Bucer, Martin, 36
Buren, Count of, *see* Egmont, Philip, etc.
Burleigh, Lord, 474
Buys, Paul, 347

C

Calendar, reform of the, 435
Calvin quoted, 472
Camarilla, the, 115
Capet, M., 325
Caron, Noël, Lord of Schoonval, 464
Catherine of Lorraine (Duchess of Montpensier), 430
Catherine de' Medici, 245, 292, 442, 475 *et passim*
Catzenellenbogen lawsuit, 18 *et passim*
Cayas, Gabriel de, 248
Cecil, Lord, 175
Chabot, Jeanne, 298 *et passim*
Champagny, Seignior of (Jerome Perrenot), 37, 40, 354 *et passim*
Charles the Bold, 10
Charles V., 1, 12, 52; abdication, 54 *et seq.*; 82, 87 *et passim*
Chiericati, Bishop, 2
Cleves, Duke of, 64
Clough, Richard, letter, 105
Coligny, Gaspard de, Admiral of France, 145, 203, 432, 477, 480 *et passim*
Cologne, archbishop of, 41, 117; refugees at, 209; negotiations at, 387
Compromise of Nobles, 161, etc.
Condé, Duke of, 291
Council of State at Brussels, 340
Council of Troubles, 192, etc.
Cromwell, Oliver, 482
Cronenburg, Hartmuth of, 21
Crue, Cécile, 298 *et passim*
Culemburg, Count, 161

Index

D

Dathenus, Pierre, 386
Delft, church at, 285
Denmark, King of, 450, 490
Dillenburg Castle, 27 *et passim*, 207, 400 *et passim*
Does, Jan van der (Janus Douza) 272 *et seq.*
Don Carlos, 69
Don Frederic of Toledo, 238, 243, 250, 271
Douay, University at, 127
Dupré, 461, 463

E

Egmont, abbey of, 120
Egmont, Countess of, 54
Egmont, Lamoral of, 59, 123; letter to Philip, 131; 138, 184, 190; trial, 199; death, 200
Egmont, Maximilian of, Count of Buren, 37 *et seq.*, 41 *et seq.*
Egmont, Walpurga of, 26
Elector Palatine, 306; letter to Charlotte's father, 306
Elizabeth of England, 225, 227 *et passim*, 411, 416, 437, 485
Elizabeth of Valois, 69, 76
Erasmus, Desiderius, 2 *et passim*, 33
Escherenne, 57, 58
Este, Isabella d', 2 *et seq.*

F

Farmoutiers, abbess of, 309
Farnese, Alexander, Prince of Parma, 153, 357; succeeds Don John, 384; 390; receives deserters, 394; 433, 455, 471
Feugheran, M., 325
Florida, 477 *et seq.*
Foreest, Dr. Petrus van, 276 *et seq.*, 425, 469
Francesca of Savoy, 14
Francis I. of France, 12 *et passim*, 16
Francis II., 76

G

Gachard, Louis Prosper, 489
Gembloux, battle of, 371 *et passim*
Genlis, 205
Gérard, Balthasar, 457 *et seq.*
Get, offers to kill Orange, 456 *et seq.*
Ghent, pacification of, 333 *et seq.*, 347; seat of Assembly, 1576, 346; enters Union of Utrecht, 386; troubles in, 387 *et passim*
Glippers, the, 274
Golden Fleece, Order of the, 22, 77, 172
Gomez, Ruy, 70
Gonzaga, 17
Gorcum, martyrs of, 232
Granvelle, Cardinal (Anthony Perrenot, Bishop of Arras), 38; and the Prince's first marriage, 41; as diplomat, 70 *et passim;* letter to, 72; influence over Orange, 84; opinion on Saxon marriage, 91 *et seq.*; letters to Philip II., 97, 131, 132, 159, 186; friction with Netherlanders (1560–63), 114 *et passim*, 135, etc.,147; created cardinal, 123; departs, 142; letters to, 150, 155, 156, 158; objects to States-General without Philip, 160; advises death of Nassaus, 247; rejoices at news of Prince's death, 423, 433, 471
Gresham, Sir Thomas, 175; letter to Cecil, 182
Guelderland, 379, 396 *et passim*
Gueux adopted as name, 167
Guion, François, 461, 462
Guises, the, 303

H

Haagpreek, 168

Haarlem, diocese of, 120; siege of, 240, 243 *et passim*
Hadamar, 101
Hadrian Junius, 279
Hainault, 379 *et passim*
Halfleiden, Jan, 273
Hames, Nicholas de, letter to Louis, 164
Hanau, Philip of, 26
Heiden, Gaspar van der, 325
Heiligerlee, 204, 259 *et passim*
Henry II. of France, 44, 59, 70, 76, 484
Henry VIII. of England, 11
Henry of Navarre, 450, 485, 490
Herlle (William Herle), 418
Hesse, Philip, Landgrave of, 20, 93, 127, 129, 133
Hesse, William, Landgrave of, 176, 198, 220, 252, 257, 324, 326
Hèze, Seignior de, 342 *et seq.*
Hildesheim, 144
Hohenlohe, Count Albert of, 281, 319, etc.
Holl, George von, 152, 197
Holland, Estates of, in 1572, 234; give new powers and allowance to Orange, 290; closer union with Zealand, 295, 335, etc.; and countship, 454, 481 *et passim*
Holstein-Schauenburg, Adolph of, 35
Hooft quoted, 244, etc.
Hooft, C. P., 454
Hoogstraaten, Count of, 77, 164, 194, 205
Horne, Count of, letter to Philip II., 131, 184: trial, 199; death, 200, 261
Hout, Jan van, 273
Huguerye, Michel de la, 239, 256, 291, *et seq.*, 314

I

Iconoclasts, 174
Isenburg, Amelia of, 30

J

Jacqueline of Holland (Jacoba of Bavaria), 10
Jarnac, battle of, 206
Jaureguy, Jean, 419 *et seq.*; his successors, 455
Johanna of Polanen, 10
Junius, Francis, 161

K

Keppel, nunnery at, 24
Königstein, 27
Königstein, Philip von, 30

L

Lafontaine, Michelle de, 301
Lalaing, George de, Count of Rennenberg, 114, 396
Lammen, fort of, 284
Languet, Hubert, 391
La Pise, Joseph de, 70
La Rochelle, 228 *et passim*
Laval, M. de, 417
Legaspi, 476
Leicester, Earl of, 415
Leiden, siege of, 251, 271 *et seq.*; University of, 386
Leiderdorp, 284
Leoninus, Elbertus, 184
Liebart, Barthélemy, 487
Liège, bishopric of, 143
Lincoln, Abraham, 482 *et seq.*
Line of Demarcation, 6
Lion Petit, 432
Lodron, Count, 193
Long-vic, Jacqueline de, 297, 300 *et passim*
Lorich, 141, 143
Lorraine, Catherine de, 303
Lorraine, Duchess of, 68
Louvain, University of, 147, 194, etc.
Lumey, William de, Baron de la Marck, 224, 227 *et passim*
Luther, Martin, 2, 8, 20 *et passim*

M

Magellan, Ferdinand, 1 *et seq.*
Mansfield, Count, 161, 169, 461
Marck, Henry Robert de la, Duke of Bouillon, 297
Marie, Queen of Hungary, regent of the Netherlands, 32 *et seq.*
Marnix, Jean de, Sr. de Tholouse, 181, 197
Marnix, Philip, Seignior of Ste. Aldegonde, 161; represents Orange in 1572, 234 *et seq.*; urges submission, 251; goes to Heidelberg for university professors, 315; escorts Charlotte to Holland, 322; represents Orange at Ghent, 347 *et seq.*; sees baptism of Frederick Henry, 451; conference with Orange, 451
Mars, John, English ambassador dismissed from Spanish court, 227
Mary of Burgundy, 11
Mary of England 69
Mary Stuart, 76, 303, 338
Matthias, 369, 411
Maurice of Saxony, 92 *et passim*
Maximilian, Emperor, 11; forbids Prince's levies, 203; mentioned *et passim*
Mayence, Archbishop of, 25
Medina Cœli, Duke of, 132
Meghen, Count of, 169
Meixnern, Dr. John, 197
Menendez, Pedro, 478 *et seq.*
Mérode, Johann van, 35
Meteren, Emmanuel van, 420
Michael, Jacob, 325
Middelburg, treasure at, 281
Miggrodus, Jan, 325
Molinet, Anne du, 301
Mondragon, 258
Montesquieu, 472
Montfort, Dirk van, 285
Montigny, 77, 104

Mook Heath, battle of, 253 *et seq.*; after the, 265
Morgan, Captain, 466
Morillon, Provost, 125; letters to Granvelle, 155, 156, 158, 336, 340, 347
Mousson, Jeanne de, 301

N

Namur seized, 355
Nassau, 9 *et passim*
Nassau Church Regulations, 22
Nassau-Dillenburg, 9
Nassau family, 8 *et seq.*
Nassau, Adolph of, 136, 185; death at Heiligerlee, 198
Nassau, Anne of, 297, 366, 490 *et passim*
Nassau, Catherine of, 98
Nassau, Catherine Belgia of, 428, 490
Nassau, Charlotte Brabantina of, 428, 490
Nassau, Charlotte Flandrina of, 428, 490
Nassau, Countesses of (by marriage): Claudia of Orange-Chalons, 14; Cunigunde of the Palatinate, 401; Elizabeth of Hesse, 19; Elizabeth, Landgravine of Leuchtenberg, 185 *et passim*, 268; her death, 396; Juliana of Stolberg, *see* Juliana; Menzia, 15
Nassau, Emilie of, 210, 297, 400, 458
Nassau, Engelbert of, 9, 10 *et passim*
Nassau, Frederick Henry of, birth and baptism, 450, 490
Nassau, Henry of, mentioned, 10, 11, 14, 17 *et passim*
Nassau, Henry of (brother to Orange), 136, 142, 143, 145, 258, 265
Nassau, John of, 10, 11
Nassau, John VI. of (brother

Nassau—*Continued*
of Orange), 63; letter to Louis, 64; becomes head of family, 79; in Dresden, 107; his letters, 136; anxious about Henry's career, 143; at Dillenburg, 185 *et passim*, 239; escapes battle of Mook Heath, 258; letter about Orange's marriage, 324; disapproval and acceptance, 321, 324, 331; arrives in Holland, 367; accepts governorship of Guelderland, 374; letter to Dr. Schwartz, 396; resigns office, 401; distrusts French alliance, 425 *et passim*

Nassau, Louis of, third son, 31; at Breda, 63; first office, 65; aids Orange, 79; mission to Dresden, 101; letter to Orange, 129, 130, etc., 134; letter to landgrave, 133, 135, 138; letters to, 143; at Spa, 151 *et seq.*; and the *Compromise*, 161; and the confederates, 174; declared disturber of peace, 194; victory at Heiligerlee, 198; difficulties, 200; defeat at Jemmigen, 201; and the French, 206, 237; submits to Alva, 238; and Charles IX., 245; plans for invasion, 252; and Anjou, 254; plans converting the bishops, 256; compared to "angel Gabriel," 265; expedition of, 258; defeated at Mook Heath, 259; his character, 260 *et seq.*; his *Apology*, 262; mentioned, 315 *et passim*

Nassau, Louise Juliana of, 359, 428

Nassau, Marie of, birth, 62; maid of honour, 145; withdrawn from court, 184; at Dillenburg, 331 *et passim*; her letters, 362, 363 *et seq.*; returns to Netherlands, 366; letters to Count John, 371, 373, 375, 424, 425; mentioned, 399, 458, etc.

Nassau, Maurice of, 269, 332, 360, 417, 470, 490, 492

Nassau, Philip William of, birth, 62; farewell to his father, 184; left at Louvain, 184; greets Alva, 189; taken to Spain, 192 *et seq.*; letter to Count John, 361; mentioned, 470, 490, etc.

Nassau, René of (Prince of Orange), 14 *et passim;* death of, 17; mentioned, 77, 87, etc.

Nassau, William of, the elder or the Rich, 11 *et seq.*, 18, etc.; death of, 79; mentioned, 261

Nassau, William Louis of, 269

Navarre, Henry of, mentioned, 291, 305; godfather to Frederick Henry, 450, 490

New Netherland, 486

Noircarmes, Ph. de, 184, 252 *et passim*

Noord Aa, 283

Nootdorp, 282

O

Orange, 86, etc.; heresy in, 126

Orange, Philibert of, 14 *et passim*, 87

Orange, Prince of (William, Count of Nassau, Catzenellenbogen, etc., called *le taciturne* or the Silent), and Philip II., 7; his family, 8 *et seq.*; inheritance, 10 *et seq.*; birth and childhood, 30 *et seq.*; *Apology* quoted, 33, 40, 52, 70, 74; education, 35; betrothal to Anna of Egmont, 37; orthodoxy, 38; marriage, 40, 46; reported visit to France, 44; his dancing, 45; first commission (1551), 46; letters to his

Orange—*Continued*
wife, 47–54, 56, 57, 59; at emperor's abdication, 55; councillor of state, 56; remonstrates with Philip II., 58; tries to raise loan, 60; loses first wife (1558), 60; letters on Anna's death, 60–62; his children, 62; relations to wife and family 62 *et seq.*; part in treaty of Cateau-Cambrésis, 67 *et seq.*; letter to Emmanuel Philibert of Savoy, 68; at Paris as hostage (1559), 71; letter to Anthony Perrenot, 72; in the forest of Vincennes with Henry II., 73; his name, *le taciturne*, 75; return to Brussels, 76; appointed stadtholder of Holland, Zealand, and Utrecht, 77; strained relations with Philip II., 78; loses his father (1559), 79; letter to Count Louis, 79; his status and character, 81 *et seq.*; relations with Anthony Perrenot, 84 *et passim;* his property, 86 *et seq.*; his financial embarrassments and lavishness, 89, *et seq.*; desires second marriage, 91 *et seq.*; letter to Count of Schwarzburg (1560), 98; urges Estates to grant supplies, 98; letters to Count Louis, 100; relation with Germany and with king *in re* religion, 102; wedding festivities, 105, *et seq.*; pledge *in re* religion of Anne of Saxony, 109; brings wife to Brussels, 110; breach with Anthony Perrenot, 112 *et seq.*; his changed position, 116 *et seq.*; his attitude towards Protestantism in Orange, 126; letter to Pius IV. (1561), 126; first child by Anne of Saxony, 128; absence at Frankfort, 128; makes protest to Philip with Egmont and Horne, 131; judged dangerous by Granvelle, 132, 139 *et passim;* letters to Count Louis, 134, 136, 141, 143, 162; plans for Count Henry show theological indifference, 143; places his daughter Marie in court, 145; desires three measures of reform (1564), 146; advice to Count Louis, 152; advises execution of royal orders (1565), 154; distrusted by people, 160; letter to regent, 162; offers resignation, 163; advises toleration after petition (1566), 165 *et seq.*; at the "Beggars'" supper, 167; at Antwerp, 169 *et seq.*; letter to regent, 171; letter to William of Hesse, 176; tries to calm troubles at Amsterdam, 178; refuses new oath, 179; resignation declined, 180; and Tholouse, 182; accused of duplicity, 183; letter to Philip (April 10, 1567), 183; goes to Germany, 184; life at Dillenburg, 185 *et seq.*; troubles with Anne, 186 *et passim;* asks for religious instruction, 189; cited to appear before Council of Troubles, 194; negligence about his son, 194; his *Justification*, 195; letter to William of Hesse, 196; plans three attacks on Netherlands (1568), 198; letter to Louis after Jemmigen, 201; proclamation, 203; his standards, 203; crosses the Meuse, 204; retreats to Strasburg, 206; his years of wandering, 206; letters to Count John, 207, 217; his ciphers, 207; letters to Anne, 210, 215; hopes to

Orange—*Continued*
keep her affairs quiet, 217; establishes navy, 223, etc.; sees chance in Alva's taxes, 231; activity after the capture of the Brill, 232; acts as Stadtholder again, 233 *et seq.*; his executive powers (1572), 235; letters to Count John, 235, 237, 241; defeated at Hermigny, 238; re-enters Holland, 239; conditions of reconciliation with Philip II., 241; letter to Count Louis, 242; professes Calvinism (1573), 243; distrusts the French, 242, 247 *et passim;* efforts to raise money, 248; epistle to king, 249; repudiates advice to lay down arms, 251; letters from Flushing (1574), 253, 254; Stadtholdership tacitly acknowledged when Middelburg surrendered, 255 *et seq.*; anxiety about brothers, 265; his frantic letters, 265; long ignorance of disaster of Mook Heath, 266, etc.; accepts fact April 22d, 268; letters to Count John, 269; plans relief of Leiden, 275; falls ill, 276; treated by Dr. van Foreest, 276 *et seq.*; condition reported by Brunynck, 279; able to write to Count John, 280; depressed, 281; writes to Leiden, 281; visits fleet, 283; receives news of relief at church, 285; visits Leiden, 285; establishes university, 286; defines his status, 288; accepts supremacy in Holland, 290; insists on proper income, 290; method of procedure described by La Huguerye, 291; negotiations with Spain, 293 *et seq.;* cannot accept conditions, 294; insists on toleration clause in articles of union, 295; decides on new matrimonial alliance (1575), 296; attitude towards Anne of Saxony, 297 *et seq.*; chooses Charlotte of Bourbon as wife, 297; his personal knowledge of Charlotte, 315; sends Marnix to Heidelberg to make his proposal, 315; reasons against the alliance, 316 *et passim;* sends Count Hohenlohe to Heidelberg, 319; his minute instructions, 320; offends Count John, 321; announces marriage, 323; accepts act of ministers as legal justification, 325; explains himself to Count John, 327; appeals to François de Bourbon, 330; unable to repay Count John, 331; his daughter Marie, 332, 362 *et passim;* takes advantage of Requesens' death in 1576, 334; receives added powers from Holland and Zealand, 335; his ambition, 336; superhuman exertions, 341; his efforts at toleration, 342; his relation to the *coup d'état*, 343; letter to States-General, 344; succeeds in obtaining provincial congress, 346; represented by Ste. Aldegonde at Ghent, 347; pleased with Pacification of Ghent, 349; cognisant of all negotiations with Don John, 350; distrusts Don John, 352; extends his own influence, 353; rated by Don John, 354; makes capital from Don John's errors, 356; enters Brussels after ten years' absence, 356; his methods not always good, 357; his family background, 358;

Index

Orange—*Continued*
finds Charlotte a helpmate, 359 *et seq.*; letters to Count John, 359, 368; his opportunism, 360; letters from Charlotte, 360, 367, 370 *et passim;* his mother (1577), 362; plans for his children, 365; Ruward of Brabant, 369; reception of Matthias, 369; needs his brother, 370; letter to Charlotte, 376; obtains Religious Peace, 379; part in the Union of Utrecht, 380, 382 *et seq.*; belief in the Confederation, 383; in Paris pantomime, 385; criticised by ultra-Protestants, 386; answers criticism, 387; refuses terms offered by Philip, 387; price set on head (the Ban, 1580), 389; *Apology,* 391, *et seq.*; letter to States-General, 393; supported by the States, 394; attacked by calumny, 394; loses many friends, 395 *et seq.*; last letter to Juliana of Stolberg, 399; loses his mother, 400; disregards John's warnings, 402; insists on Anjou as "Protector," 405, 412 *et passim;* approves abjuration of Philip, 405; governor *pro tem*, 409; at Anjou's inauguration, 415; shot by Jaureguy, 417 *et seq.*; tries to protect the French, 423; relapse, 425; recovery, 427; loses Charlotte de Bourbon, 427; sees Anjou made Count of Flanders, 432; exposed to danger, 432; difficulties with Anjou, 437; last interview with Anjou, 439; declares treachery "a misunderstanding," 441; answers Elizabeth and Catherine, 443; reluctant to discard the French, 444; advocacy evokes criticism, 445; fourth marriage, 446 *et seq.*; not daunted by anti-French feeling, 448; indignant at Antwerp's distrust, 449; establishes his family at Delft, 450; celebrates baptism of his youngest child, 450; demands inauguration as Count of Holland, 451; opposed by C. P. Hooft, 454; exposed to dangers, 455; his household at Delft in the Prinsenhof, 457; his bitterness, 458; receives announcement of Anjou's death, 459; treatment of "Guion," 460, etc.; his last words and death, 466; his appearance and age, 469; his funeral, 470; his foes rejoice, 471 *et seq.*; his relations with Philip, 473 *et seq.*; compared with Coligny, 480; compared with Cromwell and Lincoln, 482; compared with Washington, Elizabeth and Henry of Navarre, 485; his toleration, 486; his need for sympathy, 488; his "silence" 489; his children's names, 490; his luxury and courage, 491; his statesmanship, 492; as Father of his Country, 493

Orange, Princesses of:

1—Anna of Egmont, 37, 40, 46; letters to, 47 *et seq.*; death, 60 *et seq.*

2—Anne of Saxony, her family 92 *et seq.*; as a wife, 124 *et passim;* letter to her grandfather, 127; her first child, 128; resents emigration, 186; her conduct and deterioration, 187, *et seq.*; at Cologne, 208 *et seq.*; intimacy with Jan Rubens, 215; letter to Jan Rubens, 216; letter to Count John, 218; at Beil-

Orange—*Continued*
  stein, 219; removed to Dresden and death 222, 296; divorce from Prince, 323 *et passim*
    3—Charlotte de Bourbon mentioned, 256; parentage, 297; takes vows as child, 298; abbess of Jouarre, 299; appeals to Jeanne d'Albret, 303; leaves Jouarre, 305; at Heidelberg, 306 *et seq.*; plans in behalf of, 315; the objections, 316 *et seq.*; accepts proposal of Orange, 317; arrives at the Brill, 325; married at Dordrecht, 326; writes to Juliana of Stolberg, 327; has to meet criticism, 329 *et seq.*; her sister reconciled, 330; her value to the Prince, 358 *et seq.*; her first child, 359; letters to Orange, 360, 366, 367, 370; pleasant relations with step-daughters, 364 *et passim;* letters to Juliana of Stolberg, 399; to her sister-in-law, 402; despair at Jaureguy's crime, 422; succumbs to strain, 426; her death, 427; her children, 428; her will, 431
    4—Louise de Coligny, (Mme. de Téligny), her story, 446; married to Orange, 448; her journey to Delft, 450; gives birth to son, 450; notices Gérard, 465
Ostrawell, 181
Ottonian branch of Nassau family, 9

P

Palatinate, the, John Casimir of, 252, 375 *et passim;* Christopher of, 258 *et seq.*; Cunigunde of, 397, 401
Palatine, Frederick, Elector, 246; receives Charlotte de Bourbon, 306 *et seq.*
Paraclet, Abbess of, 298, etc.
Paris, pantomime at, 385
Pero Lopez, letter to Granvelle, 158
Perthuis, Catherine de, 310
Pfeffinger Dr., 109
Philip II. of Spain, the fortunate prince, 7; and Orange, 7, 45 *et passim;* succeeds Charles V., 55; makes Orange councillor of state, 56; neglects soldiers' needs, 58 *et passim;* assumes offensive in France, 59; condoles with Orange on Anna of Egmont's death, 61; marriage to Elizabeth of Valois, 69 *et seq.*; appoints Margaret of Parma his regent for the Netherlands, 76; displeased with nobles' opposition, 77; angry farewell to Orange, 78; his opinion of the Saxon marriage, 96 *et seq.*; sends proxy and present, 104; his relations with Granvelle, 112 *et seq.*; apparently favours nobles, 114; and the new sees, 117 *et seq.*; willing to aid Netherland churches with Spanish funds, 120; receives Montigny pleasantly, 131; his debts, 140; withdraws Granvelle from Netherlands, 141; reasons for new sees, 148; orders enforcement of edicts of Council of Trent, 154 *et seq.*; approves regent's course in 1566, 170; demands new oath of fealty, 179; is appealed to by Anne of Saxony, 210; and Elizabeth of England, 225; his ambassador, 226; refuses to recall Alva, 229; comment on Coligny, 248; recalls Alva, 249;

Philip II.—*Continued*
   appoints Requesens, 249; named as founder of Leiden University, 286; delays action after Requesens' death, 334 *et seq.*; appoints Don John, 337; disapproves seizure of Namur, 355; neglects Don John, 383; confirms Parma's appointment, 384; publishes Ban against Orange, 388, 390; attacked by Orange, 392 *et seq.*; abjured as sovereign, 407; and Orange, summaries, 475
Philippine Islands, 1, 5, 476
Pigafetta, Antonio, 3 *et seq.*
Poland, king of, 246, 315
Polanen, Johanna of, 10
Ponika, Hans von, 107
Pontus Payen quoted, 181 *et passim*
Pope Alexander VI., 6
Pope Gregory XIII., 436
Pope Paul IV., 118, 123
Pope Pius IV, 126
Portugal, Maria of, 153
Prior of St. John, 190
Pruneaux, M. des, 417

R

Requesens, Don Luis de, 249 *et seq.*, 255, 261; his death, 334; mentioned, 492
Rheims, archbishop of, 117
Rheineck, Philip von, 30
Ribault, Jean, 477 *et seq.*
Riedsel, Volbrecht, 191
Romans, king of the, 128
Romero, Julian, 238, 254, 294
Rossem, Martin van, 16
Roubaix, Capt., 456
Rubens, John, 215, 216, etc.
Ruzé, bishop of Angers, 298
Ruward of Brabant, 369
Rÿtberg, Mlle. de, 129

S

Ste. Aldegonde, *see* Marnix
St. André, Marshal, 67, 70
Ste. Gudule, 128
St. Trond, 170
Sarrot, Radegonde, 310
Savoy, Emmanuel Philibert, Duke of, 52, 68, 76 *et passim*
Saxony, Augustus, Elector of, 92 *et seq.*, 107, 220, etc.
Saxony, Duke Hans Frederick of, 21
Saxony, Maurice of, 46, 97, etc.
Scépeaux, François de, Marquis de Vieilleville, 44, etc.
Schauenberg, Count Ernest of, 398, 400
Schauenberg, William of, 144, 145
Schetz, Gaspar, Sr. de Grobbendonck, 128, 137
Schmalkald, league of, 22
Schomberg, Gaspar, 329
Schoore, president of council, 33
Schwarzburg, Gunther, Count of, 95 *et passim*
Schwarzburg, Catherine of, 428, 458, 466 *et passim*
Schwartz, Dr., advice to Count John, 402
Segwaert, 282
Sidney, Philip, 391, 415
Siegen, 215 *et passim*
Silva, Guzman de, 225
Sluis, 228 *et passim*
Solms-Braunfels, Count and Countess of, 400
Spa, 150, 355, etc.
Spain (1909), 479 *et seq.*
Spanish Fury, 347
Spanish soldiers, mutiny of, 268
Spes, Guereau de, 226
States-General, 135, etc.; declare Don John a public foe,

370; and the *Apology*, 393 *et seq.*; in 1584, 481
Stochem, 204
Stolberg, Juliana of, Countess of Hanau, 26; Countess of Nassau, 27 *et seq.*; and her children, 28; mentioned, 63, 104, 143, 184 *et passim*, 362, 364; falls ill, 399; her death, 400 *et seq.*; her namesakes, 401, 490
Strada quoted, 171 *et passim*
Stuart, Mary, mentioned, 225, 303, 338 *et passim*

T

Taffin, John, 201, 325
Terranova, Duke of, 388
Tholen, island of, 333
Thou, President de, 312
Tontorf, Mme., 431
Treaty of Bordeaux, 405; Cateau Cambrésis 67, 69, *et seq.*; Marché-en-Famine, 350; Passau, 24; Plessis les Tours, 405; Tordesillas, 6
Trent, Council of, 148, 151 *et passim*
Tylius, Thomas, 325

U

Union of Arras, 381
Union of Brussels (1677), 352
Union of Utrecht, 380 *et seq.*
Utrecht, 118
Uylenburgh, Rombert, 466

V

Valenciennes, 51 *et passim*
Valois *see also* under Christian names, Elizabeth of, 69, 76; Margaret of, 305, 314; efforts to further Anjou's cause, 355
Vargas, 194
Vassery, Jeanne de, 301
Vaucelles, truce of, 58
Victoria, 2 *et seq.*
Vieilleville, Marquis de (François de Scépeaux), 82
Viglius van Aytta (president of the council), letter, 150; mentioned, 154, 249, 343, etc.
Villabos, Ruy Lopez de, 5
Villiers, Pierre, secretary of Orange, 391, 394, 460
Voorne, island of, 228

W

Walramian branch of Nassau family, 9
Walsingham, Sir Francis, 474
Washington, George, 482, 485 *et passim*
Waveren, battle near, 205
Werf, Adrian van der (Vermeer), 273 *et seq.*
Wesembeck, Jacques de, 207
Wilhelmuslied, 239 *et seq.*, 495
Wiltberg, Henry von, tutor of Philip William of Nassau, 107, 190, 193
Woltersdorff, Ulrich, 107
Worms, diet of, 2, 13 *et passim*
Würtemberg, 2

Z

Zell, Nicholas, 189
Zierikzee, effect of fall of, 340 *et seq.*
Zimmermann, 422 *et seq.*
Zoeterwoude, 283 *et seq.*
Zwieten, Cornelius van, 273

A Selection from the
Catalogue of

G. P. PUTNAM'S SONS

**Complete Catalogue sent
on application**

Heroes of the Nations

A SERIES of biographical studies of the lives and work of a number of representative historical characters about whom have gathered the great traditions of the Nations to which they belonged, and who have been accepted, in many instances, as types of the several National ideals. With the life of each typical character will be presented a picture of the National conditions surrounding him during his career.

The narratives are the work of writers who are recognized authorities on their several subjects, and, while thoroughly trustworthy as history, will present picturesque and dramatic "stories" of the Men and of the events connected with them.

To the Life of each "Hero" will be given one duodecimo volume, handsomely printed in large type, provided with maps and adequately illustrated according to the special requirements of the several subjects.

For full list of volumes see next page.

HEROES OF THE NATIONS

NELSON. By W. Clark Russell.
GUSTAVUS ADOLPHUS. By C. R. L. Fletcher.
PERICLES. By Evelyn Abbott.
THEODORIC THE GOTH. By Thomas Hodgkin.
SIR PHILIP SIDNEY. By H. R. Fox-Bourne.
JULIUS CÆSAR. By W. Warde Fowler.
WYCLIF. By Lewis Sergeant.
NAPOLEON. By W. O'Connor Morris.
HENRY OF NAVARRE. By P. F. Willert.
CICERO. By J. L. Strachan-Davidson.
ABRAHAM LINCOLN. By Noah Brooks.
PRINCE HENRY (OF PORTUGAL) THE NAVIGATOR. By C. R. Beazley.
JULIAN THE PHILOSOPHER. By Alice Gardner.
LOUIS XIV. By Arthur Hassall.
CHARLES XII. By R. Nisbet Bain.
LORENZO DE' MEDICI. By Edward Armstrong.
JEANNE D'ARC. By Mrs. Oliphant.
CHRISTOPHER COLUMBUS. By Washington Irving.
ROBERT THE BRUCE. By Sir Herbert Maxwell.
HANNIBAL. By W. O'Connor Morris.
ULYSSES S. GRANT. By William Conant Church.
ROBERT E. LEE. By Henry Alexander White.
THE CID CAMPEADOR. By H. Butler Clarke.
SALADIN. By Stanley Lane Poole.
BISMARCK. By J. W. Headlam.
ALEXANDER THE GREAT. By Benjamin I. Wheeler.
CHARLEMAGNE. By H. W. C. Davis.
OLIVER CROMWELL. By Charles Firth.
RICHELIEU. By James B. Perkins.
DANIEL O'CONNELL. By Robert Dunlop.
SAINT LOUIS (Louis IX. of France). By Frederick Perry.
LORD CHATHAM. By Walford Davis Green.
OWEN GLYNDWR. By Arthur G. Bradley.
HENRY V. By Charles L. Kingsford.
EDWARD I. By Edward Jenks.
AUGUSTUS CÆSAR. By J. B. Firth.

HEROES OF THE NATIONS

FREDERICK THE GREAT. By W. F. Reddaway.
WELLINGTON. By W. O'Connor Morris.
CONSTANTINE THE GREAT. By J. B. Smith.
MOHAMMED. By D. S. Margoliouth.
CHARLES THE BOLD. By Ruth Putnam.

WASHINGTON. By J. A. Harrison.
WILLIAM THE CONQUEROR. By F. M. Stenton.
FERNANDO CORTÈS. By F. A. MacNutt.
WILLIAM THE SILENT. By Ruth Putnam.

Other volumes in preparation are:

BLÜCHER. By Ernest F. Henderson.
MARLBOROUGH. By C. T. Atkinson.
MOLTKE. By James Wardell.

ALFRED THE GREAT. By Bertha Lees.
GREGORY VII. By F. Urquhart.
JUDAS MACCABÆUS. By Israel Abrahams.
FREDERICK II. By A. L. Smith.

New York—G. P. PUTNAM'S SONS, Publishers—London

The Story of the Nations

In the story form the current of each National life is distinctly indicated, and its picturesque and noteworthy periods and episodes are presented for the reader in their philosophical relation to each other as well as to universal history.

It is the plan of the writers of the different volumes to enter into the real life of the peoples, and to bring them before the reader as they actually lived, labored, and struggled—as they studied and wrote, and as they amused themselves. In carrying out this plan, the myths, with which the history of all lands begins, will not be overlooked, though these will be carefully distinguished from the actual history, so far as the labors of the accepted historical authorities have resulted in definite conclusions.

The subjects of the different volumes have been planned to cover connecting and, as far as possible, consecutive epochs or periods, so that the set when completed will present in a comprehensive narrative the chief events in the great STORY OF THE NATIONS; but it is, of course, not always practicable to issue the several volumes in their chronological order.

For list of volumes see next page.

THE STORY OF THE NATIONS

GREECE. Prof. Jas. A. Harrison.
ROME. Arthur Gilman.
THE JEWS. Prof. James K. Hosmer.
CHALDEA. Z. A. Ragozin.
GERMANY. S. Baring-Gould.
NORWAY. Hjalmar H. Boyesen.
SPAIN. Rev. E. E. and Susan Hale.
HUNGARY. Prof. A. Vámbéry.
CARTHAGE. Prof. Alfred J. Church.
THE SARACENS. Arthur Gilman.
THE MOORS IN SPAIN. Stanley Lane-Poole.
THE NORMANS. Sarah Orne Jewett.
PERSIA. S. G. W. Benjamin.
ANCIENT EGYPT. Prof. Geo. Rawlinson.
ALEXANDER'S EMPIRE. Prof. J. P. Mahaffy.
ASSYRIA. Z. A. Ragozin.
THE GOTHS. Henry Bradley.
IRELAND. Hon. Emily Lawless.
TURKEY. Stanley Lane-Poole.
MEDIA, BABYLON, AND PERSIA. Z. A. Ragozin.
MEDIÆVAL FRANCE. Prof. Gustave Masson.
HOLLAND. Prof. J. Thorold Rogers.
MEXICO. Susan Hale.
PHŒNICIA. George Rawlinson.
THE HANSA TOWNS. Helen Zimmern.
EARLY BRITAIN. Prof. Alfred J. Church.
THE BARBARY CORSAIRS. Stanley Lane-Poole.
RUSSIA. W. R. Morfill.
THE JEWS UNDER ROME. W. D. Morrison.
SCOTLAND. John Mackintosh.
SWITZERLAND. R. Stead and Mrs. A. Hug.
PORTUGAL. H. Morse-Stephens.
THE BYZANTINE EMPIRE. C. W. C. Oman.
SICILY. E. A. Freeman.
THE TUSCAN REPUBLICS. Bella Duffy.
POLAND. W. R. Morfill.
PARTHIA. Geo. Rawlinson.
JAPAN. David Murray.
THE CHRISTIAN RECOVERY OF SPAIN. H. E. Watts.
AUSTRALASIA. Greville Tregarthen.
SOUTHERN AFRICA. Geo. M. Theal.
VENICE. Alethea Weil.
THE CRUSADES. T. S. Archer and C. L. Kingsford.
VEDIC INDIA. Z. A. Ragozin.
BOHEMIA. C. E. Maurice.
CANADA. J. G. Bourinot.
THE BALKAN STATES. William Miller.

THE STORY OF THE NATIONS

BRITISH RULE IN INDIA. R. W. Frazer.
MODERN FRANCE. André Le Bon.
THE BRITISH EMPIRE. Alfred T. Story. Two vols.
THE FRANKS. Lewis Sergeant.
THE WEST INDIES. Amos K. Fiske.
THE PEOPLE OF ENGLAND. Justin McCarthy, M.P. Two vols.
AUSTRIA. Sidney Whitman.
CHINA. Robt. K. Douglass.
MODERN SPAIN. Major Martin A. S. Hume.
MODERN ITALY. Pietro Orsi.
THE THIRTEEN COLONIES. Helen A. Smith. Two vols.
WALES AND CORNWALL. Owen M. Edwards. Net $1.35.
MEDIÆVAL ROME. Wm. Miller.
THE PAPAL MONARCHY. Wm. Barry.
MEDIÆVAL INDIA. Stanley Lane-Poole.
BUDDHIST INDIA. T. W. Rhys-Davids.
THE SOUTH AMERICAN REPUBLICS. Thomas C. Dawson. Two vols.
PARLIAMENTARY ENGLAND. Edward Jenks.
MEDIÆVAL ENGLAND. Mary Bateson.
THE UNITED STATES. Edward Earle Sparks. Two vols.
ENGLAND, THE COMING OF PARLIAMENT. L. Cecil Jane.
GREECE—EARLIEST TIMES—A.D. 14. E. S. Shuckburgh.
ROMAN EMPIRE, B.C. 29–A.D 476. N. Stuart Jones.